SOMERVILLE FOR WOMEN

Mildenham
6196

Mary Somerville

Somerville for Women

An Oxford College
1879–1993

PAULINE ADAMS

DONEC RURSUS IMPLEAT ORBEM

OXFORD UNIVERSITY PRESS
1996

Oxford University Press, Walton Street, Oxford OX2 6DP

Oxford New York
Athens Auckland Bangkok Bombay
Calcutta Cape Town Dar es Salaam Delhi
Florence Hong Kong Istanbul Karachi
Kuala Lumpur Madras Madrid Melbourne
Mexico City Nairobi Paris Singapore
Taipei Tokyo Toronto
and associated companies in
Berlin Ibadan

Oxford is a trade mark of Oxford University Press

Published in the United States
by Oxford University Press Inc., New York

© Pauline Adams 1996

All rights reserved. No part of this publication may be reproduced,
stored in a retrieval system, or transmitted, in any form or by any means,
without the prior permission in writing of Oxford University Press.
Within the UK, exceptions are allowed in respect of any fair dealing for the
purpose of research or private study, or criticism or review, as permitted
under the Copyright, Designs and Patents Act, 1988, or in the case of
reprographic reproduction in accordance with the terms of the licences
issued by the Copyright Licensing Agency. Enquiries concerning
reproduction outside these terms and in other countries should be
sent to the Rights Department, Oxford University Press,
at the address above

This book is sold subject to the condition that it shall not, by way
of trade or otherwise, be lent, re-sold, hired out or otherwise circulated
without the publisher's prior consent in any form of binding or cover
other than that in which it is published and without a similar condition
including this condition being imposed on the subsequent purchaser

British Library Cataloguing in Publication Data
Data available

Library of Congress Cataloging in Publication Data
Adams, Pauline.
Somerville for women : an Oxford college, 1879–1993 / Pauline Adams.
Includes bibliographical references (p.   ) and index.
1. Somerville College (University of Oxford)—History. I. Title.
LF741.S65A33 1996   378.425'74—dc20   95–49172
ISBN 0–19–920179–X.
ISBN 0–19–920182–X (pbk.)

1 3 5 7 9 10 8 6 4 2

Typeset by Graphicraft Typesetters Ltd., Hong Kong

Printed in Great Britain
on acid-free paper by
Bookcraft Ltd.
Midsomer Norton, Avon

To Somervillians,
past, present, and future

Acknowledgements

THE history of Somerville has been a long time in the writing. A book planned to mark the college's centenary in 1979 missed the deadline; its intended author, Anne de Villiers, was subsequently prevented by a disabling stroke from committing to paper the fruits of much research. In taking over her task in the mid-1980s, I was—frustratingly for us both—obliged to start again virtually from scratch; and also, as the centenary receded further into the distance, to find a new closing date. In this respect at least, the college's decision to admit men from 1993 seemed providential.

As college Archivist, I have been in the fortunate position of having the main sources for this book in my own charge. In my archival forays outside Somerville I have met with much kindness, and no little hospitality. I am grateful to colleagues at Lady Margaret Hall and St Anne's for allowing me access to their archives, and to the governing bodies of those colleges for permission to quote from them. Mrs Annabel Cole has made available to me the papers of her great-aunt, Margery Fry, and Miss Elisabeth Murray the letters which she wrote home as an undergraduate in 1928–32. Mrs Herbert A. Gaylord and Professor Richard Sorabji have kindly allowed me to quote from the letters of their respective aunts, Frances Sheldon and Cornelia Sorabji, and Mrs Mary Bennett from those of her mother, Lettice Ilbert. I am grateful to the staff at the British Library and the India Office Library, to Dr Anne Whiteman for granting access to the papers of Dame Lucy Sutherland, and to Dr Alexander Murray for permission to quote from the correspondence of Gilbert Murray—both collections deposited in the Bodleian Library, and consulted with the permission of the Keeper of Western Manuscripts. The quotation from Sir John Mabbott's *Oxford Memories* is by permission of Thornton's of Oxford. The plans of Somerville are by Jeanne Croft.

The bibliography records the many Somervillians who have committed their memories of college to print, whether in autobiography, journalism, or fiction. I have also drawn extensively on the unpublished recollections, deposited in the college archives, of Florence Rich (1884), Mary Skues (1884), Catherine Childs (née Pollard, 1888), Ethel Williams (née Thomas, 1909), Alice Cameron (1910), Kathleen Byass (1917), Constance Savery (1917), Evelyn Irons (1918), Hilda Whittaker (née Street, 1918), Rachel Varcoe (née Footman, 1923), Jean Redcliffe Maud (née Hamilton, 1924), Marjorie Jenkins (1927), Joan Browne (1930), Margaret Hill (née Haigh, 1937), Christina Roaf (née Drake, 1937), Joyce Sugg (1944), Ann Hansen (1959), and Hilda Bryant (Principal's Secretary 1932–58). But I owe at least as much to oral tradition and corporate memory: to conversations with colleagues at lunch, and visitors at breakfast, and old Somervillians at gaudies. In this respect I began to gather material for this book long before I knew that I would write it; and I have accumulated more debts than I can possibly repay here. The greatest of these is to the memory of Anne de Villiers herself. I have also learned something of how Somerville appears to the outsider from scholars who have come to consult the Somerville archives in the course of their own researches.

Barbara Harvey and Janet Howarth have been unstintingly generous with their time and help; I am particularly grateful to Dr Howarth for allowing me to see an early draft of her chapters on women for volumes vii and viii of the *History of the University*. I owe much to the forbearance of my husband, Robert Franklin, who can probably by now recite most of these pages by heart, and that of my colleagues in Somerville College Library—above all Susan Purver, who has on innumerable occasions rescued a mangled text from the maw of the computer.

Having entrusted me with writing the college history, the governing body has made no attempt whatsoever to influence how I should do so. There are, however, few fellows who have not, over the years, given help or support of one kind or another. Any errors remain my own responsibility, and I apologize for them in advance. Where opinions are expressed, they too are my own. I do not expect my colleagues to agree with everything that I have written; but I console myself with the reflection that it would be most un-Somervillian if they did.

Contents

Contents

List of Illustrations

46. *Dame Janet Vaughan and Mrs Pandit*, at the opening of the Margery Fry and Elizabeth Nuffield House, 15 October 1964. (Photograph by permission of *Oxford Mail & Times*.)

47. *The opening of the Wolfson Building*, 21 November 1967. Left to right: Sir Isaac Wolfson, Mr Harold Macmillan (Chancellor of the University and Visitor of Somerville), Dorothy Hodgkin, Barbara Craig.

48. *Daphne Park presiding at dinner in Hall*, 1981, beneath the portrait of Somerville's first Principal, Madeleine Shaw Lefevre. (Photograph by permission of Brian Shuel.)

49. *Somerville's first Proctor*. The Vice-Chancellor gives Joanna Innes watch and ward over the university after her admission as Senior Proctor, March 1990.

50. *Somervillians Say No*. Somerville undergraduates (with reinforcements from Newnham in the background) demonstrating outside the New Council Room on 19 February 1992, as the Governing Body ratifies its decision to admit men.

51. *Somerville's last all-women Governing Body, June 1993*. Front row (left to right): Josephine Peach, Lesley Brown, Miriam Griffin, Katherine Duncan-Jones, Catherine Hughes, Barbara Harvey, Jane Hands, Nan Dunbar, Anna Davies. 2nd row: Almut Suerbaum, Gráinne de Búrca, Fiona Stafford, Margaret Adams, Judith Heyer, Joanna Innes, Carole Jordan, Anne de Moor, Pauline Adams, Frances Stewart. Back row: Angela Vincent, Marian Dawkins, Jennifer Loach. Missing: Hilary Ockendon, Adrianne Tooke, Karin Erdmann, Aviva Tolkovsky, Sarah Gurr. (Photograph by permission of B. J. Harris of Gillman & Soame, Oxford.)

Although every effort has been made to trace and contact copyright holders in a few instances this has not been possible. If notified the publishers will be pleased to rectify any omission in future editions.

Abbreviations

ACM	Agnes Catherine Maitland
AEW	Association for Promoting the Higher Education of Women
ASM	Association of Senior Members
BDC	Barbara Denise Craig
CUF	Common University Fund
DP	Daphne Park
EP	Emily Penrose
GB	Governing Body
GM	Gilbert Murray
HD	Helen Darbishire
HT	Hilary Term
HUO	*History of the University of Oxford*
JCR	Junior Common Room*
JV	Janet Vaughan
KMEM	Katherine Maud Elisabeth Murray
LMH	Lady Margaret Hall
MCR	Middle Common Room*
MKP	Mildred Katherine Pope
MSL	Madeleine Shaw Lefevre
MT	Michaelmas Term
MVC	Maude Violet Clarke
NUS	National Union of Students
OUDS	Oxford University Dramatic Society
PF	Meeting of Principal and Fellows
SCR	Senior Common Room*
SMF	Sara Margery Fry
SSA	Somerville Students' Association
TT	Trinity Term
UGC	University Grants Committee
WUS	Women's University Settlement

* In Oxford usage, these terms can refer, confusingly, either to a body of persons or to the actual room in which they meet.

Abbreviations

Except where the context demands otherwise, Somervillians are normally referred to by the name under which they first appear in the college records; where appropriate, the date they entered Somerville is given in brackets.

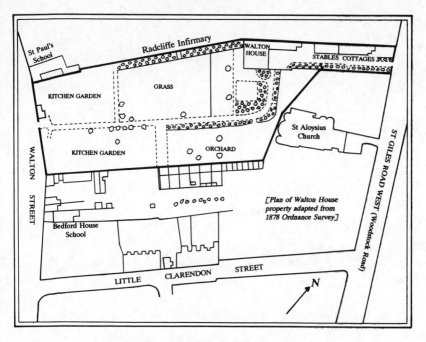

PLAN OF SOMERVILLE HALL 1879

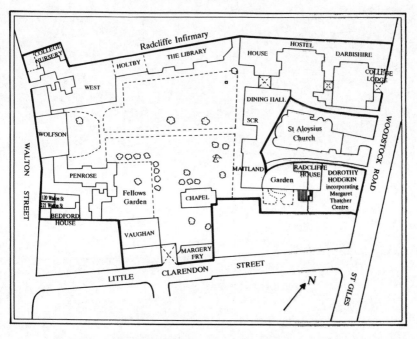

PLAN OF SOMERVILLE COLLEGE 1993

Introduction

Lady Margaret Hall for Ladies, St Hugh's for Girls, St Hilda's
for Wenches, Somerville for Women.

Oxford Proverb (*c.*1930)

THERE are several variants, not all flattering to Somerville, on this
piece of folklore which was current in Oxford between the wars.[1]
However questionable the individual attributions, they made an
important point: that—at least within the small compass of the
university—clear differences were discernible even between colleges
which might at first glance seem extremely alike. Such distinctions,
once strong, are now very blurred. It is, indeed, not always immediately apparent to the outsider which colleges were once restricted
to men, and which to women.

In the eyes of its own members, of course, any college is distinctive
and special. Somerville has always had a powerful sense of its own
identity, as is perhaps to be expected in an institution which was
founded by a splinter-group in defence of a principle. But the college
has also retained, for longer than many others, something of its
old hold on the public imagination.[2] Its reputation for producing
formidable women is such that, while counting two Prime Ministers
among its alumnae, it is frequently credited with three, or four, or
five.[3] A journalist in 1984 went so far as to opine that Queen Elizabeth
I would have benefited from a Somerville education. What he might
have had in mind, and of what other figures the same might be said,
was the subject of amused speculation in a speech by one of the

---

[1] Oxford's fifth women's college, St Anne's, developed out of what was until 1942 the
Society of Oxford Home Students.

[2] See e.g. 'Somerville: A Degree above the Others', *Now!*, 13 Mar. 1981.

[3] Sirimavo Bandaranaike, Golda Meir, and Benazir Bhutto (an LMH graduate) have all
at various times been wrongly attributed to Somerville. See e.g. 'Somerville Girls', *The
Times*, 7 Feb. 1992. Mrs Bandaranaike's daughter Sunethra read PPE at Somerville 1964–7.

I

fellows (a graduate of St Hilda's) at that summer's gaudy; this book may suggest some further answers.

It is essentially a domestic history, written by a Somervillian, from the inside. An account of how a community of women has organized itself over a period of 114 years has a certain intrinsic interest. The strategies adopted by that community, first to gain acceptance by a male university, and then to survive within a mixed one, have a wider institutional significance. Long excluded from the university, the women's colleges came to form a natural sub-group within it, set apart from their male counterparts not merely by gender but by geography and life-style, by their mode of government, sources of finance, social composition, and style of architecture. It is very easy to see them as marginal to the university's normal life. In many books about Oxford the presence of women is barely acknowledged; in the twentieth-century volume of the official *History of the University* the fine chapter devoted to women is to be found curiously sandwiched between 'Medicine' and 'Politics'.[4] Yet, as that chapter shows, the peculiarities of the women's colleges are to a large extent the product of university policy. Their history has been profoundly influenced by the fact that they are, in Oxford terms, both recent foundations and poor ones—characteristics which a number of former men's colleges share. There are few aspects of university life on which their history does not shed light, if only by contrast. To consider them always as a group is to miss other relationships which may be equally illuminating. A Somervillian of the 1930s, asked with which Oxford college she felt most affinity, would have been at least as likely to say 'Balliol' as 'Lady Margaret Hall'.

A product of nineteenth-century religious controversy, Somerville was to become a focus of late twentieth-century feminist debate. Its history involves issues deeper than the place of women at Oxford. The pioneers of higher education for women were posing a challenge to conventional views about the whole role of women in society. Changes in those views have been reflected both in the college itself, and in the lives of its individual members. Somerville has at times been in advance of public opinion, and at times lagged behind it. Sometimes, indeed, it has done both simultaneously: the generation which campaigned for women's suffrage submitted, more

[4] J. Howarth, 'Women', in B. Harrison (ed.), *The History of the University of Oxford*, viii. *The Twentieth Century* (Oxford, 1994), 345–76.

or less cheerfully, to the outdated indignity of chaperonage. While Somerville's student body has provided, for more than a century, a kind of maverick control-group for the observation of social trends, the college's institutional development has been influenced by a range of external forces: economic and financial fluctuations, government intervention, changing educational orthodoxies, the turn of international events, the operation of European Community law.

But a college, in the last resort, is something more than a set of buildings and junior members currently in residence, run by committees. The ultimate test of any institution is the quality of what it produces. Somerville has provided a common factor in lives as varied as those of Cornelia Sorabji, Eleanor Rathbone, Dorothy L. Sayers, Vera Brittain, Dorothy Hodgkin, Indira Gandhi, Iris Murdoch, Margaret Thatcher, Esther Rantzen. All of these will have been affected, to a greater or lesser extent, by the college and the people they met there. Some of them have maintained a closer connection with it than others. But it would be presumptuous to assume that, in the three years or so normally at its disposal, a college can do much more than to refine existing traits of personality. This book is therefore not so much an attempt to explain what its old members gained from Somerville as to suggest what may have prompted them to apply there in the first place.

Part I

1879 – 1919

I

Origins: A Question of Denomination

OXFORD was a late convert to the idea of educating women. The arrival there of women students in 1879 owed much to the encouragement of individual members of the university, nothing to the university as an institution. It was not until 1910 that their existence was officially acknowledged, and not until 1920 that they were admitted to university membership. The five 'women's societies' established in Oxford between 1879 and 1893 became full colleges of the university only in 1959.

The early history of women at Oxford is essentially one of infiltration—the achievement, as the historian of the process put it, of 'degrees by degrees'.[1] Local conditions determined the course of a movement which had parallels elsewhere: in the programme of extramural lectures and classes for women pioneered in the late 1860s by Miss Clough's North of England Council for Promoting the Higher Education of Women; in the opening to women in 1878 of London University and the rapid spread of coeducation in the provincial and Scottish universities;[2] in Emily Davies's pioneering College for Women at Hitchen, and the experience of its successor, Girton, and its rival, Newnham, in Cambridge. Inspired in part by a general liberal impulse to extend to women the educational advantages long enjoyed by men, these developments owed much to an urgent practical need to provide qualified teachers to staff the new girls' schools which were springing up in the wake of the publication in 1868 of the Taunton Commission Report on Middle Class Education. The

---

[1] A. Rogers, *Degrees by Degrees: The Story of the Admission of Oxford Women Students to Membership of the University* (London, 1938).

[2] Owen's College Manchester was empowered to admit women in 1871; University College Bristol was mixed from its foundation in 1876; the others followed suit in the course of the next fifteen years.

movement in support of the higher education of women was to remain, as it began, almost exclusively a middle-class concern.[3]

The prestige of the ancient universities, and their unrivalled library and teaching resources, made them natural targets for the promoters of the movement. But their collegiate structure, links with the establishment, and long tradition of obscurantism rendered them peculiarly impenetrable to the forces of change. Cambridge, initially more hospitable than Oxford to women students, was to experience a more powerful conservative backlash which delayed until 1948 their admission to degrees. In Oxford the women's cause was associated with a series of radical reforms—the abolition of religious tests, the expansion of the science professoriate, the introduction of a married fellowship, the encouragement of non-collegiate students, the rise of the University Extension movement, the creation of new honour schools—which, from the 1850s onwards had sought, often in the face of bitter opposition, to transform a clerical, quasi-monastic, university into a modern teaching and research institution. It was in this context that Dr Pusey was to describe the establishment of the women's halls as 'one of the greatest misfortunes that has happened even in our own time in Oxford'.[4] Opponents of change within the university could call on powerful allies outside: when in 1877 Mr Leonard Courtney MP proposed an amendment to the Universities of Oxford and Cambridge Bill then before parliament, to enable them 'to examine female students concurrently with male students', it was defeated by 239 votes to 119.[5]

Lack of official encouragement obliged the supporters of women's education in Oxford to resort to a policy of self-help. The creation in 1857 of the Oxford Delegacy of Local Examinations, and the opening ten years later of its examinations to schoolgirls, supplied the essential infrastructure. In 1875, with a view to providing some kind of teacher's certificate, the Delegacy was empowered to run special examinations for women over the age of 18, of a standard roughly equivalent to university finals. A key figure in these developments was the schoolgirl daughter of Thorold Rogers, former Drummond Professor of Political Economy, whose performance in the Oxford Senior

[3] See G. Sutherland, 'The Movement for the Higher Education of Women: Its Social and Intellectual Context in England, *c.* 1840–80', in P. J. Waller (ed.), *Politics and Social Change in Modern Britain: Essays Presented to A. F. Thompson* (Brighton, 1987), 91–116.

[4] Dr Liddon, *Guardian*, 23 Apr. 1884. Quoted in Rogers, *Degrees by Degrees*, 21.

[5] *Hansard* CCXXXIV 296–303, 3 May 1877.

Local Examinations in 1873 would have entitled her, had she been a boy, to an exhibition at Worcester College. (The exhibition was, indeed, offered, and hastily converted into a book prize when the winning candidate's initials, A. M. A. H., were discovered to stand for Annie Mary Anne Henly.) The incident was widely reported in the national press, and gave pause for thought to those who maintained that young women were incapable of the same level of academic attainment as young men. Four years later Miss Rogers was the sole candidate for honours in the new Delegacy examination for women over the age of 18, and gained a first class.

While Annie Rogers tested the waters of the local examination system, other Oxford residents applied their minds to the related question of teaching provision for women. The earliest venture was a series of lectures and classes for women organized in 1866 by Miss Eleanor Smith, sister of the Savile Professor of Geometry, and a friend of the future founders of Girton and Newnham. Despite the distinction of the lecturers—who included Mark Pattison, Henry Nettleship, and William Sidgwick—the enterprise proved to be short-lived, largely because at that date there were not many women in Oxford to take advantage of it. But this situation changed dramatically after 1871, when legislation was passed permitting married men to be fellows of colleges. Before long North Oxford was thickly populated with young wives hungry for self-cultivation and beginning to think about the future education of their daughters. A new set of classes and lectures organized in 1873 by Mrs Mandell Creighton, in the wake of a visit to Oxford by Ruskin to give a course of public lectures on Italian art, attracted an enthusiastic following among a group of women who, with their husbands, were later to be closely associated with the foundation of the women's halls: Mrs Max Müller, Mrs Humphry Ward, Mrs T. H. Green, Mrs Edward Talbot, Mrs Arthur Johnson, Mrs George Kitchin. Dons sympathetic to the cause of women's education gave lectures and classes, to which schoolgirls and schoolmistresses were admitted at reduced rates; ticket-holders from the lectures were admitted to read in the Radcliffe Camera. Among those who took an interest in the venture was the young Robert Bridges.[6]

By now it was becoming clear that the demand for such courses of instruction was not restricted to North Oxford residents, and the idea was mooted of establishing a 'Ladies' Hall' for the accommodation of

---

[6] G. Battiscombe, *Reluctant Pioneer: A Life of Elizabeth Wordsworth* (London, 1978), 57.

students coming from further afield to take advantage of the special facilities for study which Oxford offered. Supporters of the scheme looked naturally to Cambridge for guidance. A visit to Girton inspired the Warden of Keble, Edward Talbot, with the desire to see something similar in Oxford, but conducted on definite church principles.[7] It was to Miss Clough at Newnham that Mrs Humphry Ward (a former pupil at her school at Eller How) wrote in May 1877 for advice on how to proceed. 'It appears to me most important that the number should be small at first that the students may be unobserved till people get used to the idea', she was told in reply—'I believe that for the first two years we were very little known.'[8] Drawing on her six years experience as Principal of Newnham, Miss Clough recommended taking a furnished house if possible, in order to reduce expenses; suggested that it might be possible to find some lady who would be willing to undertake the management—'a pleasant occupation'—for the first year without a salary; and explained that she had kept down expenses at Newnham by getting students to provide their own sheets and towels.

It was in this context of calculated economy that the following year an offer of £1,000 was received for the purpose of establishing a women's hall in Oxford. But the source of the offer—the wealthy feminist Mrs Rose Mary Crawshay, acting through the mediation of the American Rationalist preacher Moncure Conway, a friend of Charles Bradlaugh and Annie Besant[9]—meant that the overriding reaction to this generosity was one of consternation. Realizing that 'any scheme evolved by these special promoters, who were persons of views little acceptable to the Oxford world, would hardly commend a women's College to the University', the local supporters of women's education were spurred on to work out a more acceptable scheme of their own.[10] On 4 June 1878 a meeting chaired by Edward Talbot agreed on the desirability of attempting 'the establishment in Oxford of a small Hall or Hostel in connection with the Church of England for the reception of women desirous of availing themselves of the special advantages which Oxford offers for Higher Education.'[11] Later that month the Master of University College, Dr Bradley, chaired a meeting attended by 'almost every one who cared for the cause', at

---

[7] Battiscombe, *Reluctant Pioneer*, 64.   [8] A. Clough to M. Ward, 9 May 1877.
[9] M. D. Conway, *Autobiography, Memories and Experiences* (London, 1904), 265–8.
[10] G. Bailey (ed.), *Lady Margaret Hall: A Short History* (Oxford, 1923), 32.
[11] Council Minute Book, LMH Archive.

which it was agreed to establish in Oxford an Association for Promoting the Higher Education of Women (the AEW) on the lines of those already in place in many other English cities. The Association's chief object would be to establish and maintain a system of instruction having general reference to the Oxford examinations for women over 18 years of age. At a further meeting on 3 December it was agreed that no student should be admitted to the AEW courses until the committee had been satisfied that suitable arrangements had been made for her residence. But the provision of suitable accommodation was to be left to other agencies; and to allow time for this, lectures were not to begin until October 1879.

After the December meeting a circular was issued appealing for funds to establish a hall for the reception of students. But it was now clear that Talbot's insistence on a specifically Anglican connection for the hall was unacceptable to many of the AEW's most enthusiastic supporters. Liberals like the philosopher T. H. Green, opposed on principle to any imposition of religious tests, argued passionately for the hall to be open to all, regardless of religious affiliation. Throughout the second half of 1878 attempts had been made to reconcile the opposing parties. A compromise in the form of a 'conscience clause' was reluctantly proposed by Talbot's committee and rejected by Green and his friends, whom nothing short of an explicitly undenominational provision would satisfy. The two parties eventually agreed to differ: the Church party went ahead with plans for what was to become Lady Margaret Hall, and in February 1879 a second committee was formed to draw up proposals for an alternative establishment 'in which no distinction will be made between students on the ground of their belonging to different religious denominations.'[12] An editorial in the *Journal of the Women's Education Union* noted with concern the intrusion of Church quarrels into the cause it had at heart.[13]

The non-denominationalist party—unlike their LMH counterparts—had strong political connections. Liberals, firmly committed to the principle of equality of opportunity in education, they saw the opening of opportunities to women in the wider context of the University Extension Movement, of which many of them were already enthusiastic supporters. In religious terms, they represented a broad spectrum of opinion, Anglican, Nonconformist, and agnostic. The Anglican members included a future bishop: Dr John Percival

---

[12] Minutes of Somerville Committee, 7 Feb. 1879.   [13] *JWEU*, 15 Apr. 1879, 54.

(Plate 1), the new President of Trinity, who as Headmaster of Clifton had been involved since its inception in 1868 with the Bristol Committee to Promote the Higher Education of Women (of which his wife had been the first secretary), and a prime mover in the establishment of one of the first university colleges in England to be open alike to men and women.[14] Dr G. W. Kitchin, currently censor of Oxford's non-collegiate students, was to become Dean successively of Winchester and Durham. A. H. D. Acland, in process of renouncing deacon's orders in the Church of England, was a member of the Nonconformist Union (later re-named 'The Society for the Promotion of Religious Equality'), a body of which Professor Legge was a Vice-President. So was Professor Green (Plate 3), arguably the most influential member of the Somerville committee, a naturally religious man who 'had little use for theological dogmas, and small sympathy with ecclesiastical institutions.'[15] Mary Ward (Plate 2), whose father, Thomas Arnold, had already at this date changed his religious allegiance three times, with traumatic consequences for the family on each occasion, had learned through bitter experience the importance of toleration.[16]

Though united in their commitment to non-sectarianism, the members of the committee were far from agreed on how the principle should be interpreted. At a meeting on 15 February summoned to consider a draft circular to be issued for the proposed hall, William Sidgwick, Henry Nettleship, and A. G. Vernon Harcourt argued unsuccessfully for a purely secular constitution. But the original proposal that students 'will be expected to be present at family prayers in the House' was modified by a series of amendments to the simple statement that 'Prayers will be read daily in the House'; and the qualifying phrase 'as a rule' was inserted to soften the obligation to attend some place of worship on Sundays. It was agreed that instruction in Holy Scripture should be provided for students who desired it. The rest of the circular was uncontroversial: no student would be admitted under the age of 17; private tuition could be arranged if necessary to supplement the instruction provided by the AEW; charges for board and lodging would be 20 guineas per term. Thanks to the generosity of Samuel Morley, the Liberal MP for Bristol and a passionate

[14] W. Temple, *Life of Bishop Percival* (London, 1921), ch. 11.

[15] H. Darbishire, *Somerville College Chapel Addresses and Other Papers* (London, 1962), 15.

[16] See M. Trevor, *The Arnolds: Thomas Arnold and his Family* (London, 1973).

campaigner for unsectarian education, the committee was able to offer at the outset four exhibitions of £25 p.a. for two years to students who were preparing to become teachers.[17]

The prospectus for the Anglican hall had claimed that 'The life of the Students will be modelled on that of a Christian family'; the non-denominational hall proposed as its model 'the life . . . of an English family.' The differences between the two halls were to be exemplified and confirmed by their respective choices of name, and later of Principal. The Anglican foundation was named after Lady Margaret Beaufort, mother of King Henry VII and a generous benefactor of both Oxford and Cambridge Universities. In the memorable words of its first Principal: 'She was a gentlewoman, a scholar, and a saint, and after having been three times married she took a vow of celibacy. What more could be expected of any woman?'[18] In adopting, on 28 February 1879, Mary Ward's suggestion of the name of 'Somerville', the founders of the non-denominational Hall chose a rather different role-model for their students. Mary Somerville had died as recently as 1872, internationally regarded as one of the greatest woman scientists of the age. A Scot, twice married, and the mother of six children, she was almost completely self-taught. She had published her first book, *The Mechanism of the Heavens*, at the age of 51, and spent the day before her death, forty-one years later, revising a paper on quaternions. She was cultivated, accomplished, and sociable, a skilled needlewoman, a thrifty housewife, and a competent cook. In religion she tended towards unitarian views, while remaining a member of the established church; in politics she was a staunch Liberal, a supporter of women's suffrage—hers was the first signature on John Stuart Mill's petition to Parliament in this cause in 1868[19]— and an advocate of women's education. She was a passionate anti-vivisectionist. On her death, her family had given her books to the recently established College for Women at Hitchen; they now befriended the new hall at Oxford, subsequently allowed it to adopt their arms and motto, and over the years presented it with many family mementoes.

---

[17] Minutes of Somerville Committee, 15 Feb. 1879.

[18] E. Wordsworth, *Glimpses of the Past* (London, 1913), 153.

[19] In 1869 Mill presented Mary Somerville with a copy of *Subjection of Women* and, in response to her letter of thanks, expressed his appreciation of 'the approbation of one who has rendered such inestimable service to the cause of women by affording in her own person so high an example of their intellectual capabilities.': M. Somerville, *Personal Recollections* (London, 1873), 315.

Having chosen a suitable name, the meeting of 28 February proceeded to elect a committee, which it charged with taking all needful steps for opening the hall in October. Like the committee of the AEW, it was to consist of men and women in equal numbers—a striking contrast to the London women's colleges, whose government was almost entirely in the hands of men.[20] A provision debarring husbands and wives from serving on the committee simultaneously ensured the widest possible spread of interest in the new hall. The university members (A. H. D. Acland, T. H. Green, G. W. Kitchin, James Legge, J. R. McGrath, Henry Pelham, John Percival, and F. H. Peters)—included two heads of house, and fellows of Balliol, Corpus Christi, Exeter, Trinity, and University Colleges. The women members (Mrs Butcher, Mrs Esson, Mrs Vernon Harcourt, Mrs Nettleship, Mrs Prestwich, Mrs Rolleston, Miss Smith, and Mrs Humphry Ward)—many of them powerful figures in their own right—included the wives of the Professors of Latin, Geology, and Anatomy, and provided links with University College, Merton, Christ Church, Corpus, Pembroke, Balliol, and Brasenose. Many of these supporters of women's education in the 1880s had only recently issued another challenge to Oxford tradition, as pioneers of a married fellowship.[21] The Somerville committee also included one extremely influential figure from outside the university: Alderman James Hughes, according to his obituary 'the most energetic and distinguished public man that the civic life in Oxford has ever produced', had already twice been Mayor of Oxford, and was to serve four more terms in that office before his death in 1895.[22] An eighteenth member, Mrs Pickard, was elected, but did not serve. Several of the members were also associated, either in person or through their spouses, with the committee of the AEW.

The Somerville committee elected Dr Percival as its chairman, appointed Mrs Vernon Harcourt and Mrs Ward as joint secretaries and Mr Acland as treasurer, and formed itself into two sub-committees, one charged with finding a Principal, and the other with finding suitable premises. It was agreed to hold the examination for exhibitions in June. The ensuing months were given up to the

---

[20] When Thomas Holloway founded the Royal Holloway College in 1883 in memory of his wife he actually stipulated that all future trustees and governors should be male: C. Dyhouse, *Girls Growing Up in Late Victorian and Edwardian England* (London, 1981), 60–2.

[21] For an account of 'young married Oxford', see the chapter on 'The Ladies of Oxford' in J. E. Courtney, *An Oxford Picture Gallery* (London, 1931).

[22] *Jackson's Oxford Journal*, 14 Sept. 1895.

search for funding, accommodation, a Principal, and—not least—for students.

As early as November 1878 the LMH committee had announced the appointment as its Principal of Miss Elizabeth Wordsworth, a great-niece of the poet. She came from the heart of the Anglican establishment: her father was a bishop and her brother was to become one. The Somerville committee, with equal but opposite appropriateness, now looked to the Liberal political world to which they themselves mostly belonged. Madeleine Shaw Lefevre was the niece of a former Speaker of the House of Commons, and the sister of a Liberal Member of Parliament. Her father, Sir John Shaw Lefevre, was an eminent public servant and a former Vice-Chancellor of London University.[23]

The committee was well aware that the hall's non-denominational status would render it doubly suspect to a university establishment which was not only exclusively male, but also—only eight years after the abolition of religious tests—overwhelmingly Anglican. Its chief concern, therefore, in appointing a Principal, was to secure someone who was capable of disarming prejudice. Miss Shaw Lefevre did not seek the post; nor, indeed, was she the committee's first choice. A number of possible candidates were suggested, of whom three were short-listed for interview on 28 April and deemed unsuitable.[24] It was almost certainly at Dr Percival's suggestion that an approach was then made to Miss Margaret Elliot, with whose father, the Dean of Bristol, he had been closely involved in the establishment of the University College of Bristol, and who had herself for many years been involved in movements for social and educational reform in that city. Miss Elliot (who had once been tipped as the future Mrs Jowett[25]) declined on her own behalf, but added her voice to those who had put forward the name of Madeleine Shaw Lefevre. Percival's experience in building up his teaching staff at Clifton had taught him the advantage of shock tactics;[26] he now descended on the Shaw Lefevre family while they were at luncheon and persuaded Madeleine to go to Oxford for interview. She declined to take with her any testimonials, or to put herself forward in any way. After the briefest of interviews, she was

[23] For an account of the Shaw Lefevre family, see F. M. G. Willson, *A Strong Supporting Cast: The Shaw Lefevres 1789–1936* (London, 1993).

[24] See Mary Ward's Diary, Mar.–Apr. 1879.

[25] Her father was a friend of Jowett, who seems to have been near the point of proposing to her in 1862, when Henry Wall was elected to the only Balliol fellowship then compatible with matrimony: G. Faber, *Jowett: A Portrait with Background* (London, 1957), 299 ff.

[26] Temple, *Life of Bishop Percival*, 17–18.

elected on 3 May, on the understanding that the appointment would be for one year only, and that she would be free to go home in the vacations; she would receive board and lodging in term-time, and be paid £100 a year. Her father welcomed the appointment as offering his daughter 'an interesting and creditable employment for somewhat more than six months of the year.'[27]

Her family traditions, as well as her own character and interests, made Miss Shaw Lefevre an attractive candidate for the post. The interviewing committee noted with approbation the distinction of her appearance and the polish and courtesy of her manner. At the age of 44 she was emphatically a woman of the world, accustomed, despite a natural tendency to shyness, to mixing in 'good' society; an obituarist was to comment that she was the only early head of a women's college who could make any claim to being 'something of the *grande dame*'.[28] Her family connections ensured that she would find a welcome in Oxford: among her friends were many of the men and women involved in the movement for the higher education of women, including members of the councils of Girton and Newnham. In the months before she took up her appointment she was able to visit both Cambridge colleges, staying for several days at Newnham, where Miss Clough not only gave her much information and advice but also took pains to enable her to meet the students (including Helen Gladstone), to see their rooms, and to discuss with them their views of college life.

The Hall was fortunate in attracting funds for exhibitions and scholarships to supplement the original four offered by Mr Morley. The Clothworkers' Company's long history of generosity to Somerville was inaugurated with an undertaking to provide an exhibition of £35 p.a. for three years, to be awarded, if possible, for proficiency in natural science. A three-year scholarship of £30 for proficiency in mathematics was given by a lady in memory of Mary Somerville. With these as bait, the committee began its quest for students. Advertisements were placed in the national and provincial press; circulars were sent out to local secretaries in Cheltenham, Crystal Palace, Leeds, Leicester, Liverpool, Manchester, Rochester, and Southampton. The exhibition examinations were held in mid-June. Mary Ward's diary

[27] Hants RO., Wickham MSS: 38M49/D19, JGSL to HFSL, 5 May 1879. For an account of Miss Lefevre's election see Willson, *A Strong Supporting Cast*, 298 ff.

[28] *Journal of Education*, Nov. 1914, 794.

for the ensuing weeks records the Secretary's complicated dealings with potential applicants, parents, guardians, and headmistresses:

Thurs 19 June . . . Announced results of Exhibition exam to Miss Baynes and Miss Macauley.

Thurs 3 July. Wrote to Mrs Macauley proposing scholarship should be put off for a year. Showed it to Mr Green.

Sat 5 July. Mrs Macauley answered accepting. Gave her leave to put notice in Reading papers.

Sun 27 July. Letter from Miss Lefevre forwarding rules & letter from Miss Pidgeon who does not wish to go in for Prelim in Dec. Wrote to offer Miss Perkins an Exhibition.

Tues 29 July. Answer from Miss Perkins declining. Wrote card to Mr Green to ask what should be done next.

Sat 2 Aug. Letter from Miss Pidgeon enquiring whether open Association Scholarship & Clothworkers' Exhibition are tenable with a teacher's Exhibition. Wrote to Mr Green about it.

Sun 3 Aug. Wrote to Miss Edwardes . . . & Miss Thompson offering Exhibitions.

Tues 5 Aug. Answer from Miss Edwardes declining Exhibition.

Wed 6 Aug. Answer from Miss Maude Thompson . . . accepting. She makes our 7th student . . .

Sat 30 Aug. Letter from Miss Frances Conway Cobbe, who desires to enter Somerville Hall in October . . .

Thurs 4 Sept. Wrote to Miss F. C. Cobbe about church going. Clause necessary but will be liberally worded.

Fri 5 Sept. Heard from Miss Cobbe that she had seen Mrs Nettleship and was reassured.

It also gives some idea of Somerville's dependence in its early days on the advice of Professor Green.

Meanwhile, the sub-committee charged with finding suitable accommodation visited a number of properties, including Cowley House—subsequently St Hilda's—which was then in the market. Eventually it was decided to settle for a five-year lease on Walton House, a St John's property built in 1826 by a Mr Taunton, and occupied for some years by the Chief Constable of Oxfordshire, Captain Mostyn Owen. Attracted by a three-acre site in the highest and healthiest part of

Oxford, and emboldened by the offer of financial backing from a friend of Miss Shaw Lefevre's, Miss Elizabeth Forster, the committee took what seemed then the rash step of acquiring the short lease of the two properties, the house and grounds and the adjoining cottages, for £600. On 19 June the purchase was confirmed, the Principal and Secretaries were authorized to draw up specifications of the furniture needed, and a sub-committee was appointed to superintend alterations to the house. In recognition of her help, Miss Forster was offered—but declined with thanks—the right to nominate two students for the Hall, and to be nominated to the vacant seat on the committee.[29]

Thirty years later Miss Shaw Lefevre produced for inclusion in the newly instituted college Log Book an account of Somerville as it was in 1879:

Walton House as I first saw it was a very different place to the Somerville of today. It was approached from St Giles' the Woodstock Road by a private road densely overshadowed with trees. The grey square stone house covered with wisteria and other creepers had a very countrified aspect. Near the house, the ground widened out into a large garden well planted with fine old trees, and the field beyond bright with buttercups and the apple trees in blossom added to the rural effect of the place. Stabling for several horses occupied the site of the present Wing. The names of the horses still hung over the stalls. At the Walton Street end of the ground was a gardener's cottage and kitchen garden. The quaint old Cottages had, we were told been occupied by undergraduates. A dilapidated coachhouse and stable filled up the space between the Cottages and the House.

For the first few years two cows and a pig formed part of the establishment, but these were later replaced by a pony and donkey which might be seen disporting themselves in the field adding to the picturesque and homely character of the place.[30]

Possession of Walton House was not obtained until August, and of the cottages until 29 September. Both needed extensive repairs and alterations. The drains had to be reconstructed and connected with the town drainage system, making the drive up to the house impassable for some time. The small rooms in the cottages were enlarged by throwing two into one, or by the addition of bow windows, to

---

[29] Minutes of 14 and 19 June 1879.   [30] Log-Book i. 14.

provide accommodation for five students, two servants, and the porteress. (The only servant in the house, Mrs Court, slept in the bathroom.) The cellar under the dining-room was converted to use as a larder by opening light and air into it. A winter lawn-tennis court was laid out in the grounds.

Before term began the household had been established and a gardener installed. The women members of the committee took charge of furnishing the house and cottages, supplying many items of furniture and ornament from their own homes. The Hall was showered with gifts from well-wishers: a garden roller from Mrs Arthur Sidgwick, a framed portrait of Caroline Herschel from the Dowager Lady Herschel, a grand piano from Miss Mary Ewart. The foundations of what was to become a superb college library were laid with a gift of 72 volumes—including Gibbon, Macaulay, Hallam's *Middle Ages*, and Guizot's *History of Civilization*—from Mrs Stephen Winkworth of Holly Lodge (with her husband, among the first subscribers to the fund for Somerville Hall); 28 volumes—including French and German dictionaries—from the Principal; and copies of Liddell & Scott and Lewis & Short from Professor Henry Nettleship. In a gesture of sisterly welcome, Miss Clough and the students of Newnham also sent a gift of books.[31]

A large importation of American walnut furniture was selected by Miss Shaw Lefevre from a wholesale firm in Limehouse, and the beds were specially made by Heal's. On 23 September the committee approved a list of house rules drawn up by the Principal, and gratefully accepted an offer by Mr Acland to undertake the management of the grounds for the first year. Mrs Humphry Ward's diary for the week 6–10 October 1879 reads simply 'Very busy all week at Hall.' On Monday 13 October Somerville's first students began their first term, and three weeks later Mary Ward's daughter Janet was born.

---

[31] Somerville Gift Book. Newnham later sent a gift of books to LMH, which, according to Miss Wordsworth, opened with two books on the shelves—a copy of *The Newcomes* and an 'unintelligible treatise on sound and colour.': Battiscombe, *Reluctant Pioneer*, 83.

2

Madeleine Shaw Lefevre and Somerville Hall, 1879–1889

UNSURPRISINGLY, work on the cottages was still in progress when the term began, and some of Somerville's first students found themselves accommodated for a time in the homes of members of the committee. During the weeks that followed leaking gas- and water-pipes gave endless trouble. Dry rot was found under two of the ground-floor rooms, but was cured by ventilation. The drainage works proved not to have been properly carried out, and had to be overhauled the following year.

The lines on which Somerville as an institution might develop were as yet very unclear. Its finances were precarious. It was housed in temporary accommodation, on a lease which was due to expire within five years. Its Principal, who had undertaken to stay only for a year, could claim little relevant practical experience beyond that afforded by membership of the Metropolitan Association for Befriending Young Servants.[1] For teaching, the halls were dependent on the—as yet, untried—provision made by the AEW. Uncertainty regarding the market value of the women's examinations, and competition from the longer-established colleges in Cambridge, threatened their ability to attract students. They had no recognition from the university, and were regarded with suspicion—not to say, hostility—by considerable sections of Oxford society.

The Somerville founders and their advisers brought to bear on these problems a formidable range of expertise and influence. Dr Percival, though new to Oxford and perhaps never thoroughly at home there, had important contacts in the City as well as in educational circles. Professor Green's pervasive moral influence on Somerville's development[2] was underpinned by valuable practical links with Birmingham

---

[1] F. M. G. Willson, *A Strong Supporting Cast: The Shaw Lefevres 1789–1936* (London, 1993), 296 ff.

[2] See H. Darbishire, *Somerville College Chapel Addresses and Other Papers* (London, 1962), 14–16.

and Nonconformity. Within Oxford, Alderman Hughes was to prove a useful source of advice on city questions, particularly in the conduct of negotiations leading to the purchase of Walton House. The Hall's first Treasurer, Mr Acland, brought to the post his experience as Steward of Christ Church, making joint arrangements for the two institutions in such matters as fish supplies;[3] at the end of his first year in charge of the Somerville grounds he was able to report an impressive profit of £51.7s.2½d on the garden account.[4] Somerville's legal affairs were in the experienced hands of William Shaen, former Clerk of Convocation at the University of London, solicitor from its foundation of the Girls' Public Day School Trust, benefactor of Girton and Newnham, and chairman from 1880 to 1887 of the Council of Bedford College—a prominent Unitarian who, according to his daughter 'could not bear to see the advantages of higher education limited by sex'.[5]

In appointing Madeleine Shaw Lefevre to the principalship, the committee had also secured the interest and support of her family, with its wide range of connections in London and Reading. When devising a (not very sophisticated) system of household accounts for the new Hall, she was able to call upon the expertise of her brother-in-law Charles Ryan, a future Auditor General, to supplement that of Mr Acland.[6] Her brother George, MP for Reading and First Commissioner of Works in Gladstone's second administration, was active in raising funds for Somerville, played a prominent part at the General Meetings of subscribers, and was responsible for the suggestion which determined the direction of its constitutional development. The idea—adopted in time by all the Oxford women's colleges—of setting up a joint-stock company to carry on the work of the hall was agreed in November 1879.[7] In 1881 the Somerville Hall Company was duly incorporated as an association not intended for profit under the Companies Acts of 1862 and 1867: it was to consist of ordinary members, who subscribed £1.1s. or more per annum; life members who subscribed £25 or £5.5s. per annum for five years; and honorary members, of whom one of the first, in recognition of his services, was William Shaen.[8] An elected council of eighteen persons was to manage the company's affairs and submit an annual report to a general meeting.

[3] MSL to EP, 11 Dec. 1908.   [4] Minutes of Council 23 Sept. 1879 and 19 Oct. 1880.
[5] M. J. Shaen (ed.), *William Shaen: A Brief Sketch* (London, 1912), 8.
[6] MSL to ACM, 17 Oct. 1889. Ryan (KCB 1887) married Jane Shaw Lefevre in 1862. He was promoted from Assistant Comptroller and Auditor to Comptroller and Auditor-General in 1888.   [7] General Meeting, 18 Oct. and 5 Nov. 1879.
[8] Minutes of Council, 18 June 1881.

The composition of the first council virtually reproduced that of the old committee, with the important addition of Arthur Sidgwick. In the years ahead, new members, recruited with a careful eye to Somerville's traditions and interests, were to include a succession of distinguished Nonconformist ministers, heads of house, scholars, scientists, and financiers. In recognition of its past generosity (and in hopes of securing its continued support), the Clothworkers' Company was invited to nominate a representative; Sir Owen Roberts served for seventeen years in this capacity, to be succeeded in 1900 by Sir William Bousfield.[9] Both of them were to prove generous benefactors in their own right. A strong Balliol connection, established at the outset in the person of T. H. Green, was maintained in later years by Sir William Markby, Edward Caird, H. W. C. Davis, and A. D. Lindsay. Women continued to be powerfully represented; Charlotte Green (Plate 4), who came on to the Council in 1884, after her husband's death, chaired many of its meetings during her long period as Vice-President from 1908 to 1926. Only one election was to prove controversial: the nomination in 1890 of Lady Burdon Sanderson, wife of the Regius Professor of Medicine, was publicly denounced by Miss Frances Power Cobbe, who regarded the animal experiments conducted by Professor Burdon Sanderson as an insult to Mary Somerville's anti-vivisectionist principles.[10]

The success of the Hall was still far from assured when in October 1879 the committee set about the task of securing permanent premises. Percival, McGrath, Green, and Hughes were deputed to negotiate with St John's about the possibility of acquiring the freehold of the existing property, and to consider possible alternatives should this approach prove unsuccessful.[11] In January they submitted details of five such sites, and reported that, while St John's was 'not disposed to regard Somerville Hall as an institution towards which the College should be expected to show any special favour', it would probably consider any offer which might be represented as in its own financial interest.[12] A valuation was commissioned, and it was agreed to make

[9] Subsequent Clothworkers' representatives were Mr P. M. Evans (1910–44) and Dame Dorothy Brock (1946–51). G. W. Child (1883–96), though not an official representative of the Company on the Somerville Council, was active for many years on the Court of the Clothworkers', which he represented on the council of Bristol University.

[10] *Somerville Hall: A Misnomer. A Correspondence with Notes* (London: Victoria Street Society for the Protection of Animals from Vivisection, 1891).

[11] Diary of Mary Ward, 24 Oct. 1879; Minutes of Council 5 Dec. 1879.

[12] Minutes of Council, 24 Jan. 1880: Report of Building Sites Committee.

an offer of not more than £8,000 for the freehold. In April the Somerville trustees put in an offer of £7,000, and the fellows of St John's—despite their bursar's advice that the offer was too low, and perhaps needled by rumours that they were trying to obstruct the establishment of a women's hall—voted to pursue negotiations.[13] In June the offer was accepted, and Somerville was able to embark on a programme of enlargement free from the kind of interference with which Lady Margaret Hall—also a St John's leaseholder—was to be beset for years to come.[14]

The financial commitment, for a fledgling institution, was very great. A London Committee was formed under the chairmanship of Rachel Vernon Harcourt's father, Lord Aberdare, a life-long supporter of women's education; and 400 invitations were issued for a drawing-room meeting. A sub-committee consisting of Mary Ward, Pelham, Acland, and Green was appointed to consider how best to canvass and organize fund-raising meetings in large towns; meetings were held at King Edward's School in Birmingham in November and in Reading the following spring. The three university members were asked to canvass the Oxford colleges, and secured a number of modest donations from individual fellows. City Companies were approached, the Fishmongers responding with a donation of 100 guineas and an enquiry as to what privileges they might expect in return.[15] George Shaw Lefevre wrote numerous letters on Somerville's behalf, raising a sum of c.£1,400 from donors—including several fellow Liberal MPs—who, he said, 'were not interested in education . . . and could not be appealed to again.'[16]

It was through his influence that the Reading meeting on behalf of the hall was held at 'The Acacias', the home of the wealthy biscuit manufacturer and MP George Palmer. The Palmers, who were later to endow the new Reading University College to the tune of £50,000, were extremely interested in education; as Quakers they might be presumed sympathetic both to the idea of educating women and to the principle of non-denominationalism; and through George Palmer's daughter Emily Poulton (a member of the Council from 1884 to 1939)

---

[13] T. Hinchcliffe, *North Oxford* (London, 1992), 154.

[14] St John's insisted, for instance, that LMH's first extension should be convertible into two separate houses if the halls did not prove a success: Hinchcliffe, *North Oxford*, 155 ff.

[15] Minutes of Council, 16 Nov. 1880.

[16] Recollections of MSL. The MP donors were J. B. Thomasson (£500), B. Samuelson (£100), Sir H. M. Jackson, M. T. Bass, W. Rathbone, S. Williamson, and J. F. Cheetham.

they were to have a long personal connection with Somerville. Significantly, the £100 donation received from this rich, generous, and well-disposed family was among the largest to come Somerville's way. The desired £8,000 took six years to raise; and for fifteen years the Hall received no single donation larger than £800—a startling contrast to the Unitarian Manchester College (with which Somerville had many potential supporters in common) which opened in Oxford in 1892 with capital of £55,000.[17] It is possible that Girton and Newnham had already absorbed such limited funds as were available for the cause of women's education. Somerville had many problems to contend with in its early days, but indebtedness to a major benefactor was not to be one of them. In November 1880 the committee agreed to seek a loan of £4,000 at 4 per cent; several members offered a personal guarantee for the payment of interest.[18]

Having initially agreed to take on the principalship for one year only, Miss Shaw Lefevre (Plate 6) in fact stayed for ten, taking a short period of leave at the beginning of her second year, and an extended period in the academic year 1885/6, which enabled her to visit relations in Ceylon. She often spoke of resigning, sufficiently seriously on one occasion for the Council to sound out Charlotte Green as a possible successor. (Mrs Green, who had received a similar approach from Girton, consulted her brother John Addington Symonds, who said he would like to see her at Somerville if she could go there '*con amore*', but doubted whether she had 'the versatility of intellectual sympathies' which the job required.)[19] It was, as she herself said, 'without a very certain or defined position as Principal' that Miss Shaw Lefevre entered upon her appointment in 1879. In so far as the Somerville committee had in mind any role-model for the post, it was Miss Clough at Newnham,[20] and it was to Miss Clough that she chiefly turned—both before and after taking up office—for advice and guidance. At her suggestion, a Newnham student who had just finished her course at Cambridge was invited spend a few days in Somerville after the beginning of the first term, to help establish good traditions quickly.[21] Miss Clough herself paid a visit to Somerville in

[17] J. Howarth and M. Curtoys, 'The Political Economy of Women's Higher Education in Late Nineteenth and Early Twentieth-Century Britain', *Historical Research*, 60 (1987), esp. 214.   [18] Minutes of Council, 27 Nov. 1880.

[19] J. A. Symonds to C. Green, 7 Dec. 1884 (copy in Somerville Archives).

[20] Diary of Mary Ward, 3 Apr. 1879.

[21] The chosen student was the sister of one of the founding members of the Somerville Council, W. F. H. Peters.

1892, and the Hall in its early days set great value on her sympathy and support.

One of her first pieces of advice was to proceed with extreme caution. Her concern in this matter was not purely disinterested, for, as the Principal herself later commented, 'there is no doubt that any false step on our part would have reacted on Cambridge and would have prejudiced the cause which she had so safely pioneered.'[22] But it chimed with Miss Shaw Lefevre's own instincts, and under her principalship Somerville deliberately maintained a low profile and embarked upon the policy of steady, but unobtrusive, infiltration which was to reap such benefits in later years.

Within Oxford, she was able to take advantage of her family's wide connections. The Dean of Christ Church and Mrs Liddell, the Talbots, the Aclands, G. C. Brodrick of Merton were all family friends of long standing. Dr Jowett was an old friend of her father's, and though initially dubious about the desirability of the women's halls, was in the event to show them much kindness, giving lectures for the students and welcoming them as guests to Balliol's Sunday concerts. Other family friends from outside Oxford were persuaded to interest themselves in the work of the new Hall; a distinguished array of early visitors included Mrs Fawcett, Miss Rose Kingsley, Mr Gladstone, Professor Bryce, Mrs Octavia Hill, Lady Stanley of Alderley, Sir Alfred Lyall, Rhoda Broughton, and Mr Augustus Hare. On the occasion of Helen Gladstone's visit, Somerville's most ardent Conservative student was produced to entertain her to a recitation.

The charm of her personality, combined with the interesting novelty of her position, made Miss Shaw Lefevre, like Miss Wordsworth, a welcome guest at Oxford dinner parties. She has left in her Recollections a humorous account of the first such occasion she attended:

The first time I dined out in Oxford was at a dinner given by the Vice-Chancellor, Dr Evans of Pembroke College. A Fly which I had ordered failed to appear in time. It was pouring with rain. I felt it would never do to be late at a formal dinner when caps and gowns are always worn when the Vice-Chancellor is present. There was nothing for it but to tuck myself up with a waterproof and umbrella and to run at full speed all the way down the town to Pembroke. I arrived breathless but in time to be taken in first by the Vice-Chancellor:—a graceful

---

[22] Recollections of MSL.

compliment on his part to mark the first appearance of the Principal of Somerville—and which I was so near losing.

But, however lightly worn, her social poise was an important weapon in the cause she had at heart; and her students recognized this. 'There is no doubt that through her womanliness and moderation and quiet ways the Hall took from the first a place in Oxford, which might easily have been missed under other guidance,' wrote one of them, Eleanor Powell, in an obituary tribute.[23] Elizabeth Wordsworth, writing in the *Oxford Magazine*, struck a similar note:

> She was the very antipodes of the clumsy, masculine blue-stocking who was the favourite bugbear of the opponents of women's education. It would be difficult to imagine a more womanly woman; and the importance of such a figure-head to a recently formed women's college, exposed as it was to the freest criticism from both friends and foes, can hardly be over-estimated.[24]

Among Miss Shaw Lefevre's most notable conquests was John Ruskin, whom she first met at a dinner party in November 1884. She later described their encounter:

> I was told that he was not much in favour of women's colleges—but I persuaded him to come and see Somerville which he did a few days later. I took him to see some of the rooms and several of the Students having joined us as we went along, he sat down in one of their rooms and discoursed to them in his delightful way while they gathered round him and literally sat at his feet.[25]

A few days after this visit, Ruskin presented the Hall with a picture; this was followed by some geological specimens, and a case of precious stones, cut but unset. Considering the latter to be a loan, Miss Shaw Lefevre returned them to the house where Ruskin was staying; but he sent them again, saying that he wished them to remain as a permanent 'regalia' for Somerville. More gifts followed: a copy made by himself of the Head of St Ursula from a painting by Carpaccio, a set of his own works—nineteen volumes bound in blue morocco—and some of his favourite books. But the following year the Principal was asked to return the case of cut stones to Nockhold the diamond merchant in Soho; and when she did so she was told that they had never

---

[23] *SSA Report*, 1914. [24] Obituary by 'E. W.', *Oxford Magazine*, 16 Oct. 1914, 5–6.
[25] Recollections of MSL.

been paid for. In 1887 Ruskin sent another case of cut sapphires as a permanent gift, this time enclosing with them his cashed cheque of £100. Miss Shaw Lefevre took care to preserve the letters relating to this gift (treasuring them, as she said, for their autograph value), and when a doubt subsequently arose as to whether Ruskin had really intended giving the sapphires away, was able to prove Somerville's claim.[26] The 'Ruskin jewels', thus retained, came to form the basis of the Principal's regalia on formal occasions; in 1920 a group of old students subscribed for them to be set as a pendant.

If the dispelling of prejudice in the world at large—and the Oxford world in particular—was the major achievement of Miss Shaw Lefevre's ten-year term of office, she was also largely responsible for what her obituary in the *Times Educational Supplement* called 'the wise establishment of precedents in the conduct of life in a women's college.'[27] The early student community, beset by fluctuating numbers and considerable ambiguity of status, cannot have been an easy one to preside over, or, indeed, to keep track of. 'I feel sure we were only twelve students the first year', recalled Helen Baynes many years later:

—and I fancy Miss Pidgeon did not stay the whole year. I rather think Miss Brailey had a room out of College—she and her sister already had a school at Banbury, so she generally went home for the weekend. . . . The two Miss Bruces (Isabel and Lily) lived with their sister Mrs Vernon Harcourt, attended our lectures, and often lunched at College, joined the Tennis etc: but were never in residence.[28]

This first group of students ranged in age from 17 to 36. They included a number of intending schoolmistresses, and some experienced teachers (Miss Brailey being an extreme case) in pursuit of a formal qualification. Students who were free from the prospect of having to earn a living were able to regard Somerville as a kind of academic finishing school. The flexibility of the AEW courses enabled students who so desired to dabble in a range of subjects. There was no obligation to sit the Delegacy examinations. Some students used their time at Oxford to work for the examinations of the University of London; Frances Conway Cobbe came to Somerville in order to prepare for the Girton entrance examination. There was a very high drop-out rate. Emma Pidgeon did indeed leave after a term, her mother—a widow—

[26] Recollections of MSL.   [27] *Times Educational Supplement*, 6 Oct. 1914.
[28] H. Baynes to EP, 29 July 1923.

discovering that she could not manage at home without her.[29] Miss Cobbe had to leave in the course of her second year to take care of her sick father.[30] The death of Florence Macauley's father obliged her to leave Somerville after two terms and earn her living as a teacher.[31] Only two of the first group of twelve students—Maude Thompson and Mary Watson—were to remain for a full three years.

To establish—in the glare of potentially adverse publicity—a mode of life which could accommodate this diverse group of women was no inconsiderable achievement. Miss Shaw Lefevre, conscious of the difficulties of dealing with a body of students who were 'old enough to be independent, and yet requiring some restraint,'[32] made little outward show of government. Rules were kept to a minimum, and when exceptions to them were necessary, she tried to ensure that they were made as discreetly as possible. 'Everything', recalled Eleanor Powell, 'went on very quietly, and I can recall but one or two stormy episodes; and even these were quietly dealt with.' After one such episode Miss Shaw Lefevre poured out her troubles to her opposite number at LMH: 'We ought to change students', commented Miss Wordsworth in a family letter, 'as I think I could snub *hers* and mine do not need any snubbing. . . . I would not be in her place for any money.'[33] The Somervillian reputation for cussedness was evidently established very early on.

Despite bouts of irritation at the 'second-rate . . . ways and ideas' of her charges, and their tendency to form 'sets and cliques',[34] Miss Shaw Lefevre's concern for her students, and for their individual problems and difficulties, became legendary. But she was far too reserved and shy for them to get to know her easily. After a visit to LMH an early Somerville student contrasted the two heads: 'Miss Wordsworth . . . seemed a very genial lady, much more get-at-able than Miss Lefevre.'[35] 'I think we all loved and I know we all respected her', wrote Mary Skues, who as Senior Student in her final year saw a good deal of the Principal,—adding 'I should not have liked to incur her displeasure.'[36] As an administrator, colleagues found her 'clear-headed if not hard-headed'.[37] Lilian Faithfull worked for a year as her secretary before

---

[29] Note in College Register. [30] Sheldon, 5 Dec. 1880.
[31] Sheldon, 22 Mar. 1881. She returned for a year in 1886 as a Morley Exhibitioner.
[32] Willson, *A Strong Supporting Cast*, 304.
[33] E. Wordsworth to 'Susie', n.d. (?1879) (Wordsworth MSS., LMH).
[34] Willson, *A Strong Supporting Cast*, 304.   [35] Sheldon, 13 Mar. 1881.
[36] M. T. Skues to HD, 26 Mar. 1941.   [37] *Oxford Magazine*, 16 Oct. 1914, 5–6.

embarking on the teaching career which would take her to the principalship of Cheltenham Ladies' College, and found the experience an educative one:

> The Principal was slow when I wished to be quick, and very deliberate in making decisions. Dictated letters which I eagerly wished to despatch were often kept for a day, or even two, for reflection. It was soon apparent to me, however, that such delay was really an economy in work, and that one letter sufficed where two or three might otherwise have been needed.[38]

One clue to Miss Shaw Lefevre's success was the care she took to cultivate good relations with the governing body of the Hall, and with its members individually. She made frequent appeals to them for guidance, and later paid tribute to 'the great advantage we possessed in having a Council of large-minded, wise and influential men and women, resident in Oxford, who were always ready to give help and advice and to stand by us in any difficulty'[39]—('a body of infinitely wise and learned persons', as Margery Fry was to put it, 'legislating for a little band of frail women in a dangerous world').[40] Miss Shaw Lefevre's diplomatic approach was well-judged. Though not a member of the original Somerville committee, she was regularly invited to attend its meetings; and when the committee was superseded by the council in 1881 she was immediately elected to membership. Girton, whose foundress, Emily Davies, fought for years to keep the Mistress off the college's executive committee, served as a reminder that the relations between a principal and her governing body were not always so painless.

One of the greatest challenges which confronted the halls in their early days was to convince the public at large, and parents in particular, that a college education was not actually harmful for women. The view that the female brain was incapable of sustained intellectual effort, and the female physique unsuited to the pressures of academic life, was widespread in the (male) medical establishment. Higher education, it was argued, would render women unfeminine and unmarriageable, endanger their health, and almost certainly impair their reproductive capacity. These were subjects on which the women's halls tended, understandably, to be defensive. When appealing for

[38] L. M. Faithfull, *In the House of my Pilgrimage* (London, 1924), 74.
[39] Recollections of MSL.
[40] SMF to MKP, 4 Mar. 1908 (Representation of Tutors file).

funds for a new building in 1885, the Council gave details of the academic successes of the sixty-two students who had passed through Somerville since 1879, and went on to emphasize that 'throughout, thanks mainly to the unceasing care of the Principal, . . . the health of the students has been excellent, and not a few have benefited much in body as well as in mind by their Oxford residence.'[41] Miss Wordsworth, writing in *The Monthly Packet*, conceded that there were cases on record of breakdown from overwork, but drew attention to the 'many other cases where regular, moderate, and congenial study, has had the best possible effects in establishing health and keeping off fancied illness.'[42] In 1890 Somerville and LMH co-operated with Girton and Newnham in a survey, conducted under the secretaryship of Mrs Sidgwick, which compared details of former students with those of a control group of sisters and cousins close in age who had not attended college; its conclusions reassuringly confirmed those of an earlier American survey—that a college education posed no particular threat either to health or to the ability to raise children.[43]

It did, however, show that the marriage rate among former students was significantly lower than that achieved by their non-university sisters and cousins (10 per cent as compared with 19 per cent), thereby supplying ammunition for those who argued that higher education was unconducive to matrimony. Five years later Alice Gordon conducted a nationwide survey of 1,486 ex-students, found that 208 had married while 680 were currently engaged in teaching, and concluded that 'if a mother sends her daughter to one of the universities, she is more likely to become a teacher than a wife.'[44] But many of the women who embarked on higher education at this period were already —for social, temperamental, or economic reasons—predisposed to spinsterhood; and many of those who did marry married late. A longer perspective may give a different picture. Of the 155 students who entered Somerville between 1879 and 1890, 59 are recorded as having become teachers (though some only briefly); 51 married (though some relatively late in life); ten did both (though not, generally, concurrently). In succeeding years the proportions of both categories

---

[41] Special Appeal leaflet, Apr. 1885.   [42] Quoted in *Lady's Pictorial*, 2 Jan. 1892.

[43] Mrs H. Sidgwick, *Health Statistics of Women Students of Cambridge and Oxford and of their Sisters* (Cambridge, 1890). The American survey was carried out in 1885 by the Committee of Health Statistics in Boston.

[44] A. Gordon, 'The After-Careers of University Educated Women', in *The Nineteenth Century*, 37 (June 1895), 955–60.

increased, until for the generation up between 1911 and 1920 they were exactly equal at 44 per cent.[45] The war years, of course, both increased the number of teaching posts open to women, and drastically reduced the pool of potential husbands.

But this was an argument which the women's halls could not hope to win. Once parents ceased to assume that education would make their daughters unmarriageable they began to question the economic sense of wasting an expensive education on domesticity. In warning the parents of a prospective LMH student that 'few of our girls marry really well' Miss Wordsworth was perhaps hedging her bets.[46] Somerville, which was to acquire a reputation for the professional efficiency with which it sought to equip its students for a life in which 'women must fight women's battles',[47] took care not to interpret its mission too narrowly. A college education, maintained Miss Lefevre's successor, prepared students 'alike for motherhood and the care of children, for the work of breadwinning when needed for the support of themselves and others, and for that unpaid labour charitable, philanthropic and social of which . . . the claims upon women grew yearly stronger.'[48]

At a time when the education of daughters was a low priority in many families, the support, advice, encouragement, or even bullying, of teachers and headmistresses was often crucial in overcoming parental objections. Florence Rich, encouraged by her headmistress—Miss Connolly of Aske's Hatcham School—to try for the Somerville scholarship examination in 1884, was warned by her parents that, though they did not wish to deny her the pleasure of sitting the examination, there was no question of her being able to take up a scholarship should she be successful; she was the eldest of five children, and the family finances could not stretch to sending her to Oxford. In the event, Miss Connolly overcame their objections, and Miss Rich came to Somerville to read chemistry, conscious none the less that there were people who thought it unjust to her brothers and sisters that she should be allowed to do so: 'An aunt of whom I was very fond considered it selfish of me at the time, but forgave me three years later when she heard that I had a resident teaching post at a

---

[45] *Somerville College Register.* 175 of the 395 students who entered Somerville 1911–20 married and 175 became teachers.   [46] Battiscombe, *Reluctant Pioneer*, 87.

[47] H. Deneke, *Grace Hadow* (London, 1946), 28.

[48] A. Maitland, speech on 'The Student Life of Women in Halls of Residence', *National Union of Women Workers Report for 1894.*

salary of £70 a year.'[49] The economic argument in favour of higher education gained ground as women demonstrated their ability not only to earn their own living, but also, when necessary, to support dependent relatives.

Within Oxford, the women's halls had many potential enemies. Dean Burgon's celebrated allocution to women in New College Chapel on Trinity Sunday 1884—'Inferior to us God made you, and inferior to the end of time you will remain. But you are none the worse off for that'—was not taken very seriously by his congregation, which is reported to have laughed aloud.[50] The well-intentioned, but misguided, actions of friends were at times more embarrassing. Looking back years later on the early difficulties with which the halls had to contend, Miss Shaw Lefevre instanced the episode shortly after they had opened, when, in the course of a debate at the Union, a proposal was made that women students should be admitted as subscribers to the Union library. A violent opposition was led by George Curzon, then one of the Union's most prominent speakers, in terms which, according to Miss Shaw Lefevre, were 'neither courteous nor respectful to us.' The ensuing debate was described by one witness as discreditable and vulgar, and it ended in an adverse vote, whereupon the minority who were in favour of the admission of women insisted on a poll of all the members. At this juncture the Principal, on the advice of members of the Council, wrote to the President of the Union, Edward Cook (who had in the mean time sent a present to Somerville of Warton's *History of English Poetry* as a mark of his personal goodwill), begging that the subject might be dropped, as the women themselves had neither solicited nor wished for admission to the library. But it was now too late; the printed notice announcing the poll had already been circulated. The poll this time was in favour of the motion, but the offer was declined by the women's halls with thanks. Even so, they did not escape a great deal of unfriendly comment, including a hostile article in the *Saturday Review*. Recalling the episode shortly before the Great War, Miss Shaw Lefevre commented wryly on the current newspaper headlines 'Lord Curzon announces his intention to propose that Oxford University shall be opened to women on the same terms as it is open to men.'[51]

Initially, the only lectures open to women in Oxford were those

---

[49] Recollections of Florence Rich.
[50] A. Rogers, *Degrees by Degrees: The Story of the Admission of Oxford Women Students to Membership of the University* (London, 1938), 18–19. [51] Recollections of MSL.

provided by the AEW. The Association's first lecture-room, situated over Mr Marlowe's baker's shop at 35 Little Clarendon Street, provided welcome camouflage for early students, who could attend classes on Greek history under the socially more acceptable pretext of buying cakes. Larger premises, incorporating a former Baptist chapel, were subsequently found in Alfred Street, off St Giles's. The lecturers were for the most part dons sympathetic to the cause of the higher educa-tion of women: the first lecture list included the names of Henry Nettleship for Latin and Greek, A. C. Bradley for English, and Arnold Toynbee for political economy. Their lectures were often a simple repetition of those given to their male undergraduates.

Such duplication was plainly an uneconomical use of time. But public opinion was not yet ready for the idea of women students being admitted to university lectures and classes, and an offer by H. B. Dixon to admit women to his lectures in the Balliol–Trinity laborat-ory was vetoed by both Jowett and Percival. A decisive break was made in 1880 when A. G. Vernon Harcourt simply refused to repeat his class in the Christ Church chemistry laboratory in order to maintain the separation of the sexes. Arts subjects followed suit in 1882, when J. Franck Bright and George Kitchin persuaded their colleges to allow them to admit women to their lectures. This revolutionary move was deemed to require special safeguards, and—partly as a sop to pro-priety, and partly as a precaution against what Vera Farnell called 'a faint or a fit or some other feminine fuss'—the chaperone at mixed lectures became a feature of Oxford life. The presence of a chaperone was obligatory until 1893, and up until the Great War might be re-quired at any lecture at which only one woman was present.

Initially, the rule was taken very seriously, and chaperone duty became an important, if tedious, part of the work of the women Principals and the female members of their Councils. At some lec-tures, indeed, chaperones were so numerous as to give rise to com-plaints that there were not enough seats left for the undergraduates.[52] Miss Wordsworth—who was in the habit of interrupting the lectures with questions and comments—went on strike after sitting five times through Professor Nettleship's lecture on the Greek philosophers. When Miss Maitland was Principal of Somerville, her presence as chaperone at a course of lectures on Rabelais enabled her to reassure a father, anxious about the reading matter to which his daughter

---

[52] ACM to B. Johnson, 29 Oct. 1891 (Johnson Papers, St Anne's).

was being exposed, that she had 'heard nothing which could offend'; the edition used as a set text was, she said, 'more than expurgated'.[53] Charlotte Green, whose training as a nurse was thought to make her particularly qualified for chaperone duties, used to say that she knitted throughout the lectures and never remembered any Somervillian giving any trouble.

There are many comic accounts of the early appearance of women at undergraduate lectures. Emily Kemp, a student in the early 1880s, described how some of the men attending Dean Kitchin's lectures at Christ Church were so terrified when the first women students came in (by a different door) that they ran away, and how, 'attending Dr Bright's lectures on English History at Queen's College, we were taken through all manner of dark and dingy passages and through his house . . . and when we got into the hall we sat at one end and the men at the other.'[54] At some colleges the women were required to sit at the high table, looking down on the rows of men below (and enjoying, as one of them commented, a much better view of the noble architecture). One Somerville student—Constance Tod—whose brother was a fellow of Oriel, was, however, dispensed from the services of a chaperone when attending his lectures, on the grounds that her strong resemblance to the lecturer was sufficient guarantee of propriety.

Most of the tutorial work organized by the AEW was also done—with appropriate safeguards to propriety—by men. Not all of these were equally successful in adapting their teaching methods to their pupils' needs. Frances Sheldon reported in 1881 that the mathematics students were 'in a terrible commotion about their prospects', being taught by a professor who was 'lazy, lacks sense, and has no interest in the girls' work.'[55] But in general, overwork was a more common complaint than lack of interest. 'Dr Wright gives us so much more Anglo-Saxon to do than we can manage without sitting up late at night, and such a long paper of questions besides, that we are going to *strike*' reported Cornelia Sorabji in 1889. One of their other lecturers had advised them to object, and said that Dr Wright was probably waiting for them to do so—'and so we mean to do now we are up to his little game.' By this date it was already, apparently, 'proverbial' in Oxford that 'the Ladies' Halls work harder than the Men's.'[56]

About the teaching function of the halls themselves there had

[53] ACM to an unknown father, 7 Feb. 1901.
[54] Press-cutting in College Log Book, 1921.   [55] Sheldon, 13 Nov. 1881.
[56] Sorabji, 3 Nov. 1889 (India Office Library MSS Eur.F.165/1).

always been an element of ambiguity. Somerville and LMH were initially envisaged purely as halls of residence for students whose teaching would be organized by the AEW. They had no tutorial staff of their own, and their Principals had no formal educational role, though early prospectuses indicated that they were prepared to arrange extra coaching to supplement the classes and lectures sponsored by the Association. As, with the growth of student numbers, the burden of administration and supervision became too great for the two Principals to cope with unaided, the halls began to employ resident members of staff to provide the necessary assistance. At LMH, as at Newnham, these were known as 'vice-principals'; with the appointment in 1882 of one of its own former students, Lilla Haigh, Somerville opted instead for the title of 'tutor'.

Despite her title, Miss Haigh, a 22-year-old who had taken a third in history the previous year, was engaged primarily as a general administrative assistant to the Principal. But the Hall provided plenty of scope for elementary coaching, and it was soon assumed that tutors would supplement their income by teaching. (At a time when the going rate of pay was £5 a term with board and lodging, most of them, indeed, needed to do so.) In the years which followed, as Somerville recruited some of its brightest students to the staff, the balance between administration and teaching began to shift. Margaret Seward, having taken a first in chemistry in 1885, stayed on as tutor and chaperone to Somerville's science students; two years later she applied for a teaching post at Holloway, and, in an unsuccessful attempt to keep her, the Council hastily doubled her salary to £10.[57] Isabella Don, with a first in English, joined the staff as librarian and tutor in English literature. Eleanor Powell, with a first in history, replaced Lilla Haigh in 1886 and was considered the following year as a possible vice-principal.

In the roll of early Somerville tutors a special—and specially ambiguous—place is occupied by Clara Pater, the younger of Walter Pater's two sisters. A member of the AEW Committee from 1879 to 1885, Miss Pater taught for both Somerville and LMH from her brother's house in Bradmore Road. During Miss Shaw Lefevre's absence on leave at the beginning of Michaelmas Term 1880, she agreed to move temporarily into Somerville as her deputy. Another temporary appointment as Acting Principal during Miss Lefevre's more prolongued period of leave in 1885/6 enabled her to stay on in Oxford

---

[57] Minutes of Council, 14 May 1887.

after her brother's departure for London; she was assisted on this occasion by Lilla Haigh, who took special charge of the students living in the Hostel, and by Isabella Don, who was put in charge of household management. On the opening of the new West Building in 1887 Miss Pater was appointed Resident Tutor at a salary of £45 plus board and lodging, on the understanding that she might 'take such an amount of private tuition as will not interfere with the due performance of her duties.' Although she is often referred to as 'Vice-Principal', the title was never officially conferred on her; she remained as Resident Tutor in the West until her resignation and departure for London in 1894. Miss Pater's austere dignity, combined with what a friend described as a 'picturesque truthfulness in speech', made her a stimulating—if sometimes intimidating—figure to students, though by the 1890s her teaching methods were coming to be seen as something of an anachronism.[58] When she left, friends and students commissioned a portrait by Lowes Dickinson (who was considered particularly suitable because of his links with the Pre-Raphaelites and with Liberal causes), which, according to Emily Penrose, did not 'give the least idea what she looked like'; a more satisfactory likeness, a watercolour drawing by Blake Wirgmann, was presented to the College in 1929. At the time of Miss Shaw Lefevre's death, Elizabeth Wordsworth paid tribute to the combined influence which she and Miss Pater had had on Somerville's early students and their reputation in the wider world:

> To the tone of refinement and sympathy, the love of work, and the high sense of honour fostered by them it is largely due that the presence of women students in Oxford has given so few openings to the caricaturist, and so little cause of offence to the severest censor of morals and manners.[59]

The practice of attaching former students to the college in a capacity partly tutorial and partly administrative continued for many years: Mildred Pope, Alice Bruce, Margery Fry, Vera Farnell, and Evangeline Evans (later Lady de Villiers) were all to begin their careers in this way. But in the early days it gave rise to ambiguities of status which were bound to strain relations with the AEW. So long as tutors confined themselves to chaperone duties and marking the linen there was no

---

[58] F. Perrone, 'University Teaching as a Profession in Oxford, Cambridge and London 1870–1930', D. Phil. thesis (Oxford, 1991), 145.   [59] *Oxford Magazine*, 16 Oct. 1914, 5–6.

problem; once they began to take on the direction of studies they were in danger of encroaching on the jealously guarded territory of the Association and its Lady Secretary, Mrs Johnson. As Somerville gradually built up its own teaching strength, the Principal assumed increasing control over tutorial arrangements. Students, thought Miss Shaw Lefevre, should look to their hall for guidance and advice in educational matters, the AEW being regarded as 'an august and independent body not lightly to be applied to in matters of detail.'[60] Mrs Johnson, meanwhile, continued to insist on interviewing all students at the beginning of term to arrange their work, maintaining that

> since it is the Association Committee which organises the lectures and teaching, appoints and alone has the power of dismissing the teachers, keeps the purse and supplements the expenses of education . . . the decisions of the Committee in its province of education are held to be final, without any appeal to the Councils of the Halls.[61]

The two positions were plainly incompatible. In Miss Shaw Lefevre's time open conflict was avoided; Mrs Johnson found her 'a most kind and sympathetic lady, delightful to work with.'[62] But in 1888 the withdrawal of an AEW lecturing appointment from Somerville's Eleanor Powell, on the grounds that many college lectures in history were already open to women, fuelled a resentment which was to come to a head in the time of her successor.[63]

The women's examinations administered by the Delegates of Local Examinations were of the same standard as that of the university examinations for men. It soon became clear, however, that they did not have the same standing in the eyes of the public. In particular, the failure of many school authorities to recognize the value of the women's examination appears to have deterred intending teachers from embarking on the expense of a three-year course of study at Oxford—a disadvantage which was felt still more acutely after 1881, when Cambridge University examinations were opened to women.[64]

---

[60] MSL to ACM, n.d. (AEW Box II).

[61] B. Johnson, *A Reply to Professor Pelham's Suggestions* [1892] (Johnson Papers, St Anne's: 'AEW and Somerville').

[62] B. Johnson, 'The First Beginnings', in G. Bailey (ed.), *Lady Margaret Hall: A Short History* (London, 1923), 34.

[63] AEW Minute Book, 2 Mar. 1887 (Bodleian MS.Top.Oxon. d.1047). The opportunity for Miss Powell to lecture for the AEW was first refused, then withdrawn in 1888 after she had given a single course.

[64] This decision was hailed in Newnham as 'the great crisis in the history of the women's colleges.': see A. Phillips (ed.), *A Newnham Anthology* (Cambridge, 1979), 17–19.

Three years later Oxford agreed to follow suit, largely in response to representations that the two women's halls might otherwise be obliged to close. Miss Lefevre's diary records the historic vote in Convocation:

> I thought it best to keep away. There was a very large attendance and a large majority in our favour which we hardly expected. 100 to 46. Mr Brodrick voted for us which was very doubtful to the last. Canon Liddon spoke against it. In sciences and mathematic we shall have the same papers as the men.[65]

The news was received at Somerville with great rejoicing. Twenty-four years later, at the 1908 Gaudy, Arthur Sidgwick (whose brother Henry had witnessed the earlier Cambridge celebrations) recalled the triumphal celebration in the garden at night, 'where invisible dancers carrying Chinese lanterns ran to and fro to the tune of a ballad whose burden was;

> "In spite of all temptations to avoid examinations
> We will do them if we can . . ."[66]

Professor and Mrs Thorold Rogers presented the college with a vase to commemorate the victory in Convocation; and for some years afterwards the anniversary of the day when the first examinations were opened to women was kept as a major feast in Somerville's calendar, the entire student body converging—on foot, bicycle, train, or charabanc—to some local beauty-spot, such as Wheatley or Nuneham, for a celebratory picnic.

It was, however, a limited concession, affecting only candidates for honour moderations, history, and mathematics; students offering English or modern languages or ancient history and philosophy—subjects unrecognized as yet by the university—had still to enter for the existing Delegates' examinations. The decision none the less gave new life to the women's halls. Within a year women had gained access to the university laboratories and also to many college lectures—Balliol, Exeter, and Corpus taking a lead which was followed in the next few years by most of the other colleges. By 1897 only Magdalen continued to forbid its fellows to admit women to their lectures. In October 1884 Margaret Seward was the first Oxford woman student to be entered for the honour school of mathematics; the

---

[65] MSL diary, 29 Apr. 1884. [66] *SSA Report*, 1908.

following year she was the first to obtain a first class in the final honour school of natural science. Other academic honours quickly followed. In 1888, hailed in Somerville as 'the most brilliant [year] on record', Somerville and LMH between them achieved a total of seven firsts and six seconds out of the fifteen students they had entered for honour examinations during the year.[67] The first in classical moderations gained by Somerville's Elizabeth Hodge was particularly important, for it resulted in Greats being opened to women, without any of the opposition which had been made on the previous occasion. When in 1890 Miss Hodge achieved a second in Greats, the Oxford Correspondent reported proudly: 'She is the first women who has attempted this school, probably the highest of its kind in the world.'[68]

Those students who chose to study science were doubly pioneers. A suggestion by the Clothworkers' Company in 1879 that their first exhibition should be awarded for proficiency in natural science had to be rejected on the grounds that no AEW teaching was yet available in this subject.[69] Nor were there many potential candidates. The sciences were not widely taught in girls' schools, and those students who had been well taught in science frequently lacked the language and other qualifications necessary to get them through the women's first examination. Florence Rich, awarded a scholarship to Somerville in 1884 on the strength of the zoology she had learned at school under Miss M. A. Macomish, a former pupil of Huxley's, found herself obliged to spend the greater part of her first year at Oxford keeping up her French and learning German from scratch. Neither she herself, nor the Somerville authorities, had any very clear idea what, beyond passing this examination, she should do in Oxford. Mr (later Sir Edward) Poulton, who had examined her scholarship papers and was anxious for her to continue to study zoology, urged her to apply for the school of animal morphology, assuring her and Miss Lefevre that he was sure the school would be opened to women if only application were made. Dreading the fuss and publicity of being the first woman to take the examination (and the awful humiliation of not doing well in it), Miss Rich begged to be allowed to take some branch of science which was already open. So she came to read chemistry, for which Miss Watson and Miss Seward provided precedents,[70] and in which

---

[67] Oxford Letter, 1888.   [68] Ibid. 1890.   [69] Minutes of Council, 23 Sept. 1879.
[70] Mary Watson (Mrs Style), one of Somerville's first students, took a first in geology in 1882 and a second in chemistry in 1883, going on to become science mistress at Cheltenham Ladies' College.

Somerville had a staunch ally in the person of the Lee's Reader, Mr Vernon Harcourt.

'I had been accustomed' she later wrote 'to a large, well-organised school, with a highly experienced staff, and one thing that struck me when I first came to Somerville was the extreme amateurishness of it all.' She also disliked the conspicuousness engendered by the need for special arrangements being made for each individual student. In her second year she was coached in physics by Margaret Seward, and attended the lectures given at Balliol by Mr H. B. Dixon, a newly married man whose wife's desire to attend his lectures neatly solved the problem of chaperonage. The viva at the end of the year was an ordeal socially rather than academically: the examiners were, she recalled, very nice to her, but the porter at the Examination Schools greeted her arrival (with Miss Seward in attendance) with the words 'What do you ladies want here?' In contrast, her preliminary exam in chemistry the following term took place in the Principal's Lodging at Hertford, and was interrupted by the butler bringing in tea.

In her second year Miss Rich was the only woman in a class of eight studying quantitative analysis in Mr Harcourt's laboratory at Christ Church. Mr Harcourt, whose refusal to lecture separately to women students had hastened their admission to university lectures, had equally strong objections to allowing chaperones in his laboratory; an arrangement was therefore arrived at by which, at times when Miss Rich was in the laboratory, Miss Seward carried out research with Mr W. H. Pendlebury on the rate of chemical change. When in her third year Miss Rich was at last able to devote herself exclusively to chemistry she found herself 'frightfully handicapped by being the only woman; always having to depend on someone to accompany me to lectures or library, never being able to talk over my work with my fellow students, and not fitting into any pre-arranged scheme or plan.' Once again, it was the encouragement of an individual tutor—Dr Watts of Merton—to which she attributed her successful completion of the course. In 1887, having sat the same papers as her male undergraduate contemporaries, and achieved a second, she was awarded a certificate in the Second Public Examination (Honours) which was the nearest a woman at Oxford at this date could get to a degree. In 1938 she presented to the college archives the Latin *testamur* for prelim. physics which she had been sent the previous year—partly, she believed, as a joke:

The University did not recognise the existence of women candidates, and my examiners only obtained a form from the clerk by leading him to suppose they had spoilt one of those with which he had supplied them. It was of course in Latin, and I heard there was some discussion as to the correct rendering of my name,—should it be Florentia or Firenze? But the difficulty was overcome when they realised that my first name was Mary, and the *testamur* is headed 'Rich, Maria F.'[71]

The circumstances in which the school of animal morphology was eventually opened to women is recounted in the recollections of one of the pioneers, Catherine Pollard, who in 1888 won a science scholarship to Somerville after a year spent at Holloway College London:

Up till my arrival no attempt had been made to gain entry into the School of Animal Morphology (Zoology), and it is most unlikely that it would have met with success, for the professor in charge of this subject was known to have no sympathy for the claims of women for higher education. At that particular moment, however, he had a serious breakdown in health. His deputy, a younger man, was willing, even ardent to help. Also, by a piece of great good fortune, at that particular moment there was another student at Somerville [Jane Willis Kirkaldy] who had set her heart on the same course. What would almost certainly have been refused to one, for it was a subject for which no chaperone would have been readily forthcoming, certainly not for the long daily hours in the laboratory, was conditionally permitted to two. We took a risk, for there was no certainty that when the professor returned we should be allowed to continue the course. One could only hope that once there, it would be a difficult thing to unseat us, and we had firm friends who gave us every encouragement. So we went ahead, and had the honour of 'opening the School' to women.[72]

Precarious as was the position of women scientists in Oxford, Miss Pollard found it preferable to Holloway, which at that early date had 'no adequate library, no museum, . . . only a makeshift laboratory and a weekly visit from an outside lecturer.' What London could, of course, offer, was a degree, and while at Oxford—where she, like Miss

[71] Recollections of Florence Rich.
[72] Recollections of Catherine Childs (Pollard, 1888).

Kirkaldy, took a first in 1891—Miss Pollard studied simultaneously for an external London B.Sc.

The acquisition of the freehold of Walton House in June 1880 enabled Somerville to build to keep pace with rising student numbers. In 1881 a new wing by T. G. Jackson—later described by Miss Lefevre as 'the best bit of building we have'[73]—was built on to the south front of the original house, providing additional students' rooms and a sitting room for the Principal. In 1886 work began on a new building in the north-west corner of the gardens, and the rural character of Somerville finally disappeared. Designed by the architect Harry Wilkinson Moore, and constructed in two stages, West Building—long known simply as 'The West'—was over the years to inspire greater affection among its residents than any other college building. Significantly, it has never been renamed to commemorate any principal or benefactor.[74]

In commissioning the West Building, with its separate dining-room (Plate 12) and drawing-room, the Council took a conscious decision to develop Somerville on the lines of Newnham rather than those of Girton. 'There were many considerations which determined the Council to adopt this plan rather than to add to the existing buildings' explained the *Somerville Report* for 1884–5,

> But the main reason was that a very large addition to the numbers under one roof would have seriously modified the relations between the Principal and the Students and gone far to destroy that intimate personal knowledge and care, those constant and easy opportunities for influence and advice which have hitherto been possible and to which we attribute so much of the success of our Hall.

The policy of separate dining-rooms was to be defended by Miss Shaw Lefevre in 1910, when Somerville's future development was again under discussion. 'I have always dreaded becoming like an institution', she wrote to the then Principal: 'The idea of exactly copying the men's colleges was the Girton idea but was never the Newnham idea.'[75] Convinced though she was of its merits, she had discovered the disadvantages of the system early on. 'I wonder if you will find it possible to mix the WB [West Building] people any more than I did?'

[73] MSL to EP, 26 May 1911. Jackson was the architect of the Examination Schools, the Acland Nursing Home, and the Oxford High School for Girls.

[74] For Moore's extensive work in North Oxford, see Hinchcliffe, *North Oxford*.

[75] MSL to EP, 17 Mar. 1910.

she wrote to her successor in October 1889: 'There is a tendency to become separate. I sometimes thought whether it would answer for them to change rooms for a few nights!'[76] Her farewell presentation included a portrait to hang in the Hall, and a clock, bearing her name, for the West—proof, as she said, 'of the considerate thought which has determined that I shall not be forgotten at either Hall.'[77]

The commissioning of these gifts—which were accompanied by an album containing photographs of all the students who had passed through Somerville during her principalship—was one of the first corporate acts of the Somerville Students' Association. Instituted in March 1888, with membership open to any student, past or present, who had been three terms in residence, the SSA soon became the main channel of communication between Somerville and its alumnae, sponsoring co-operative ventures ranging from sporting fixtures to the Women's University Settlement, circulating news and addresses, and even for a time renting a house in Walton Street to accommodate former students visiting Oxford. The members resident in Somerville were required to elect each year from among themselves an 'Oxford Correspondent'—usually one of the staff—who was charged with writing a summary of the past year's Hall news for circulation at the beginning of the long vacation: the Oxford Letter, a mine of information about Somerville life, survived numerous constitutional changes until in the 1950s it was replaced by an annual JCR Newsletter. The establishment of the SSA marked an important step in the development of that 'network of people spreading all over the world and through several generations' which some historians see as the defining characteristic of an Oxford college,[78] and which is perhaps what the Association's first honorary secretary, Jane Sharp, had in mind when she referred in her Report to 'the great link of Villianship'.[79]

---

[76] MSL to ACM, n.d. (1889). [77] MSL to President of Council, 26 June 1890.
[78] See B. Harrison's Introduction to *Corpuscles: A History of Corpus Christi College, Oxford in the Twentieth Century, Written by its Members* (Oxford, 1994), p. ix.
[79] Secretary's Report, *SSA Report*, July 1889.

3

Collegiate Ambitions: The Principalship of Agnes Maitland, 1889–1906

AT the end of ten years, the Somerville Council could look back with some satisfaction on the fruits of a successful policy of infiltration. The women's halls had, on their own quite modest terms, gained general acceptance in Oxford society. Scandals had been avoided, and many early fears had been allayed. The halls themselves, maintaining—unlike Girton or Holloway—a deliberately domestic aspect, merged unobtrusively into suburban North Oxford. The atmosphere within them was still preponderantly that of a family, the founding Principals—again unlike their Cambridge counterparts—assuming a quasi-maternal responsibility for introducing their young charges into polite Oxford society. Women students, soberly dressed and decorously behaved, had become a familiar sight in the streets of Oxford. They were gradually becoming less unfamiliar, though necessarily conspicuous, in the lecture halls, laboratories, and libraries of the university. While the university itself studiously ignored their existence, individual dons and their wives vied with each other to show them support and hospitality.

The strategy paid off. By 1890 Somerville was poised ready for a fresh eye and a change of pace; the resignation of Miss Shaw Lefevre gave the Somerville Council an opportunity to take stock of its position and branch out along new paths.[1] Seventeen years later the college Treasurer, Dr Woods, was to recall the Council meeting at which Agnes Maitland appeared as a candidate for the principalship:

> There came into the room a lady who seemed to stand apart from the other candidates. We were conscious of a capacity and tact, a sweetness and strength, a presence and manner, which came up to our ideal: *vera incessu patuit principalis*.[2]

[1] LMH's founding Principal, in contrast, remained in office for thirty years.
[2] Obituary in *SSA Report*, 1906.

The records of the election show that the matter was not quite so clear-cut as his account suggests. The Council interviewed eight candidates (including James Bryce's sister), and it was only on the fifth ballot that Miss Maitland secured the necessary majority of votes. Testimonials written on her behalf included one from Miss Amelia Edwards, one from Lord Aberdare, who described her as 'a thorough lady', and one from Professor Romanes, who gave it as his view that 'intellectually it would be hard to find a woman who is her superior.'[3]

It was clear from the outset that Miss Maitland's style would be very different from that of her predecessor (see Plate 7). 40 years old at the time of her appointment, she had already worked for some years in her native city of Liverpool in connection with a movement for the better teaching of cookery and domestic economy, lecturing on these subjects, and holding a post as inspector of classes for them in elementary schools. Her interest in the practical aspects of primary education was to remain with her for the rest of her life: towards the end of her time at Somerville she took an active part in making known the need for more women inspectors of schools, and very shortly before her death she helped to draw up for the Education Section of the British Association a scheme for the better teaching of hygiene in schools. She was Secretary of the Egypt Exploration Fund and a writer of stories and cookery handbooks, with publications ranging from *Ella's Half-Sovereign* to *The Afternoon Tea Book*. Unlike Miss Shaw Lefevre, who only once in her life made a platform speech (at the opening of Aberdare Hall in 1895), and hated it, Miss Maitland was an experienced and accomplished public speaker. A Presbyterian by upbringing, and a staunch Liberal in politics, she was a passionate advocate of the many causes which she had at heart. As a young woman in Liverpool she had attended the very first course of lectures organized by Miss Clough's North of England Council for Promoting the Higher Education of Women, and the excitement of this experience remained with her through life. Her appointment to the principalship of Somerville opened up to her a new range of interests and responsibilities, but—in the view of Margery Fry, who in many ways resembled her—it altered less than might have been expected the general aim of her work:

> For, from first to last, education in all its grades appealed to her most strongly as a preparation for the conduct of affairs, and for the

---

[3] ACM file: Appointment.

business of ordinary life. The idea of pure scholarship, of learning as an end in itself, commanded her respect rather than her allegiance; and thus, while she was second to none in her love and reverence for Oxford, there were some of its traditions in respect of which she was always something of a rebel.[4]

Miss Maitland also differed from her predecessor in having no independent means. Whereas Miss Lefevre had looked on the Oxford terms as a more or less enjoyable interruption of family life, for which she was diffident in accepting payment, Miss Maitland was a working woman for whom Somerville provided not only a livelihood but also a home. At the Council meeting following her appointment it was resolved that 'the Principal shall be entitled to reside in Hall all the year round on the same conditions as in full term.'[5] The Principal's salary, which had not changed during Miss Shaw Lefevre's period of office, was increased by £75 from October 1890 and thereafter kept under review.

Miss Maitland brought to the office qualities quite different from those of her predecessor. People seeking to describe Miss Lefevre almost invariably hit on the word 'ladylike'; what struck them most about Miss Maitland was her energy. At the opening of the Maitland Building in 1913, the Vice-Chancellor, Dr Heberden, said of her: 'Everyone knows how great was her administrative capacity, how excellent her judgment, how great her energy; and those are qualities which are specially needed in a young and growing institution.'[6] On her death Dr Woods paid tribute to the clearness and soundness of her judgement, her strong grasp of finance, and an administrative capacity which, he said, 'amounted almost to genius':

Step by step she organised each department of her many-sided work. The serving of tables, the social life of the students, scholarships, lecture lists, tutorial arrangements, building schemes, co-operation with other Women's Colleges, and a multitude of other subjects, occupied her thoughts in turn, and were gradually built up into a well-considered and well-ordered system. Each new suggestion came before the Council clearly thought out and pointedly put, and one frequently felt (what one does not always feel at the end of a meeting) that a definite step forward had been made.[7]

[4] Obituary by Margery Fry, *Oxford Magazine*, 24 Oct. 1906.
[5] Minutes of Council, 8 June 1889.   [6] Log Book, 1913.   [7] *SSA Report*, 1906.

As Treasurer of Somerville for the first eight years of Miss Maitland's principalship, Woods was well-placed to observe what he believed to be her one failing—an inclination at times 'to be too rigid an economist in small matters'. Elizabeth Lee, in the *Dictionary of National Biography*, described her as 'something of an autocrat' who, nevertheless, 'worked in full harmony with her staff, won the complete confidence of her students, and showed faith in democratic principles.'

During her time as Principal the number of students at Somerville grew from thirty-five to eighty-six, the teaching staff was consolidated and increased, the first research fellowship was established, and the library was built. Symbolic of these changes was the decision of Council in 1894 to adopt the title of College, on the grounds that this would 'not only improve the educational status of Somerville in the eyes of the public, but would be understood as implying the desire of the Governing Body to raise it above the level of a Hall of Residence.'[8] Two years previously, Council had acceded to the desire of the student body for 'a crest or badge and motto', and obtained permission to adopt the Somerville coat of arms and colours;[9] the 1892 Oxford Letter reported a burgeoning of red and black stripes to replace the previous buff and blue 'which were so trying to many complexions', and Somervillians made their first attempts to interpret the baffling Somerville motto *'Donec rursus impleat orbem'*. Another milestone in the forging of college spirit was the institution in 1903, as a result of a competition set by Miss Bruce, of a college song, the joint composition of three undergraduates, Helen Darbishire, Margaret Moor, and Margaret Robertson.

Agnes Maitland's ambitions for Somerville were to find fitting posthumous commemoration in the naming of the Maitland building, with its splendid hall. But it was her influence which ensured that Somerville's first collegiate building should be not a hall, but a library; and it was her efforts which raised the money necessary to finance it. Her key role in all these developments was summed up by Dr Woods in 1906:

> Whatever has been done at Somerville for sixteen years, each step in
> the unmistakeable and unbroken progress, has always been more due

---

[8] Report of Council, 1894.
[9] Bedford College adopted a badge and colours in 1895, early in the principalship of Emily Penrose (Somerville 1889–92).

COLLEGE SONG

(To the Welsh Air, ' Cwynfan Prydain')

Omnes laetae nunc sodales
  Concinentes gaudio
Uno corde conferamus
  Laudem huic collegio;
Conditum quod olim jure
  Nunc integritate stat
Atque permanebit orbem
  Donec rursus impleat.

Enitentes ut sorores
  Simus sapientiae
Jungimus labori ludum
  Juvenes et impigrae.
Doctae floreant 'Tutores',
  Principalis floreat,
Semper venerandae donec
  Orbem rursus impleat.

Floreant Oxonienses
  Urbs et Universitas
Ac nobis piis alumnis
  Sit fides, sit veritas!
Omnes laudis studiosi
  Nunquam laude careant—
Aedes Somervillienses
  In aeternum floreant!

HELEN DARBISHIRE.
MARGARET F. MOOR.
MARGARET ROBERTSON.
1903.

to Miss Maitland than to anyone else, and often has been entirely her work. She summed up Somerville in herself: she *was* Somerville. She embodied its spirit and informed its traditions. She stimulated and controlled and gave direction to its expanding energies. No Council could possibly have done what she did.

What the Council could, and did, do was to throw its support behind her in the succession of battles and enterprises in which she engaged.

After several anxious years in which the women's halls had found considerable difficulty in filling the places available, 1890 saw a sudden upturn in the number and quality of applicants, and Somerville was able to announce the prospect of beginning the academic year with full numbers for the first time.[10] Though this came as a relief, the possibility of further expansion which it raised was controversial; Eleanor Powell the next year prefaced a report of steady increase in student numbers with the words 'Some people approve and some think it is a pity.'[11] With greater choice of applicants, Somerville could afford to be more selective. In 1891 the Hon. Grace Tollemache, whose family according to student report were 'such society people that they had to seize the opportunity of being in mourning to educate their daughter',[12] was asked to leave in order to make way for a 'working student'. The following year Somerville became the first of the halls to require entrance candidates to pass a qualifying examination before coming up.

A growing tendency to adopt an independent line, particularly in the matter of tutorial arrangements, brought Somerville increasingly into conflict with the AEW, and the Principal with the Lady Secretary. Miss Maitland, though perfectly civil, lacked her predecessor's emollience. 'I am very sorry we seem fated to have these collisions over our work' wrote Mrs Johnson to her in 1893, in the course of a chilly correspondence on the conditions for students attending college lectures: 'I have not been accustomed to it, but have always enjoyed so much working with the other friends of women's education for our students up here, so I feel it a good deal, more than I should if I were younger perhaps, and more combative.'[13] Two years previously, in a difference of opinion over the work programme of a Somerville student, she had referred dismissively to Miss Maitland as 'one of our body who is not

[10] *SSA Report*, 1890.   [11] *SSA Report*, 1891.
[12] Sorabji, 24 Jan. 1891 (India Office MSS Eur. F. 165/4).
[13] Johnson to ACM, 27 Oct. 1893.

yet accustomed to our Association methods of work.'[14] But, though a new voice in Oxford, Miss Maitland's was not a solitary one. Her strategy of polite non-cooperation with the Lady Secretary was supported by Miss Lefevre and the Somerville Council, which included a number of members—or spouses of members—of the AEW committee. One of the latter, A. G. Vernon Harcourt, had already independently come to the conclusion that 'the Association should gradually resign the tutorial care of the Hall students to the Heads and Tutors of the Halls, retaining the provision and negotiation of lectures and examinations and the tutorial care of the unattached.'[15] When Eleanor Powell distributed the AEW Calendar around Somerville in December 1890 she found the students indignant about the description of the halls as 'approved by the Association'. 'They do not seem to consider that the Halls need such a testimonial at this point of their lives', she reported to Mrs Johnson—'and I agree with them.'[16] One of the topics proposed for debate at the students' Sharp Practice debating society in 1894 was that 'This Society, whilst recognising the service rendered to the cause of education in the past by the AEW in Oxford is of opinion that the time is now come when its connection with Somerville Hall should be severed.'[17]

In 1893, in an attempt to improve relations, the women Principals were invited to sit on an education sub-committee to oversee teaching arrangements, and a meeting was called to thrash out in detail the respective responsibilities of the Association and the halls. However the meeting may have clarified the position, it did nothing to promote goodwill. 'I grieve over the bad manners of my colleagues at S. Hall' wrote Charlotte Green, who as a member of the Somerville Council and a former Secretary of the AEW had a foot in both camps: 'What can be done? A. Rogers asks me to improve them! It seems to me like stroking the dome of St Paul's to please the Dean and Chapter. I thought I had stroked Mr Pelham—and now I hear he is worse than ever.'[18] But two weeks later it was Miss Maitland and Pelham who acted as 'restraining and oil-pouring influences' at a meeting of the Somerville Council which considered the report of the joint committee and took exception to the words 'The Resident Tutors at the Halls

[14] Johnson to E. Ray Lankester, 13 Dec. 1891.
[15] Vernon Harcourt to Johnson, 9 Feb. 1891 (Johnson papers, St Anne's).
[16] Powell to Johnson, 7 Dec. 1890 (Johnson Papers, St Anne's).
[17] *Fritillary*, June 1894.
[18] Green to Johnson, ?21 Jan. 1893 (Johnson Papers, St Anne's).

shall, as heretofore, be considered as part of the Association staff.'[19] Mrs Green described the meeting to Mrs Johnson as 'trying'; she was particularly outraged by the conduct of Dr Percival, Dr Fairbairn (the Principal of Mansfield), and Mr Child,[20] who 'from dense ignorance . . . treated the Hall as on a desert island alone.' 'How can people ever understand the relations of Association and Halls' she asked, 'if a man like Dr Percival, who once knew the working, ignores everything but the Principal and students as in a boarding school.'[21]

The following year an unsuccessful attempt was made to find someone with Somerville connections willing to share with Mrs Johnson the Secretaryship of the AEW, the idea being to 'give that Hall a means of keeping more closely in touch with the work of the Association.'[22] But Somerville's decision to adopt the title of College was symptomatic of its desire for independence. When Clara Pater left Oxford in 1894 the Council resolved to by-pass the teaching arrangements of the AEW and to appoint instead new college tutors in classics and modern languages. Outraged at what she saw as Somerville's duplicity in trying to 'pose as a self-supporting college' while taking advantage of the work and energy of the AEW, Mrs Johnson resigned. 'Their whole position seems to me so dishonest and dishonourable' she complained to her successor Annie Rogers, 'that it is quite impossible to trust in any promise of theirs now.'[23]

The irritation was mutual, and was observed with dismay by the other halls and the Society of Home Students. Poorer than Somerville, and lacking both its tutorial resources and its collegiate aspirations, they relied on its continued use of common teaching arrangements in order to make up viable lecture classes. A compromise was eventually agreed, by which the Association relinquished its claim to excercise a central control over teaching, but all students were required to pay a fee towards the cost of its administration and lectures. Looking back, many years later, over the acrimonious correspondence of the 1890s, Mrs Johnson acknowledged her own shortcomings—in particular the intrusion of 'too personal an element'. 'Still', she concluded, 'at that

[19] Minutes of Council, 6 Feb. 1893.
[20] Medical officer of health to the Oxford Local Board, and an active member also of the St Hilda's Committee. See obituary in *Jackson's Oxford Journal*, 5 Dec. 1896.
[21] Green to Johnson, [6] Feb. 1893 (Johnson Papers, St Anne's).
[22] Johnson to Grose, 29 Nov. and 22 Dec. 1893 (Johnson Papers, St Anne's).
[23] Johnson to Rogers Oct./Nov. 1894 (summary of correspondence in Johnson Papers, St Anne's).

time the breaking away of Somerville would have been *very* serious for the others, financially and otherwise.'[24]

Her successor as Lady Secretary adopted a more direct approach. 'I gave Miss Maitland the benefit of my remarks' she reported to Mrs Johnson during the 'fuss' of 1893, 'and told her that the less S. H. was like a girls' school & the more it was like a college the better it would stand in the University.'[25] In her view, Somerville's policy put the tutors too much at the mercy of their Principal, who, she suspected, wasn't perfectly sure of her authority. As AEW Secretary, Miss Rogers did much to promote the interests of women dons, with whom she had considerable sympathy. The establishment of a tutorial system ensured that each student's work was directed by a tutor (often from one of the women's halls) in the appropriate field. Women tutors were increasingly employed as AEW Lecturers, and in 1904 were given the right to elect representatives to the Association's education sub-committee. But such measures only served to fuel their growing aspirations beyond the point which Miss Rogers herself considered acceptable. Increasingly impatient at the powerful non-academic element in the AEW Committee, the women tutors were to form themselves in 1909 into a separate Society, and succeeded, against her advice, in restricting the electorate for the AEW Committee to teaching members of the Association and the Hall Councils. When the Delegacy for Women Students was established in 1911, they pointedly—and woundingly—refrained from putting her name forward for election; it was at the nomination of the vice-chancellor and proctors, not as a representative of the tutors, that she came to serve on a body for whose existence she was largely responsible.

Against this background, Miss Maitland and the Somerville Council set about building up the college's own tutorial strength. The first generation of tutors had been appointed largely to share the administrative and social burden of the Principal. Their stay in Somerville tended to be brief, for they were much in demand as headmistresses and such elsewhere. Lilla Haigh, after four years as Assistant Mistress at Maida Vale High School, became Headmistress of Reading High School in 1891; Isabella Don became Principal of Aberdare Hall, Cardiff in 1887; Sara Melhuish left Somerville in 1895 to become Principal of Mount Vale School York, ending her career as Head of the Education

[24] Cover note to file on 'AEW and Somerville' (Johnson Papers, St Anne's).
[25] Rogers to Johnson, 1893 (Johnson Papers, St Anne's).

Department at Bedford College London and University Reader in Education; Margaret Seward married after four years as lecturer in chemistry at Holloway College, taught at Bradford Grammar School and Roedean, and was appointed tutor in chemistry at King's College London in 1896. But from the 1890s a series of appointments was made of tutors who were to devote the whole—or the greater part—of their working life to Somerville, and to mould decisively its character for the next forty years. To Miss Maitland must go the credit for some inspired talent-spotting, and for considerable ingenuity in finding means of attaching to the college promising young scholars for whom there was no immediate academic opening. Mildred Pope, after gaining a first in modern languages in 1893, was kept on as librarian until a tutorship became available the following year; she was to remain at Somerville—universally acknowledged as the most beloved of all its tutors—until 1934, when Manchester claimed her as professor. In 1894 Jane Willis Kirkaldy was appointed tutor in the sciences, a post which she held for thirty-five years; one of her last pupils was Dorothy Hodgkin, who remembered her as 'a formidable but still beautiful old woman whose care of us was somewhat remote.'[26] Alice Bruce was appointed college secretary in the same year, at the start of an equally long, but still more varied career, most famously from 1898 to 1929 as Vice-Principal. In her retirement speech at the college jubilee in 1929, Miss Bruce was able to claim: 'Since I joined the staff in 1894, I have held, by appointment or as deputy, singly, in pairs, or in accumulations of three or four, for periods varying from three weeks to thirty years, every office in the College, except Tutor of Science or Classics.'

Among Miss Maitland's protégées were two future Principals. The creation in June 1892 of an additional tutorship with responsibility for the library and for secretarial assistance to the Principal was largely designed as a means of enabling Emily Penrose to stay on in Oxford to continue her studies after Greats.[27] In the event, Miss Penrose did not need to take up the offer; but a similar approach was made to Margery Fry in 1899, rescuing her from the stultifying round of family obligations and social calls to which she had returned at the end of her time as a student. As librarian, Miss Fry found herself entrusted with a range of tasks from marking hand-towels to coaching in mathematics;

[26] D. Hodgkin, 'Crystallography and Chemistry in the First Hundred Years of Somerville College' (James Bryce Memorial Lecture, 1979).

[27] Minutes of Council, 14 May and 10 June 1892.

she sought advice about the latter from a family acquaintance, Mr Bertrand Russell.[28]

These early tutors were all themselves Somervillians. The appointment in 1894 of Florence Hallyar to teach classics, and in 1896 of Beatrice Lees to teach history, introduced an LMH element into a senior common room in which native Somervillians were long to predominate. In the years to come there was to be much interchange at senior level between the two colleges, each providing the other with some outstanding tutors. In 1896 came Somerville's first import from Cambridge. Hilda Lockhart Lorimer, described by Vera Brittain as 'one of the most brilliantly eccentric of women dons', was a Scot, a Girtonian, a classicist, and a passionate ornithologist, whose 'solitary Saturday cycling expeditions with binoculars to the remoter fastnesses of Oxfordshire became a College legend in her picturesque and dauntless prime.'[29] The tradition of Girtonian classicists at Somerville was to be maintained unbroken for only one year short of a century.[30] With the appointment of Phoebe Sheavyn—a product of the University College of Wales, Aberystwyth, and Bryn Mawr—as tutor in English in 1897, the SCR extended its catchment area both academically and socially. The daughter of a draper, 'Phoebus' was one of the very few Oxbridge women academics of the period to emerge from the lower middle class.[31]

In thus consolidating its tutorial strength, Somerville played a leading role in establishing regular conditions of employment in what was essentially a new profession for women.[32] A committee to consider and report on conditions of tutorships was appointed by the Council in 1894. In the same year, tutors were accorded honorary membership of the college, and thereafter played an increasingly prominent part in General Meetings; in 1902 they gained the right to elect one of their number to serve on the Council. In 1904 it was established that tutorial appointments should be made for a probationary period of two years, renewable every five years thereafter. Somerville

---

[28] E. Huws Jones, *Margery Fry: The Essential Amateur* (London, 1966), 51–6.

[29] V. Brittain, *The Women at Oxford: A Fragment of History* (London, 1960), 91.

[30] Mildred Hartley (Mrs Taylor) succeeded Miss Lorimer in 1934, and was herself succeeded by Nan Dunbar (an ornithologist and a Scot, but—at least in her Somerville days—no cyclist) in 1965. Her successor, in 1995, is a Wadham graduate, Edith Hall.

[31] For the social origins of women academics at this period see F. Perrone, 'University Teaching as a Profession for Women in Oxford, Cambridge and London 1870–1930', D. Phil. thesis (Oxford, 1991).   [32] See Perrone, 'University Teaching', 147.

was a pioneer in the matter of sabbatical leave, granting paid leave in 1900 to both Miss Lorimer and Miss Pope; a second period of leave in 1902 enabled the latter to work in Paris on the thesis on *Frère Angier* which earned her in 1904 the degree of *Docteur de l'Université de Paris*. In 1917 Somerville was to become the first of the Oxford women's colleges to provide pensions for its staff through the Federated Superannuation System for Universities (FSSU), the others following suit after the recommendations of the Asquith Commission in 1921.[33]

In certain fields of scholarship women dons were themselves pioneers at this period. English literature and modern languages, taught by the AEW from the outset, were not established as honour schools in the university until 1897 and 1903 respectively. The position of women scholars like Mildred Pope, widely acknowledged as Oxford's leading authority on the French language, yet with no official standing in the university, became increasingly anomalous. As a student she had been dependent for philology teaching on a correspondence with Dr Paget Toynbee in Cambridge; her further studies during her time as librarian at Somerville were conducted during the long vacation under Professor Fritz Neumann at Heidelberg. Even after the establishment of the modern language school she was for some time the only tutor of Old French in Oxford. Margery Fry wrote of her at this period: '[She] is the only person in Oxford who knows about considerable parts of the subjects (she had been coaching the Reader in French, himself a Frenchman, on some of them)—but she can only be consulted in a backstairs way.'[34] When Hilda Lorimer came to Somerville from Girton she consulted Professor Pelham about her research, and was told that it was not necessary (or, indeed, desirable) for her to take up any, since all advanced teaching would be provided by friends from the men's colleges.[35] Fortunately, Professor (later Sir John) Myres proved more encouraging, and set her on her future career. It was perhaps because the women dons felt a greater need to prove themselves as scholars that by 1914 the proportion of them who engaged in research was actually higher than among the equivalent cohort of men.[36] But the disadvantages under which they laboured were graphically spelled out in a joint submission by the Principals of Somerville and Newnham to the Asquith Commission in 1920:

---

[33] Ibid. 240. Girton established a pension scheme for its staff in 1910.
[34] Huws Jones, *Margery Fry*, 62.   [35] Lucy Sutherland, paper read at seminar, 1973.
[36] Perrone, 'University Teaching', 46.

It is not easy to convey to anyone who has not been in close contact with it how irksome, one may almost say how humiliating the position of these women may be and often is, a position brought about quite unavoidably by their exclusion from the University. As an instance illustrating this we should like to point out that senior members of these college staffs, teachers of many years standing, scholars who may have made contributions of value in their own subjects, not only are ineligible for any official position but have not that share in matters concerning their own work which may be enjoyed by quite junior members of the University. They are not consulted and may not take part in any discussion formal or informal, with regard to the courses of study to be followed by their pupils. They are informed of decisions arrived at and arrangements made and receive instructions as to the work to be done often naturally from members of the University of much less experience than themselves. They have no prospect of ever having any influence in questions concerning the studies which are the occupation and interest of their lives, or of any further scope for their abilities, and only by the rarest chance can they have the opportunity of proving their capacity as teachers beyond the bounds of their own Colleges. Thus there is little encouragement given to any effort on their part to attain distinction in their own branch of learning and since they are for the most part cut off from the work and thought of the University they are without its help in or stimulus to such efforts which they might otherwise receive.[37]

In 1893 Hebdomadal Council took a first step towards recognizing the women's societies, when it offered to appoint one of its own members to serve on their governing bodies as a representative of the university. It was a small gesture, putting the college, as Emily Penrose later said, on the same footing as 'the Newbury Girls' School . . . the Ewelme Almshouses, and the National Trust for the Preservation of Places of Historical Interest and Natural Beauty'.[38] The LMH Council none the less declined the offer, for fear of giving offence to the AEW. Somerville accepted, and Professor Odling, Waynefleet Professor of Chemistry since 1872 and, in his private capacity, a supporter of

---

[37] Universities Commission: Report of Sub-Committee on Women's Colleges (Miss Penrose and Miss B. A. Clough).   [38] EP 'Talks to Students', 1910.

Somerville since its foundation, joined its Council as the first of a distinguished line of 'University Representatives'.[39]

The opening of university examinations to women in 1884 had been achieved largely because the women's supporters refrained from raising the more controversial issue of admitting them to degrees. By the 1890s the range of examinations open to women had greatly increased, and the question of their being permitted to supplicate for the BA degree had become a live one.[40] It was a subject on which the women in Oxford, and their supporters, were themselves divided. The initiative for a campaign in favour of degrees for women came from the AEW President, T. H. Grose; the Association's former Secretary, Mrs Johnson, was among its most passionate opponents. The Councils of Somerville and St Hugh's were in favour of pressing for degrees for women, the Council of LMH, by a small majority, opposed. The newly established St Hilda's took little part in the debate, but in a private letter to the Vice-Chancellor, its founder, Miss Beale, expressed fears that the requirements of a degree course would pressure girls' schools into specializing in classical rather than modern languages.[41] The women tutors at all the halls were solidly pro-degree; some of the AEW's male lecturers, like A. L. Smith, claimed to support the idea in principle, but thought the time inopportune. No one at this time seriously raised the question of the MA, which posed complex constitutional problems.

In May 1895 Hebdomadal Council, having been presented with a petition begging for the admission of properly qualified women to the BA, and with a number of counter-petitions and memorials (one of them proposing, with disastrous implications for the women's halls, that a diploma might be obtainable without any residence requirement), appointed a committee to consider the matter further. Somervillians whose views were canvassed were solidly of the opinion that the usefulness of women educated at Oxford was seriously

---

[39] Odling himself was distinguished for carrying out no research during his 40-year tenure of the Waynefleet chair (*HUO* viii, 40). His successors as University Representative on the Somerville Council were: Professor Gotch, 1908–13; Professor Geldart, 1913–22; Professor Sir A. E. Garrod, 1922–8; Sir W. Buchanan Riddell (Principal of Hertford), 1928–30; Professor Brierly, 1930–5 (on Council in own right since 1924); A. H. Smith, 1935–8; J. H. Wolfenden, 1940; Sir E. F. Buzzard, 1940–3; A. S. Russell, 1943–51.

[40] See Rogers, *Degrees by Degrees: The Story of the Admission of Oxford Women Students to Membership of the University* (London, 1938), ch. 2: 'The Move for Degrees'.

[41] M. Rayner, *Centenary History of St Hilda's College, Oxford* (Oxford, 1993), 21.

hampered by their lack of university recognition; the student body, led by Eleanor Rathbone, drew up a petition for the college Council to present to the university on their behalf.[42] Examination of the evidence left the university committee more or less evenly divided; but when the question came to Congregation in March 1896 a resolution in favour of admitting women to degrees was soundly—though, on the whole, unrancorously—rejected. The women's halls took what comfort they could from the many flattering remarks made in the course of the debate about the excellence of the work they were doing, and from the fact that a substantial volume of hitherto latent support for their cause had been brought into the open. Annie Rogers, the historian of the movement, thought that the episode reflected little credit on the university's statesmanship, but was at least no discredit to its dignity and good manners. 'It is doubtful' she concluded, 'if any hotly contested women's question has been treated with so much good humour and cheerfulness.'[43]

Two years later the Cambridge Senate, with rather less good humour, rejected a proposal to grant degrees to women by 1,713 votes to 662. Outraged by the obduracy of the ancient universities, Bishop Percival—who was still a member, though no longer President, of the Somerville Council—wrote to *The Times* advocating the establishment of a Queen Victoria University for Women, with Royal Holloway as its first constituent college. Henry Pelham, his successor both at Trinity and as President of the Somerville Council, wrote him a brief letter of reproach. Miss Maitland, writing at greater length, drily expressed the hope that any millionaire who responded to the bishop's letter would 'consult women concerned in education before taking hasty action':

> You and others of our kindest friends are blinded, I fear, by your kindness, and believe that women have already achieved what they are aiming at. Your scheme is a beautiful one for the future, but we are not ready for it yet and I do not think we shall be for the next 50 years.
>
> As you know—no one better—the university education of women has only existed at all for 25 years and the beginnings were so small that it is only within the last 12 or 15 years that the effect has been appreciable, and even yet, as was strongly asserted by our enemies in the recent controversy, women do not carry on their studies after leaving the university or distinguish themselves in research or other

---

[42] College Meeting, 12 May 1895.   [43] Rogers, *Degrees by Degrees*, 54.

original work. The reason is obvious to those who are engaged in the work—nine-tenths of the women who distinguish themselves at college must at once proceed to earn their daily bread, and that usually under exhausting conditions which entirely preclude them from carrying on their own studies. We have not yet the material for a Women's Teaching University of the high standard at which we should like to aim. Money is indeed wanted for women's education, but it is for fellowships to enable them to continue their studies—or some other form of endowment of research—better buildings, better libraries and so forth.

The number of women really fitted to take up the highest studies will never, I think, be very large—but of these a large proportion thirst to go on with their work, but are unable to do so for want of means.

The experiment of women's universities has been freely tried in America, and with what result? Americans will not say this publicly, but privately they admit that the standard in these exclusively women's universities is always tending to drop, because they are in the same position as ourselves and have not a sufficient body of women educated up to the standard of the men teachers in a university of the highest class.

In the exclusively women's universities, there is no outside standard to be aimed at. Every drop, in what is required of the pupils, reflects and perpetuates itself in time among the staff.

I should very much dread, at present, the founding of a University for Women only, though 50 or 100 years hence we may be ready for it, if your millionaire can help us with endowment now. We can work on without the degree, which was largely asked for as a help to bread winning, if we can only get endowment for continuance of study.[44]

Philosophical in defeat, Miss Maitland was to concentrate for the remainder of her principalship on the priorities mentioned here: buildings, library facilities, and opportunities for research.

The degrees debate left the position of women *vis-à-vis* the university fundamentally unchanged. In lieu of a degree, Somerville issued its students with a college certificate stating the number of terms during which they had resided, and the examinations which they had passed—a new source of friction with the AEW, which began to issue

---

[44] ACM to Percival, 28 May 1897. Quoted in W. Temple, *Life of Bishop Percival* (London, 1921), 275–7.

similar certificates at much the same time. 'I fear some danger from Somerville' Annie Rogers wrote in March 1896 to the Somervillian Principal of Bedford College, Emily Penrose: 'This certificate ought it seems to me to come from the central body. We don't want each College or Hall to give a degree certificate. . . . It would lead to any amount of confusion.'[45]

None the less, the Somerville Council persisted in its policy. When in 1904 the Registrar of Trinity College Dublin entered into a correspondence with the AEW Secretary on the subject of degree certificates, Miss Maitland wrote drawing his attention to the fact that 'in this matter the Association only represents the students of the Women's Halls and the Home Students, and not the students of this College—the largest institution for women students in Oxford.'[46]

In 1896, following the example of Girton, Somerville adopted new Articles of Association by which all former students who had resided for three years and taken an honours examination were eligible to become Members of the College with the right to take part in the election of the Council. The change preserved the old joint-stock principle, and was greeted by the current students as making Somerville 'one of the most democratically governed Colleges in Great Britain.'[47] The new constitution was to remain in force for 25 years, old students steadily exercising their voting rights, and a number of them being elected to serve on the Council.[48] The decision also had important financial consequences, by securing the continued support of a large body of former students who in the coming years were to respond generously to appeals on behalf of the new research fellowship (in 1902), the library (in 1904), and the Hall (in 1913).

But from the point of view of official recognition, the Oxford woman remained vulnerable. Not only was she unable to claim a degree at the end of her course, but new regulations which came into effect in 1902 with regard to teacher registration threatened to put intending teachers from Oxford at a disadvantage compared with those who had done Higher Locals and then spent a further year

[45] Rogers to EP, 20 Mar. 1896 (Degrees file).
[46] ACM to the Registrar, TCD, 22 Oct. 1904 (Degrees file). [47] *Fritillary*, 9 Dec. 1896.
[48] Somervillians elected to the Council between 1896 and 1921 included Eleanor Powell 1896–1902, Eleanor Rathbone 1899–1908, Mrs Marett (Nora Kirk) 1902–14, Margery Fry 1904–31, Lady Evans (Maria Lathbury) 1908–19, Evelyn Atkinson 1909–30, Mrs H. D. Leigh (Alice Bayliss) 1912–23, Helen Darbishire 1913–45, Grace Hadow 1914–29, Mrs H. A. L. Fisher (Lettice Ilbert) 1916–22, Mrs A. J. Jenkinson (Hilda Turner) 1917–19. Mildred Pope represented the Somerville staff 1903–13.

at a training college. An important initiative, however, was soon to come from Ireland. When in 1904 Trinity College Dublin admitted women to full membership, it made transitional arrangements in respect of students from the Royal University of Ireland and elsewhere who were unwilling to lose the benefit of the work they had already done. Acting on these temporary provisions, an Irish student at Cambridge applied for a degree under the *ad eundem* arrangements which existed between Trinity College and the Universities of Oxford and Cambridge. She stated that she had been obliged to go to England to receive the university education then denied to women by Trinity College, and that she had fulfilled the conditions as to residence and examinations which, had she been a man, would have entitled her to receive the *ad eundem* degree. Her request was granted, and the transitional arrangements were modified to the effect that 'Women educated at Oxford or Cambridge will be treated, until Michaelmas 1907, as if they had been admitted to the Academic status in these Universities corresponding to their educational exercises.' The qualification was twelve terms' residence and an honours examination; the fees were £10.3s. for the *ad eundem* BA, and £9.16s.6d. for the MA. The additional expenses of the trip—return fare from London to Dublin, two nights' accommodation, and the hire of robes—were calculated at £7.2s.0d., to meet which, the Clothworkers' Company, with characteristic generosity, granted a bonus of £10 to any of their former scholars or exhibitioners who wished to travel to Dublin to claim their degree. By 1907 some 720 women—the great majority of them from Girton and Newnham—had 'taken the boat' from Britain for this purpose; in Dublin they were known as the 'Steamboat Ladies', and their graduation fees were used in 1908 to purchase a residence for Trinity's women undergraduates.[49]

After several precarious years, Somerville's own finances were now entering into a phase of greater stability. Student fees gained in real value from the fall in prices, and by the early 1890s were providing an annual surplus of over £700. An application to the Pfeiffer Trust in 1892 brought in an endowment of £2,500, which was used initially to finance scholarships and later diverted, with the consent of the trustees, to the building of the library.[50] Some other notable benefactions,

[49] C. H. Holland (ed.), *Trinity College Dublin and the Idea of a University* (Dublin, 1991), 123, 333–5. Somervillians claiming an *ad eundem* degree included Emily Penrose, Margaret Seward, Lilla Haigh, Lilian Faithfull, Ethel Hurlblatt, and Lady Evans.

[50] See B. Herbertson, *The Pfeiffer Bequest and the Education of Women: A Centenary Review* (Cambridge, 1993).

received in the course of the decade, enabled the Council to embark on an ambitious policy of expansion. In 1891 the old entrance gates on the Woodstock Road were replaced by a gateway and porter's lodge (Plate 9), the Clothworkers' Company contributing £50 towards the expense. In the same year a lease was taken on one of the block of three houses just outside the carriage drive gate to provide accommodation for six additional students, and three tables in the Hall dining-room were lengthened to make room for them at meals. With this addition Somerville could accommodate forty-eight students, twenty-seven in the old part and twenty-one in West. Two years later more drastic alterations were embarked upon, and the Oxford Correspondent for 1893 reported, with evident mixed feelings, that the Old Hall was being 'remodelled and altered almost beyond recognition':

> The offices which straggled in picturesque untidiness down the drive; the music room with its sweet, though damp, associations, the old front door which opened with such generous determination to leave no corner unswept by the wind—all these have vanished; and with them, alas, has gone the beautiful wisteria, which used to hang its blossoms so bravely over the front entrance.

A new drawing-room was created on the first floor, with an iron staircase leading down from the window to the garden; the drawing-room, dining-room, and store room on the ground floor were knocked into one to create a large new dining-room; and a reading-room for the books which had hitherto been housed in the dining-room was created to the left of the entrance, between the wing and the house. The new extension provided much-needed servants' accommodation, and also bathrooms to replace the unattractive 'coffin' on the ground floor in which students had bathed and the housekeeper had slept. 'Best of all' reported the Oxford Correspondent, 'electric light is to take the place of the malodorous and perilous oil lamp.' In February 1894 the second stage of the West Building was opened by the Lord Chancellor, Lord Herschell, in a grand ceremony which prompted LMH's Miss Wordsworth to reflect on 'what a prosy thing the Higher Education of Women is without religion.'[51] Three years later a legacy from Miss Eleanor Smith, together with donations from Professor Dicey, Miss Shaw Lefevre, and Miss Powell, enabled the college to undertake the building of the 'Eleanor Smith Cottages'; in the

---

[51] Incomplete letter, 21 Feb. 1894 (Wordsworth MSS., LMH).

event, it was decided to retain the existing cottages so long as they were habitable, and the project never advanced beyond its first stage ('Hostel'). In a later memorandum, Miss Lefevre set out the cost of these early building operations:

> The whole of the West Buildings cost only £8,543 although built in two detachments.
>
> Looking at the cost of the six additions in 1882—1886—1890—1892—1894—1898 (not counting the Gymnasium & Library) one might consider that a Student's room was built for from £100 to £150. The Eleanor Smith Cottages were only £100 per room.[52]

Meanwhile, the possibility of future development was secured when in 1897 an anonymous donor (Miss E. J. Forster) purchased and made over to the College the strip of land and houses between the southern boundary of the college grounds and Radcliffe Row, and the Ropewalk beyond the Row.[53]

By the turn of the century the college was experiencing pressure not only on its living accommodation but also on its public rooms. The dining-room tables could not be extended indefinitely. The crunch finally came in 1900. It had long been the custom to hold a Council dinner in the Hall dining-room on the evening of the General College Meeting. To do so on the occasion of Somerville's 21st birthday meeting in December 1900 would have meant the exclusion of almost all the current students. After a heated discussion and 'repeated protests against the establishment of that College bugbear, a precedent' it was eventually agreed to hold the dinner itself at the Randolph Hotel and then return immediately to an 'At Home' in the West.[54] The incident brought home to past and present members of the college its need for a large hall.

Other needs, however, were considered still more pressing. When Margery Fry was summoned by Miss Maitland in Trinity Term 1899 to take charge of the college library, she found this to consist of some 6,000 books scattered around the shelves of the dining-room and various corridors. Somerville had been library-conscious from the start, steadily building on the nucleus of its early gifts. A Library Committee—consisting of two tutors, two students, the librarian, and one outside member—was set up in 1894 with Mr Peters as chairman.

---

[52] MSL file, *c*.1910.
[53] In 1904/5 Radcliffe Row was closed and the cottages bordering it demolished.
[54] Oxford Letter, 1901.

The Council allocated £100 a year to the library from the college's income, and was active in soliciting gifts on its behalf. The Clothworkers' Company was one of its earliest institutional benefactors, as were the publishers Macmillan and Blackie. The practice of students presenting a book to the library on leaving was established early on. 1884 saw two major benefactions: some 400 books from Mark Pattison's library, selected by his widow and Professor Bywater, and some books of Ruskin's presented by himself. Individual members of the Council were generous in donating books and money for books: Margery Fry's arrival coincided with that of two collections of classical books from the libraries of Mr Peters and Lewis Nettleship, the latter presented by his sister-in-law Mrs Henry Nettleship.

Coming to the task of librarian with little initial enthusiasm—she once remarked that books came to her as cats went to people who liked them least—Miss Fry found that within a few weeks she had developed a 'desire for more good *editions* of books, because it does seem rather well worth while to have curious and original copies in a library that's likely to go on for a very long while in some form or another.'[55] In her spare moments—fired by Miss Maitland's determination to provide fitting accommodation for Somerville's growing collection of books—she sketched elevations of library buildings. A bequest of £1,000 from Isabella Don, who died in 1896, was put towards the Principal's Library Fund, which was brought up to £2,000 by a cheque for £50 presented by Sir John Evans at the 1901 gaudy; the Board of Education agreed to the use for library purposes of the capital sum received in 1892 from the Pfeiffer Trust. Basil Champneys, architect of the John Rylands Library at Manchester and Newnham College Cambridge, was commissioned to draw up plans for a building on the College's northern boundary to link the original Hall with the West.

Work began early in February 1903 and continued through a summer of torrential rain, the prospect of a covered way through college doing much to reconcile residents to the destruction of the old boundary wall and the removal of the main walk. When the new building emerged from its scaffolding at the end of the long vacation the façade was found to be adorned with the words *Donec rursus impleat orbem* picked out in white bricks. 'I could weep at the sight of those horrid white words' wrote Margery Fry, her artistic sensibilities

---

[55] Huws Jones, *Margery Fry*, 52.

thoroughly offended. The President of the Council, called in to mediate between architect and librarian, failed, in her view, to come up to scratch: 'Mr Champneys . . . came down but Mr Pelham after all his fulminations about the motto was as meek as Moses over it when it came to the point—never even stipulated that the swellings of the letters should come off.' In the end Miss Fry had her way, and the library stood 'simple and jolly' as she had wanted it, though Champneys was furious and Miss Maitland lamented the unnecessary expense.[56]

The library was the first to be built by a women's college in Oxford, and—at a time when most men's colleges maintained their libraries solely for the use of fellows—one of the first in any college to be built with the needs of students in mind.[57] Its official opening by John Morley on 11 July 1904, in the presence of the vice-chancellor and proctors, gave ceremonial form to Somerville's collegiate aspirations. Robert Bridges, the husband of Margery Fry's cousin Monica, was prevailed upon to compose a masque for the occasion (see Plate 14), having been assured that the Somervillian actresses could 'probably be relied upon to perform simply and without any stage-tricks or vulgarity.'[58] He was given as his subject the myth of Demeter and Persephone; the music was composed by [Sir] Henry Hadow, and the Greek costumes were submitted to Lady Evans for approval; the Librarian was producer. The occasion, attended by over six hundred people and widely reported in the local and national press, was generally judged a great success—though Sir Edward Fry intimated to Bridges (whom he did not like) that the audience had found the carrying-off of Persephone rather funny, causing the poet to complain to Margery Fry that he did not pretend to understand the Oxford audience.[59]

In opening the library, John Morley expressed the hope that it would come to have 'a voice and physiognomy of its own.'[60] The occasion was marked by the current students with the gift of a clock, and followed closely by two major benefactions: the books and papers of the writer and Egyptologist Amelia B. Edwards, and—thanks to the

---

[56] Ibid. 62–3.

[57] Some colleges did not open their libraries to undergraduates until the 1930s, though a few provided separate rooms for their use. Until 1902 Oriel kept one cupboard of books for junior members: P. Morgan (comp.), *Oxford Libraries outside the Bodleian: A Guide* (Oxford Bibliographical Society, 1972), p. xii.

[58] SMF to Bridges, 21 Jan. 1904 (Demeter file).

[59] Huws-Jones, *Margery Fry*, 64–5. See also C. Phillips, *Robert Bridges: A Biography* (Oxford, 1992), 199–200. *Demeter* was subsequently acted at Liverpool three times in 1908, together with Shelley's version of Euripides' *Cyclops*.

[60] Report in *Fritillary*, 32, June 1904.

good offices of Morley himself—the library of John Stuart Mill. The huge task of dealing with these collections fell, after Miss Fry's departure in 1904 to take up the wardenship of University House, Birmingham, to Rose Sidgwick and Lucy Kempson, her successors as Librarian.[61]

The acquisition of Mill's library—or, rather, of that part of it which was in England at the time of his death—increased Somerville's bookstock by nearly a third.[62] It was offered by his step-daughter, Helen Taylor; and it came without condition, to be used as a working library for students. Unlike the Edwards library, which the donor insisted should be kept together as a collection, Mill's books were duly issued with classification numbers and dispersed through the library. Duplicates and works (such as cookery and travel books) deemed inappropriate for a college library were disposed of. It was not until 1969 that, with the help of a grant from the Pilgrim Trust, the remaining collection was reassembled and restored to something like its original state. In the mean time, generations of Somerville students had enjoyed the inestimable privilege of actually using Mill's superb library. The gift was hailed in 1906 as 'a fitting memorial of his generous championship of women';[63] the manner of its use, however offensive to bibliographical orthodoxy, may perhaps be considered a memorial to his utilitarian principles.

Amelia Edwards bequeathed her Egyptological books to University College London; it was, presumably, her friendship—through the Egypt Exploration Society—with Miss Lefevre and Miss Maitland which prompted her to leave her fine general library to Somerville. The collection, for which a special room was constructed at the eastern end of the new building, is described in the *SSA Report* for 1907:

> It is the library of a person interested in many subjects, who read everything that came her way and made the utmost of the comparatively limited opportunities of a woman of the mid-Victorian era. One understands the more easily as one makes acquaintance with her books, why Miss Edwards was anxious to bequeath a possession so precious to her as her library to a College which should give to the women of a later generation much that she was able to attain only with great difficulty and much that never came within her reach.

---

[61] Rose Sidgwick was temporary tutor in history 1903–4 and Librarian 1904–5; Lucy Kempson was Librarian and Principal's Secretary 1905–14.

[62] The rest of his books found their way to the Bibliothèque nationale and the Avignon public library.   [63] Oxford Letter, 1906.

Her books included fine editions of standard authors, classical and modern, rare antiquarian items, and precious association copies (for she counted many celebrated authors among her friends). Along with them came an important manuscript collection, an interesting collection of pottery acquired in the course of her travels, particularly in the Mediterranean, and many of her own charming water-colours, including the original illustrations for her book *A Thousand Miles Up the Nile*.

Meanwhile, efforts were in train to supply the other great need of the women's colleges: the provision of opportunities for research. At an informal meeting of old members, tutors, and final-year students in 1902 it was agreed to pursue the possibility of raising funds to finance a research fellowship; and a provisional committee, including Eleanor Rathbone and Margery Fry, was set up to this end. Despite the many other calls on their generosity—the committee was particularly anxious that the fellowship should not be launched at the expense of the Women's University Settlement, to which many old members already subscribed—Somervillians responded enthusiastically to the new appeal, and the college was able to advertise a three-year appointment at £140 p.a. In 1903 Miss Evelyn Jamison of Lady Margaret Hall, a historian of medieval Sicily, was elected Oxford's first woman research fellow. In reporting her election, the Council expressed its view that 'the Old Students have rendered a most important service both to the College and to the Higher Education of Women by this timely and generous benefaction.'[64] An editorial in *Fritillary* hailed the election as 'the most interesting event of the term,' and complimented Somerville on following 'the graceful custom said to be peculiar to our university' of electing a member of a sister college.[65]

The principal conditions of the fellowship—known at first as the 'Somerville Research Fellowship', and from 1914 (to distinguish it from the Carlisle Fellowship) as the 'Mary Somerville Research Fellowship' —were that the holder should devote herself to some line of research and should publish the results. The proposers of the scheme were also concerned to provide the fellow with some defence against unreasonable family demands. 'I don't think the Council realizes quite the position many women are in towards their families' wrote Eleanor Rathbone, urging the desirability of imposing on the Fellow at least a moral obligation to stay for the full three years, 'nor what advantage

[64] *College Report*, 1903. [65] *Fritillary*, 29, June 1903.

to the Fellow herself strict regulation may be, to enable her to resist domestic pressure.'[66] In an article in *Fritillary* Mildred Pope and Margery Fry defended the use of a title which might be considered simply 'a new case of our borrowing the names and forms of masculine institutions, whose essence has escaped us'. While conceding that the new fellow would have no powers of government in the college beyond those of an ordinary member, they voiced the conviction of the subscribers that

> the foundation of Fellowships on the lines of the present one would do much to invigorate and widen both the intellectual and the corporate life of our women's Colleges. They have undoubtedly suffered hitherto in comparison with men's Colleges, from the restriction of their members to those who are either learning or teaching subjects necessary for Schools, and nothing could tend more directly to remove the narrowness which is too often the reproach of work done for examinations, than the presence in our Colleges of a body of women engaged in work more advanced and of a wider scope than is possible for the average student.[67]

Initially restricted to Oxford women, the fellowship was opened in 1909 to women students from Cambridge and Trinity College Dublin, and in 1920 to graduates of any British university. Though its finances, based on a multiplicity of small donations, were frequently precarious, the fellowship has survived, with two war-time intermissions, to this day, supporting a long line of distinguished scholars in a wide range of subjects. Miss Jamison was succeeded in 1906 by the mineralogist Florence Isaac, and in 1909 by the anthropologist Barbara Freire-Marreco. At a time when Somerville had no other fellows of any kind, these three in turn were known simply as 'The Fellow'.

The growth in student numbers and proliferation of buildings made it increasingly difficult to maintain the family atmosphere which had characterized Somerville in its early days. Miss Maitland, however, if less constantly present to her students than her predecessor had been, was very much more approachable; and the pastoral aspects of her work were ones to which she attached particular importance. Her dealings with students—by whom, uniquely in Somerville's history, she was known as 'the Warden'—were characterized by what Margery Fry called 'an invincible hopefulness which often

---

[66] Quoted in Huws Jones, *Margery Fry*, 61.   [67] *Fritillary*, 29, June 1903.

brought about its own fulfilment'—'Again and again she was justified in her belief that the most tangled character will often straighten itself out if time and freedom be given to it, and her most anxious thought often issued in a policy of wise inaction.'[68] Even Lady Rhondda, scathing about most aspects of her brief stay at Somerville, admitted that she had liked and admired the Principal.[69]

In September 1897 Miss Maitland was taken ill, and, at the request of the Council, Miss Shaw Lefevre agreed to deputize for her in Michaelmas Term. Characteristically, she refused to accept the £50 honorarium offered:

> I never thought of it except as a matter of friendly cooperation in an emergency. . . . I am glad to have had the opportunity of renewing my interest in the College, and I have much enjoyed seeing my old friends in Oxford. The work has not been heavy and I have been much helped by Miss Bruce.[70]

Miss Maitland returned to work in the new year; but a second illness eight years later was clearly more serious, and in Hilary Term 1906 she was obliged once again to withdraw from college. Miss Bruce was appointed Acting Principal, and an old student, Evelyn Atkinson, came—as the Council recorded with gratitude, 'at a moment's notice during a time of stress and difficulty'—to be her assistant.[71] Plans for the gaudy that summer were abandoned. At their meeting in May the Council agreed to appoint a bursar to take over some of the domestic responsibilities—particularly with regard to conferences in vacation—which had hitherto rested with the Principal; Mrs Ralph was appointed to this post in June. On 19 August Miss Maitland died of cancer, at the age of 57.

---

[68] *Oxford Magazine*, 24 Oct. 1906.
[69] Viscountess Rhondda, *This was my World* (London, 1933), 107.
[70] Minutes of Council, 7 Feb. 1898.   [71] Ibid. 12 Mar. 1906.

4

Towards University Recognition:
The Early Principalship
of Emily Penrose, 1907–1914

Miss Maitland's death shocked the college. The Standing Committee—afforced by Sir William Bousfield, Mr Fisher, Miss Fry, and Miss Cooper—was asked to consider whether any changes might be made in the conditions of the principalship, and how best to set about making an appointment. They concluded that fees should be raised in order to increase the Principal's salary, 'which all agreed was at present very inadequate', to £400 a year, and that the post should be offered to Miss Emily Penrose; in the event of her refusing, it should be advertised.[1] Among other names mooted by members of the Council was that of Margery Fry herself.[2]

Miss Penrose accepted on certain conditions: that she might postpone taking up her duties until Easter 1907; that, in view of the recent appointment of a bursar, she would not be bound to remain in Oxford during vacations to superintend conferences and summer schools; and that board and lodging should be provided for her maid (for whose wages she herself would remain responsible).[3] Her terms were accepted by the Council, and on 12 November 1906 she was elected unanimously—the first of a distinguished line of 'home-grown' Principals.

She was the obvious choice for the job. Now in her 49th year, Emily Penrose had entered Somerville as a student when already in her 30s, having previously enjoyed what Miss Darbishire called 'the rather erratic but thoroughly stimulating and enriching education that came the way of fortunate girls of her generation.'[4] Her grandmother was the writer 'Mrs Markham'. Her grandfather's sister, Mary Penrose, had married Dr Arnold of Rugby, and as a child Emily was a frequent visitor to the Arnolds at Fox How. Her architect father, Dr F. C.

---

[1] Minutes of Council, 15 Oct. 1906.
[2] She was the choice of Mrs Green: Huws Jones, *Margery Fry*, 80.
[3] EP to H. Pelham, 8 Nov. 1906. Minutes of Council, 12 Nov. 1906.
[4] Obituary by HD, *Oxford Magazine*, Summer 1942.

Penrose, was the first director of the British School of Archaeology at Athens; her brother Francis was to become a distinguished physician. With little formal schooling, Emily was nevertheless able to study languages and the arts on long visits to France, Germany, and Italy; her father taught her drawing and painting as well as the rudiments of architecture and archaeology; and she shared the scientific interests of her brother. When the family moved to Athens she learned Modern Greek. She acquired many of the usual—and some less common—feminine accomplishments: a fine needlewoman, a skilled water-colour artist, an accomplished skater, she was also an intrepid mountaineer. In Athens she looked after the family business; back in England she taught literature, languages, and drawing in a girls' school near Brighton.

Her father's friendship with Professor Pelham determined the course of her future career. At his suggestion she came up to Somerville in 1889 to read *literae humaniores*. Starting with no Latin and a little Modern Greek, and choosing an archaeological special subject for which she could draw on her experience in Athens, she became in 1892 the first woman to be placed in the first class in Greats. The following year she was appointed Principal and lecturer in ancient history at Bedford College, London; in 1898 she moved to the Royal Holloway College, where she remained as Principal till 1907.

During these years her administrative talents were developed, and she won a high reputation not only in the colleges of which she was head, but in the wider sphere of university politics and administration. She helped to steer her two colleges into the full stream of university life, and herself played an active part on the London University Senate.[5] On her return to Oxford, she soon came to be acknowledged as the leading representative of the women's colleges, a position confirmed by the retirement of Elizabeth Wordsworth in 1909. In 1911 she was invited to serve on the Advisory Committee on University Grants, and in 1916 as the only woman member of the Royal Commission on University Education in Wales. After the War, she was a natural choice for membership of the Royal Commission on Oxford and Cambridge.

Though Somervillian vanity may regard her return to Oxford in 1907 as a natural progression, from Miss Penrose's own point of view

---

[5] See M. J. Tuke, *A History of Bedford College for Women* (London, 1939), esp. ch. 10, 'The Tide Turns'; and C. Bingham, *The History of Royal Holloway College 1886–1986* (London, 1987), esp. ch. 4, 'The Larger Life of a University: The Principalship of Miss Emily Penrose'.

the move was by no means an obvious, or indeed an advantageous one. As Helen Darbishire was to point out: 'To an ambitious woman it might have seemed a step down—from a large College to a small one, from a University where women worked on an equal footing with men to one where women were only enjoying the hospitality of the University by courtesy'.[6] Fortunately for Somerville, Miss Penrose was not, so far as her own personal interests were concerned, ambitious. Whether her acceptance of the principalship was motivated by affection for Somerville and for Oxford, or by the wish to play a part in the movement—in which she heartily believed—for the admission of women to membership of the university, her twenty-year period of office was to make a profound impact on college and university alike.

Emily Penrose was the first woman head of house in Oxford or Cambridge to combine high administrative ability with high academic achievement. She was also a consummate tactician, 'the wise director of policy, the counsellor of action or delayed action', whose generalship in the movement for the admission of women to membership of the university was to prove decisive. The 1920 statute by which this objective was achieved was the culmination of many years' work by many people; but it would not, in Helen Darbishire's judgement, 'have been the fair and generous instrument that it was if Miss Penrose had not used her powers and her position as she did.' 'We feel it was you' wrote Helen Waddell in 1925, 'who made it inevitable that women should be recognised in the University.'[7]

Her influence derived as much from personal example as from her acknowledged political skills. In her presence it was not easy to make out a convincing case either for the intellectual inferiority of women, or for their unfitness for university business. So great were her abilities, indeed, that they were often paid the ultimate tribute of being described as 'masculine' by writers who hastened to stress the femininity of her accomplishments. The quality which impressed people above all was statesmanship:

> Anyone who has worked with Miss Penrose on a committee will have been struck by her statesmanlike vision. Where the ordinary person sees one step ahead, and where you or I . . . see two or three, Miss Penrose sees nine or ten, or as far ahead as there can possibly be any consequences that matter. This gift, like all the best gifts, has been earned as well as given. Her intellectual swiftness and strength are

---

[6] *Oxford Magazine*, Summer 1942.   [7] H. Waddell to EP, 27 Dec. 1925.

backed by a patient and deliberate mastery of detail, and the combination is invincible. . . . Impartiality, a strong sense of justice, a desire to get at the truth of a case and to examine all the facts fairly—these are the foundation of her recognised power, as distinct from mere efficiency and ability, in affairs.[8]

The letters written to her on her retirement in 1926 bear witness to her importance as a role-model to the rising generation of women academics. 'Six years ago' wrote Maude Clarke,

> I would have thought it absurd that anyone should claim to have gained a moral education by serving on committees. Now I know that the time spent in discussing College business, and in watching your unswerving justice, patience and complete obliteration of self has been the best thing I have ever known.[9]

It was perhaps this training which developed the strong sense of constitutional propriety, combined with 'delicacy of perception regarding individual claims' which a young colleague was to recognize as Maude Clarke's own distinctive legacy to Somerville.[10] Bertha Phillpotts, with experience of Westfield and Girton behind her, wrote: 'I didn't know until I began my own struggles as Head of a College how much I should owe to the memory of your way of looking at University politics and people.'[11] Arthur Gillett thought it a sad reflection on a male-dominated society that such abilities had not been pressed into service on the international scene.[12] There were, however, chinks in Miss Penrose's armour: an ability to see all sides of a question which sometimes made it difficult for her to make up her mind;[13] a susceptibility to disabling headaches; an almost total lack of small-talk; and a terror of cats.

Much of Miss Penrose's public reputation rests on the part she played in the movement for the admission of women to membership of the university. When she took up office in 1907, however, her immediate concerns were more purely domestic. Somerville, still reeling under the shock of Miss Maitland's death, had suffered a second severe loss in the death in February 1907 of its President, Henry Pelham. At his funeral a special place in the University Church was

---

[8] 'Isis Idol', *Isis*, 1 Mar. 1922.   [9] MVC to EP, 24 Nov. 1925.
[10] M. Lascelles, *A Memoir* (privately printed, 1989), 47.
[11] B. Phillpotts to EP, 11 Jan. 1927.   [12] A. Gillett to HD, 2 Feb. 1942.
[13] Notes by Lady Evans, 1942 (Penrose file).

reserved for Somerville students, in recognition of his affection for the college; they in their turn subscribed towards an enlarged photograph to perpetuate his memory in Somerville. Miss Penrose used the college history as one means of restoring a sense of continuity to a community whose life had recently undergone so much disruption. Throughout her time as Principal, she took pains to make her students aware of the history of the college, and that of women at Oxford more generally. At the suggestion of the Librarian, Miss Kempson, a log-book, recording term by term the events of college life, was started; press-cuttings for the earlier period were collected, and Miss Lefevre was approached to write her recollections of the earliest days of Somerville. Inviting her back to attend a Log Book Evening in Trinity Term 1909, Miss Penrose explained:

> We particularly want a large set of good students who are going down this term to be here. They came up during Miss Maitland's illness and to some extent will form the bridge between the old and new regime.
>
> We have been talking to them about the old days and I think it will mean a great deal to the College if you will do us the great kindness of coming. . . . We do want this particular set of students to realise you and to understand a little of what the College owes to its first Principal.[14]

In writing to thank Miss Lefevre for coming to speak to the students, she added 'You will understand how much it means to me to hear that you were pleased with what *your* Somerville has grown into.'[15] A further reminder of the college's debt to its first Principal came with the establishment by her cousin, Lady Wantage (sole heir in 1883 to the huge fortune of her father, Lord Overstone) of a Shaw Lefevre scholarship, to be awarded to a candidate 'who has already given proof of special capacity either at Somerville or elsewhere'. The first Shaw Lefevre scholar, Constance Watson, who came to Somerville in 1907 to read Greats, having already achieved a first in Classics at Manchester University, died in mid-course shortly after achieving a first in honour mods. Future holders of the award included Margaret Roberts, who as an undergraduate in 1945 impressed her tutors with her ability as a chemist, and later—as Mrs Thatcher—was to give proof of special capacity on a somewhat wider stage.[16]

[14] EP to MSL, 29 Apr. 1909.   [15] EP to MSL, 14 May 1909.

[16] Dame Janet Vaughan's well-known dismissiveness of Margaret Roberts as a scientist was perhaps coloured by her dislike for Mrs Thatcher's politics; the records of Education Committee tell a different story.

Miss Penrose also had to deal, in her early years as Principal, with the administrative consequences of her predecessor's illness and sudden departure from office. Business had been left unfinished, documentation incomplete. Uncertainties emerged about tutorial appointments: whether Miss Kirkaldy, for instance, was responsible for all Somerville's science students or only for the biologists—a matter of some importance for relations with the AEW.[17] 'Unfortunately, Miss Maitland left very few written memoranda of any kind at the College', Miss Penrose wrote in 1912 in the course of an embarrassed correspondence with Mrs Henry Nettleship about the fate of three statues which the latter had loaned to Somerville seventeen years before. Concerned at their battered and dangerous condition, and finding no record of their provenance, she had herself recently authorized their disposal. Mrs Nettleship expressed surprise that Miss Maitland had kept no record of the transaction and that the college had not taken greater care of the statues (of one of which, she said, Miss Pater had been particularly fond), but hastened to exonerate Miss Penrose herself from blame: 'I have no doubt the damage was done by the servants in the vacation.' In her reply Miss Penrose made it clear that she thought students and vacation visitors more likely culprits.[18]

Within the university at large, and in Somerville in particular, Miss Penrose made the raising of academic standards one of her chief objectives. Like Emily Davies in earlier days at Cambridge, she believed firmly that women should aim at taking the full degree courses, even when the degree itself was denied them. 'I believe we have suffered less from having no degree than from the fancy courses which most of us have taken', she wrote to Miss Maitland from Bedford College in 1895, when invited to give evidence to the committee considering the question of admitting women to degrees.[19] Her insistence as Principal that Somerville students should observe all university regulations as to residence and preliminary examinations, as well as proving their quality in the final honour schools, though irksome at the time, was to pay dividends in the long run. Building on the foundations laid by Miss Maitland, she steadily consolidated the college's teaching strength, early appointments including two former members of her staff from Holloway: Helen Darbishire in English and

---

[17] Correspondence with J. W. Kirkaldy, Oct. 1912.
[18] Correspondence with Mrs Henry Nettleship, Dec. 1912.
[19] EP to ACM, 9 Sept. 1895 (Degrees file).

Margaret Hayes Robinson—'the best loved member of [Holloway] staff ever'—in history.[20] In 1907 the Oxford Correspondent reported that:

> The Staff has been increasing until it has attained dimensions so imposing that the question of accommodation in the SCR has become a matter of serious difficulty. It has also lately developed a positive passion for the making of many books and for the acquiring and wearing of Academic gowns of various types.

The latter was in response to popular demand: in May the students had requested at College Meeting 'that the Principal and all members of the Staff who are entitled to wear the academic dress . . . [should] do so at Sunday prayers.'[21] In 1912 the 'President and Faculty' of Somerville were represented by an American Old Somervillian, Miss Almy, at celebrations to mark the 75th anniversary of the founding of Mount Holyoke.[22]

The tutors' powers at home, however, were still very limited. In 1902 they had gained the right to elect one of their number to serve as their representative on the college Council; in 1907 the advocates of increased staff representation were dissuaded from pressing for major constitutional change at a time when both the Principal and the President were new.[23] Sending the relevant papers to Miss Pope for safe keeping against the day when the issue could be raised again, Margery Fry expressed the view that 'while some admixture of outsiders, and certainly of men, is useful, there is something a trifle ridiculous in the absence from its deliberations of almost all the tutors.'[24] Miss Penrose would undoubtedly have agreed with her. It is characteristic of her methods that, instead of engaging in controversy on Council, she provided the staff with an alternative mode of operation. As Principal of Holloway, where women were excluded by the foundation deed from serving on the governing body, she had used the Education Council as a Trojan horse to bring women tutors into the policy-making of the college.[25] She now adopted a similar tactic at

---

[20] Bingham, *Royal Holloway College*, 98. Vera Brittain, who was taught by Miss Hayes Robinson at Somerville, thought her 'nearer to the ideal type of woman—to the woman we hope the future will bring—than at any rate any don I have ever met.': Brittain, *War Diary 1913–1917*, ed. A. Bishop and T. Smart (London, 1981) 125–6.

[21] College Meeting, 22 May 1907.   [22] Oxford Letter, 1912.

[23] See letters from C. Green and Sir William Markby in Constitution: Representation of Tutors file.   [24] SMF to MKP, 4 Mar. 1908.

[25] Bingham, *Royal Holloway College*, 95.

Somerville. Emily Overend, tutor in German for the first three years of Miss Penrose's principalship, later recalled the 'somewhat stormy' tutors' meetings of the period, claiming to have 'grown up quite a lot' simply from observing how, as chairman, the Principal did things and got them done: 'You had such a wonderful way of being perfectly impartial and yet sympathising with each of us and moreover of getting the business through.'[26] Throughout her principalship, the status of the tutors was steadily enhanced, and their familiarity with college business extended, until in 1921 it seemed natural for them to be accorded membership of the Council. The long view came naturally to Miss Penrose: at Bedford College in the 1890s she had worked to ensure that her successor as Principal should have—what she did not have herself—an office of her own;[27] at Somerville she ensured that her successor should be the first Principal to take the chair at meetings of Council.

In the year that she took office, eight Somervillians achieved firsts in the final honour schools—a triumph which Council acknowledged by granting permission for the first-ever college ball. 'It is possible' commented the Oxford Correspondent,

> that when the tradition arose that seven firsts should win a College ball this was considered equivalent to deferring to the Greek Kalends. But Somerville has played the part of the indomitable third son in a fairy story, has accomplished its task, gained its reward, and the ball has become a reality.[28]

(The fact that the occasion 'combined pleasure with solvency' was seen as an additional triumph.) In 1908 Somerville signalled its academic expectations by the decision to hold an entrance examination in conjunction with its scholarship examinations, the first of the Oxford women's colleges to do so.

In 1912 it became the first of them to attract endowment for research, with the establishment by Gilbert Murray's mother-in-law, Rosalind Countess of Carlisle, of a research fellowship, tenable for five years and open to any unmarried or widowed woman of European race and British nationality, and to naturalized Jewesses. 'No gift could have taken a more welcome form than this endowment of research' commented the writer of the 1913 Oxford Letter, announcing

---

[26] E. O. Lorimer to EP, 3 Nov. 1923.   [27] Tuke, *Bedford College for Women*, 166–7.
[28] Oxford Letter, 1908.

the election as the first holder of the fellowship of Miss Bertha Phillpotts (later Dame Bertha Newall), a distinguished Icelandic scholar and the future Mistress of her own old college, Girton. With an income of £120 a year the Carlisle fellowship, as Miss Phillpotts' successor Mary Winearls Porter told a friend triumphantly in 1919, was at that time 'the best fellowship in the country for women.'[29] It should in fact have been even better, Gilbert Murray explained in 1954 to Janet Vaughan: 'Lady Carlisle left in her will £20,000 to Girton. I persuaded her to give another £20,000 to Somerville, to which she agreed. She paid the £20,000 to Girton and forgot to alter the clause in her will, so that Girton got it twice and Somerville was badly starved.'[30] But at the time, Somerville could only rejoice in its good fortune. No less welcome was a bequest by Miss Mary Ewart of £10,000 for the foundation of scholarships. The first application of the fund, in 1912, was the award of a travelling scholarship to the Somerville Research Fellow, Barbara Freire-Marreco, to enable her to continue for a fourth year her research on the Amazonian Indians. But the primary purpose of the Mary Ewart Fund was the support of undergraduate scholarships; and it was with some dynastic pride that in 1913 the Oxford Letter announced the holder of that year's scholarship to be 'the first College grand-child', Margaret Leigh, whose mother, Alice Bayliss, had been a Clothworkers' scholar from 1881 to 1884. Miss Leigh's first cousin, Dorothy L. Sayers, preceded her to Somerville as a Gilchrist scholar in 1912.

Such benefactions were the more valued because they came at a time when the college was losing some of its traditional support. Enthusiasm for educating women was not invariably accompanied by a desire to grant them the vote. The prominence in campaigning against votes for women of Somerville's founding secretary (and Miss Penrose's cousin), Mrs Humphry Ward, was a source of keen embarrassment to a college the majority of whose current members—staff and students alike—were committed suffragists; relations were not improved when her offer of a paper putting the anti-suffrage case was turned down by the college debating society.[31] Somerville's high pro-suffrage profile offended a number of other friends and benefactors who shared her views, or who—like the current Secretary of the

---

[29] M. Porter to F. Bascom, 8 May 1919. Quoted in L. B. Arnold, 'The Bascom–Goldschmidt–Porter correspondence 1907–1922', *Earth Sciences History*, 12/2 (1993).

[30] GM to JV, 17 Feb. 1954 (Carlisle Fellowship file).

[31] Massie to Gillett, 26 July 1914 (EP2–Suffrage).

Council, Mrs Massie, and her husband—believed that colleges had a duty to hold aloof from controversial political questions.[32]

This view certainly prevailed at Newnham, where a student up in the early years of the century was horrified at the 'indifference or opposition' of the dons to votes for women.[33] Appealed to by Mildred Pope in 1912 for support for a scheme to involve the Oxford and Cambridge women's halls in a joint suffrage campaign, Mrs Sidgwick sounded a note of warning about 'people engaged in one kind of work associating together to use the weight of their position to promote another object not connected with the first':

> I may be wrong, but I think that both objects might suffer more than either would gain. At any rate, the womens' colleges might suffer, for some of their supporters would undoubtedly feel aggrieved. . . . It would be different if it could clearly be seen that the cause of the colleges would be advanced by the vote and if they joined together to press for it for that reason. But this is not really clear, and it is a view which frightens some university men I fancy who are quite good friends of the colleges educationally.[34]

Apologizing for writing 'such a cold-watery letter', Mrs Sidgwick attributed her caution to the fact that 'here at Newnham . . . we have always kept the questions of education and the vote so carefully apart.'

Somervillians were markedly less circumspect. By 1910 membership of the Somerville Women's Suffrage Society, exclusive of former students, stood at seventy-five out of a total student body of ninety-four. Its members took part in national demonstrations, and at home organized debates and lectures and 'special effort weeks', when lucrative forms of labour and penance were devised in aid of the National Union of Women's Suffrage Societies. In 1911 this culminated in an American tennis tournament of mixed doubles, with twenty-eight couples competing to receive from the hands of the Principal a copy of John Stuart Mill's *Essay on the Subjection of Women*. Reporting the unprecedented sight of male undergraduates dining in Somerville in tennis kit, a writer in *Fritillary* commented that 'Somerville had the appearance of a co-educational college, and

---

[32] Massie to Gillett, 16 July 1914.
[33] A. Phillips (ed.), *A Newnham Anthology* (Cambridge, 1979), 51.
[34] Sidgwick to MKP, 24 Oct. 1912.

moreover a co-educational college of devoted suffragists, as the red, white and green badges testified.'[35]

When in 1911 the women's colleges combined to form the Oxford Women Students' Society for Women's Suffrage, they commissioned Edmund New to design a splendid banner, showing Oxford's spires in gold on a dark blue background. It made its first public appearance at the procession of women's suffrage societies in London in June, and the following spring was taken to a great meeting organized—with the support of all the women principals and vice-principals—by the Oxford town branch of the National Union, when the chief speaker was Lord Haldane. In April a number of OWSSWS members defeated efforts to keep them out of an anti-suffrage meeting at which the chief speaker was Mrs Humphry Ward, and raised a series of questions which, by their own account, 'were not altogether appreciated by the speakers.'[36] The prominence of Somervillians in such activities prompted a letter in the *Times* complaining that in one of the Oxford women's halls 'meeting after meeting in favour of votes for women has taken place, usually with the help of notable suffragists imported from outside', and deploring the tactics of 'peaceful persuasion' which, he alleged, were brought to bear on students unsympathetic to the cause. In consequence of such behaviour:

> While pioneers are sad and sorry to see that the recently developed training of girls is deteriorating their sense of proportion, and is often bulging into self-sufficiency and self-assertiveness, parents are beginning to shrink from planting their daughters in hot-beds of feminism, and pious benefactors are altering their wills and diverting intended bequests to other objects.[37]

Somerville was indeed beginning to pay for its notoriety. In November 1913 press reports of a suffrage meeting held on college premises under the chairmanship of the Principal of St Hilda's, Miss Burrows, prompted Mr Frederick Conybeare to announce his reluctant intention to discontinue, as soon as the tenure of the current holder expired, the scholarship which he had established in 1888 in memory of his first wife Mary, the daughter of Professor Max Müller.

---

[35] *Fritillary*, 53, June 1911. For the voting record of the Union on suffrage issues at this period see John Draper's BA thesis, 'An Educated Male Elite: Oxford University Undergraduate Behaviour in the Formative Years of the Women's Colleges' (Oxford, 1994), esp. 18–19. [36] Article by Ruth Giles on the OWSSWS, *SSA Report*, 1912. [37] Letter from 'Educationalist' in *The Times*, 12 Apr. 1912.

Somerville, he protested, was being given up, 'not exclusively to the educational purposes for which it was founded, but also to a propaganda which, by reason of the degradation of countless poor girls incidental to it, is abhorrent to myself and, I am sure, would have been no less abhorrent to my late wife.'[38] The following year, Mr and Mrs Massie cancelled their annual subscription to the college on hearing that a meeting of the OWSS had been held in Somerville during term-time.[39] Such a gesture, coming from someone who had served for fifteen years as Secretary of the College Council, was particularly embarrassing. The President and Treasurer engaged in a placatory correspondence; but in Michaelmas Term 1914 Miss Penrose again gave permission for the OWSS to meet in Somerville, and the Council again steadfastly upheld her authority to do so.[40]

The whole suffrage affair was an extraordinary episode in Somerville's history. That Miss Penrose—normally prudent to a fault in discouraging any activity which might rebound unfavourably on the movement to secure degrees for women—should have thrown her weight so unreservedly behind the suffrage campaign, cannot be attributed simply to her personal enthusiasm for the cause. She must have been very confident that those people whose opinion counted most in the matter of degrees were on the right side in the matter of the vote. In 1923, when the controversy was over, Mrs Massie sent a donation of £100 for the college Endowment Fund.[41]

The university, meanwhile, was finding it increasingly difficult to ignore the presence of women in its midst, and was beginning to realize that only by recognizing their existence could it bring them under any kind of control. In 1908, on the proposal of H. T. Gerrans, Secretary to the Oxford Local Examinations Delegacy and a member of the Somerville Council, a committee was appointed to consider the relations of the University to women students, particularly in the matter of examinations. Miss Penrose was involved in consultations from an early stage, being enlisted by Gerrans to restrain the AEW from engaging in a premature agitation which might prove counterproductive. 'Advised me at all costs to stop AEW from proclaiming its views at this stage' she noted, after a conversation on 20 November, going on to state her own, very characteristic, determination 'not to

---

[38] F. C. Conybeare to the Secretary of the Council, 22 Nov. 1912.
[39] Massie to Gillett, 16 July 1914.
[40] Minutes of Council, 28 Nov. 1914 and 2 Feb. 1915.
[41] Finance Committee, 16 Oct. 1923.

put weapons into hands of opponents'.[42] Her diplomatic mission was aided by good working relations with Annie Rogers, with whom she had dealings while still Principal of Bedford, and by the fact that she was personally uninvolved in Somerville's earlier tussles with the AEW. After lengthy deliberations, the committee recommended the establishment of a Delegacy for the supervision of women students, and a statute to this effect was promulgated in May 1910. The Delegacy was to consist of the vice-chancellor and proctors, nine members of Congregation, and—for the first time in the University's history—nine women members: the Principal of the Society of Home Students *ex officio*, two women nominated by the vice-chancellor and proctors, and six elected by a board consisting of women engaged in teaching and administration in connection with registered students. Miss Penrose was one of those elected to serve under this provision.

One of the functions of the Delegacy was to keep a register of the women students entitled to use its examinations, and a record of examinations passed by them. In future women were entered for examinations under the University of Oxford instead of through the Local Examinations Board; and in Trinity Term 1911 their names were for the first time included in the Schools lists. The *University Gazette* abandoned its practice of including women under the 'Unofficial Notices'. Somerville felt that the seal had been put on its acceptance by the university when in 1912 the college porter, Scroggs, was invited to the College Servants' Dinner.[43]

Whether the establishment of the Delegacy was likely to bring women any nearer to being admitted to degrees was a question, wrote the Oxford Correspondent for 1910, 'about which our foes speak a good deal and our friends keep a discreet silence.' The previous year the Chancellor, Lord Curzon, had examined the position of women students in his *Memorandum on University Reform* (nicknamed 'The Scarlet Letter' from the colour of its binding), and made conservative proposals for admitting them to a titular degree, though without any constitutional privileges. Hebdomadal Council pledged itself to bring the question before Congregation, and in 1913, after 'due deliberation, characteristic of its movements at all times' (as the writer of the Log Book put it), the university agreed to grant to women Certificates of Merit in Letters and Science, corresponding to the degrees of Bachelor

[42] EP, Notes on conversation with Gerrans, 20 Nov. 1908 (Delegacy file).
[43] Oxford Letter, 1912.

of Letters and of Science. The outbreak of war cut short further discussion, an interruption disappointing at the time, but which proved in the event to be positively advantageous.

These modifications in the status of women students at Oxford were accompanied by a radical change in the character of Somerville itself. Early in 1910 Council received a letter signed by a number of old members, urging the need for a hall large enough for the whole college to take its meals in, and to accommodate a large audience for lectures. The signatories also drew attention to the need for a new suite of Principal's rooms, and the desirability of providing additional accommodation sufficient to bring the number of students up to a hundred. Their proposal was a controversial one. The argument in favour of a hall capable of accommodating the whole college on special occasions was generally accepted, as was the desirability of moving the college kitchen from the immediate vicinity of the Radcliffe Infirmary dust-heap.[44] Miss Shaw Lefevre was one of those who deprecated further expansion, and also disliked the idea of a central dining hall. 'Would it not be better to make it more of a privilege to enter the College by some process of selection, rather than to increase our numbers?' she had written in response to an earlier proposal for expansion: 'I know it is difficult to devise such a process—but quality rather than quantity is what one would like to aim at, now that we are in the happy position of having many more applicants to choose from than we can possibly take in.'[45] She now—citing the corroborative authority of Mrs Sidgwick of Newnham—rose to the defence of the old system of separate dining-rooms:

The noise and greater distraction of a large party (over a hundred in our case perhaps) is not desirable. I was told by an American student from Vassar, that the effect on the nerves of meeting large numbers of students in the passages, stairs, etc was very trying and thought to be too exciting. Also I think it does not tend to good manners. I used to think that whatever the social position of the students was, manners were often deficient and that the little formality of assembling for dinner was a help in this way . . . A large Hall would certainly be a great gain—and a central kitchen, if the Newnham plan is found to answer of serving the Halls from one kitchen—but I am quite against

---

[44] Minutes of Council, 7 Feb. 1911.   [45] MSL to EP, 19 Nov. 1907.

doing away with the present dining-rooms for every day use, and in any case they would be wanted for breakfast?[46]

The future, however, lay with the signatories, who, in proposing a new building, had gone on to suggest how it might be financed. They acknowledged that not many Somervillians were sufficiently wealthy to make large donations for such a project, but thought that there were probably many who would be able to advance sums of money at a moderate rate of interest. Their suggestion that debentures should be issued to secure the financial side of the scheme was adopted by the Council, and the building of the Maitland Hall was in fact financed entirely by the contributions of members and friends of the college, £6,000 being received in donations and £11,000 raised by debentures. 'If any doubt should exist in any mind as to whether a women's college in Oxford is capable of evoking the same feelings of affection in its members as are evoked in the case of generations of old Oxford men for the foundations to which they are attached' said the President of the Council, H. A. L. Fisher, at the official opening ceremony, 'this building supplies a sufficient answer.'[47]

Work began in the summer term of 1913 with the felling of trees, the sight of which, wrote the Oxford Correspondent, 'harrowed our feelings whilst it fascinated our eyes.' In the course of digging the foundations a gravel pit was discovered, and it became clear that, under such unfavourable conditions, the cost of the work would be much greater than expected. Council had no choice but to substitute brick for stone in the contract, and with this modification the eventual cost was almost exactly as originally estimated. On 24 May 1913 the college organized an 'At Home'—with a display of morris dancing on the lawn—for the workmen engaged on the new buildings and their wives. (Children were deliberately omitted from the invitation in order to keep the numbers down and to give their mothers a holiday.)[48] In the course of the afternoon it was discovered that the clerk of the works had worked as a young man on the Hostel building, and that in the case of one of the workmen three generations of his family had been employed in building for Somerville.[49]

The new buildings, designed by H. A. L. Fisher's brother Edmund, and named after Miss Maitland in posthumous tribute to her

[46] MSL to EP, 17 Mar. 1910.   [47] *Oxford Magazine*, 16 Oct. 1913.
[48] College Meeting, 25 Apr. 1913.   [49] Oxford Letter, 1913.

ambitions for the college, consisted of a dining-hall, private dining-room and senior common room, kitchen premises, and a block of over 20 new rooms for staff and students. There was a general post as the Principal moved to the Hall end of college and the Vice-Principal to the West, every member of staff changed rooms, the old Hall lecture room was converted into an entrance hall, and most of the public rooms changed their character and function.

The official opening, by the Vice-Chancellor Dr Heberden (himself a former President of the college Council), took place on Saturday 4 October 1913. 'I do not intend to allude to the aesthetic qualities of this building' said H. A. L. Fisher in his opening address, 'partly because I know too little about architecture, and partly because I know too much about the architect.' Other speakers, unhampered by family ties, were less restrained in their admiration for the new hall. 'No building committee could have made it much better than it is' asserted Gilbert Murray:

> We are proud of its dignity and beauty, of its severity and magnificent proportions. It seems to me unlike any other hall in Oxford; it does not ape the manner of another age, but stands on its own foundations, with its own character, as a fine specimen of the work of the early 20th century. . . . We are fit to take our place among the great halls of Oxford. And I have thought that, though we have not their associations, we have something of our own; that, as against their picturesque darkness, as against their somewhat fitful heating arrangements (laughter), it is something that we have here a modern hall, warm, well-aired, and flooded with light.[50]

Pride of place on the south wall was given to the newly acquired portrait of Mary Somerville by John Jackson, presented by an anonymous donor on condition (satisfied by reference to Christies' sales records) that the authenticity could be proved. Other gifts flooded in: a Jacobean oak chair for the Principal, presented by old students living in Oxford; light fittings for the hall presented by the Principal; a handsome Indian carpet (copied from an old Persian one) given by Cornelia Sorabji for the new senior common room; a fender stool given by Miss Cooper; a copper coal-scuttle given by Mr and Mrs Chapman. A writer in the *Oxford Magazine*, predicting that tourists

---

[50] *Oxford Magazine*, 16 Oct. 1913.

would flock to gaze at the new buildings, could not forbear to mention their one generally acknowledged defect: 'Between the two blocks of the new structures protrudes a glimpse of that excessively ugly edifice, St Aloysius. This must be hidden—by walls or trees or trellis.[51]

The Maitland buildings, hailed as a monument to college enthusiasm and loyalty, were to change radically the character of Somerville as an institution. Their importance as a turning-point in Somerville's perception of its future development was noted by the Vice-Chancellor in his speech at the opening. 'I am not at all sure that you will agree with me in what I am going to say', he told his audience of somewhat euphoric Somervillians, after paying due tribute to Miss Maitland, Henry Pelham, and other past heroes:

> The thought that I have in my mind is whether the College has now attained its full stature, whether you will contemplate adding in the future to its numbers and its buildings. Well, if there are any members of the College who cherish visions of that kind, although it may be very impertinent for me to offer them any advice, I should be inclined to say to them, 'Resist your ambition'. . . . I am quite certain . . . that as soon as you begin adding to your members beyond a certain number you alter the character of the college. . . . Therefore, if you value the traditions which have been set up in the thirty years or more during which this college has existed, I should say to you, or I should be inclined to say to you, 'Be content'.

Dr Heberden's suspicion that this message might be unwelcome to his audience was well-founded; many of those present, according to the report in the *Oxford Magazine*, 'seemed to doubt whether Somerville might not expand a good bit further before it lost any such advantages.'

With the movement for degrees apparently on the point of success at last, Somerville had good cause for such confident optimism. On 22 June 1914 the new hall was proudly used for a commemoration ball. Some ninety couples danced till 4 a.m. to the music of Herr Maurice Wurm's band; refreshments were served in the Hall common room and ices on the Maitland balcony. At dawn those who had survived the evening assembled on the steps of the library loggia for a group photograph (see Plate 16). Many of them would not survive the next five years. And within a few months the new hall itself was to be in use as a hospital ward.

---

[51] *Oxford Magazine*, 16 Oct. 1913.

5

Interlude at Oriel,
1915–1919

THE outbreak of war in August 1914 caught even Miss Penrose unprepared. When college reassembled at the start of Michaelmas Term it
was entertained to mock-heroic accounts of the Principal's adven-
turous journey home from Switzerland, 'wheeling her luggage on a
trolley for a couple of miles and making quite a triumphal progress
through France in company with some other English in military
trains',[1] and of the Bursar's hasty return from Iceland, via the Faroes
and Leith, with the Lady Carlisle research fellow, Miss Phillpotts. It
was some months before the Mary Ewart travelling scholar, Marya
Czaplicka, engaged in anthropological fieldwork on the Yenesei River
in Siberia, was able to return to Oxford. Four students failed to return
to college in October for reasons connected with the war: Charis
Barnett left to work as an interpreter for the Women's Emergency
Corps; Grace Procter was granted a year's leave to work at a local
branch of the Soldiers' and Sailors' Wives' Association; a Canadian
student, Constance Reid, was unable to get to England as all available
steamships had been requisitioned for the transport of Canadian
troops; and Vera Siordet was obliged to withdraw for lack of money,
her fees coming from a family fund in Germany which had been
seized by the German government.[2]

  The impact of the war on the daily life of the college, however, was
initially slight. The AEW organized a series of intercollegiate lectures on subjects connected with the war, for which Somerville, whose
new hall was the largest possessed by any of the women's colleges,
provided accommodation. Large audiences attended to hear such
speakers as W. D. Ross on 'International morality', Mr Grant Robertson on 'Economic problems connected with the War' and 'The future
of British civilization', and Mrs Creighton on 'Women and the War'.
Somervillians threw themselves enthusiastically into work for the

---

[1] *SSA Report*, 1914.   [2] Minutes of Council, 20 Oct. 1914.

Oxford-based Belgian Relief Committee, which was organized by Miss Bruce's sister Pamela. Dorothy L. Sayers, part of a team entrusted with the task of preparing accommodation for a refugee family of nine, described as 'like a page out of *Punch*' the process whereby Lady Mary Murray's cook explained the workings of the kitchen range to the Somervillians, who translated her explanation into French for the benefit of the mistress of the house, who in turn translated it into Flemish for the cook and housemaid.[3] In Michaelmas Term the college held an 'At Home', at which Miss Penrose and the staff received Belgian adults in the hall, while the students entertained the children to tea and games in the gymnasium, the occasion ending with vigorous renderings of the Belgian and English national anthems. Later in the war groups of somewhat reluctant Belgian women were taken to a camp near Broadway run 'with strict military discipline' by Miss Lorimer and Miss Lodge of LMH, to be trained to live in primitive conditions, as a prelude to their eventual repatriation.[4]

Somerville's position next door to the Radcliffe Infirmary ensured that this gentle introduction to wartime conditions would be short-lived. At the end of Hilary Term 1915 Council was alerted to the possibility of the college buildings being required by the War Office for hospital purposes, and the President and Principal were empowered to take such measures as were necessary for the temporary housing of the students. The arrival of a sanitary inspector on Saturday 27 March to take measurements signalled the start of a busy fortnight. Next day, the Administrator of the 3rd Southern General Hospital, Colonel Ranking, made a full inspection of the college buildings, and notified Miss Penrose that he proposed to recommend that they should be requisitioned for use as a military hospital for the duration of the war. By now, the college's contingency plans were well advanced. An emergency committee was summoned that afternoon, and learned that the Treasurer, Mr Gillett, had unofficially sounded out the Provost of Oriel about the possibility of renting the St Mary Hall Quadrangle, which stood virtually empty in consequence of the wholesale departure of its undergraduates for the war.[5] Arrangements were made for the Principal and Bursar to visit Oriel on Monday morning;

[3] B. Reynolds, *Dorothy L. Sayers: Her Life and Soul* (London, 1993), 61.

[4] E. Lodge, *Terms and Vacations* (London, 1938), 146 ff.

[5] In 1915 Oriel could claim the highest percentage of military service of all the colleges in Oxford. By the end of Trinity Term it had only fifteen men still in residence (*Oriel Record*, 1915).

a formal application by the Treasurer was considered by a special meeting of the Provost and fellows of Oriel the following day, and by Tuesday evening a letter had been written and received agreeing to the occupation by Somerville for the duration of the war and three months after of the St Mary Quadrangle 'except only the Junior Library and the coal cellar'.[6]

Mr Gillett meanwhile communicated to Colonel Ranking the terms on which Somerville was prepared, for the duration of the war and not more than two months after, to place its premises—with the exception of the library—at the disposal of the War Office.[7] These were agreed to by the War Office Finance Committee on 6 April and formally accepted by Colonel Ranking on 9 April.[8] The handover took place on 12 April. A letter was dispatched to all Somerville students to tell them of the impending migration to Oriel and warn them that, as no sanatorium was available in the new premises, any student contracting an infectious illness would be expected to pay for lodging and nurse. The Bursar entered upon a phase of feverish activity. Removal expenses amounted to £226. As Miss Penrose later said, the episode gave the lie to the common charge that academics were incapable of quick and decisive action.

Before its incorporation into Oriel, St Mary's Hall had been a separate college, and it was a relatively easy task now to shut it off from Oriel's two other quadrangles and restore to their original uses the old dining-hall and kitchens. In the words of the *Oriel Record*: 'Mrs Grundy was appeased by two massive walls of brick in the passages between the quads';[9] according to the Somerville version (as relayed by Miss Farnell) the fortifications were installed 'to allay the Provost's expressed fears of the possibility of any "Pyramus and Thisbe" incidents'. The thoroughness with which Somerville's new quarters were isolated from the main Oriel buildings was the subject of amused comment by a reporter from the *Oxford Times* who visited St Mary Hall two days before the Somerville students came into residence:

> In the rooms and corridors tenanted since the fourteenth century only by men, there were now to be seen the strange signs of women's occupation in the shape of certain luggage that could never by any possibility belong to a man. A straw basket, of which the lower part

[6] Phelps to Gillett, 30 Mar. 1915.   [7] Gillett to Ranking, 29 Mar. 1915.
[8] The terms were re-negotiated in November 1917. (See Treasurer's Statement respecting the arrangements made with the War Department for taking over the College Buildings as a temporary hospital.)   [9] *Oriel Record*, 1915.

fits into the upper, an umbrella tied on to it, and a small feminine box stood boldly in a little ante-room that had been hurriedly made up by a stage property kind of wall thrust along one side of it. In other rooms, women's furniture had arrived . . . Here was modernism, women students in possession of a college hitherto solely for men, and yet—down on the ground level workmen were bricking up arch-ways with a purpose and determination that were worthy the mediae-val bricking-up of a nun. One really couldn't feel comfortably sure that some unhappy Somerville student, arriving a little previously, had not been seized and immolated. Where archways should lead into Oriel proper one was confronted with the smooth even surface of a newly-made brick wall painted over with yellow wash—the most forbidding venture-no-further kind of wall ever seen. . . . There was but one place left from which an undergraduate could command a corner of St Mary's Hall quad, and we wondered whether the author-ities would discover it in time to block it.[10]

He went on to speculate on what the Somerville students would make of their new surroundings, contrasting Somerville's 'own magnificent dining-hall, with its noble proportions, its air of stateliness' with 'the depressing addition [to Oriel] perpetrated in the name of Cecil Rhodes':

It is easy to imagine that they will love the quiet little quad, with its oval lawn and its cosy and dark dining hall, and the great oriel win-dow on the east side. The comfortable domestic architecture of the old house on the west side has great charm, but the big new pile, with its ugly yellow shiny 'art' tiles, its ill-proportioned rooms, with glass lights over the doors, its dull walls washed into the semblance of quarters in some institution—what will women of culture think of this?

In fact, only about half of Somerville's staff and students could be accommodated in 'Skimmery' itself (where, however, some of them had the unaccustomed luxury of two rooms or a shared sitting-room and small bedroom).[11] A number of third-year scientists lived with Miss Buckley, the Senior Student of the West, at 18 Merton Street; a few lived at Oriel Street and came into St Mary's for meals. The rest

[10] *Oxford Times*, 1 May 1915.

[11] 48 students, six members of the SCR, and six maids were accommodated in St Mary Hall; 52 students and four members of the SCR in lodgings (report by Miss Penrose to Council, 11 May 1915).

were allocated rooms in nearby 'outhouses', Miss Bruce presiding over Canterbury House (8 King Edward Street), Miss Jebb over 4 King Edward Street, Miss Darbishire over Micklem Hall, and Miss Pope over 16 Turl Street. The occupants of the two King Edward Street houses rapidly became noted for a 'cheerfulness of disposition accompanied if not accounted for by the excellence of their cuisine'; the view glimpsed through lace-curtained windows from the street, of a row of girls on either side of the long dining-table, earned them the nick-name 'The Girls' Friendly Society'.[12] The Turl Street House was notable for having a waiter to serve meals. In Michaelmas Term 1916 a third house in King Edward Street was taken over as accommodation for graduates.

After dinner on their first evening in Oriel—an occasion whose strangeness was mitigated by the familiarity of the college soup—Miss Penrose addressed the assembled students on the subject of their changed circumstances: 'She intimated that people were vaguely expecting us to do something unsuitable—she wasn't quite sure what, but anyhow she was sure we wouldn't do it.'[13] Students gradually accustomed themselves to the new patterns of life, to the strangeness of living on staircases instead of corridors, and to the inconvenience—deeply felt—of living without access to gas-rings. In the absence of a common room, the hall provided the focal point of college life, for coffee after dinner and for college meetings. Some books were kept at the lecture rooms at 10 Oriel Street; others were fetched from Somerville library on request. The vicar of the University Church allowed college prayers on Sunday evenings to be held in the church room at St Mary's. The JCR constitution was modified to take account of the new arrangements, it being agreed that from Michaelmas Term 1915 there should be only one Senior Student, who would be elected in the usual way and would live in Oriel; and that each lodging-house should elect a student from among themselves to be responsible for the business of that house.[14]

The 1916 Oxford Correspondent reported that the greatest difficulty was 'getting to know the students who have only come up since the migration', adding that 'the darkened streets have added to the difficulties of our scattered community life and have made journeys to and from the lodgings—even with the aid of a torchlight—a service

---

[12] 'Somerville to Oriel', *SSA Report*, 1916.   [13] Ibid.
[14] College Meeting, 28 May 1915.

of danger.' This danger was compounded (though others doubtless were prevented) by a rule forbidding women students to be out alone after dinner. Constance Savery describes the complications of an outhouse student accepting an invitation to dine with her tutor in St Mary Hall: 'Getting to Skimmery from 19 Holywell was always a difficulty, . . . so another girl from Holywell had to be persuaded to come with me to dine in Quad., and then two people from Skimmery had to be persuaded to take our vacant places in 19 Holywell.'[15] Though a member of the Oxford Inter-Collegiate Christian Union (OICCU), she was unable to take part in its activities, because it was based at St Aldate's 'which was out of bounds for Somerville students, who were discouraged, though not positively prohibited, from atten- dance there, on the ground that one might pick up germs in such a rough part of the town.' Some of her contemporaries, however, took college rules less seriously:

> Miss Starkie told us that she had a bath every night in quad, and then walked home to Teddy Street, where she lives, lightly but elegantly attired in her nightdress and an overcoat! We hardly knew how to believe her. Fancy anyone walking up the High in the face of all the world in a nightdress and an overcoat and nothing else. If the Pen heard, there'd be the most unholiest row that ever was. We're not allowed even to cross Oriel Street without a hat on.[16]

Even as a student, Enid Starkie was plainly a law unto herself, on one occasion letting off a red gas-filled balloon during a formal dinner, and on another inviting two men into hall, disguised as women. She had, concluded Constance Savery, 'all the Irish charm and doubtless she used it on the Pen.'

From their new quarters south of the High, members of the college took a keen interest in the Somerville hospital (Plate 17). 'I think some of us would hardly recognise it now', reported the writers of 'Somer- ville to Oriel':

> Passages have sprung into being, rooms have been divided into two, walls have been demolished. The Hall (in which a bathroom has been built), makes a splendid ward—and the hospital authorities have informed us that they have thoughtfully covered with deal some at least of the oak floor and panelling.

---

[15] Recollections of Constance Savery (1917).
[16] Letter to her family, quoted in Recollections of Constance Savery.

Vera Brittain, visiting it in June 1915, thought it much better as a hospital than as a college: 'It is all so sweet & clean & fresh that it must be quite a joy to be convalescent here.'[17] Access to the Radcliffe Infirmary was gained by knocking a hole in the north wall of the college, thus enabling stretchers to be wheeled directly into the operating theatre next door. Because it had a large number of small rooms, Somerville was deemed by the military authorities to be particularly suitable for use as a hospital for officers, and in 1916 the whole college (and not just the Maitland building, as hitherto) was reserved for this purpose.[18] The Somerville hospital was to have some distinguished occupants. Siegfried Sassoon, recovering from gastric fever in August 1916, thought that 'to be lying in a little white-walled room, looking through the open window on to a College lawn, was for the first few days very much like Paradise';[19] Robert Graves, a year later, took advantage of the warm weather and the hospital's easy discipline to stroll down the Cornmarket in pyjamas and dressing gown for morning coffee at the Cadena.[20] Somerville student volunteers wheeled out wounded soldiers in Bath chairs, and helped organize motor drives in the country for the more mobile; back at Oriel, a 'comforts' table was instituted for such articles as stamps, magazines, stationery, and novels.

The absence of so many male dons on war service opened up new academic opportunities for the remaining women dons. Vera Brittain, attending Miss Darbishire's lecture on Milton in May 1915, thought she seemed a little nervous; she later discovered that it was not only the first university lecture that Miss Darbishire had ever given, but that she was only the second woman whom the university had entrusted with the task of lecturing.[21] As the war progressed, women were given responsibility not only for lecturing but even, on occasion, for coaching the few remaining male undergraduates. Charles Grant Robertson of All Souls was regarded as particularly enlightened in this respect, meeting regularly with the women history tutors to discuss plans of work and lecture lists, and to arrange for them to undertake some of the university courses.[22]

These new academic responsibilities were often undertaken in

---

[17] V. Brittain, *Chronicle of Youth: War Diary 1913–1917*, ed. A. Bishop and T. Smart (London, 1981), 208.   [18] Oxford Letter, 1916.
[19] S. Sassoon, *Siegfried's Journey 1916–1920* (London, 1945), 5.
[20] R. Graves, *Goodbye to All That* (London, 1929), 304 ff.
[21] Brittain, *Chronicle of Youth*, 187.   [22] Lodge, *Terms and Vacations*, 142.

conjunction with demanding war work of their own. The National Registration in Oxford was organized—according to press reports, with unique efficiency—by Miss Penrose, assisted by Miss Darbishire and Miss Walton, in the long vacation of 1915.[23] Miss Bruce moved to London during the vacations to help with the organization of the Red Cross and the Joint Women's Committee of the Voluntary Aid Detachment. College raised a subscription to enable the Mary Somerville research fellow, Ethel Jones, to undertake a short training at Guy's Hospital before working as a nurse and interpreter with the French Red Cross at Yvetot, where her colleagues included the librarian, Miss Kempson. Miss Pope spent some weeks in Northern France working under Margery Fry with the Friends' War Victims Relief Expedition. During the spring and summer of 1916 Miss Lorimer divided her time between Oxford and London, working four days a week for the Admiralty; the summers of 1917 and 1918 were spent further afield, nursing with the Scottish Women's Hospital Corps in Salonika. The history tutor, Miss O'Loughlin (later Lady Woodward), helped to run a canteen, and Miss Farnell a settlement. Payne, the college porter, spent the war near Southampton, training recruits to shoe horses and mules.

Students spent their vacations, according to the season, in fruit-picking and farming, in office work for the Oxford Higher Local Examinations Board or the Ministry of Pensions, in factories and canteens. During term, a number of them volunteered for work packing and unpacking cases of china and hardware at the Military Supply Depot at Didcot. Sewing meetings were held in hall on Saturday evenings, at which shirts and tray-cloths were made, bandages rolled for the Scottish Women's Hospital, and socks knitted for the Somerville hospital or Russian prisoners of war. An appeal at College Meeting in January 1918 for digging volunteers produced an immediate show of thirty-two hands.[24]

Wartime conditions increased the need for economies of all kinds, and College Meetings heard constant injunctions to exercise restraint in such matters as coal and light, and to avoid any suspicion of extravagance in matters of entertainment. Efforts were made to maintain standards: flowers continued to be provided for the common room (though it was suggested that money could be saved if students

[23] The National Registration Act 1915 required a return for every civilian male between the ages of 15 and 65; it revealed that almost 2 million available men had not yet volunteered for war service.   [24] College Meeting, 23 Jan. 1918.

themselves provided flowers or berries for this purpose), and students were reminded that they were expected, if not to change for dinner, at least to come tidy without their jerseys.[25] The JCR continued to subscribe to *Punch* during term-time, salving their conscience by sending back issues to a hospital. As the war moved into its third year, austerities began to bite. Domestic staff became increasingly hard to find; and in January 1917 students were asked to make their own beds, to enable the college to manage with one maid fewer. At College Meeting the Senior Student gave a warning—directed in particular at the first year—as to 'the extreme inadvisability of giving elaborate and expensive teas or parties of any sort'.[26] Sacks for the collection of waste paper were provided on each landing, and volunteers were sought to help with waste-paper sorting at the depot in St Aldates. After a heated debate as to whether college should display one of the ration cards issued by the Food Controller guaranteeing the observance of the voluntary ration order, it was decided to do so, on the grounds that the example of Somerville, thus made public, might have a good effect on the passer-by; a motion to the effect that 'While relaxing no effort, we do not display the cards' was defeated.[27] Somerville food, never noted for its sophistication, entered a particularly unappetizing phase in which boiled beetroot formed a staple of the menu; at dinner one evening Thilo Bugnion, a Swiss student unaccustomed to English plain cooking, was heard to ask, in ringing tones that rose above the chatter round the hall, 'What *ees* this bloodee stuff?'[28] In the summer of 1917 Somerville for the first time allowed students to stay up during the vacation, an acknowledgment of the increasing difficulties of rail travel.[29]

A Somerville War Savings Association was established in 1916; during the first year of its existence an average of ninety members was maintained—the domestic staff showing, according to the Oxford Correspondent, 'a keenness which might well be emulated by some of the slacker student members'—and 133 certificates were bought.[30] In November 1917 the Association was addressed by the Provost of Oriel, who 'dealt with the dangers as well as the advantages of saving; and indicated new lines of economy along which we might still advance.'

[25] College Meeting, 21 Oct. and 9 Dec. 1915.   [26] College Meeting, 24 Jan. 1917.
[27] College Meeting, 16 May 1917.
[28] E. Irons, 'Somerville, 1918–1921', *ASM Report*, 1993, 62.
[29] Oxford Letter, 1917; Minutes of Council, 8 May 1917.
[30] Oxford Letter, Nov. 1917.

The occasion was memorable as the first time that the Provost had been entertained to dinner in St Mary Hall since Somerville had taken up residence there two-and-a-half years before. 'We were glad', recorded the Log Book, 'to have the opportunity of thanking him ourselves for his generous hospitality, and also of hearing renewed expressions of welcome from his own lips.' Fifteen members of the Somerville branch of the Association—two of them carrying a specially designed banner—took part in the procession through Oxford in March 1918 to promote the sale of war bonds, the college raising £100 of the £150,000 which Oxford was called upon by the Government to contribute towards the cost of a destroyer.[31]

Most students had relatives or friends on active service; the bitter succession of losses recorded so poignantly by Vera Brittain in *Testament of Youth* was an extreme case of a common experience. When she, and later Winifred Holtby, broke off their Oxford courses to volunteer for war service, it prompted many of their contemporaries to question whether they themselves were doing the right thing by remaining in Oxford. Margaret Philp later recalled the circumstances of her hurried departure from Oxford in the Easter vacation of 1916:

> I remember at home in Scotland, seeing the postman (who always had breakfast in our kitchen, after a long round) sitting with his head on his arm and sobbing his heart out. Afterwards I asked the cook what was the matter with him, and she said that he had delivered 'one of those letters' to every house on his round. . . . Our local regiment, the Gordons, had been wiped out completely, and I felt I could not stand taking my degree in such terrible circumstances, . . . I left Somerville then and there.[32]

Such unrest among women students was taken sufficiently seriously to warrant a letter to Miss Penrose from H. A. L. Fisher, now President of the Board of Education. Clearly intended for a wider audience, it was quoted in *The Times* in February 1917 under the headline 'Robbing the Future':

> I gather that there is a feeling of some uncertainty among the students of Somerville, and probably among the women students of other colleges and universities, as to their true path of duty in this time of public anxiety. It is very natural that students engaged upon courses of study which have no immediate bearing upon the war

---

[31] Log Book, HT 1918.   [32] M. Mills (Philp, 1914) to P. Adams, Dec. 1979.

should be asking themselves the question as to whether they could not be more usefully employed either as workers upon the land or as nurses or as Government clerks or in some other capacity in which they would be brought into direct connexion with the machinery of public affairs. My own view is that for the present women students at the universities should continue their academic courses until such time as they may be called up by the branch of the National Service Department presided over by Mrs Tennant, and I am glad to say that Mrs Tennant and Mrs Neville Chamberlain entirely concur in this opinion.

If anybody had been sceptical as to the advantage of academic training of the higher kind in practical life, that scepticism must assuredly have been dispelled by the remarkable services which women trained in our universities have been able to render to the country during the war, and in view of the great importance to the nation of securing an ample stock of highly-trained and highly-cultivated women in the teaching profession, it would be deplorable if the women's colleges at our universities were to be closed until the absolute necessity for such a step had been established beyond doubt. It should be remembered that women training for the high profession of teaching are in a very real sense equipping themselves for a valuable and expert branch of National Service. The gifts and aptitudes which go to the making of a teacher are none too common, and it would be an ill-measure of national economy to deplete our colleges of students who are designed by their qualities and discipline for a career so exacting in its demands upon brain and character.[33]

A few weeks later Fisher reiterated these views in person to an audience of women students in the Sheldonian Theatre. 'The importance of the meeting' commented the *Oxford Magazine* 'can be recognized by the fact that *The Times* gave half a column to reporting it.'[34] Mr Fisher's letter, amplified, Latinized, and transformed into a royal proclamation, was to provide an appropriate climax to the college going-down play that summer.[35]

News of the armistice reached Oxford soon after 11 a.m. on November 11 1918. In a general outburst of patriotic enthusiasm, Somerville congratulated itself upon the 'optimistic forethought' of Miss Penrose

[33] *The Times*, 8 Feb. 1917.   [34] *Oxford Magazine*, 16 Mar. 1917.
[35] Log Book, 1917.

which enabled St Mary Hall to be among the first buildings in the High Street to display the flags of the allies from its windows. Hilda Street, then in her first term, recalls that, while several of her friends ventured out to join the celebrations in the streets, she herself was terrified at the noise of rejoicing—'the like of which I had never heard'—and remained immured in her room until Eileen Gonner came to join her in a prayer of thanksgiving.[36] That evening the Christian Union organized a service in the JCR, which was followed by a festive dinner in hall with 'a beautifully and patriotically decorated High Table and a speech by the Principal, followed by a sing-song in which large numbers rejoiced together.'[37]

The agreements entered into with the War Office and Oriel in 1915 had stipulated that Somerville should regain its own buildings within two months, and vacate St Mary Quadrangle within three months, of the end of the war. It soon became plain that this timetable was unrealistic. 'A young officer who was in my office today told me that he had been informed by one of the senior matrons that the Military were trying to evacuate the Somerville College buildings by the end of January, but you will know what such information is worth' reported Gillett to Miss Penrose at the end of November.[38] Though Dr Phelps had just assured him privately that Oriel did not expect to need the St Mary Quadrangle until the following Michaelmas Term, and that Somerville was welcome to stay until the end of July or beginning of August, Oriel's official line was that it must regain possession of its buildings by the end of June at the latest.[39]

As in the course of Hilary Term 1919 undergraduates began to reappear in Oxford, demobbed from the various theatres of war, Oriel became markedly less tolerant of the presence of Somerville in its midst. 'Oriel is pressing very hard to get rid of us', reported Constance Savery in a letter home: 'Miss Biggs found a man in her room the other day, who stalked all round very sulkily, saying that the furniture in it was his, "but I suppose I ought to be glad it's here at all," he ended gloomily.' Writing to tell her family of a 'simply awful' tea-party which she and Florence Duncan had just had for Miss Penrose (in the course of which the Principal consumed two pieces of scone, a slice of bread and jam, three cups of tea, a chocolate cake, and a piece of dough cake), she reported:

[36] Reminiscences of Hilda Whittaker (Street, 1918).   [37] Log Book, MT 1918.
[38] Gillett to EP, 28 Nov. 1918.   [39] Lyon to Gillett, 30 Nov. 1918.

She says that if the Government does not let us have Somerville in time for the October term, Oriel will turn us out—just think of that. It will take six months to get it papered and cleaned and repaired, so if they aren't quick we shall be in a very sorry plight.[40]

Early in January 1919 Miss Penrose called on Colonel Ranking and was told that he was powerless in the matter, that it was no use making any further representations to the medical authorities, and that she should write to the Secretary of the War Office direct. A letter having met with no response, in February Miss Penrose requested an interview at the War Office with the Director General of the Army Medical Service. The meeting took place on 7 February; on 8 February instructions were sent to the officer in charge to take immediate steps for the very early surrender of the college buildings. On 25 February Miss Penrose was able to report to Council that 'the evacuation was in fact rapidly taking place.'[41] Negotiations over Somerville's claim for dilapidations continued through the summer (delayed by the loss of one of Gillett's letters behind a cupboard in the War Office); it was not until 10 July that the agreed sum of £2,050 was at last received.[42]

In Trinity Term Miss Penrose presided over a joint debate between the Somerville and Oriel debating societies—a fitting celebration, the *Oriel Record* reported, 'of the connection between the two institutions, which have for four years been bound together like the Siamese twins, each institution possessing its independent organisation, but bound to the other by a physical bond.'[43] 'If Oriel's manners left something to be desired, it was, in the circumstances, excusable' reported Constance Savery, describing the occasion less diplomatically as 'more of a rag than a debate.'

A still more anarchic celebration marked the final days of this enforced co-habitation. The Somerville Log Book contains a relatively laconic contemporary account of what came to be known variously as 'the Oriel Raid' and 'the Pickaxe Incident':

On the night of Thursday June 19th 1919 certain members of Oriel JCR expressed their desire to return to S Mary Hall in a somewhat unusual but practical manner. After prolonged bombardment on the intervening wall a breach was effected through which several undergraduates jumped into the quad. After cheering Somerville and implying

---

[40] Reminiscences of Constance Savery.   [41] Minutes of Council, 25 Feb. 1919.
[42] Captain Atkey (Directorate of Lands, War Office) to EP, 10 July 1919.
[43] *The Oriel Record*, 1919.

the mixture of their feelings with regard to our impending departure they were induced to return to their own side by the authorities of both colleges. Further disturbance was prevented by the watchful guardianship of the Somerville SCR.

Vera Farnell, who as Miss Penrose's secretary played an active role in the night's events, left two accounts—one in prose and one in verse—for the college record, though for reasons of discretion she omitted them from her book *A Somervillian Looks Back*:

A hot summer night in mid-June had tempted a number of the 'Young Ladies' to drag their bedding into the grassed quad preparatory to sleeping there. Towards midnight all was quiet, and but few lights burning, save that of Miss Lorimer the classical tutor, busy with her dictionaries.

Next door in Oriel 'there was a sound of revelry by night'—the young men were celebrating a triumph on the river, which culminated in an attempt to make a hole through the dividing wall. The young ladies, alarmed, began hastily to return to their rooms. The Portress, roused by the commotion, and seeing Miss Lorimer's light in a ground-floor room, hurried to warn her of the situation. Accordingly Miss Lorimer donned her hat with the pendent ostrich feather, and went to survey the scene. By this time a number of somewhat inebriated young men had crawled through the hole they had made and were dancing triumphantly round the pickaxe by means of which they had effected their entry and which they had cast to the ground in the middle of the quad. Miss Lorimer's appearance and her words 'Gentlemen have the courtesy to return to your own quarters without delay' routed the revellers, who turned and fled, scuttling back through the hole they had made. Wasting no time, Miss Lorimer returned immediately to her work.

It was at this point that Viola Garvin, one of the students, darted down from her room on the first floor and seizing the pickaxe which she had seen lying abandoned in the quad, bore it back to her room as a trophy.

Meanwhile the Portress had climbed the stairs to report the incursion to Miss Penrose, whose bedroom was on the first floor, facing the High Street. She dressed herself hurriedly in a grey coat and skirt and put on her second best hat, a Dolly Varden straw. She came down to my room, which was below hers, where I was asleep. I woke to see her tall form standing erect beside my bed. 'There are men in the quad' she said, 'Please get up and come with me.' In a minute I was out of bed and, seizing a dressing-gown and slippers, announced myself as ready. As we walked together to the quad Miss Penrose said 'Do you think this will get into the papers?' 'Oh, yes, most certainly' I said unsympathetically, feeling it would make a good story. The quad was now empty and Miss Penrose said 'We must visit the hole.' We heard scufflings and voices from the other side and before very long the Oriel porter arrived. Apologising for our disturbance, he asked what he could do.

'Kindly ask the Provost to come and speak to me' said Miss Penrose.

Meanwhile an increasing number of our students were appearing, anxious to miss nothing of the fray. As Miss Penrose stood awaiting the arrival of the Provost, there appeared at her feet a dishevelled head and a form struggling its way through the hole and making vain attempts to rise.

'Kindly keep to your own side' said Miss Penrose.

'Which ish my side?'—digging her in the ribs.

With one of her masterly gestures Miss Penrose said 'That!' He toppled backwards and shuffled ignominiously back to the Oriel side, and that was the end of him.

A longish pause ensued before the Provost arrived on the Oriel side.

'Is that you, Provost?'

'Yes. Is that you, Principal?'

'Yes.'

'I am sorry about all this. What do you want me to do?'

'I should like you to come through and speak to me.'

'Oh no, I won't do that, it's nothing much, the men have quieted down now.'

'Won't you come through and talk to me?'

'Oh no, I will just go and make sure that all is quiet', and he departed.

Miss Penrose quickly made her plans. She turned to the students who were arriving one by one behind her and said 'You must all go to bed', and to the few tutors who had also arrived on the scene 'We must guard the hole throughout the night, we'll take an hour each. I will take the first, Miss Pope the second, Miss Lorimer the third and Miss Farnell the fourth. I will now return to my room and change my hat. I will put on a squash hat.' The students thereupon arrived with coffee and cushions and rolled up an armchair which they placed in front of the hole. Very soon Miss Penrose arrived, squash hat on head, and took her place in the armchair. She then sent everyone to bed.

The hours went by without a sound, and by the time my turn came it was perfectly clear that further vigil was quite unnecessary, so I stayed on in bed.[44]

> A flushed excited band of Oriel men
> Fresh from the celebration of a 'bump',
> Wielding a pick-axe 'lifted' without leave,
> Batter'd their rude way through the bricked-up wall
> And danced around our neat quadrangle lawn,
> A midnight rout of red-faced revelry;
> But, daunted, one by one crawled their way back,
> Before Authority in feathered hat—
> (Miss Lorimer, summoned from midnight toil
> On dictionaries, and donning for the fray
> As 'twere a helmet, her best black straw hat
> With ostrich feathers hanging down behind).
> Silence or whispering quiet reigned awhile
> Till, at the hole's mouth, crawling on hands and knees,
> Appeared two ruffled heads of Oriel men
> Who found themselves confronted from a height
> By two tall figures—upright, stiff and straight—
> Our Principal in Dolly Varden hat,
> Her Secret'ry in dressing-gown and plaits.
> (Thus had these two, roused from their first sweet sleep,
> Decked themselves out for action prompt and strong.)
> All unaware, and full of merry wit,
> Th'adventuring pair rose stumbling to their feet
> In mood to dig all comers in the ribs;
> But ere established on a steady stance
> Received, with gesture sudden, swift and true,
> A condign intimation to *which* side
> Of hole in gaping wall was theirs to keep.
> Back through the hole these fuddled fumblers fell,
> And later on gave place to Pyramus.
> They stood—the Provost-Pyramus in Oriel—
> Thisbe—the Principal, in St Mary Hall—

[44] Rewritten by Vera Farnell in October 1975, shortly before her death, the original version having been lost.

The Wall between them with its gaping hole,
Low down through which behold! we see
Each decent pair of Principalian legs.
Then words are heard, first whispere'd, then aloud,
'Is that you, Provost?' 'Yes, Principal, it's me.
And pray what is there I can do for you?'
'Please, Provost, I should wish that through this hole
You'ld come and speak to me, and after that . . .'
'No! no! not that—I'ld rather keep this side—
I'll go at once and send my men to bed.'—
And Pyramus is gone—while Thisbe, left,
Issues directions how throughout this night
Guard shall be kept upon the gaping hole:
'Myself will watch from one till two o'clock;
Miss Pope from two till three, Miss Lorimer
From three till four, and following close on her
Miss Stonedale will keep guard from four till five;
Last on the list will come my Secret'ry,
Miss Farnell . . . Now let us change our clothes.

When in 1979 another eyewitness of these stirring events, Dr Cicely Williams, gave a talk in Somerville on 'Somerville at Oriel', she presented to the college library the very copy of the *Oxford Book of English Verse* with which Miss Penrose had whiled away her long vigil by the hole in the wall.

The incident caused deep embarrassment in Oriel, and a flood of letters of apology to Miss Penrose. 'It is difficult' wrote the Provost, 'to find words which are adequate to express our regret for the deplorable incident of last night.'[45] 'I should have infinitely preferred' wrote the classics tutor, Marcus Tod (a member of the Somerville Council), 'that the College should not have won its success rather than that in the celebrations of its victory it should thus have imperilled its good name.'[46] It is not known under what pressure the President of Oriel JCR wrote to express the sincere sorrow of the culprits, and their hopes that the regrettable incident would not 'be allowed to mar the very cordial relations which have existed up to the present time between Somerville and Oriel.' It was, he assured Miss Penrose, 'done in a thoughtless spirit.'[47]

---

[45] Phelps to EP, 20 June 1919.   [46] Tod to EP, 20 June 1919.
[47] Martin Gilkes to EP, 20 June 1919.

Miss Penrose hastened to assure her correspondents that 'We fully realise that it was the thoughtless action of a few individuals and would be condemned by the public opinion of the undergraduates.'[48] Of the subsequent history of the pickaxe itself two distinct versions have survived. According to one, the Provost of Oriel, attending the Encaenia luncheon the day after the raid, overheard one of the guests entertaining her host with a lively account of the night's events. On his protesting that 'You mustn't believe all this young lady says, it was a very slight affair', Viola Garvin (for it was she) retorted 'Well, at least we've got the pickaxe as a proof that something happened.' A day or two later the Oriel porter appeared at St Mary Hall and asked for the pickaxe, telling a sad tale of a workman who could not get on with his job without it. Miss Garvin ruefully surrendered her trophy. According to the second version, Somerville retained the pickaxe for some considerable time, carrying it around as a kind of mascot to inter-collegiate debates. What is certain is that Somerville's next boat—a sculler—was named 'Pickaxe'.

The Pickaxe incident provided a dramatic climax to Somerville's residence in Oriel. Skimmery retained a firm hold on the affections of the Somerville students who had lived there, and one of their first acts on returning to Somerville in Michaelmas Term 1919 was to present a clock to the Oriel JCR as a memento of their stay and in token of their appreciation of Oriel's hospitality. In writing to thank the Senior Student, Miss Spicer, for this gift, the Provost expressed the hopes that the relations established during the past four years between the two colleges might be continued and developed.[49] It is perhaps significant, in the light of this early experiment in co-residence, that Oriel was to be the last of the men's colleges, and Somerville the last-but-one of the women's, to remain single-sex.

[48] EP to Phelps and to Gilkes, 21 June 1919.   [49] Phelps to Spicer, 24 Oct. 1919.

6

'The Life of an English Family', 1879–1919

WHEN fundraising for Somerville in 1879, T. H. Green described as the founders' objective the establishment of a mode of life which would be 'quiet, healthy, economical, and at the same time refined'.[1] The model which they proposed was that of the ordinary—viz. middle-class—English family. Miss Shaw Lefevre came from a more sophistic-ated background: 'Daily intercourse in College', she thought 'should be something like that of a country house party—many independ-ent hours, much cooperative occupation, all the deference to "the College" which we would accord to a hostess and all the care to con-tribute to the common life which would be given by fellow guests.'[2] An early account of the daily life of the Hall—written with some-thing of the detached fascination of the social anthropologist—is contained in the letters home in October 1880 of Somerville's first American student, Frances Sheldon:

All room-work is done for us. When I come up to bed, there is a good-sized tin tub set out on a large flannel rug, near my washstand. Next morning at 7 . . . housekeeper tiptoes in with a big can of boiling water. . . . When the bell sounds . . . I descend to prayers. This con-sists of reading of the prayers of the day by the Principal, in the pres-ence of the whole crew, servants included. They all get up from their knees and look at the servants put breakfast into the room; for on the side table they set cold joints or ham; on another place is deposited a dish of hot meat or fish. On the table are put bread (uncut), butter, coffee, tea and cocoa (and eggs, if any), and a lot of toast and a pot of jam or marmalade. Then two or three of a table wait quickly upon the rest and themselves, to meat. Someone cuts bread; the head serves drinks, and so we eat a good breakfast, sort of free and easy. . . . After breakfast, till lunch one puts in whatever work they own. . . . Then,

---

[1] T. H. Green to Mr Martineau, 22 Nov. 1879 (copy in Somerville Archives).
[2] Note (? by Ethel Hurlblatt) on Miss Lefevre written for her sister Emily in 1914.

as soon as possible, between 1 & 2, comes lunch. . . . Bells ring. Go in. Meats arranged and helped as before. On the table is a cake or pudding; bread, etc—likewise a great wedge of cheese, from which they cut as wanted. Sort of unceremonious affair. . . . Dinner: servants in attendance, bringing around a dish of fish or of soup for each one. . . . Remove first plates; servants process around, No 1 with platter of chicken, or something, from which you . . . supply your own plate; No 2 bears potatoes; No 3 vegetables (greens, they call them). Eat it all up. By the way a chunk of bread has been by your plate from the beginning, which you dispose of as you will, but without butter. Fish is eaten, in this Hall at least, with fork alone, except for the assistance you can get from your bread. Plates removed; pudding circulates. We have fruit puddings almost entirely; eat them with fork and 'dessert' spoon. Afterwards come apples, very good ones. Pure whole apples. Lay it on a plate. Attack it with knife and *fork*; convey small pieces to mouth with fork. . . . Dinner done. All flock to the really handsome and artistic drawing room; Turkey carpet on the floor . . . lots of nice little pictures and 'chiny' set up for show in the corners of the room; tea kettle sings on its rack in front of the fire. The big triple window is all walled up with ponderous solid panels for the evening. Gas is lit. Then there's a social sort of time, till maid brings in tea-pot at 8; then people wait on each other to tea, which somebody makes by pouring from kettle upon the dry or only partly-steeped leaves. The tea is delicious; and with it are served wafer-thin slices of ready-buttered bread, also crackers. After tea, which . . . is taken sitting wherever you like about the room, we soon begin to scatter to our own rooms. . . .[3]

Though tin bath-tubs gradually gave way to fixed plumbing, the routine described here was to survive with little modification until shortly before the Great War. Students were expected to shake hands with the Principal before morning prayers, and to sit at her table for at least one meal a day; some kissed her before retiring to bed.[4] An article in *The Queen* in September 1887 fills in some of the details of life between lunch (at which 'beer or wine could be obtained, as an extra, by those who did not care for pure water') and dinner:

Walks or drives, tennis or other amusements, according to the season, were the order of the day, until 4 o'clock when afternoon tea was

---

[3] Sheldon, 17 Oct. 1880.   [4] See E. S. Bosanquet, *Late Harvest* (n.d.), 49.

brought into the drawing room, where a good many students generally gathered to enjoy it, though any one was at liberty to make tea
in her own room and invite her friends to join her, if she preferred
it. . . . Then one by one each girl retired to her own room, and for the
next two hours or so applied herself to hard reading until it was time
to dress for dinner.[5]

Dinner was generally followed by half an hour of conversation and
music before students returned to their rooms to work. Mary Skues
recalled how Miss Lefevre's arrival in the drawing room after dinner
would be accompanied by a soft rustle through the room, as students,
relaxing in their chairs, instinctively uncrossed their legs 'as a token
of respect for one (for she was most broad minded) of our Principal's
early Victorian prejudices.'[6] The hour between 10 and 11 p.m. (by
which time all students were supposed to be in their own rooms) was
the accepted time for paying social calls, and giving what Cornelia
Sorabji called 'supper parties', more generally referred to—from the
staple beverage consumed—as 'cocoas'.

With minor local variations, this routine would have been familiar
to students at any of the residential women's colleges of the period in
Oxford, Cambridge, or London.[7] At Girton there was greater formality, at LMH and Westfield more prayer, and at Newnham (if the
accounts of early students are to be believed) worse food.[8] As the colleges developed, each acquired a distinctive tone, which in the early
days was largely set by the personality and interests of the Principal.
Miss Shaw Lefevre was a less dominant character than Miss Wordsworth, and had a much shorter period of office, but in the domestic
life of Somerville her influence and taste were all-pervasive. A talen-
ted artist, she took a personal hand in the decoration and furnishing
of the house; and for many students the delight of having for the first
time a room of their own—a luxury at this date even for the well-
to-do—was enhanced by the prettiness of the room itself. Frances
Sheldon's first letter home to her family in America describes in detail
one of the original rooms in the old Hall:

[5] *Queen*, 24 Sept. 1887. In 1908 the time for dinner was changed from 7 p.m. to 7.15 p.m.
(College Meeting, 15 Feb. 1908).   [6] Recollections of Mary Skues (1884).
[7] See M. Vicinus, *Independent Women: Work and Community for Single Women 1850–1929*
(London, 1985), 140–1.
[8] The awfulness of the food is a recurring theme in A. Phillips (ed.), *A Newnham
Anthology* (Cambridge, 1979).

There are fine points and possibilities about this room, even if it has very little over six square feet of window . . . Its carpet is subdued, being mottled finely in two dull shades of red with black. The paper is light and cool in effect, with a graceful, flowing honey-suckle pattern, on very high walls; ceiling handsomely corniced with white mould-ing. My little bed is covered with a big chintz cover of wild thorn pattern; this, for handsome, unsuggestive effect in day-time, as we only have single rooms. The furniture is walnut; and the floor which, nicely polished, appears for two feet or so around the carpet, is dark, too. . . . Everything in the room harmonious, which is a comfort. There is one marvelous creature in the shape of a tall, wide rack for towels or whatever. This they stand up in front of the washstand daytimes, for obvious reasons; and if you have any bright drapery, a shawl, for instance, like mine, to hang over it, full spread, the artistic effect is stunning. A *tall* dark olive-green curtain, hung from rings that run on a brass-knobbed bar, has a rather toney look.[9]

The room's most striking feature, she reported, was the fireplace, 'which is unusually gorgeous and jolly in this room, because this is the chimney end of a very large stately room which has been divided into two.'

With the building of the Jackson wing in 1881 came added amenit-ies. The new rooms had flower balconies outside and cushioned window-seats with lockers for boots and shoes; coal-bunkers were concealed below the window-seats in the passageways. Eleanor Powell years later recalled 'the pleasant impression made on me by my first sight of the room I was to inhabit, with its simple American walnut furni-ture, yellow paper and orange curtains, and the strange but attractive brass shutters to the fireplace.'[10] The idiosyncrasies of the shuttered fireplaces—which were designed by Dr Vernon Harcourt and more noted for attractiveness than for efficiency—are a recurrent theme in the recollections of Somerville's early students. Catherine Pollard described the fireplace as the one mistake in her otherwise charming room:

The design was a tall upright into which metal plates were introduced at intervals, fuel being packed between every two plates. The fire was

[9] Sheldon, 17 Oct. 1880.

[10] *SSA Report*, 1914. Tastes, of course, varied: a few years later Margery Fry's artistic sensi-bilities were to be offended by the yellow wallpaper and brick-red curtains of her room in West. (E. Huws Jones, *Margery Fry: The Essential Amateur* (London, 1996), 39.)

lighted at the top storey, and when that section had burnt itself out or nearly so, you removed the first plate and the second storey came into action. The scheme was far from being the success hoped for. Often the draught was inadequate to start the fire going at all, or it might be that once started it would proceed to spread from storey to storey without intention or the removal of the plates, and a fiery furnace would result which it was impossible to control.[11]

She was, none the less, delighted with the accommodation provided by Somerville, not least for the contrast it presented to the much more institutional rooms she had previously occupied for a year at the Royal Holloway College.

A strict code of etiquette governed the internal relations of this closely-knit community. Addressing and referring to each other formally as 'Miss——', students mimicked the social conventions of their parents' world, as they paid and repaid calls, left visiting cards, issued and accepted invitations. Eighty years after going up to Somerville, Ethel Thomas recalled her astonishment when 'a second-year from my home town of Liverpool, but previously unknown to me, *called* on me formally, announcing "I am Miss Jones"—followed by the Senior Student, once at my old school, doing exactly the same thing.'[12] Charis Barnett, who came up in 1912, said that she and her friends much preferred this formality to 'the indiscriminate use of Christian names in the other women's colleges.'[13]

With greater familiarity came the use of simple surnames—'I'm going for a bike ride with Fry this afternoon' wrote Lettice Ilbert of a future Principal in 1895—or of nicknames; a contemporary of Ethel Thomas who fell asleep at a cocoa party was thereafter known as 'Dormouse'. Even among close friends the adoption of first names was rare, and subject to the ritual formality of a 'proposal'. 'Today I proposed to Miss Jaeger and Miss Cotterell proposed to me' recorded Charis Barnett in her diary towards the end of her first term. Muriel Jaeger was her contemporary, but to have been 'propped' by a fourth-year like Margaret Cotterell was a tremendous social coup. For a junior to take the initiative in 'propping' her senior was simply unthinkable.[14]

[11] Recollections of Catherine Childs (Pollard, 1888).
[12] Recollections of Ethel Williams (Thomas, 1909).
[13] C. U. Frankenburg, *Not Old, Madam, Vintage* (Lavenham, 1975), 59.
[14] For the operation of the 'proposal' system at Newnham, see Phillips, *A Newnham Anthology*, 66.

Seniority was taken with almost comic seriousness. 'I feel most responsible as a Senior now' wrote Cornelia Sorabji at the beginning of her second year, confiding to her family her anxiety about one of the freshers whom she had been asked to look out for: 'She is a dear little girl but *very* green indeed and rather conceited. . . . I had the painful duty of speaking to her about it the other day, as she is, in a way, my Fresher. . . . She took it nicely—but I fear she did not like it'.[15] At a similar stage in her college career, Lettice Ilbert apologized to her family for a disjointed letter home: 'It's frequently interrupted by freshers coming to return their calls. I really *must* have some of them to cocoa soon.'[16]

'Cadbury and Rowntree must have benefited greatly from us' commented Ethel Thomas, recalling the extent to which Somerville's social life was based on the consumption of cocoa.[17] In her early days at college, a fresher would be invited to cocoa by a succession of neighbourly seniors; etiquette required her to wait at least until her second term before returning the invitations. When, in her second term, Lettice Ilbert plucked up courage to issue an invitation to the hockey captain, Elsbeth Philipps, her boldness 'gave rise to much envy in the bosoms of Miss Davies and Miss Fry.'[18] Miss Ilbert held her own contemporaries in somewhat less respect, reporting to her family in December 1894 that she had joined with Margery Fry and Hilda Chappel in holding a 'scum cocoa' to which they invited 'all the objectionables—[fifteen out of a total first-year of twenty-four]—and polished them off'.[19]

There was, from the start, a less decorous side to community life. In 1890 a noisy midnight Hallowe'en party in West was broken up by Miss Pater 'most wroth'; an uncomfortable interview between the perpetrators and Miss Maitland took place next day.[20] Within a week, however, the same girls were celebrating Guy Fawkes night with a pillow fight in the passages with the gas down: 'They did look such a comic sight—in varied attire playing like great babies with their pillows and scattering the passages with feathers' commented Cornelia Sorabji, with the self-righteousness of one who was trying to write an

---

[15] Sorabji, 19 Oct. 1890 (India Office Library, MSS.Eur.F.165/3).

[16] Ilbert, 10 Oct. 1895.

[17] Cf. Joyce Sugg of the 1944 generation: 'Over in West and Penrose they swore by Van Houtens, but in Maitland we preferred Bourneville.'   [18] Ilbert, 3 Feb. 1895.

[19] Ilbert, 9 Dec. 1894.

[20] Sorabji, 2 Nov. 1890 (India Office Library, MSS.Eur.F.165/3).

essay the while.[21] The corridor-based West buildings were better adapted for such larks than the warren-like Old Hall, where the Principal was an even more inhibiting presence than a wrothful Miss Pater.

Community life was not to everybody's liking, and, inevitably, some students found it distasteful or oppressive. 'The worst down has been the monotony of Hall life; that is, the uninterestingness of the chatter' complained Frances Sheldon, who later moved out into lodgings:

> I like chatter when there is anything original about it; but when everyone talks in diminutive tones, and giggles over commonplace little pleasantries . . . and when everyone is constantly broaching the question whether something is proper; then one feels like being a 'critter' in a crockery shop. . . . The thing that oppresses one the most [is] the sense that the girls and women are always in a suppressed attitude. They lack gush fearfully—generally speaking.[22]

But, although she found her fellow-students 'very *stiff* compared with American girls', she thought them 'not excruciatingly proper', and she appreciated their qualities: 'They are in earnest about their work, don't make a fuss over it, and don't ape boys.'[23]

Lady Rhondda, who as Margaret Thomas spent two unhappy terms at Somerville in 1904–5, was less charitable in her judgement:

> Somerville smelt frousty to me. I disliked the ugliness of most of the public rooms, and I disliked the glass and the crockery and the way in which the tables were set. I disliked the food, and, more still, the way in which it was served. . . . And I disliked the dowdiness of the dons, and still more that of the other girls. . . . I could not bear the cloisterishness of the place; and felt irritated by the cautious way in which we were shut off from contact with men, the air of forced brightness and virtue that hung about the cocoa-cum-missionary-party-hymn-singing girls, and still more the self-conscious would-be naughtiness of those who reacted from this into smoking cigarettes and feeling wicked. And I disliked the slightly deprecating and dowdy, and again very self-conscious, atmosphere of ladylike culture that hung about the dons at play.[24]

Somerville, she concluded, was not her spiritual home. But, writing in 1933, even she admitted that she had liked and admired Miss Maitland,

---

[21] Sorabji, 2 Nov. 1890 (cont. 6 Nov.).   [22] Sheldon, 9 Nov. 1880.
[23] Sheldon, ?17 Oct. 1880.   [24] Rhondda, *This Was My World*, 107.

and rather liked her tutor; and that her intolerant youthful contempt had been directed at 'the awkward adolescence of something infinitely worthwhile.'

Miss Shaw Lefevre conceived one of her duties to be that of introducing her charges into polite Oxford society. Students were expected to attend the Principal's Wednesday afternoon receptions, taking it in turns to arrange the flowers and attend to the needs of the guests. For the shy, these could be nerve-racking occasions. Florence Rich and her contemporaries were, as she says, 'rather non-plussed' by John Ruskin's enquiry over tea: 'Do any of you study *nasty* Physiology?' His alleged comment on another occasion—'So glad to be old enough to be let come and have tea in Somerville and watch the girlies play at ball' passed rapidly (and, it would seem, inaccurately) into Oxford legend.[25] Equally disconcerting was the Principal's habit of calling in unexpectedly to students' rooms with distinguished guests in tow. Mary Skues, recalling how 'if we had a garden party or other function I would be sent off to show round and entertain one of the most formidable guests', said that she herself was not always grateful at the time for these attentions, though she had come to appreciate them since.

But it was not only the students who found such occasions disconcerting. Jacques Bardoux, a Frenchman who visited Oxford in 1895, has left an account of a Somerville Reception from the point of view of a guest:

> The lady student who showed me over Somerville Hall hardly troubled to conceal the disdain my astonishment inspired. Here is the gymnasium with its parallel bars, its horse, and its bicycles; the drawing room, plain but comfortable, and provided with pianos and violoncellos. As we went up a delightful staircase she asked me about the most famous French geometrician. I muttered the name of M. Poincaré, but acknowledged my ignorance. My guide's disdain became more marked. After showing me one or two rooms . . . the student handed me over to the care of one of her friends, who hastened to speak to me about the chief manuscripts of the 'Chanson de Roland'.[26]

His overriding impression of Somerville was one of 'happiness and comfort', and of its marked superiority over comparable Parisian establishments.

[25] Vera Farnell's version (*A Somervillian Looks Back* (Oxford, 1948), 9) may record a fuller oral tradition, but what the Birthday Book actually says (Feb. 8) is 'So glad to be old enough to be let come and have tea at Somerville Hall.'

[26] J. Bardoux, *Memories of Oxford*, trans. W. R. Barker (London: F. E. Robinson, 1899), 14 ff.

Some students, indeed, were in little need of 'drawing out'. At the official opening of the second stage of the West building in October 1894, the visiting grandees included many family friends of Lettice Ilbert, then in her first term. She described the occasion in a letter home:

> We little freshers didn't know where to go, and just as we reached the drawing room door, we were told by a severe senior that we were all to go upstairs, as there was no room. . . . Just then arrived another agitated senior, saying that Miss Pope wanted Miss Ilbert *at once*. I fled back into the drawing room, and from that moment till the end it was 'Miss Ilbert' a good deal, as heaps of people somehow seemed to know that I was here, and to wish to see me. Much to the amusement of the freshers, also their envy, and very much to the astonishment of the seniors, who had regarded me as a mild nonentity! I . . . was very happy.[27]

The influx of visitors on this occasion evidently sated the students' hospitable impulses: at College Meeting the following week it was agreed by a large majority that 'there shall be no entertainment of any form given by the students this term'.[28] The students' At Home was a normal feature of Michaelmas Term, providing them with an opportunity to invite their own friends, and to organize their own form of entertainment. As the years went on the occasion became more and more ambitious, to the extent of hiring of professional entertainers and caterers; when in 1910 the planned At Home was found to clash with the Oxford polling day (an occasion on which, by convention, male undergraduates were gated, thereby robbing the Somerville party of many of its intended guests), it was only the threat of compensation claims which deterred the students from a last-minute postponement.[29]

Whether they enjoyed their social responsibilities or not, Somerville students learned to accept them with a good grace. 'I tried to swot a bit after lunch but it was our At Home day and people poured in. I swore at them inwardly, but received them smilingly' reported Cornelia Sorabji in December 1890.[30] They received a great deal of hospitality in return for their efforts. 'The movement [for higher education for women] was still so new that we were looked upon as

---

[27] Ilbert, n.d. (Oct. 1894).   [28] College Meeting, 27 Oct. 1894.
[29] College Meeting, 28 Nov. 1910.
[30] Sorabji, 4 Dec. 1890 (India Office Library, MSS.Eur.F.165/3).

curiosities, and people were anxious to sample us' recalled Florence Rich. The fact that many people in Oxford were hostile to the presence of women students in their midst spurred on the sympathetic to redouble their welcome. Somervillians were particularly appreciative of Mrs Max Müller's habit at parties of mentioning the name of their college when introducing them to their fellow-guests, 'just as she did with the men undergraduates.'[31]

Cornelia Sorabji, as the first Indian woman to study at an English university, was lionized more than most.[32] Quickly taken under Jowett's wing, she was a frequent visitor at Balliol; and in 1890, at Sir William Anson's invitation, she became the first woman to be admitted as a reader to the Codrington Library at All Souls. 'The people there are so kind to me', she reported to her family: 'The men give up a book if the Librarian says I want it—so I do not tell him what I want now till I know it is disengaged for I think it is rather rough on the poor men who have the same books to read for lectures.'[33] Earlier in the term she had left the Philharmonic Society, 'partly because I have no time for it, and partly because Dr Roberts (the Musician of Magdalen, who teaches us) will pay me such very grossly untrue compliments that it insults my dignity. He means kindly I daresay—but I think it coarse to say the least.'[34] Florence Rich's experience was more typical:

> When I went up [in 1884] I had introductions to Mr & Mrs Chavasse, then living at the vicarage of St Peters-le-Bailey in New Inn Hall Street . . . and to the two Miss Thomases in Norham Gardens . . . The Poultons and the Vernon Harcourts were most good about inviting me, and so were the H. B. Dixons, the James Walkers and Miss Weld. I also visited at the house of the Odlings (he was Professor of Chemistry) and the Percivals at Trinity College [who were 'at home' to Somerville Students for tea each Tuesday]. Dear Mrs A. H. Johnson and beautiful Mrs T. H. Green I got to know much better after I went down. Dr and Mrs Darbishire showed me much hospitality in their charming house in the High opposite Magdalen College, and there were three dear little people, named Helen, Arthur and Rachel, who used to emerge from the nursery for dessert and at other times.[35]

[31] Recollections of Emily Kemp (1881).
[32] C. Sorabji, *India Calling* (London, 1934), 21 ff.
[33] Sorabji, 2 Nov. 1890 (India Office Library, MSS.Eur.F.165/3).
[34] Sorabji, 19 Oct. 1890 (India Office Library, MSS.Eur.F.165/3).
[35] Recollections of Florence Rich (1884).

Writing in 1938, Miss Rich saw this social network as one of the greatest contrasts between 'then' and 'now': 'In those days we saw much more of the university people; if you were one twenty-fourth of the whole number you would naturally have more opportunity of being invited out than if you were a mere one hundred and fiftieth.' If the early generations of women students had no formal contact with the university they were very familiar indeed with North Oxford drawing-rooms.

Many of them, indeed, went on to establish North Oxford drawing-rooms of their own. Remarking on the high incidence of matrimony between Oxford tutors and their women pupils, Alice Cameron (a student in 1910–14) was inclined to attribute it to the 'chivalrous, almost romantic, spirit' in which many young dons sympathetic to the cause of women's education offered their services to the fledgling women's colleges. In the years before the Great War, Somerville provided wives for—among others—R. R. Marett of Exeter, H. A. L. Fisher of New College, A. D. Lindsay of Balliol, G. H. Stevenson of University College, and M. N. Tod of Oriel[36]—the latter taking punctiliousness to the point of calling on the Principal to request the use of her room for the purpose of proposing to one of her students.[37] All except the Stevensons were, in the fullness of time, to send daughters to Somerville; Fisher, Lindsay, and Tod were all to serve on the college Council, as were Mrs Fisher and Mrs Marett.[38]

A strict code of chaperone rules ensured the extreme propriety of any tutorial—or other—courtship. The conventions governing the social activities of women students evolved only gradually, and the life of the first generation of Somervillians (or 'Somervillains' as they originally called themselves)[39] was in many respects less regulated than that of their successors. The earliest college rules simply stipulated that students should consult the Principal before accepting invitations from friends, and that they should not be out of Hall after sunset without leave—rules which any middle-class Victorian family would have taken for granted. Prudence and experience soon suggested further refinements. 'I wrote [to one of the new students] and

[36] Nora Kirk (1891) m. R. R. Marett in 1898; Lettice Ilbert (1894) m. H. A. L. Fisher in 1899; Erica Violet Storr (1898) m. A. D. Lindsay in 1907; Phoebe Wadsworth (1907) m. G. H. Stevenson in 1912; Mabel Byrom (1906) m. M. N. Tod in 1909.

[37] Recollections of Alice Cameron (1910).

[38] Fisher 1900–13 (President 1910–13); Tod 1913–31 (Vice-Chairman 1930–1); Lindsay 1915–22 and 1926–51 (Vice-Chairman 1931–51). Mrs Marett served on the Council 1902–14, Mrs Fisher 1916–22.   [39] See correspondence of Frances Sheldon, 1880–3.

explained some of the unwritten rules, or rather traditions which the students observed, such as the younger students not walking alone in the town but two together, without leave from you, and this also if going to station or long expeditions or Church in the country' wrote Miss Shaw Lefevre to Miss Maitland in the course of the 1889 hand-over.[40] Three years later, Miss Maitland assured a reporter from the *Lady's Pictorial* that there was no truth in the allegation that 'girls who reside at Oxford Halls are allowed to visit at College rooms with very insufficient chaperonage':

> The girls do visit their brothers, but never without a chaperone who is personally known to the Principal, and who is exceptionally qualified for her somewhat responsible duties. Every possible care is taken of these girls, and rules for their guidance, without being at all strict or in any way severe, are so emphatic and so rigidly enforced, that the most careful parent need not be afraid to trust his daughter to the guidance which awaits her at Somerville Hall.[41]

The rules—and the reason for them—are spelled out in Miss Penrose's letter of welcome to her first intake of students in 1907:

> Students never go into Colleges alone. They do not attend College chapels nor walk in College gardens without permission and in some cases not without a chaperon. They do not walk 'by the Barges' nor along the towing path. They do not take long country walks or bicycle rides quite alone and if they want to go out of Oxford by train, they must always ask leave. As a rule, they do not walk much about the city alone.
>
> When attending College lectures, they do not go in singly but two or three together. They sit all together and it is understood that even if they have relatives or friends attending the same lectures they do not speak to them. . . . This is by the wish of the Colleges which give the privilege of attending their lectures. We are always anxious that new students should understand this and realise how completely the reputation of the College passes into their hands. We have many privileges but no rights.[42]

Avoidance of anything which might seem like an assignation with a member—particularly an undergraduate member—of the opposite

---

[40] MSL to ACM, 7 Sept. 1889.

[41] L. T. Meade, 'English Girls and their Colleges, v. Somerville Hall, Oxford', *Lady's Pictorial*, 2 Jan. 1892.   [42] EP to K. F. Jones, 6 Sept. 1907.

sex was strictly enjoined, and taken, on occasions, to comic lengths. Frances Sheldon described how a fellow-Somervillian, Jane Sharp, who had accompanied her to evening service at St Philip and St James, found herself coming out of church immediately in front of a childhood friend from home, now an undergraduate:

> Now she is so very proper that she never bows to him here in Oxford. It is a way Somerville girls have of being oblivious to all mankind on the street. Sunday night, as we came out from our seats, I looked up and there . . . stood Harry Kennedy. . . . When I saw him, I was shocked and looked straight at little Jane. She was beaming and trying to conceal a broad grin. Glancing back at Harry, I perceived a reflection of her expression. We went down the aisle in front of him and said not a word, either, then or ever. . . . I imagine the coincidence will occur again. But there is no intrigue about it, and Jane will always march straight home as dumb as a mummy.[43]

There were, of course, loopholes of which the less scrupulous did not hesitate to take advantage. One of the delights of skating in Christ Church Meadow, reported Lettice Ilbert, was 'the way all the little rules of etiquette depart':

> Unchaperoned, we skate with any youth we know, and do just as we like. . . . Miss Scott's brother I have skated with a good deal, and as she and I go together, he sort of looks after us both. Phil [Elsbeth Philipps?] and that lot seem to have *dozens*. I see them skating with a different youth each time! . . . We danced a Lancers on the ice yesterday—it was *very* mad.[44]

The college authorities for their part were prepared to exercise a certain discretion in applying the rules. At a time when attendance at dances during term-time was forbidden, Florence Rich was enabled to accept an invitation to a dance on the last Saturday of term by being allowed to go down two days early and stay with the Darbishires.[45] In 1890 Cornelia Sorabji was not only allowed to attend a hallowe'en party unchaperoned except by her brother Dick, but was entrusted with a key to the gate, to let herself in to Somerville at the 11 p.m. deadline—the earliest recorded instance of a College late key.[46] For chaperone purposes, it was accepted that 'special cousins may count

---

[43] Sheldon, 17 May 1881.   [44] Ilbert, '3 Feb'.
[45] Recollections of Florence Rich.
[46] Sorabji, 2 Nov. 1890 (India Office Library, MSS.Eur.F.165/3).

as brothers at parents' request'.[47] Charis Barnett was allowed to invite a fellow of Trinity, the unfortunately named Mr Raper, to tea in her room alone after assuring Miss Penrose that he was over 70 and had been her father's tutor.[48] The arrival at Somerville in 1912 of Mrs Radhabai Subbarayan, a married Indian student whose husband was an undergraduate at Wadham, caused a considerable stir among her fellow-students when it was learned that the rules had been waived to enable the couple to have tea together in her rooms from time to time, without a chaperone.[49] After the move to Oriel in 1915, students who had separate bedrooms were allowed to entertain male visitors in their sitting-rooms—subject to the usual chaperone conditions, and on the strict understanding that a return to Somerville would mean a return to the old rules. A wartime student, Constance Savery, reported in a letter home that

> One of the second-year students is engaged to a man who is taking Greats at the same time as she is. They have tea in Miss Penrose's room once a week, and also in Miss Farnell's; then Miss Penrose or Miss F. discreetly departs. Everyone complains bitterly that you dare not go to Miss Penrose's room now for fear of interrupting one of these nice little tête à têtes. I saw them strolling along arm-in-arm the other day.[50]

It was perhaps to this couple that Vera Farnell was alluding when she related how, in the course of a none-too-happy career as a chaperone, it had once even fallen to her to assist, with mixed feelings, at a proposal of marriage.[51]

There were, of course, some people to whom the ordinary rules simply did not apply. Chief among these for nearly fifty years was Professor Gilbert Murray, who first visited Somerville as an undergraduate to take tea with Miss Shaw Lefevre, joined the college Council in 1908 and served—the last of its life members—until his death in 1957. Alice Cameron records how in 1912 he allowed himself to be smuggled secretly into college to direct and stage-manage the second-year play—his own translation of Aristophanes' *The Frogs*—which had, traditionally, to be kept as a surprise for the rest of the college; as an

---

[47] Notebook kept by Miss Penrose. Students were reminded from time to time that 'the brother of one is not the brother of all'.

[48] Frankenburg, *Not Old, Madam, Vintage*, 60 (where Raper is wrongly attributed to All Souls). [49] Barnett, 12 Oct. 1912.

[50] Letter home, quoted in Recollections of Constance Savery.

[51] Farnell, *A Somervillian Looks Back*, 48.

official guest on the night of the actual performance, he rose from his seat beside the Principal to express his thanks with the words 'It was so good that we all felt we really *were* in Hell' (the scene of the last act). When in 1946 *The Frogs* was chosen as the first major post-war production of the college Dramatic Society Gilbert Murray was again present, and 'crowned the very spirited performance by a delightful and characteristic speech.' Perhaps he redeployed the same joke? Over the years, the college provided him with a succession of classicist graduate secretaries, while generations of devoted Somervillians enjoyed the teetotal, vegetarian hospitality dispensed at Yatscombe, refrained from consuming alcohol in his presence, and, whatever their politics, addressed envelopes on his behalf in his five attempts to win the Oxford University vote for the Liberals.

The college's oversight of its students' conduct extended to matters of dress. They were exhorted to steer a difficult middle course between the dowdy and the flashy, avoiding the eccentricity which was said to have exposed some of the pioneers of higher education for women to ridicule. (Mark Pattison claimed—not intending it as a compliment—that in a large party he could at once detect a Newnham or Girton girl by her dress.)[52] 'The dresses worn at Somerville Hall, whether for morning or evening, are always exceedingly simple, though they often display a great deal of taste on the part of the wearers' wrote a former student in an article in *The Queen* in 1887, stressing that, though there were no actual regulations as to dress, 'the antiquity of the place is supposed to be reflected with certain modifications in the dresses of the students, and their costumes, though certainly not nun-like, yet generally present that amount of cloistral simplicity, which to a casual observer would leave no doubt as to the *status pupillaris* of the wearer.'[53] Enterprising Oxford tradesmen seized—albeit with some aesthetic misgivings—upon a welcome commercial opportunity. 'Tradesmen . . . who do their best to gratify the caprices of the fair sex will have reason to grumble if they are not well patronised by Somerville Hall' wrote a commentator in *Jackson's Oxford Journal* in 1886: 'The aesthetic greens, and drabs, and blues, if they can never gratify our sense of beauty either in colour or shape, may nevertheless help to replenish the empty exchequer, and keep Oxford trade on its feet.'[54]

[52] J. E. Courtney, *An Oxford Portrait Gallery* (London, 1931), 219–20.
[53] *Queen*, 24 Sept. 1887.
[54] *Jackson's Oxford Journal*, 16 Oct. 1886.

In Miss Shaw Lefevre students had a prime example of understated elegance set before them. Eleanor Powell recalled in an obituary notice the pride taken by early Somerville students in their 'distinguished looking Principal, especially when she was going out in the evening in one of her quiet, rich, well-made dresses.' Miss Shaw Lefevre's gardening clothes, as described by Mary Skues, were scarcely less impressive: 'a purple dress of some very soft material with an unbelievably long skirt, a . . . three-quarter length black jacket, velvety and lacey . . . and a black straw hat trimmed with black lace and purple flowers and tilted to one side with a slightly rakish air.' If this was a style to which few students could aspire, Miss Pater, with her blue dresses and amber beads, provided an alternative model of fashionable pre-Raphaelite simplicity.

'The Principal liked us to dress tastefully, but she was always quick to notice anything that she thought in the least conspicuous' recalled Emily Kemp. She herself was told that if she wished to go to a garden party in a white flannel tennis dress, carrying a racquet and shoes—which was considered to be aping the men—she must drive and not walk through the streets. A student who was determined to show that 'prettiness in dress was not incompatible with serious work' was rebuked for wearing too becoming a hat, and offered the use of one of the principal's bonnets in its place.[55] 'Of course, I need not tell you that Oxford is like London in matters of dress and that one could not walk about the streets except in the quietest of clothes' wrote Miss Shaw Lefevre to a prospective student from what she described as a 'smart, rather dressy' family.[56] To her successor she confided her fear that 'a dressy student of a better social position than some may set such a bad example.'

Vera Brittain, who over the years was to make an impact on the college in a number of ways, first impressed it by her style of dress. In *Testament of Youth* she describes an after-dinner interview with Miss Penrose in the summer of 1913 to discuss the possibility of applying to Somerville:

Being quite ignorant of the plain-Jane-and-no-nonsense conventions of Oxford women dons, I had carefully changed, in accordance with

[55] Recollections of Florence Rich.
[56] See MSL to ACM (Discipline file). Incorrectly quoted in Farnell, *A Somervillian Looks Back*, 12. For the risks women ran of being mistaken for prostitutes at this period if they were 'gaily-dressed', see L. Nead, *Myths of Sexuality* (Oxford, 1988), 180–2.

the sartorial habits of Buxton, into evening dress, and was wearing a flimsy lace frock under a pale blue and grey reversible satin cloak, and an unsubstantial little pair of high-heeled white suède shoes. So unlike the customary felt hat and mackintosh of the average 1913 woman student was this provincially modish attire, that the Principal actually referred to it when she interviewed me during the Scholarship examinations in the following March. 'I remember you' she said immediately, 'you're the girl who came across the lawn in a blue evening cloak.'[57]

Miss Penrose on the whole exercised a more indirect censorship than had Miss Shaw Lefevre. Her disapprobation of some rather dashing earrings—scarlet and green parrots in pendent gilt cages—sported by the youthful Dorothy L. Sayers was mediated through an older student, Vera Farnell; later, as Principal's Secretary, Miss Farnell was required to remonstrate with a student on the subject of her 'unnecessarily, even outrageously, conspicuous behaviour and attire', and was greeted with the response 'I won't, I *won't*, I won't be a Dowd.'[58] In 1918 it fell to the Senior Student to explain at College Meeting that objections had been raised to the wearing of blazers at lectures and examinations (and, indeed, in the town generally), and to request students to wear them only in the house or for athletics; after the college returned to its own premises in 1919 it became the rule that 'Blazers were to be worn only north of Somerville'.[59] On one occasion when Miss Penrose intervened personally to express concern that an undergraduate whom she knew to be penniless should be so well dressed, she apologized handsomely on learning that the clothes were all either home-made or hand-me-downs.[60]

Though women students enjoyed much North Oxford hospitality, university clubs and societies were in general closed to them. For their social life they were largely dependent on each other. Social contacts with students from the other women's halls were developed by the establishment of joint societies, by participation in inter-university sporting and debating fixtures, and by the founding in the 1890s of a joint magazine, *The Fritillary*. The establishment in 1887 of the Women's University Settlement brought Somervillians into contact not only with the poor of Southwark, but with fellow-volunteer

---

[57] Brittain, *Testament of Youth: An Autobiographical Study of the Years 1900–1925* (London, 1978), 66.   [58] Farnell, *A Somervillian Looks Back*, 13.
[59] College Meeting, 24 May 1918, 22 Oct. 1922.
[60] Recollections of Rachel Varcoe (Footman, 1923).

workers from LMH, Girton, and Newnham.[61] Many students had sisters or cousins at Cambridge; and through Emily Penrose contacts were established with both Bedford and Holloway. All these colleges drew their students overwhelmingly from the same social group, through the same select network of girls' schools; and the institutions which grew up within them were, in essentials, remarkably similar. They were also highly competitive. Somervillians, proud of their liberal and non-denominational tradition, were inclined to take a rather superior view of the Anglican foundations. (The college did not model itself on Balliol for nothing.) For the first forty years of its existence, college loyalty was paramount.

It was based on a communal life which involved senior and junior members alike. Many of the tutors, recruited straight from college, were scarcely—if at all—older than the students under their supervision. There was at Somerville no 'high table', of the kind insisted on from the start (when it had only two occupants) by Emily Davies at Girton. Principal, staff, and students lived and ate together; and if the chaperone rules threw them together at times willy-nilly, they often voluntarily shared each other's company during their leisure hours. Tutors took an active part in college societies of all kinds: Miss Pope—celebrated for 'her pace on the wing in the hockey-field [and] her pertinacity and level-headedness in debate'[62]—was a founding member of the discussion group known as the 'Associated Prigs'; Miss Lorimer was among the group of gym enthusiasts who, 'dressed in peculiar tunics', wound up their regular Wednesday afternoon exercise with a run in single file through the garden;[63] the Principal presided solemnly at State Openings of the Somerville Parliament, of which Miss Bruce was the first Speaker. All of them were active members of the Somerville Suffrage Society, and worked alongside present and former students in the Women's University Settlement. When in 1898 the tutors at last acquired a common room of their own, the JCR marked the occasion with the gift of a picture for which thanks were recorded in verse:

> Thank you, kindly JCR.
> What delightful folk you are!
> It was very kind to bring
> Botticelli's 'Verdant Spring'.

[61] See G. Barrett, *Blackfriars Settlement: A Short History 1887–1987* (London, 1985).
[62] Farnell, *A Somervillian Looks Back*, 24.   [63] Ibid. 7.

It reminds us of the past,
Beauteous, but too bright to last,
Yet renewed from day to day,
When we see you at your play.

As you fly with garments loose,
Bear with you the thanks of *Bruce*.
As you write your themes with ease,
Freely use the tips of *Lees*.
When to win a match you hope,
Take the blessing of the *Pope*.
When you wish to join the gods,
Lorimer will coach for Mods.
All your life with joy to leaven
Be the grateful task of *Sheavyn*.

All the Senior Common Room
Praise you till the crack of doom![64]

From 1886 until the opening of the Maitland Hall in 1913, the fundamental division in Somerville was not between staff and students, but between the Hall (later 'House') and the West. The college consisted of two largely independent communities, one presided over by the Principal and the other by the Vice-Principal. New students living outside the two main buildings were assigned on arrival either to the House or to the West, according to the position of their room in college. When Vera Farnell arrived in 1911, Miss Penrose was presiding over West, and Miss Bruce over House. Miss Farnell, who had a room in what later became part of the library, has left an account of her first interview with the Principal:

Miss Penrose, always addicted to alarmingly abrupt questions, asked me: 'Will you belong to the West or to the House?' Completely ignorant of College customs, for I knew then not one single Somervillian, I asked her what would be involved in my decision: her reply came, direct, explicit, with all the alarm of the Unknown that was now upon me: 'If you belong to the West, you will come under my care and supervision; if you belong to the House, you will come under that of Miss Bruce; which will you choose?' I felt my fate to hang upon that choice; I saw Miss Penrose, infinitely alarming and awe-inspiring to a Fresher; I had not yet seen Miss Bruce. Conscious, a

---

[64] Quoted in *Fritillary*, 13, Dec. 1898.

second later, how tactless my reply might seem, I shot out: 'I'll belong to the House, Miss Penrose'.[65]

Each community elected its own Senior Student and its own news-paper representative, and organized a rota of volunteers to arrange its common-room flowers. A messenger service operated between the two buildings to deliver internal mail. Hall and West challenged each other in sport (West won the annual hockey match for the first time in 1911) and in fire-fighting, which for all practical purposes counted as a competitive sport.[66] (The College Fire Brigade was established in 1903, with separate corps for the Hall and the West, and held weekly practices in term-time; any student who failed to attend the call-over of a general fire alarm was liable to a fine of 2/6.)[67] The two commun-ities endlessly sought to out-do each other in hospitality. Cornelia Sorabji described to her family plans for an end-of-term supper party to be given by the West for the inhabitants of the Hall:

> We are to appear in gym costume and those who have not gym dress in fancy dress: but to begin with we are to have a *Phantom Dance* in the Hall at 9 p.m. We all come as phantoms, in sheets and masks, with pillow cases on our heads: we will dance for an hour or thereabouts to weird music by blue lights, and then adjourn to the Gym where we will throw off our masks and appear in our other costumes. During supper we shall *lark* and be as rowdy as we can . . . A banjo and comic songs in the gallery. To bed at *11.30*.[68]

She later reported the evening to have been a great success, and the supper 'very recherché'. Having helped her compatriots the Princesses Bamba and Catherine Duleep Singh to dress as a Gujarat Ranee and a peasant, Miss Sorabji herself appeared as Mephistopheles, with burnt cork moustache and eyebrows, and 'skipped about supremely happy, unburdened with skirts' to the accompaniment of claps and loud cheers.[69] 'The Hall will have to return our invitation' she wrote home: 'I don't know how they will do it quite. They can't conceive better plans than ours—unless they do tableaux. Even that will be common place.'[70]

Attempts to break down the barriers between the two communities

[65] Farnell, *A Somervillian Looks Back*, 36–7.
[66] Cf. Phillips, *A Newnham Anthology*, 46.
[67] College Meeting, 24 Nov. 1903, 18 Oct. 1911.
[68] Sorabji, ?9 Mar. 1891 (India Office Library, MSS.Eur.F.165/4).
[69] Sorabji, 16 Mar. 1891, ibid.   [70] Sorabji, ?9 Mar. 1891, ibid.

often served merely to accentuate the differences between them. 'West Dining Rooms & Drawing Room both seemed enormous to us who lived in the Hall' commented Miss Penrose on the requirement of her student days that all Somervillians should dine once a week 'at the other end'.[71] In the complex constitutional discussions following the opening of the Maitland Hall in 1913 serious objections were raised to the proposal (which was eventually adopted) that the Senior Students should in future be both nominated and voted for by the whole college, on the grounds that 'Hall and West did not know each other sufficiently to judge the merits of candidates coming from the other end.'[72] But at least they didn't have to cross a road to get to the other end, as was the case in the early days at Newnham; nor did Somerville have the sense which prevailed among Newnham's constituent halls, that each community catered for (or produced) a different kind of student.[73]

An important milestone both in breaking down the Hall–West division and in developing a sense of separate student identity was the establishment in 1894 of College Meeting, the remote ancestor of the JCR. Originally open to all college members—including visiting former students—it soon became accepted that dons would only attend if specifically invited.[74] Like most student bodies, the College Meeting was deeply obsessed with its own constitution. But, in the intervals between devising electoral procedures, it assumed responsibility for many of the practical details of daily life: the use and re-sale of newspapers and magazines, the running of the fiction library, the allocation of bicycle stalls, the purchase of hymn-books for Sunday Prayers, the tipping of scouts, the rules governing the popular practice in fine weather of sleeping out in the garden. It raised money for the Mary Somerville Research Fellowship and the WUS, made collections of old clothes for charity, entertained children from the Cowley workhouse, organized social discussion classes for the college maids, and encouraged members to patronize the boot-making services of the St Crispin Workshop. It also acted at times as an important initiator of college business. The move in October 1894 to exclude dons from meetings seems to have been prompted by the desire for uninhibited discussion of a current grievance, and was followed by an appeal to the Council to appoint someone with nursing experience to take care of sick

---

[71] EP, Notes for Tour round College, 1926.   [72] College Meeting, 1913–14.
[73] 'Clough for games, Sidgwick for brains, and Old for silk petticoats.': see Phillips, *A Newnham Anthology*, 21, 53.   [74] College Meeting, 27 Oct. 1894.

members of the college. (Council compromised by laying this responsibility on the housekeeper.[75]) Soon afterwards the students campaigned
successfully, under the generalship of Gertrude Pesel and Eleanor
Rathbone, for relaxation of the rule prohibiting attendance at dances
in term-time. A petition submitted to Council cited the example of
Girton, whose students were allowed to attend dances provided that
the college hours were adhered to, before touching on a more general
source of discontent: 'We are . . . already subjected to a large number
of restrictions from which undergraduate members of the University are free and we feel it hard that we who can claim to have shown
ourselves not more easily distracted from our work are placed under
legislation.'[76] In 1895 the College Meeting, again on the proposal of
Eleanor Rathbone, urged the Council to institute a biennial gaudy to
replace the college picnic which traditionally marked the anniversary
of the opening of university examinations to women.[77]

In the course of a heated discussion in March 1913 of the unpopular
rule enjoining silence at 11 p.m., it transpired that many students
were unaware that the rules about work-hours had been made not
by the college authorities, but by their own predecessors in College
Meeting.[78] The extent to which Somerville was prepared to allow its
students to make their own rules is most strikingly illustrated in the
matter of smoking. Widely regarded as a symptom of advanced feminism, smoking posed an obvious quandary to a college which was at
once committed to liberal principles and anxious to propitiate public
opinion. Early Somervillian smokers included Eleanor Rathbone, who
had already acquired what was to be a life-long habit when she came
up to college in 1893. Miss Maitland, who 'thought it best not to make
an absolute rule . . . about smoking, [but] short of that did all she
could to discourage it',[79] recognized a hopeless case when she saw one
and turned an unresponsive nose to the wreaths of smoke emanating
from the room above hers.[80] In the case of another confirmed smoker,
Eleanor Cropper, she confined herself to remarking 'Odours of Araby,
my dear' as she kissed her goodnight.[81]

As smoking became increasingly prevalent the women's colleges

---

[75] College Meeting, 3 Dec. 1894 and 25 Jan. 1895.
[76] College Meeting, 25 and 30 Jan. and 5 Feb. 1895.
[77] College Meeting, 15 June 1895. [78] College Meeting, 28 Mar. 1913.
[79] EP to Miss Stephen(s), 16 Jan. 1913 (Discipline file).
[80] M. D. Stocks, *Eleanor Rathbone: A Biography* (London, 1949), 39.
[81] Bosanquet, *Late Harvest*, 49.

at Oxford and Cambridge reviewed their position, and in 1914 no-smoking rules were introduced at Girton and LMH. Miss Penrose, who had continued her predecessor's policy of non-legislation, was reluctant to follow suit: 'No rules at S.C. Proud of it' reads a note on the subject in her hand. College convention, however, distinguished between smoking alone, which was countenanced, and a 'smoking party', whether in public or private rooms, which was not. 'There is absolutely no objection to smoking, except in Common Room. Isn't that grand? One better than Girton, eh?' wrote Dorothy Sayers in an early letter home.[82] Mindful of the need to set a good example, members of the Senior Common Room at this date exercised a self-denying ordinance whereby they refrained from smoking not only in Somerville itself but anywhere in Oxford. (At Newnham, where smoking was strictly forbidden, Miss B. A. Clough was reduced to hiring a hansom to take her out into the country to indulge her habit.)[83] Appealed to in 1914 for their views, the SCR pronounced that, much as they deprecated the practice of smoking in college, they were still more strongly opposed to making a rule prohibiting smoking.[84] Miss Penrose, reiterating her opposition to rules 'except perhaps in public rooms', referred the question back to the student body. At College Meeting, two distinct points of view emerged, one party holding that smoking was accepted by the outside world as a matter of course, the other that it attached a stigma to college, and was highly prejudicial to its reputation—'Somerville was getting the name of a smoking college'. It was reported that most of the other women's colleges had a definite rule against smoking, though in some it was not strictly kept. The discussion ended with the passing of a characteristically Somervillian motion 'that the whole matter be left to the individual conscience, with due regard to the fact that outside opinion is in a transitional state.'[85]

As the students made their own rules, so they made their own entertainments. Charades and dressing-up games and music and dancing—the conventional leisure-time occupations of middle-class households of the period—were popular in college from the start. The opportunities presented by institutional life to join clubs and societies, to take part in drama and debate and competitive sport, still had the excitement of novelty for any student who had not been to one

---

[82] Quoted in B. Reynolds, *Dorothy L. Sayers: Her Life and Soul* (London, 1993), 47.
[83] Phillips, *A Newnham Anthology*, 45.   [84] College Meeting, 30 Apr. 1914.
[85] Ibid.

of the more progressive girls' schools. Cornelia Sorabji listed for her family the range of college societies available to the fresher of 1889:

> There are the Debating Society, a Knitting or Working Society (for the poor), the Sharp Practice (a debate without preparation—anyone called upon must speak at this for three minutes or stand looking a fool), the Hockey Club, the Browning Society, and the Practising Society (to keep up Music); also the Historical Society.[86]

The 1892 Oxford Letter reported a number of recent changes:

> The old Shakespeare Society has revived, and now finds it possible to live in harmony with the Literary Society, whose creation killed it several years ago; but the latter has changed its name and its character, and is now partly an essay-reading society called the Mermaid Club; it is limited to twelve members, and its promoters hope to keep it alive by this idea of selectness, by holding only four meetings in the term, and those at the festive hour of 10, and by supplying the members with refreshments.

It is clear that by this early date many of the standard features of college societies were already well established: their essential impermanence; their tendency to recur and to overlap; their founders' optimistic initial estimates of the likely attendance at meetings, and more realistic subsequent acknowledgment of the need to woo members; the crucial importance of providing refreshments.

The same year saw the establishment of one of Somerville's most distinguished early societies, the Scientific and Philosophical—a select group of science students who set up a small museum of curiosities and scientific objects, and held meetings at which an introductory essay was followed up by appropriate experiments or practical demonstrations. In Trinity Term 1893 the society achieved a tremendous coup by securing Professor Poulton to lecture on 'Mimicry in Animals', in what was in effect his inaugural lecture as the newly appointed Hope Professor of Zoology. The lecture, preceded by music, was attended by members of Council and outside friends, the Oxford Correspondent greeting as a welcome sign of the times the fact that this prestigious lecture 'should be in Somerville Hall and to women'.[87] For a few years the 'Sci-Phi' went from strength to strength, abolishing in 1895 'the enervating practice of refreshments',[88] and publishing

---

[86] Sorabji, 1889 (India Office Library, MSS Eur F.165/1). [87] Oxford Letter, 1893.
[88] Oxford Letter, 1895.

an annual record of its learned proceedings. But in 1897 it met the
fate of all student societies, and the Oxford Letter reported the end
of its 'brilliant, though all too short career'. It should not, perhaps,
have held refreshments in such contempt.

The Sci-Phi was unusual in a number of respects. Somerville's earliest societies were preponderantly literary in character, some, like the
Browning Society, surviving virtually unchanged for years, others,
like the Literary Society (1901)—which 'ran a successful course on a
ground cleared for it by the extinction of many earlier societies with
similar aims'—and its successor the Literary and Philosophical Society (1908), undergoing constant transformations and amalgama-
tions. Of the college's non-literary societies one of the most popular
—and certainly the hardiest—was the Archaeological Society, popu-
larly known as 'the ARK'. The 1904 Oxford Letter commented on the
numerous expeditions into the Oxfordshire countryside with which
the society's lectures from distinguished outside speakers were interspersed; in 1917—when many college societies were collapsing under
the pressures of wartime—ARK was described as continuing to flourish
in spite of advancing years; and though thought to be languishing
in 1923, it was still extant ten years later and pursuing 'its traditional
mysterious and occult practices.'[89] The practices of a society called
'The Witches' Cauldron' became the subject of considerable speculation when in 1907 one of its objects—'to make Somerville more
womanly'—came to the notice of the popular press. In fact it was a
cooking syndicate, whose ten members met once a week to try out
recipes. Their successes included Welsh rabbit cooked by Mary Anson
(later Lady Bosanquet), and buttered eggs cooked by Ruth Pelham-
Pearson (the future head of English at St Leonard's School); of the
fruit salad prepared by Elizabeth Macleod it was reported that 'everything not spilt on the carpet was successful.'[90]

Perhaps the most remarkable of the early college societies was
a small group 'for discussing things in general' which called itself
the Associated Prigs. The founder members included Edith Deverell,
Mary O'Brien, Eleanor Rathbone, and Mildred Pope (newly elevated
to the SCR as Librarian); the first topic proposed for discussion was
'Provisional Socialism'. Membership was by invitation only, later recruits including Margery Fry, Lettice Ilbert, and Hilda Oakeley. The
society was characterized by high moral earnestness and a passionate

[89] Oxford Letter, 1932/3.   [90] *Fritillary*, 39, Dec. 1906 and 40, Mar. 1907.

concern for the social issues of the day—a concern which, in the case of many of its members, remained manifest through life. In one of their more frivolous end-of-term meetings they held a 'prolongued and interesting discussion' on the subject of dress:

It was maintained on the one hand that we, as women students, should dress as well as possible, lest, among other considerations, carelessness in this matter should bring discredit on the cause of women's education. On the other hand, it was urged that it was our duty to act so as to protest against the costliness of dress at the present day. The former view received the greater support, and it was pointed out that it might be so put into practice as to gain the end aimed at by the second proposal.[91]

Nearly twenty years later, and in a rather different spirit, Dorothy L. Sayers was the leading-light in the 'Mutual Admiration Society'— so called on the grounds that if its members didn't give themselves this title the rest of college would.[92] Consisting originally of a small group of first-years who met once a week (with refreshments) to read their own works, the MAS soon attracted applications from other years. Election was decided by the members on the merit of an original entry in prose or verse. 'An awfully nice child who writes quite good stuff' was the comment on one successful applicant, Muriel St Clare Byrne—a future honorary fellow of the college, who was to go on writing good stuff until her death in 1983 at the age of 88. One of Dorothy Sayers's own contributions to the MAS took the form of a conversation between the three Magi, a clear anticipation of *The Man Born to be King*. All the members except Amphilis Middlemore, who died tragically young, were in fact to publish their mature work.

In 1902 the students ventured beyond charades into 'theatricals'. The Oxford Letter for that year notes a 'new departure in College amusements':

At the end of Hilary Term, a few enterprising students gave, in the gymnasium, scenes from Jane Austen's novels, from Anthony Hope's *Heart of Princess Osra* and from *The Girls of St Wode's* (a novel whose travesties of college life never cease to delight the heart of Somerville); and it must have been the success of this venture which prompted the more ambitious and very amusing entertainment given to the

---

[91] Minutes of the Associated Prigs, 23 June 1895.
[92] Frankenburg, *Not Old, Madam, Vintage*, 62–3.

College at the end of the Summer Term by all the students who were going down.

Immediately Schools were over placards appeared in college giving notice that something was about to happen; and, after several days of feverish, but secret, activity the finalists emerged to regale the rest of college with a topical morality play, *Most of Us*. In an obvious parody of *Everyman*, four college 'types' were presented: 'Flanelette' (the athletic girl), 'Fritilla' (the frivolous young lady, attended by 'Fine Clothes' and 'Candy'), 'the Stodger', and 'the Meddler'. The evening ended with a college version of Cock Robin, which 'enabled the performers still further to point any morals which they wished to enforce.'[93]

Thus began what was to be a thirty-year tradition of the college 'going-down play'. The following year's entertainment was hailed by the Oxford Correspondent as 'the crowning glory of the year':

Attired each as her own totem, i.e. the animal which she was considered by herself or her friends most closely to resemble, the departing students were exhibited to their friends by a humorous showman, who in each case read an instructive and somewhat incisive dissertation on the manners and customs of the creature in question.[94]

Helen Darbishire appeared as an old grey sheep, Grace Hadow as a gosling, Rose Macaulay as a caterpillar. The costumes, hastily assembled by the performers in the interval between the end of Schools and the last Saturday of term, were described as 'triumphs of ingenuity', which 'should have convinced the most ardent Conservative (had there been any to see) that a college education does not unfit our sex for the use of the needle.'

In the years that followed the going-down students experimented with a number of different formats. The 1904 play took the form of a Chaucerian prologue describing the various actors under the guise of pilgrims; the 1905 finalists, more ambitiously literary, provided impersonations of characters in fiction, in which Jeanie Deans jostled Miss Mattie, and Becky Sharp exchanged pleasantries with the Woman in White; the 1906 students opted not for a play, but for a dance, at which each guest was provided with a button-hole and a motto— 'the latter being not always greeted with enthusiasm by the recipient, though as a rule it afforded much pleasure to her friends.'[95] Of

[93] Oxford Letter, 1902.   [94] Oxford Letter, 1903.   [95] Oxford Letter, 1906.

Pantodaemonium, the 1907 play, the Oxford Correspondent reported that it would 'long live in the memories of the SCR as a vision of College as it really is'; *The Swing of the Pendulum; or Mummies* in 1911 gave 'a delightful and amusing vision of Somerville in the future when it has become truly womanly.' Two standard features had by now become established. The plays served as a vehicle for satirical comment on college institutions or the events of the past year; and they were interspersed with songs set to familiar tunes—the popular songs of the day, hymn tunes, parodies of Gilbert and Sullivan—with choruses in which all could join. On 14 June 1913 the old Hall dining-room was used for the last time for a going-down play whose title, *Past, Present and Future*, itself commemorated a turning-point in the college's history. The play introduced many celebrities, including Mary Somerville, the College Ghost, and the Fisher Baby (Mary Laetitia Somerville Fisher, the infant daughter of the President of the Council); there was a contest between three Senior Students; and 'a note of cheery optimism with regard to the Future dominated the whole.'[96]

Theatrical performances and fancy-dress balls flourished in college during these years. In 1904 the gymnasium platform was enlarged and a curtain rod put up in order to provide a stage for college theatricals. A wardrobe was established, and accommodated in the ottoman in the Gatehouse. It became the fashion to entertain the helpers in the termly 'library dusting', not only with the traditional cocoa and cakes, but also with some form of 'mental diversion' which ranged from Punch and Judy on the lawn to scenes from George Eliot in the gymnasium.[97] A fancy-dress dance at the beginning of Michaelmas Term had become an annual event by 1913: Vera Brittain, accustomed to the social sophistication of Buxton, found it 'very dull dancing with girls after having been to proper dances.'[98]

With the performance by the second-year students in Michaelmas Term 1906 of *The Critic*, followed by a sketch called *A Modern Faustina*, in which the title-role was filled by the authoress, Miss Overend, another Somerville institution came into being: the second-year play. 'There is never any doubt that the Second Year will produce a play at the end of the Michaelmas Term' wrote the Oxford Correspondent for 1910–11, showing how rapidly an immemorial custom can become

---

[96] Log Book, 1913. [97] Oxford Letter, 1905.
[98] Diary for Sat. 24 Oct. 1914, Brittain, *Chronicle of Youth*, 119.

established. That year's offering, *Trelawney of the Wells*, was one of the most successful in Somerville's annals, its memory perpetuated by the naming after it of a new college boat. Hilary Term, inevitably, became the province of the first-year students, who were required to entertain their seniors at the beginning of their second term. Nor were the dons exempt from the obligation to entertain. In Trinity Term 1910 Miss Penrose directed the classics students in a mock Athenian trial, which the Oxford Correspondent politely described as 'an exceedingly interesting performance.' Later the same term the combined SCRs of Somerville, LMH, and St Hilda's put on a performance of *Everyman* in the garden of Radcliffe House. 'It really was a most tremendously sporting thing to do' wrote a student reviewer in *Fritillary*: 'We must have been a very difficult audience to play before—mostly pupils of the cast: but it is the fact that nobody felt the least desire to laugh, even when Good-deeds' [viz. Helen Darbishire's] toes peeped beyond a too scanty curtain.'[99] Miss Walton, the Somerville Bursar, was—it was reported—'terribly convincing' as Death.[100]

An enthusiasm for debating went back to the very early days of the Hall, when in 1882 a group of Somerville students joined with three unattached students to found a women's debating society. This developed into the Somerville and Lady Margaret Halls' Debating Society, and by 1892 had grown sufficiently self-confident to challenge the Cambridge debating societies to the first inter-university debate, held on neutral territory at the Upper Baker Street High School in London. Somervillians were prominent in the debate, Miss Muncaster speaking for the motion (which was lost) 'That the advance of Democracy destroys true liberty'; Misses Lacey, Kirkaldy, and Don against.[101] On the next occasion, in March 1897, Margery Fry proposed and carried the motion 'That the foreign policy of the present government is false to England's highest interests.'[102] St Hugh's Hall—whose students were initially excluded from the society's private business and debarred from holding office—was admitted to full membership in 1893, when the society was transformed into the United Halls' Debating Society (subsequently the Oxford Students' Debating Society). In June 1904, as part of an effort to revitalize the flagging OSDS, the Principals of Lady Margaret Hall and Somerville took part in a special debate on the motion, proposed by Miss Wordsworth (seconded by

[99] *Fritillary*, 50, June 1910.   [100] Oxford Letter, 1910.   [101] *SSA Report*, 1892.
[102] Oxford Letter, 1897.

Annie Rogers), and opposed by Miss Maitland (seconded by Miss Pope), 'That this world would be a howling wilderness without conventionality.'[103]

Aspiring debaters had ample opportunity to sharpen their skills within their own college, through institutions such as Sharp Practice, designed to accustom students to extempore speaking. The format of Sharp Practice meetings varied over the years and from college to college: in Ethel Thomas's time (1909–12) Somervillian participants met in a room with two bowls, one containing names, the other topics; a name and a topic were drawn at random, and the student on whom the lot fell then had to speak for two minutes on the allotted subject. A writer in *Fritillary* in 1897 looked forward, perhaps not entirely in jest, to the day 'when the Leader of the women's party in Parliament shall acknowledge that her exalted position is due entirely to the fluency and assurance gained in the weekly Sharp Practice Debates.'[104]

Though political clubs were discouraged in college, discussion of political issues was fostered. A special lecture on Socialism arranged in 1895 by Lucy Papworth (a future General Secretary of the Women's Industrial Council) was attended by a French visitor to Oxford, who professed himself astonished that a young ladies' college should open its doors to a socialistic meeting:

> The hall [gymnasium] of Somerville was transformed. High up in the gallery the lady students had taken their places; merry and happy, they exchanged pleasantries with those of their friends who were doing the honours of the place. The undergraduates were more serious and were gathered on the floor of the hall round the platform. It was a very curious meeting, owing to the place where it was held, the number of the ladies among the audience, as well as for the peculiar physiognomy of the Fabians.[105]

College Meeting subsequently voted to hold more meetings on the same lines, provided 'that the subject be political rather than Socialistic'; suggested topics included Bimetallism, the Protection system, and Industrial Peace.[106] In 1896 the convention of excluding political topics from Sharp Practice debates was abandoned, following a successful experiment on the subject of 'The Czar's scheme of disarmament'. On a wider stage, Somervillians were particularly prominent in the suffrage movement and in the Oxford Women Students' Fabian

---

[103] *Fritillary*, 32, June 1904.   [104] *Fritillary*, 10, Mar. 1897.
[105] Bardoux, *Memories of Oxford*, 48.   [106] College Meeting, 3 Nov. 1896.

Society, of which in 1908 they filled the offices of president, secretary, and treasurer.[107]

But by the turn of the century the most important forum for political debate in college was unquestionably the Parliamentary Debating Society, soon known simply as 'Parliament'. Copied from Newnham, where it had been going strong since 1884 (inspired perhaps by the presence on the staff of Mr Gladstone's daughter, Helen),[108] the society modelled itself closely on Westminster, with debates conducted on strictly parliamentary lines and members addressing each other formally as 'Honourable Gentlemen'. For the twenty years or so of its existence, Parliament played an important role in fostering an interest in current affairs and canalizing political enthusiasms; it also promoted a grasp of parliamentary and constitutional procedure, on which many were to draw in later life. (Margery Fry claimed to have learned more of definite use in life from the Somerville Parliament than from any direct instruction at Oxford.)[109] Parliament was instituted too late to enable Eleanor Rathbone to practise the skills which in 1927 were to take her as Somerville's first real MP to Westminster. But the judgement of contemporaries may have persuaded the student Member for Aberystwyth, Rose Macaulay, that her talents lay elsewhere: 'On the subject of privilege of Parliament, the torrent of somewhat incoherent language poured forth by Mr Macaulay was truly characteristic of that decidedly erratic politician.'[110]

Parliamentary proceedings were conducted with extreme seriousness. 'It is a wonderfully radical kind of Conservatism that Somerville produces' commented the Oxford Correspondent of an early Conservative government which in 1902 nationalized the railways before resigning upon the passing of a vote censuring its Indian policy; the Liberals in their term of office brought forward a budget at one meeting and a bill for the reform of the House of Lords at another. In the course of 1904/5, when both parties held office, home rule was granted to Ireland, the problem of unemployment was solved by the introduction of a scheme of labour colonies, and alien immigration was regulated. 'The work done by the Somerville Parliament in two short sessions' commented the Oxford Correspondent 'puts St Stephen's to shame.'[111] In 1908 an Irish University Bill was introduced, of which

---

[107] *Fritillary*, 12, Dec. 1897 and 14, June 1908.
[108] She did not attend meetings 'in case her presence should be embarrassing': Phillips, *A Newnham Anthology*, 29.   [109] Huws Jones, *Margery Fry*, 55.
[110] *Fritillary*, 28, March 1903.   [111] Oxford Letter, 1905.

she said that the measure subsequently passed at Westminster seemed but a feeble imitation.

High-minded debates were interspersed with comic set-pieces, important none the less for instilling a sense of constitutional procedure. Hilary Term 1908 was enlivened by the impeachment of 'Stephen Marmaduke, Baron Fry of Failand [a reference to Margery Fry's family home in Somerset], for high crimes and misdemeanours.' The prosecution was conducted by six managers, and the accused defended by Mr G. Hadow, KC and Mr E. Jamison, KC. After a vigorous cross-examination which, it was said, 'shed a lurid light on the past history of certain members of the SCR which would never be forgotten by those privileged to be present', Baron Fry was found guilty of bribery and corruption, and consigned to the Gate House during His Majesty's pleasure.[112]

This period was the heyday of the Somerville Parliament. 'We have never taken anything quite so seriously as we took the Poor Law in the autumn' reported the Oxford Correspondent in 1910—'the huge subject was thrashed out with a thoroughness really admirable.' An indication of Parliament's growing fame came in Hilary Term 1912, with an invitation from the Arnold Society of Balliol to take part in a joint debate on the subject of women's suffrage. It was held on neutral ground, in the Masonic Hall, with the Dean of Balliol, A. L. Smith, in the chair; in his speech of welcome he pointed out 'what a great gulf separated the time when the appearance of a woman student in Balliol caused the Senior Fellow to take to his bed, and the present unique and unprecedented occasion.'[113] To avoid a straight contest between the colleges, two speakers from each spoke for, and two against, the motion 'That this House is resolved that in matters of franchise no distinction should be made between man and woman.' The occasion attracted a good deal of publicity, and was fully reported in the *Westminster Gazette* under the headline 'A New Movement in Oxford'. The Balliol speakers included the President of the Oxford Union, F. K. Griffith, and its Junior Treasurer, W. T. Monckton, both of whom had distinguished political careers before them; but according to the reporter, 'for grasp of the subject and lucid exposition nothing has lately been given equal to . . . [the speeches] of Miss Hunter, Miss Dismorr and other ladies on both sides.'[114] When, after a keen debate,

---

[112] Oxford Letter, 1908.   [113] Report in *Fritillary*, 55, Mar. 1912.
[114] *Westminster Gazette*, 24 Feb. 1912.

a division was taken, eighty-six votes were recorded for the motion and twenty-six against. 'Not a few undergraduates' commented the reporter 'left the hall in deep thought'.

An invitation from the Twenty Club of New College quickly followed, this time to debate, under the chairmanship of H. A. L. Fisher, the motion 'That in the opinion of this House compulsory arbitration between members of the Hague Conference is both practicable and desirable.' Somerville basked in the fame brought by these encounters: 'Apart from the enjoyment that [they] . . . gave us, we are pleased at the courtesy which prompted the invitations.'[115] In Hilary Term 1913 Balliol members of the Arnold Society were invited into Somerville itself, to attend a session of Parliament at which the Unionists brought in a resolution in favour of imperial federation. The guests participated in the debate, and were subsequently entertained to coffee in the West common room.[116] In a return visit the following year, it fell to Dorothy Sayers to propose the motion 'That in the opinion of this House the educated classes at the present time sadly lack enthusiasm'. According to the college Log Book, the evening was not a great success:

> Enthusiasm did not seem to extend beyond the first four speakers, and the large number and gorgeous attire of the Somerville contingent served rather to emphasise their silence, while the somewhat perfunctory and unwilling speeches from the small number of members of the Arnold Society present suggested without conviction the male talent for rising to the occasion in matters of eloquence. There was no division.[117]

A visit to Ruskin College earlier in the term to debate the motion 'That in the opinion of this House the tendency of recent legislation is to produce a servile state' was deemed to have been more successful. Somervillians were clearly more at ease with serious than with frivolous topics.

Preoccupied on the one hand by the activities of their own Parliament, and on the other by these novel expeditions into undergraduate society, Somervillians came increasingly under censure from the other women's colleges for their slack attendance at the Oxford Students' Debating Society. At College Meeting in June 1909 Matilda Snow spoke of 'a feeling abroad among the other Colleges that Somerville

---

[115] Oxford Letter, 1912.   [116] Log Book, HT 1913.   [117] Log Book, HT 1914.

did not take its fair share in Debate', and, after much discussion, it was agreed that one meeting of Parliament should be given up in order that more attention might be devoted to the United Debate.[118] Any improvement was short-lived. The three meetings of OSDS held in the 'rather blighting' atmosphere of the Oxford High School in Trinity Term 1914 attracted five, three, and three Somervillians respectively, most of them officers of the society attending officially. When at the end of Trinity Term 1914 a motion was proposed at College Meeting that Somerville should retire from the joint society, Miss Scott Stokes, quoting these figures, said that no one would notice if it did. The motion was defeated, on the grounds that it would be a pity to emphasize Somerville's difference from the other colleges by not taking this opportunity of mixing up:

> We certainly had a feeling of superiority where OSDS was concerned —but the inferiority of OSDS existed only because of our superiority. . . . We certainly are rather different from the other colleges— more different than they are from each other—and for that very reason we ought to go in larger numbers and mix up with them when we have the chance.

concluded Miss Chubb with—not uncharacteristic—Somervillian condescension.

Sport provided another outlet for Somerville's competitive instincts.[119] An early picture in *The Graphic* (see Plate 5) of 'Life at Somerville Hall' shows a game of lawn tennis in progress in the shade of St Aloysius Church, the players as elaborately be-hatted as the spectators. An annual inter-university match between the women's halls of Oxford and Cambridge was inaugurated in 1883, with a doubles match on a private court in Essex; the gold medal and silver owl prizes presented by two members of the Girton Committee for the first and second champions on the winning side are the earliest recorded challenge trophies in women's inter-university sport.[120] The match soon became a social as well as a sporting highlight of the year, and one in which former students took a keen interest. When the Somerville

---

[118] College Meeting, 17 June 1909.

[119] For the importance of sport in the advancement of women in the late 19th century, see K. E. McCrone, *Sport and the Physical Emancipation of English Women* (London, 1988), esp. ch. 2, 'The Lady Blue'.

[120] McCrone, *Sport and Emancipation of English Women*, 27. Girton's silver owl was exhibited, together with some of Somerville's sports cups, in the 'Sporting Trophies' exhibition at the Victoria and Albert Museum in 1992.

Students' Association was set up in 1888, its rules provided for two social meetings a year in London, one to be held early in January and the other on the evening of the tennis match; and one of the duties laid upon the Oxford Correspondent was to report the result of the match.[121]

Somerville's future Vice-Principal, Alice Bruce, first made her mark in the college annals in 1890 as one of the tennis champions who, after defeating LMH and St Hugh's, went on to beat united Girton and Newnham by three sets to love at a match hosted at Lambeth Palace by the Archbishop of Canterbury.[122] The *SSA Report* for that year contained an appeal by an old student, Lilian Faithfull, for the provision of silver cups or bowls as prizes for the inter-university lawn tennis match, to supplement the owl and brooch presented 'in the infancy of the Halls'.[123] Her proposal that 'some badge should be decided upon, which only those who have played in a University Match would have a right to wear', as a means of showing that a girl had 'got her blue' was implemented the following year.[124] Somerville's facilities were gradually upgraded, and after alterations to the level of the courts in 1908 home matches no longer had to be played through the branches of the cedar tree. In 1914 an old Somervillian, Miss Wolferstan, presented the tennis club with a silver cup to be competed for as a championship cup in college.

As a student during 1883–7, Lilian Faithfull had been Somerville's first captain of hockey. In her autobiography she recalled the excitement of the first inter-collegiate hockey match,

—our disgust at the defeat of Somerville after her captain had been laid low with a black eye from someone else's stick, and our triumph on hearing that Lady Margaret in the flush of its first victory had imitated the undergraduates and had a bonfire in the garden, with the result that hockey had been forbidden for the ensuing term.[125]

At this date, hockey matches were played on the Somerville tennis courts, which Eleanor Lodge of LMH recalled as including 'one or two little banks and a bush or two', though she does not mention

---

[121] SSA Rules (1888).

[122] Archbishop Benson hosted the match in memory of his daughter, a former student at Lady Margaret Hall: McCrone, *Sport and Emancipation of English Women*, 28.

[123] *SSA Report*, 1890, 12.

[124] McCrone, *Sport and Emancipation of English Women*, 44.

[125] L. M. Faithfull, *In the House of My Pilgrimage* (London, 1924), 62.

the cedar.[126] In 1894 Somerville hired a hockey field by the river, and supplied four of the players in the first university match against Cambridge—an event reported in the *St James's Gazette* with much greater emphasis on what the teams wore (in Oxford's case 'dark blue skirts and shirts, with white collars and cuffs, and dark blue caps embroidered in white with crossed hockey sticks and the letters OHHS') than on how they played.[127] By 1898 the college hockey club had so many members that it was able to institute second and third eleven matches—though the availability of so much talent did not prevent the students' team from losing, for the first time on record, the 'Past v. Present' hockey match which was held on the day of the SSA General Meeting. In 1908 a coach was engaged, in an attempt to improve the standard of play; and the following year Miss Bruce offered prizes for a competition in such essential skills as passing and hard-hitting. In 1910 the appearance of the Somerville hockey teams was transformed, with the substitution of red serge skirts for the old black ones.[128] The new skirts, worn twelve inches off the ground, were called 'frills' and considered very daring.[129] In 1912 the women's inter-university hockey cup, instituted fifteen years before, came for the first time to Oxford. Four Somervillians played in the winning team, and, to celebrate, a 'cup dinner' was held in college, with Miss Pope, herself a former blue, proposing the health of the team.[130]

Somerville's initiation into the pleasures of the river is also recorded by Lilian Faithfull:

> A boat on the river was much coveted, and a sympathetic Professor selected four of us, and himself acted as cox. The authorities considered it imperative that our first appearance should be at a time when we should not meet any of the undergraduates, and we had one glorious hour of coaching before breakfast on a May morning on the Cherwell, but why it was never repeated and no race ever took place we never knew.[131]

Racing, for women in Oxford, was still far in the distance. But in 1889 the hiring of a boat on the Cherwell brought their ambitions a step nearer to fulfilment. Eleanor Powell, the Oxford Correspondent that year, reported that considerable progress had been made in the arts

---

[126] E. C. Lodge, *Terms and Vacations* ed. Janet Spens (London, 1938), 57.

[127] *St James's Gazette*, 15 Mar. 1894. Cambridge won 3–1.   [128] Oxford Letter, 1910.

[129] Frankenburg, *Not Old, Madam, Vintage*, 68.   [130] Oxford Letter, 1912.

[131] Faithfull, *In the House of My Pilgrimage*, 62.

of rowing, sculling, and steering by those students who had succeeded in passing the preliminary fifty feet swimming test, and that
Somerville had engaged a place in a new boat-house which was to
be built. 'We look forward' she concluded, 'to having a boat of our
own at no distant date if the fates are propitious.' It was not in fact the
fates but Miss Powell's own generosity which was responsible for the
acquisition soon afterwards of the 'Urmila'—Somerville's first, and
most celebrated, boat—which, in commemoration of the presence
in Somerville of three Indian students (Cornelia Sorabji, and the
princesses Bamba and Catherine Duleep Singh), was given the San-
skrit name for the lotus flower, one letter of the word being inscribed
on each of the six sculls in English and in Gujarati characters.

Somerville students took to the river with passionate enthusiasm,
and by 1895 the boat club had grown so much that it felt obliged to
remodel its constitution on more democratic lines, and to accommodate its increased numbers by hiring another double scull outrigger.
In 1898, with the help of a loan from Council, a boat-house capable of
holding six boats was built on a site adjoining the hockey-field. An
article in *The Ladies' Field* stressed the care taken to avoid offending
the sensibilities of the men's colleges:

> A Somerville boat would be very much disliked on the river, so,
> though the college owns five boats, two canoes and a punt, these are
> kept on the Cherwell. . . . On the lower river these boats never
> appear; they sometimes go on the upper river for picnics, but that is
> all.[132]

Somerville steadily increased its stock of boats, their names often
commemorating recent college events: 'Demeter' in 1905, 'Outdoor
Relief' in 1910 (the year in which Parliament attempted to deal with
poor law reform), 'Trelawny' in 1911. Two new outrigs, 'Thyi' and
'Donec Rursus Impleat' were presented by Mr Watson in 1910; and in
the glorious summer which followed College acquired a punt and a
canoe, and built a punt-shed on to the wooden paling of the Rhea
bathing place. The practice of hiring a four for a month in Hilary
Term became so popular that in 1914 the more strenuous members of
the boat club expressed the wish to have it for both winter terms in
future.[133] Proficiency tests for boating became more severe, with the
addition of tests in canoe paddling and punting, and the institution

---

[132] *Ladies' Field*, 31 Dec. 1898, 106–8.   [133] Oxford Letter, 1914.

of a 'degrading test' for half-captains.[134] In 1910, in response to a series of river accidents, and the 'not infrequent confession of the victims that at the critical moment "they forgot how to swim"', a stringent reform in the swimming test was made.[135]

The possibility of indoor exercise in bad weather was opened up in 1890 with the erection at the eastern end of the West building of a college gymnasium—the gift of Miss Shaw Lefevre's friend, Miss Forster. In a first flush of enthusiasm, students rushed to Elliston & Cavell to have gym costumes made: 'I think' reported Cornelia Sorabji 'they are to sort with our emblem the blackberry and be a bluey black with ribbons and material of pale pink and green.'[136] The following week she announced the acquisition of 'blue knickerbockers, a short pleated skirt above the knees—like a child's sailor suit—and a loose blouse . . . with light collar and cuffs'—the latter chosen in preference to the 'sailor blouses with buff fronts' affected by some of her friends.[137] A sergeant from the Cowley military school was imported to give lessons to those students who wanted them. His classes were somewhat fitfully attended, though fencing lessons proved popular.[138] Once the novelty had worn off, the gymnasium was less and less used, and in 1922 it was converted to provide two students' rooms and a lecture room.

Cycling, which hit Oxford in the course of the 1890s, was to enjoy a longer future. By 1896 the coach house at one end of the drive, and the stable at the other, had been commandeered as bicycle sheds, and learner riders wobbled perilously along the paths between. As Somerville's cyclists became more adept, the college garden became more hazardous: 'Cycling has . . . been practised with much vigour, and the garden has been rendered dangerous to the peaceable inhabitant by the perpetual gymkhana feats attempted by the more skilful riders,' reported the Oxford Correspondent the following year. It would be difficult to over-estimate the sense of liberation which mastery of a bicycle gave to women of this generation. For years to come an immense amount of time at College Meetings was taken up by the question of bicycles: where to house them, where not to ride them, what sanctions to apply to those who 'borrowed' other people's. In 1900 control of the college bicycle stalls was vested in the recently established Amalgamation Committee, which administered the funds

---

[134] Oxford Letter, 1905.   [135] Oxford Letter, 1910.
[136] Sorabji, 15 Jan. 1891 (India Office Library MSS Eur.F.165/4).
[137] Sorabji, 24 Jan. 1891, ibid.   [138] *Lady's Pictorial*, 2 Jan. 1892.

of the common room and the amalgamated games' club, special responsibility for bicycles being given to one of the three elected student members.[139] During Dorothy Sayers's term of office as Senior Bicycle Secretary in 1915 (the burden of work having by that time become too great for one person) the rules were enforced with notorious severity: her policy of impounding any bicycles found in the gatehouses or the Maitland loggia, and releasing them only on payment of a fine, featured prominently in that summer's going-down play:

BICYCLE SECRETARY'S SONG

It's well to be methodical where culprits are concerned
So I've made a little list! I've made a little list!
Of members of this commonwealth who ought to be interned
And who never would be missed! Who never would be missed!
The brutes who borrow bicycles without their owners' leave,
Who get their own in pound and come and ask for a reprieve;
Who take their breakfast on the Cher at half-past six A.M.,
And say they thought the general rule did not apply to them.
The people with excuses that you simply can't resist,
I'm sure they won't be missed, I'm sure they won't be missed.

CHORUS
She's got them on her list, she's got them on her list, And we're sure they
won't be missed, we're sure they won't be missed.

The folk who leave their bikes about say twenty times a term
I've got them on the list! I've got them on the list!
Who say they had a label once, which wasn't tied on firm—
I'm sure they won't be missed, I'm sure they won't be missed.
Who let your notice stare them in the face a week or more,
And then complain they've never seen the beastly thing before;
Who think the fines augment the Secretary's bank account;
Who ask more foolish questions in a day than you can count;
Who rise at College meetings and who argue and insist,
I'm sure they won't be missed, I'm sure they won't be missed.

---

[139] The Committee, established in Michaelmas Term 1898, consisted of the Senior and Junior Treasurers, the Senior Students of the Old Hall and of the West Buildings, the Presidents of the Boat and Tennis Clubs, the Captain of the Hockey Club, the Secretary of the Gymnasium, and three students elected annually by the College.

CHORUS

But these are not the only pests that poison College life,
And I've made a little list! I've made a little list!
Of those who shake the midnight air with dialectic strife,
And who never would be missed, who never would be missed.
The nymphs who stroll at breakfast-time in nightgowns made of silk;
The people who remove your books, your matches and your milk;
The blighters who drop catalogues and whisper in the Bod.,
Or whistle Bach or Verdi as they walk across the quad;
The superficial sceptic and the keen philanthropist,
They'll none of them be missed! They'll none of them be missed!

CHORUS

Student life in all its aspects was profoundly affected by the war.
Rules governing the conduct of women students were modified,
though not always in the direction of greater freedom: after the move
to Oriel the George Café was put out of bounds.[140] With staff and students scattered in lodging-houses around Oxford, many of the old
college institutions could no longer be maintained. The second-year
Christmas play was abandoned. Societies found it increasingly difficult to secure outside speakers. The Literary and Philosophical Society,
which in 1915 heard papers on 'The Elder Edda and Icelandic Saga'
from the Lady Carlisle research fellow, Miss Bertha Phillpotts, and on
'Belgian Poetry' from a refugee from the University of Louvain, Professor Doutrepont, was reduced in 1916 to discussions among the
members themselves of such topics as Japanese drama, Myths, and
Australian literature, and shortly afterwards came to an end. There
was a party truce in Parliament, and controversial matters were elimi-
nated from debate; the parliamentary highlight of the war years was
the impeachment in Michaelmas Term 1917 of Miss Lorimer, who was
eventually acquitted by her peers of the charges of starting the fire in
Salonika and of seditious dealings with the enemy.[141] The move to
Oriel placed Somervillians at a greater distance than ever from their
playing-fields; and sport—despite the encouragement of Somerville's
athletic new Bursar, Miss Stonedale—inevitably suffered from the
demands made by war work on students' time. The closure of the
Merton Street swimming baths in 1916 dealt a blow to the boat club by
preventing many students from taking their annual swimming test.

---

[140] College Meeting, 29 Apr. 1915.   [141] Log Book, MT 1917.

One notable new enthusiast for the river emerged, however, against the trend: the Oxford Correspondent reported in 1915 that 'Miss Penrose has acquired great skill in the art of canoeing, and the Boat Club are delighted with her ardour for the river—an ardour which even the most unpropitious weather fails to damp.'

One college institution survived intact: the going-down plays, transformed into open-air events performed in the St Mary quadrangle, were, if anything, enhanced by the peculiar domestic circumstances in which Somerville now found itself. The 1915 play, *Pied Pipings, or the Innocents Abroad*—a skit emphasizing the futility of modern research—was partly written by Dorothy Sayers, who in the role of the Pied Piper gave a memorable impersonation of the conductor of the Bach Choir, Sir Hugh Allen (Plate 24). The 1916 play, *A Mess of Pottage*, had as its theme the poverty of the university in wartime and the consequent advantages of giving degrees to women, a secondary theme being the absence on war service of so many of the Somerville dons. The weather during Somerville's last week at Oriel was so bad that the 1919 play, *Paradise Regained; or, It's a Long Way to Tipperary*, was transferred at the last minute to a hall in St Aldates. Among the many topical allusions was an interlude consisting of the Bally Flu Ballet, in which the maidens were overcome by malevolent germs, but finally rescued by two deliverers armed with gigantic thermometers. But the play's main theme was the college's impending return to its own premises; as staff and students joined together in the celebratory grand finale 'Way back to Somerville' they might well (had they not been too excited) have reflected on the gulf—now much greater than that noted by A. L. Smith in 1912—which separated their own circumstances from those of Somerville's first arrivals forty years before.

Part II

1920 – 1939

7

University Membership and
College Charter, 1920–1926

SOMERVILLE celebrated its return to its own buildings in the summer of 1919 with an orgy of destruction. In the process of unpacking there emerged from wartime storage what Vera Farnell termed 'certain unsightly relics of the past'—furniture, pictures, plaster casts—which were ceremonially burned in a great bonfire in the garden. There was particular rejoicing at the dispatch of a much-despised oil-painting from the JCR known as 'Junior Cows' under whose paralysing stare generations of schoolgirls had been obliged to sit the Somerville scholarship examination.[1]

So far as the status of women was concerned, the Great War had been a 'wonderful period of progress'.[2] The extension of the parliamentary franchise to women above the age of 30 gave rise, however, to an anomalous situation at Oxford and Cambridge, where women, though still not admitted to degrees, were now entitled under certain conditions to vote for the parliamentary representatives of the university.[3] On 13 March 1918 the *University Gazette* published a letter from the Vice-Chancellor to the effect that 'all women who have been admitted to and passed the final examination, and kept the period of residence necessary for a man to obtain a degree at a University, are entitled, provided they have attained the age of 30 years, to be registered as Parliamentary Electors for the University.' By the beginning of September, 163 Somervillians had claimed their entitlement.

Among the factors now working in favour of the women's cause was a potent economic one. Wartime inflation had halved the value of the university's endowment and fixed income, and when in 1918 the newer state-aided universities formed a deputation to ask the

---

[1] V. Farnell, *A Somervillian Looks Back* (Oxford, 1948), 45.

[2] *Daily Telegraph*, 21 Feb. 1920, quoted in R. McWilliams-Tullberg, *Women at Cambridge: A Men's University—Though of a Mixed Type* (London, 1975), 151.

[3] The privilege, granted to the University by James I in 1604, of sending two Burgesses to Parliament, was abolished by the Labour Government of 1945–51.

Government for an increase in public funding, Oxford and Cambridge accepted an invitation to join in the request. After submitting applications based on their financial needs, both received interim awards from the government; but the price of state aid was an acceptance—which many found unpalatable—of a much greater degree of public interference in their internal affairs. One of the questions on which the press now focused its attention was that of degrees for women:

> At Oxford and Cambridge the old illiberal exclusiveness, alien to the country as a whole, still lingers in many minds. But now that these two universities are appealing to the nation for aid from its taxes, it would not be unreasonable for the nation's stewards to ask that a share in the benefits of any contributions it may make should be equally open to the future citizens and ratepayers of either sex.[4]

In Oxford, at least, the champions of degrees for women were by now preaching to the converted. During the war, with most male undergraduates and many male dons away on active service, it was to a large extent the women who had kept the wheels of academic life turning. Women tutors had lectured for the university; the fees of women students provided it with a crucial source of revenue. One of the last bastions of male exclusivity had fallen in 1917, when, on the initiative of the faculty of medicine, the first BM examination was opened to women. (The Professor of Human Anatomy insisted, nevertheless, on a separate laboratory for women students, to meet which requirement the Clothworkers' Company undertook to provide a dissecting-room for their use.) That June a statute allowing for the matriculation of women students was provisionally approved by the Hebdomadal Council, its progress being delayed for over a year while the university took legal advice on whether such a step required the sanction of Parliament. The Sex Disqualification (Removal) Act of 1919, which contained a clause expressly permitting the ancient universities to matriculate women without further legislation, resolved this legal uncertainty. A statute was drawn up in Michaelmas Term 1919, and after considerable redrafting was submitted to Congregation the following Hilary. It was passed without a division.

The University, which had taken so long to act, did so in the end with unexpected generosity. The 1920 statute opened up to women not

---

[4] *Manchester Guardian*, 28 July 1919.

only matriculation and all degrees (except that of Divinity, which was still the exclusive preserve of those in holy orders), but also membership of Convocation and Congregation, faculties and faculty boards. A certain amount of opposition to the statute was encountered; but amendments intended to exclude women from serving on delegacies, boards, and committees, and from acting as university examiners, were soundly defeated. An editorial in the *Oxford Magazine*, congratulating Council on its decision to introduce the statute, paid tribute to those 'who have organized women's education in Oxford with such signal tact and success':

> The staffs of the women's colleges can claim that the proposal of 'full privileges' (or something very like it) comes unsolicited, in response to no deputation or agitation of theirs or their pupils. It is pleasing, but perhaps presumptuous, to hope that the privileges may be granted with the same grace with which their prolongued refusal has been endured.[5]

Somerville presented its first candidates for matriculation on 7 October, and its first degree candidates the following week (Plate 19), and held a great dinner in hall at which real cream was served with the pudding and toasts were drunk in lemonade to celebrate what the *Oxford Magazine* described as 'a victory won by courtesy, patience, and merit alone'.

Vera Brittain, whose relations with Miss Penrose had not always been easy, attended the ceremony in the Sheldonian at which the degree of MA by decree was conferred upon the Principals of the five women's societies (none of whom had satisfied the full requirements of the statute):

> What a consummation of her life-work this was for her! I reflected, with a feeling of partisan warmth towards the intellectually arrogant college whose Principal, more than any other Oxford woman, had been responsible for the symbolic celebrations of that morning. Brought up in the nineteenth-century educational tradition, she was an academic Metternich of an older regime—but it was a Metternich that the War and post-war periods had required. Her task, during those complicated years, of reconciling college and University, don and student, man and woman, war-service and academic work, conscience and discretion, had been colossal in its demands upon tact

[5] *Oxford Magazine*, 28 Nov. 1919.

and ingenuity, and probably no woman living would have done it so well.[6]

In the 1920 Oxford Letter Somerville expressed particular gratitude to the two members of its Council, Professor Geldart and Mr Lindsay, who had introduced the statute in Congregation; and in the following year was able to report that:

> the woman undergraduate in her soft square cap and scholar's or commoner's gown is no longer a sight to arouse wonder among the passers-by. The unfailing generosity and courtesy of the University has made our entry within the charmed circle a singularly pleasant one, and despite inevitable mistakes and blunders, we are settling down in our new position with ease and great happiness.[7]

The soft cap—'a judicious compromise between Portia and Nerissa'— in fact constituted something of a grievance, forced upon the women by proctorial authority when their own strong preference was for the traditional mortar-board.[8] In the years ahead even such a stickler for correctness as Miss Penrose avoided wearing the offensive headgear whenever she could.

Under the provisions of the statute, those women who had in the past fulfilled all the university conditions of residence and examinations were entitled, for a limited period, to claim their degree. Once again Somerville reaped the benefits of Miss Penrose's foresight, and in October 1920 it had some 300 past students—the largest number of all the women's colleges—qualified to proceed immediately to the BA. Many other women, determined to complete their qualifications, took up temporary residence in Oxford and submitted themselves, years after having done Schools, to the indignity of sitting 'Smalls', 'Divvers', and 'A1'.

Women hastened to take advantage of the opportunities and university prizes now open to them. In 1923 a recent Somerville graduate, Margaret Hobling, became the first woman to receive an Oxford University Studentship at the British School at Rome. In 1924 May McKisack was the first woman to win the Lothian Prize, in 1931 her fellow-medievalist Naomi Hurnard the first to win the Stanhope Prize. Even so, it was to be some time before women—particularly at senior

---

[6] V. Brittain, *Testament of Youth: An Autobiographical Study of the Years 1900–1925* (London, 1978), 507–8. [7] Oxford Letter, 1921.
[8] A. Rogers, *Degrees by Degrees: The Story of the Admission of Oxford Women Students to Membership of the University* (London, 1938), 114–15.

level—came to exercise fully the rights and privileges which their membership of the university in theory conferred. Experience in lecturing (Plate 43), examining, and administration which would enable women to play an effective part in the university and qualify for its senior posts, was gained only slowly. The way was led by Miss Pope, who was appointed as Taylorian Lecturer in 1920 (while taking on temporarily the work of the Professor of Romance Philology), and an examiner in the final honour school of French in 1922; in 1927 she became the first woman to hold a university readership. Miss Darbishire, one of the first three women to be appointed to a university lecturership, later became the first woman chairman of a faculty board. But, even in traditional 'women's subjects' like modern languages and English, such appointments were exceptional. Ironically, Cambridge, which in December 1920 decisively rejected proposals to admit women to full membership of the university,[9] showed greater initiative in this respect. Muriel Bradbrook had already examined for Cambridge when, at the age of 26, she came to Somerville for a year in the mid-1930s, and was astonished to find that such an opportunity had never come the way of many, much more senior, Oxford women dons:

> 'I prefer justice to favours' one of them haughtily remarked to me, with a flash of old feminist spirit; but Cambridge felt it was more important to revise the Tripos syllabus than to protest at Q's habit of addressing his audience as 'Gentlemen'.[10]

In the course of almost thirty years as a tutorial fellow in English, from 1932 to 1960, Mary Lascelles was to have only one three-year stint of examining in the final honour school. The experience, which came late in her teaching career, gave, she said, 'much needed insight into a seemingly mysterious system. Without this, we seemed to be teaching in the dark.'[11] It was not until the 1960s that women dons were fully absorbed into this most important aspect of university life; there is little doubt that both they and their pupils were handicapped by their unfamiliarity with the system.

But such reflections were far in the future in 1920, as the rhythms of college life and hospitality, so long disrupted by wartime conditions, were gradually resumed. In May 1921 the university conferred

---

[9] In 1923 they were made eligible instead for titular degrees which gave them no voice in university government.
[10] M. C. Bradbrook, *That Infidel Place: A Short History of Girton College 1869–1969* (London, 1969), 70–1. 'Q' was the Professor of English Literature at Cambridge, Sir Arthur Quiller-Couch. [11] M. Lascelles, *A Memoir* (privately printed, 1989), 65.

the degree of DCL by diploma on Queen Mary, who afterwards visited Somerville (Plate 20) and met a number of Somervillian grandchildren —among them the seven-month old Anthony Huxley (grandson of Julia Arnold), of whom the Queen was twice in the course of the afternoon heard to remark 'If heredity predicts rightly, he will become a great man.'[12] Trinity Term 1922 saw the revival of the pre-war institution of 'Somerville Saturday', with a garden party to which were invited, besides Old Somervillians, Mr George Trevelyan and the members of a delegation of Italian mayors and representatives of commerce on a visit to the chief cities of England and Scotland. During the long vacation of 1924 the Principal and SCR gave tea to an overseas party from the Imperial Education Conference, and hosted the annual dinner of the Federation of University Women. When an Indian student of the College, Mary Chandy, married Mr George Matthai in St Giles' Church in 1924 she anticipated Harriet Vane by over ten years in choosing to be given away by the Principal.

Among the long-postponed projects which were now put in hand was the construction of a garden in memory of Miss Shaw Lefevre, who had died at the beginning of the war. In 1922 the ground on Somerville's southern boundary was cleared, levelled, and laid out with lawns and wide beds of flowers around a sundial inscribed with her name. A yew hedge was planted on the eastern side to divide the Shaw Lefevre memorial garden from the main college garden; a boundary to the north was provided by the old stone wall (into which was set an ancient door which Miss Lefevre had discovered in the cellar beneath Walton House, and which was thought to be a relic of an earlier building on the same site), and to the west by a line of old trees (soon to be demolished to make way for the Penrose building); to the south the garden looked out over open ground including part of the old ropewalk. The college porter, Payne, who had known Radcliffe Row as a boy, was able to locate the position of the old ropemakers' boiler from the pitch which was dug up in the course of preparing the ground. An old leaden waterhead belonging to the cottages which had once occupied the site was set up again as a pump.[13]

Two new tutors joined the college at the end of the war, Charlotte Young moving direct from the JCR to succeed Eglantyne Jebb as assistant tutor in English, and Maude Clarke (formerly of LMH)

---

[12] Juliette Huxley, *Leaves of the Tulip Tree* (London, 1986), 100–1 (where the occasion is wrongly described as a party to celebrate Somerville's 50th jubilee).
[13] Oxford Letter, 1923.

returning to Oxford from Belfast, where during the war she had deputized for the Professor of Modern History, to take over from Mary Coate as tutor in history. (She was later to describe as 'like coming from darkness to daylight' her move to Somerville 'from the selfish intrigues of a provincial university, demoralised by the war.'[14]) With the establishment in 1921 of the new honour school of philosophy, politics, and economics (PPE, or 'Modern Greats'), Somerville appointed as its first tutor in economics and political science a young Girton graduate, Miss Doris Rhodes.

Within the college, the status of the tutors was now enhanced by their admission to membership of the Council. The initiative for this development—long advocated by Margery Fry—came from the new Secretary of Barnett House (and future Principal of the Home Students), Grace Hadow, who at the 1920 General Meeting proposed the appointment of a committee to consider the best method of altering the articles of association so as to provide for the representation on Council of the college staff. A new constitution, based on the committee's recommendations, was adopted on 19 December 1921: the *ex officio* members of Council were retained, but the number of 'outside' members was reduced to fifteen, and provision was made for the election of not less than six and not more than nine 'official fellows' from among those holding teaching or administrative posts on the college staff. At the next meeting of Council Miss Bruce, Miss Pope, Miss Lorimer, Miss Darbishire, Miss Clarke, and Miss Stonedale were elected as Somerville's first official fellows. A further step towards self-government was made later in 1922, with the appointment of Miss Helene Reynard—a former junior bursar of Girton—as the college's first full-time Secretary and Treasurer. Miss Penrose, in reporting these changes to the SSA, put on record Somerville's indebtedness to the succession of honorary Treasurers[15] and Secretaries[16] who had so generously served the college for the first forty-three years of its existence.

Throughout the university, finance was to be a major preoccupation of the post-war years. The Somerville Council, faced with a deficit of £1,776.8s.6d. on the revenue account, and no prospect of

[14] MVC to EP, 24 Nov. 1925.
[15] A. H. Acland (1879–85), Dr Woods (1885–97), Sir William Markby (1897–8), Dr Heberden (1898–1907), Professor Henry Miers (1908), H. T. Gerrans (1908–12), and A. B. Gillett (1912–22).
[16] Mrs Humphry Ward (1879–80), Mrs Vernon Harcourt (1879–96), Mrs Massie (1896–1911), Mrs Leigh (1912–18), Miss Darbishire (1919–20) and Mrs Leys (1920–2).

substantial improvement, agreed in Michaelmas Term 1919 to solicit voluntary payments from the parents of students on top of the increased fees already announced.[17] By October 1922 the annual fee, which pre-war had stood at £102, had risen in line with inflation to £150. In response to an appeal for the enlargement of the Radcliffe Infirmary, the Treasurer replied in November 1919 that 'in its present state of insolvency the College could not now offer any donation', though it would wish to reconsider the matter in a year's time.[18] It was to be in no better position then; in November 1920 the finance committee asked Council to sanction the sale of £2,000 worth of stock, part of an anonymous gift from an old student, to meet the current deficit on the revenue account. Apart from a few scholarships, Somerville's endowment income at this date amounted to £25 p.a. It was probably the richest of the women's colleges.

No one, in fact, had seriously considered the financial implications —which were now becoming painfully obvious—of admitting women to university membership. Most pressing was the question of academic stipends. The income (including fees from outside pupils) of resident tutors at the Oxford women's colleges at this date varied from £257 to £438, with an average of £349; the minimum scale of salaries for university lecturers recently proposed by Sir Michael Sadler's Committee of the Association of University Teachers was £400 rising by increments of £25 to £650.[19] With a view to making joint representations to the government for a Treasury grant, the five women's societies spent the Michaelmas Term of 1919 drawing up statements of need based on expenditure on stipends and pensions as well as capital expenditure on buildings, equipment, and libraries. In November they were advised to wait to lay their case before the newly appointed University Commission; but the Somerville Council had an answer ready prepared when in the same month it received an enquiry as to what use it could make of a capital sum of £20,000, or an annual income of £1,000. The query was made on behalf of the trustees administering a gift of £500,000 by Sir Ernest Cassel for educational purposes, one of which was 'the promotion of the higher education of women by the assistance of Colleges for Women'. St Hilda's received a similar approach; LMH and St Hugh's were ineligible by virtue of

---

[17] Minutes of Council, 23 Sept. 1919; Finance Committee, 19 Dec. 1919 and 6 Feb. 1920.　　[18] Minutes of Council, 29 Nov. 1919.
[19] Memorandum by EP on Women's Colleges at Oxford, presented to the Universities Commission.

their denominational status. By the end of November the trustees had confirmed an annual grant to Somerville of £1,250, the first call on which would be to make provision for academic stipends and pensions, and which would be reviewed after five years in the light of any changes brought about by the Royal Commission.[20] The tutors, in expressing gratitude to the Council for the consideration shown them in the allocation of the Cassel grant, expressed the hope that the salaries of the administrative staff would be reviewed as soon as possible.[21]

Since Miss Penrose was herself a member of the Royal Commission, it fell to Dr Heberden and Miss Bruce to give evidence on Somerville's financial needs, estimated by the Council at £2,400 per annum.[22] The Commissioners were impressed by the women's case, and when in 1923 a government grant of £60,000 p.a. to the University was announced, £40,000 of it was earmarked to give temporary assistance for the next ten years to the women's colleges, half of this sum being set aside for stipends and pensions. The grant was made on the understanding that the colleges would make every effort in this period to increase their endowment so as to make themselves self-supporting.

They had already begun to take steps to do so. In October 1920 the Principal of LMH wrote to the Councils of the other women's colleges proposing a joint appeal for the endowment of women's education in Oxford. Somerville agreed to co-operate in this venture, while making a special college appeal at the same time. On 17 January 1921 an appeal on behalf of the women's colleges was published in the principal daily newspapers; signatories included the Chancellor of the University, Lord Curzon, Lord Bryce, H. H. Asquith, A. L. Smith, Professor Gilbert Murray, and Lady Rhondda, the Treasurer of the Appeal. A circular issued at the same time to old members and friends of Somerville spelled out in greater detail the specific needs of the college: loan repayments, amounting to £1,100 a year, on its property and buildings; endowment for the library, scholarships, and research; the provision of adequate stipends and pensions for the staff; expansion of the college's teaching strength to enable Somerville 'to take its full share in University teaching and to help meet the growing demands of new subjects.' In all, a foundation fund of £80,000 would be

---

[20] Special Meeting of Council, 29 Nov. 1919.
[21] Extraordinary Meeting of Council, 15 Mar. 1920.
[22] Meeting of Council, 19 Oct. 1920.

required to meet these needs, and to relieve the 'harassing uncertainty' of the college's current financial position.[23]

By the summer of 1923 Somerville had received some £8,000 from the two appeals. It was a relatively small return for a great deal of effort. Past students had thrown themselves enthusiastically into organizing fund-raising dances, concerts, lectures, and sales of work; current undergraduates donated to the endowment fund the small proceeds of tennis tournaments and 'special effort weeks'. A sale of Christmas presents held in the JCR in December 1921 raised £150: Miss Penrose contributed some sketches of Switzerland, and Helen Waddell some embroidery and lace sent specially from Ireland; Miss Farnell conducted an auction of *punto* work done by the Principal; undergraduates supplied interludes of music and drama, and Hilda Reid told fortunes on the Hall staircase. A similar event was held in London later in the week. In reporting the use of the college in the long vacation of 1923 by a group of University Extension students and three summer schools, the Oxford Correspondent noted that the conferences had all subscribed generously to the endowment fund. But the world at large—as the organizer of the joint appeal, Cecil Percival (a former LMH student and the daughter-in-law of Somerville's first President), discovered—regarded the needs of the women's colleges with 'absolute indifference.'[24] In corresponding with the Cassel trustees about the proposed conversion of their annual grant into a capital sum, Miss Reynard explained, in words that were to echo down the years, 'The lack of capital endowment is the weakest spot in the financial position of the College.'[25]

There was also a weakness in its constitutional position, which was still that of a joint-stock limited-liability company. The creation of fellows in 1922 fitted awkwardly into the old framework, underlining a generally felt need to place the women's colleges on a more regular constitutional footing. The reverberations of the 'St Hugh's Row' of 1923–4, when a popular tutor was summarily dismissed for allegedly attempting to undermine the principal's authority, brought home forcefully the shortcomings of existing arrangements, and in particular the desirability of establishing some kind of visitatorial jurisdiction.[26] In

---

[23] 'Somerville College Endowment Fund' Appeal document.
[24] Somerville Appeal File.
[25] H. Reynard to A. E. Twentyman, 21 Dec. 1923 (Finance Committee Minutes).
[26] See the chapter by Rachel Trickett in P. Griffin (ed.), *St Hugh's: One Hundred Years of Women's Education in Oxford* (London, 1986).

1924 a committee of the Somerville Council recommended that the existing incorporation of the whole body of Somerville members be replaced by that of the Principal and Council. A draft charter was submitted to an extraordinary meeting of Members of the College on 7 November 1925; incorporation took place on 7 June 1926 with its approval by the King in Council. Further meetings were held on 8 June and 3 July to authorize the voluntary liquidation of the old limited-liability company; and a final meeting on 9 October received the report of the liquidators and concluded the transition period between the death of the old company and the birth of the new corporation. In embarking on these complicated constitutional proceedings Somerville was fortunate in having as President one of Oxford's most experienced administrators, the University Registrar, Edwin Craig. The last chairman under the old dispensation, he now became the first vice-chairman under the new, and was elected (together with Mrs Green, Mrs Poulton, and Professor Murray) one of Somerville's four life-members under the terms of the charter.

One of the committee's chief concerns in drafting the charter had been to safeguard the close relationship with the college of the member-shareholders of the old dispensation. To this end, a new body —the Association of Senior Members of the College—was established to replace two existing (and largely overlapping) ones, the Members of the College and the Somerville Students' Association.[27] At the time of the change, there were some 460 Members of the College who were also life members of the SSA (and who had paid life membership fees in both societies), and some 300 SSA members who were not Members of College. Membership of the ASM was now offered to all except the undergraduate members of the SSA. It was agreed that the SSA should hand over to the college the balance of its funds representing the life subscriptions of its members, and that the college in return should accept full financial responsibility for the new Association and its meetings. The ASM was to have its own chairman and hold two meetings annually; it was empowered to elect a total of six members of Council and to submit resolutions to Council. The ASM came into being with the charter, and existed side by side with the SSA until the meeting at Oxford on 9 October, when the chairman and committee were elected, and it became a fully organized Association.

The granting of the college charter provided a fitting climax to Miss

---

[27] *SSA Report*, 1925, 'The SSA and the Somerville College Charter'.

Penrose's principalship. When she retired in June 1926, the University conferred on her an honorary DCL—a gesture which was seen not only as a tribute to the esteem which she personally enjoyed, but as an official seal on the status of women academics in Oxford. Miss Penrose attended the ceremony wearing John Singer Sargent's gown, presented to Somerville the previous year for the use of the first Somervillian DCL.[28] The Oxford Letter described the scene with pride:

> Large numbers of men and women assembled in the Sheldonian, eager to take the opportunity of expressing publicly by their presence and applause, something of the gratitude and admiration we all feel for Miss Penrose and for the work she has done in Oxford and elsewhere. It was an impressive moment when the great doors of the Sheldonian opened and preceded by the Bedels and accompanied by the Public Orator, Miss Penrose in Sargent's robe of scarlet and crimson and the black velvet hat of a Doctor, advanced to be admitted by the Vice-Chancellor to the degree of DCL, *honoris causa*.

Among the many Somerville undergraduates in the audience was the future Erasmus scholar, Margaret Mann, who wrote home to her parents with a rather less reverent account of the proceedings: 'We had a wonderful time on Tuesday—the Degree Ceremony (giving the DCL to the Pen) was the funniest thing I ever saw, and we sat and giggled in a ribald manner.'[29] She was more impressed by the subsequent celebrations in Somerville itself:

> At night there was a Dinner, with the Council present. They wore gowns, and the Pen looked lovely at the centre of the table in her scarlet, with Fisher of New College (who was Minister of Education) on her right, and Gilbert Murray (with the Bruce) on her left, and the Master of Balliol facing her. We had cider (first time in my knowledge of Somerville) and drank a health to the King and to Dr Penrose, which was proposed by Fisher and by a woman, some old Somervillian . . . [Grace Hadow]. The Pen replied in a charming speech, comparing herself to a flagstaff ('a poor wooden pole') on which, to honour a mighty building (the women's colleges) a gorgeous flag had

---

[28] Minutes of Council, 20 Oct. 1925.   [29] Mann, 3 June 1926.

been hung; and she paid very courteous tributes to the two past principals, to the Council, to Miss Bruce (loud acclamation) and to 47 generations of students—after which, on the invitation of the President of the Council, we sang 'For she's a jolly good fellow' lustily, and cheered her out. It was really very good, and there was no monotony—no-one said too much, and everyone was pleased.

'I hope the dear old soul was happy', she concluded, with the condescension of youth—'I think she had reason to be.' The following month the University of Sheffield conferred on Miss Penrose the Honorary Degree of LL.D. as part of its 21st anniversary celebrations; in 1927 further civil honours were added to the academic when the King created her Dame of the Order of the British Empire.

On her doctor's advice, Miss Penrose had formally notified the college Council in November 1925 of her wish to retire at the end of that academic year, 'or any earlier date more convenient to Council.' In December a committee of Hebdomadal Council recommended placing a limit on the total number of women undergraduates in the university, and the restriction of each of the four residential colleges to 135. The recommendation posed a serious threat both to the autonomy of the women's colleges and to their financial viability. An *ad hoc* committee—consisting of the President, the Principal, Mr Tod, Professor Brierly, and Miss Fry—was appointed by Council to consider the report, and to confer with any similar committee in the other women's colleges.

In proposing Margery Fry to serve on this committee, the Council was securing the involvement of the person whom most members saw—some with enthusiasm, and some with trepidation—as Somerville's next Principal.[30] Her name was one of five put before a special election meeting of Council held on 15 January 1926. She herself had grave doubts as to her suitability for the post, and wrote begging to withdraw. A motion proposed by Miss Bruce and seconded by Miss Pope, that her name none the less be retained on the list, was carried by eighteen votes to one; a motion by Mr Poole, that Miss Hadow's name be added to the list, despite her known unwillingness to stand against Miss Fry, was likewise carried by a large majority. The

---

[30] See letter from HD (writing from Wellesley, Mass.) to EP, 2 Dec. 1925: 'Margery Fry . . . seems to me the most distinguished person and the most full of life and power of anyone available.'

contest was essentially between these two, Miss Fry receiving twelve votes and Miss Hadow six. In the final vote, it was resolved, with four dissentients, to offer the principalship to Miss Fry. She eventually accepted, thanks to the urging of Mildred Pope, who told her that three years would be worth doing it for,[31] and the reassurance of her brother Roger: 'Du reste, ce n'est que pour la moitié de l'année; car les vacances à Oxford sont gigantesques.'[32]

[31] SMF, 17 Jan. 1926 (Fry MSS).
[32] E. Huws Jones, *Margery Fry: The Essential Amateur* (London, 1966), 134.

8

Limitation and Jubilee:
The Principalship of Margery Fry,
1927–1931

IN November 1926 there was a celebrated debate in the Union on the motion that 'The Women's Colleges should be razed to the ground.' Opposing the motion was the first woman undergraduate ever to be invited to speak at the Union, the president of the Somerville debating society, Lucy Sutherland. Supported by Richard Acland and Dingle Foot, she championed the rights of the women, according to the *Oxford Magazine*, 'in a manner peculiarly charming and amazingly clear.'[1] The motion was carried by a majority of 25, but—as Dame Lucy herself later said—'No-one minded in the least. . . . It was one of the Union's frivolous (if sometimes heavy-handed) debates, full of rather bad jokes, and everyone seemed to enjoy it.'[2] But the same term saw the beginnings of a university debate which was no joke at all, when 210 members of Congregation, following the recommendation of the committee of Hebdomadal Council on the number of undergraduates in residence, petitioned Council to impose a permanent limit on the number of women in the university.

Though the petitioners included some notable anti-feminists—such as Principal Hazel of Jesus, who spoke in Congregation of 'locking the stable door'—they also included a number of dons whom the women's colleges had been accustomed to regard as friends. The rapid growth in the number of women at Oxford since the war had given rise even in sympathetic quarters to anxiety about pressure on university lodgings and libraries and lecture halls.[3] Diehards who observed with distaste the new fashions for dancing and frequenting cafés for morning coffee—indulging, as Vice-Chancellor Farnell put it, 'in

---

[1] *Oxford Magazine*, 25 Nov. 1926: 'They [women students] were, she said, a very harmless race, whose chief recreation was brass-rubbing. Various reasons had been advanced for and against their remaining in Oxford. She would like to suggest a further reason for their being allowed to stay—because they wished to'.

[2] L. Sutherland, 'Women in Oxford', talk at seminar, 1973.

[3] See Editorial in the *Oxford Magazine*, 27 Jan. 1927.

unnecessary and unmanly food'—were inclined to attribute them to the demoralizing influence of women undergraduates.[4] The university was beginning to fear for its reputation with parents and the public schools; and Cambridge was said to be capitalizing on Oxford's image as 'socialistic, weak in athletics and be-womaned.'[5] At senior level, the activities of Annie Rogers in canvassing for a women's 'slate' in the 1926 Hebdomadal Council elections gave some colour to suspicions that a 'women's party' was being built up in Congregation. 'It is no doubt true that experience proves that whenever a large new element of the population is admitted to a position of privilege and power it takes time before the old traditions and conventions are assimilated by the new element. But there are certain elementary principles of fair play which no *man* can ignore without eventually bringing retribution on his own head', wrote W. T. S. Stallybrass in a letter to the *Oxford Magazine*.[6]

But the real question at issue, as another writer in the *Oxford Magazine* put it, was whether Oxford was to be 'a man's University with a certain number of women in it', or a 'mixed' university open to the talents regardless of sex.[7] On 14 June 1927, after an—at times—acrimonious campaign and a heated debate in Congregation, the former option was endorsed, by a crushing majority of 229 votes to 164. A move to force an actual reduction in the number of women at Oxford—which might well have meant bankruptcy for the women's colleges—was averted; but numbers were frozen at the 1927 figure of 840, and a quota (in Somerville's case, 150) was allotted to each college. The statute further provided that no new women's college might be founded which would increase the ratio of women to men students in residence beyond one to four.

With minor modifications during and after the War, the freeze persisted for nearly thirty years. It kept the women's colleges, which had no endowment, poor; it depressed the stipends of women academics; and it deprived many able girls of the chance of an Oxford education. The animosities which had been aroused in the course of the debate seriously sapped the new self-confidence of the women's colleges, and gave rise to a much more self-conscious feminist and anti-feminist feeling in the university than had previously existed. Reporting on the debate and its aftermath to Dame Emily (now in retirement), Alice

---

[4] L. Farnell, *An Oxonian Looks Back* (London, 1934), 295–6.
[5] A. Rogers to EP, 29 Oct. 1926.   [6] *Oxford Magazine*, 10 June 1926.
[7] *Oxford Magazine*, 9 June 1927, 558.

Bruce said that many of the supporters of the statute were thoroughly ashamed of themselves: 'our chief opponents are positively smarmy when one meets them.'[8] One of them, Sir Walter Riddell, the Principal of Hertford, subsequently expressed a wish to be on the Somerville Council, and was appointed as University Representative the following year; Somerville suspected 'a slight element of regret if not remorse'.[9]

The only woman to speak in the debate was Somerville's new Principal, Margery Fry (Plate 34). Miss Fry had had an almost uninterrupted connection with the college since July 1894, when her parents called on Miss Maitland to explain that, now that their daughter had qualified for entrance to Somerville, they wished her to sit for no more examinations.[10] As Librarian from 1899 to 1904 she had been chiefly responsible, with Miss Maitland, for the building of the library; and since her departure from Oxford in 1904, she had served continuously—and actively—on the college Council. The only woman member since its foundation in 1919 of the University Grants Committee, she had a wide experience of the institutions and problems of higher education in this country.[11] Her interests, however, were not primarily academic. Like her Somerville contemporary and lifelong friend, Eleanor Rathbone, she was a crusader and social reformer, and since 1919 she had been the honorary secretary of the Howard League for Penal Reform. During her time as Principal she served on the Street Offences Committee, causing an undergraduate to complain that 'she was more interested in prostitutes than in us.'[12]

The *Oxford Magazine* welcomed the election of one 'who combined intellectual distinction, a fine eloquence, and academic experience with the force of character and sympathy which the post demands.'[13] The Somerville Council, which knew Miss Fry well, could not have elected her in expectation of a quiet life. It may, even so, have been unprepared for the rapidity with which complications began to arise. In May 1926 she wrote asking to delay taking up office until the end of Michaelmas Term; Miss Penrose, a few weeks away from retirement, agreed to stay on for a further two months, and the Principal-elect set out for British Columbia to visit her nephew Julian Fry. There, a riding

---

[8] AMB to EP, 17 Sept. 1927 (Limitation file).   [9] SMF, 21 Nov. 1927 (Fry MSS).
[10] E. Huws Jones, *Margery Fry: The Essential Amateur* (London, 1966), 36.
[11] She was still the only woman member of the committee, and the last of its original members, when she resigned in 1948.   [12] Huws Jones, *Margery Fry*, 156–7.
[13] *Oxford Magazine*, 4 Feb. 1926, 251.

accident came near to overturning her plans completely; as she lay awaiting rescue one of her first thoughts was 'I shall not have to go to Somerville after all'.[14] When she did arrive in college to interview entrance candidates in November, her predecessor—with whom she confessed herself never quite at ease—was still in post, her scrupulous efforts to keep discreetly in the background rendering her all the more intimidating.[15] 'Miss Penrose is a lover of routine, and [I] hope that the filling up of forms looms larger in her view of the duties of a Principal than it need in mine,' she confided to her mother in the course of the hand-over, somewhat overwhelmed by the amount of administration which seemed to be involved.[16] She found institutional life uncongenial, and the Principal's quarters unsuitable for the kind of informal entertainment which she was anxious to introduce.[17] A solution to this problem was found when Miss Darbishire offered the use of Radcliffe House as a Principal's residence. Having been assured by the Vice-Chancellor that a leasehold property would satisfy the statutory requirement for a head of house to be 'resident within the buildings of the Society within Full Term',[18] provided that the land and buildings on each side of the path over which there was a right of way were the property of the college, Council purchased the lease for the remaining thirty-nine years, and opened negotiations with University College for the purchase of the freehold.[19] The story current among undergraduates was that the Principal needed to move out of college in order to play the flute.[20]

For senior and junior members alike, Miss Fry's vitality and passion and zest, her interest in art and music, her commitment to social concerns, came as a breath of fresh air after the heroic but austere rule of Miss Penrose. 'It was clear from the first', wrote Vera Farnell 'that the change would keep us alive.'[21] One of her first acts as Principal was to

[14] Huws Jones, *Margery Fry*, 136.

[15] SMF, 19 Dec. 1926 (Fry MSS): 'I wish I ever really felt really comfortable with her, she has a disapproving voice which always chills my marrow a little.'

[16] SMF, 13 Nov. 1926 (Fry MSS).

[17] SMF, 30 Jan. 1927 (Fry MSS). 'I find the students have hardly any of them been beyond the office in their dealings with the Principal.'

[18] Stat. Tit. XXIII, II 'Of Societies of Women Students', 2(c).

[19] The previous year Council had turned down the option of purchasing the lease of Radcliffe House, on the grounds that 'the house was not sufficiently suitable for College requirements, and that the Council was unwilling to purchase leasehold property.': Minutes of Council, 3 Nov. 1925.

[20] Conversation with Marian Sykes (1929), May 1991.

[21] V. Farnell, *A Somervillian Looks Back* (Oxford, 1948), 52.

hand over to SCR volunteers responsibility for taking Sunday evening prayers in hall. She abolished the old practice of undergraduates queuing up in the JCR before dinner to be taken in to hall by members of the SCR. Students—as she persisted in calling undergraduates, in defiance of Oxford convention—were invited in groups to drink coffee and listen to records after dinner in the Radcliffe House sitting-room, which one scout was said to have described as 'more like a circus than a lady's room'.[22] She urged them to activities outside their work—encouraging, for instance, the formation of a University Dance Club—and to careers outside what she described as 'eternal school-marming'.[23] She suggested that they should try painting their parents' drawing-room fireplaces in gold paint. Concerned at their ignorance in matters of sex, she invited Dr Winifred Cullis to give two lectures on health and elementary physiology; an impersonation by Nancy Samuel of Dr Cullis addressing the College on 'Ourselves and our Bodies' was to be the high point of the 1928 going-down play: 'The genial eloquence with which she adjured us (gracefully swinging the tea-strainer which served as her lorgnette) on the subject of eating, "*never* to miss an opportunity" will not soon be forgotten.'[24] She encouraged the JCR to join in the formation of an inter-collegiate committee of JCR officers which was to lead, through affiliation with the National Union of Students, to the creation of organized university undergraduate opinion.[25]

'It is always nice to hear Miss Fry talk' commented Elisabeth Murray after the Principal had addressed the college at the beginning of Michaelmas Term 1929,—'she is so direct, vigorous and sincere.' The following term, having been awarded a grant from the Eileen Gonner fund, Miss Murray was summoned, together with other award-winners, to tea in Radcliffe House:

> She told us what she knew of Eileen Gonner, which wasn't much. She also gave us a sentimental leaflet about her . . . The Fry said we must excuse its sentimentality as it was written just after her death, and that we needn't feel we had to preserve it for the rest of our born days.[26]

[22] Huws Jones, *Margery Fry*, 140.   [23] SMF, 5 Feb. 1928 (Fry MSS).
[24] College Letter, 1928.   [25] Farnell, *A Somervillian Looks Back*, 55.
[26] KMEM, 23 Feb. 1930 (Murray MSS). The Fund established in memory of Eileen Gonner, who died in 1920 while still an undergraduate, provided grants for students who 'have proved themselves valuable members of the College'.

But what most impressed the undergraduates was the Principal's skill in bringing the party to an end:

> The Fry was really supreme the way she got us out. She first gave us our leaflets then she called our attention to her bulbs (which she grows in stones and water instead of fibre) and we stood up to look at them—and having looked at them and being on our feet it was obviously time to go—and go we did!

Whenever Miss Fry herself addressed a meeting in Oxford, she was supported by large numbers of admiring Somerville undergraduates, earning the college a reputation for 'following its Principal around'. (She had had much the same effect on her charges in Birmingham years before; towards the end of her life she was to compare herself ruefully with St Ursula, 'who, you will remember, went about with 11,000 virgins'.)[27]

There were, none the less, limits to her effectiveness in dealing with the young. She herself suspected that the undergraduates considered it rather undignified of her to wish to get to know them better.[28] And, notwithstanding her wide experience of human nature, she retained some of the prejudices of a world very different from their own. When Audrey Withers went to discuss with her the choice of a career she was disappointed at the Principal's simple assumption that this would—and should—take the form of some kind of unpaid social work. Surely, she said—in response to the objection that what was wanted was paid employment—Miss Withers's parents could afford to keep her; it seemed not to occur to her that an undergraduate who did not have to earn her own living should wish to do so. 'The different viewpoints of that conversation' reflected Audrey Withers many years later—after a career beginning in a bookshop and ending as editor of *Vogue*—'showed that even a progressive thinker of one generation can be out of touch with another.'[29]

There is a revealing account of Miss Fry's methods in the memoirs of Sir John Mabbott, who as a young don in the 1920s did some of Somerville's philosophy teaching. The rule established in Miss Penrose's time was that a male tutor might teach a pair of Somerville pupils in his own college rooms, but that if teaching only one he had to come to Somerville and use a special room set aside for the purpose. Mabbott became increasingly irritated by this requirement, and

---

[27] Huws Jones, *Margery Fry*, 67.   [28] SMF, 30 Jan. 1927 (Fry MSS).
[29] A. Withers, *Lifespan* (London, 1994), 33.

on the arrival of Margery Fry as Principal, determined to do something about it:

> So, at the start of her first term, I went to Somerville and asked to see
> her. I knocked at the door marked 'Principal' and went in. I saw a very
> lively looking girl, sitting in a corner and typing furiously, with her
> hair all over the place. I said 'I should like to see Miss Fry. I know this
> is very difficult. She must be very busy and I have no appointment.
> But I shan't take more than a minute. I just want to deliver an ulti-
> matum. Do you think you could smuggle me in?' She said 'I am Miss
> Fry. Who are you?' Somewhat shaken, I told her. 'And what's all this
> about an ultimatum?' I said 'Miss Fry, you know the rule about hav-
> ing to come here to give tuition? Well, I had intended to say that I was
> not going to teach Somerville pupils any longer under these insulting
> and inefficient conditions.' She said that, as a College Fellow, I must
> be aware that a Principal was not a dictator, and could not change
> College rules unaided. She would have to see how far she could carry
> her colleagues with her. Meantime, would I suspend my ultimatum. I
> said of course I would, but for how long (expecting a year or so)? She
> said . . . 'well, ring me up in three weeks and see where we have got.'
> I rose to go. As I reached the door, she said 'Mr Mabbott, how long
> have you been teaching people under these . . . conditions?' I told
> her five years, and I left. After three weeks I rang up and she said
> 'Ah yes, the ultimatum. Well, we have reached what you might call
> a compromise; and that is that anyone who has taught Somerville
> pupils for at least five years, without disaster, may teach them singly
> in his own room. Will that do to be going on with?' . . . My first
> Somerville pupil under the Fry regime thought my success augured
> well. She said they had heard that the new Principal was an authority
> on Food Reform and Prison Reform, and these were the two things
> Somerville needed. In later years, I broadcast once or twice with Miss
> Fry, and once, awaiting our green light, I recalled the ultimatum.
> 'Without disaster', I said, 'Now what did you mean by that?' 'Well',
> she replied 'You didn't have to marry any of them, did you?'[30]

Margery Fry herself acted as moral tutor to Somerville's small body
of mathematicians, whose studies were directed, together with those
of maths students from the other women's colleges, by the LMH lecturer, Dorothy Wrinch. Such inter-collegiate arrangements tended to

---

[30] J. Mabbott, *Oxford Memories* (Oxford, 1986), 81–2.

be unsatisfactory, not least because of the variations in pay scales and policy between the participating colleges. The impending retirement of Jane Willis Kirkaldy, who had been director of studies for all the women's colleges for over thirty years, now prompted an urgent review of teaching in the sciences. Invited to attend a meeting of the women Principals to advise on future arrangements, Miss Kirkaldy recommended that each college should have a science fellow on its governing body, aiming to provide between them an organic and an inorganic chemist, a physiologist, a zoologist, and a botanist; all, she said, should have Oxford degrees, the physiologist a BM.[31] The financial implications of such a course were alarming, and, without much hope, the Principals agreed to seek advice about possible approaches to the Rockefeller and other Foundations. How to make tutorial provision for their science students was to be a major preoccupation of the women's colleges in the years ahead. Somerville seemed to have found a solution when in 1929 it attached to itself as a research fellow a promising young botanist from St Hugh's, Christine Mary Pilkington, and the following year appointed her tutor in natural sciences. But Miss Pilkington inconsiderately chose this moment to get married; and though, as Mrs Snow, she continued to teach for Somerville until 1958 she never became a tutorial fellow. The other recruits to the teaching staff during Miss Fry's principalship were all in the humanities, and all Somervillians: Lucy Sutherland (already an MA of the University of Witwatersrand), was invited in her final year as an undergraduate to apply for the post vacated by the resignation in 1926 of the PPE tutor, Doris Rhodes; Enid Starkie returned to Somerville from Exeter in 1928 as Sarah Smithson lecturer in French; and in the same year Kathleen Constable began, as assistant tutor in English, the distinguished career which would take her (as Kathleen Tillotson) to the Hildred Carlile chair in the University of London.

The main building project of these years—Harold Rogers's Penrose building—had been planned before Miss Fry took up office. It was informally opened in Michaelmas Term 1927 on a dark night of relentless rain, when 'an intrepid but somewhat disorderly procession of members of Council, Staff and ASM trooped in mackintoshes down the garden, headed by Dame Emily; who, with one decisive blow on the door, declared the building open, and was answered by an instantaneous illumination at every window.'[32] The Penrose building pro-

---

[31] Principals' Meeting, 26 Oct. 1926.   [32] College Letter, 1927–8.

vided—at the cost of the fine line of poplars which had hitherto marked the college's south-west boundary—twenty-one students' rooms, two tutors' sets (whose first occupants were Miss Lorimer and Miss Pope), a common room, and an SCR guest-room. From the outset opinions differed as to the architectural merits of the exterior of the new building, but its interior amenities—and in particular its plumbing—were generally agreed to be beyond praise. The generous allowance of bathrooms, separate washrooms, and laundry and ironing rooms, drew attention by contrast to the deficiencies of the West, where alterations were rapidly put in hand to provide extra bathrooms and some new rooms for maids.

Miss Fry's own taste was given rein in 1929 when the newly enlarged entrance hall was paved in sea-green mosaic by Italian workmen; and it was at her suggestion that the ceiling of the barn-like West common room was lowered to provide a better-proportioned JCR and four additional students' rooms above. In 1930 money to build and furnish a reading-room over the loggia between Maitland and Hall was given anonymously by a going-down student,[33] and college took the opportunity to build a fellow's flat on the floor above—an ingenious piece of infilling, which had the incidental advantage of blocking out the hated view of St Aloysius from the college garden. The architect, Morley Horder, was recommended to the college by Roger Fry.

At a preliminary discussion in May 1928 of the college's forthcoming jubilee, Council took the decision that this should not be an occasion for any public appeal for funds. The generosity of old Somervillians, however, was not to be curbed. A Jubilee Gift Fund was opened, and 660 members of the ASM and 42 friends of the college contributed a total of £4,200. The meeting of Council to which the final figure was reported learned also of a bequest from Canon Gamble of £3,000; it was agreed to combine the two sums as a Founders' and Benefactors' Fund, the first call on which would be to provide for the appointment of a tutor in Greats.[34] £200 was set aside to establish a T. H. Green prize in *literae humaniores* and a Canon Gamble prize in PPE; £50 was allocated for the purchase of art books for the library; and £1,000 was held in reserve for structural developments. Possession of these funds emboldened the Council to lay the foundations of future expansion, by the purchase from University College, for just over £8,000, of two sites in Little Clarendon Street, and from St John's

---

[33] E. R. Cochrane (PPE 1927) migrated to Christ Church 1941.
[34] Minutes of Council, 3 Feb. 1930.

College of Bedford House School. The departure in September 1930 of the tenant of Akers' baby-linen shop enabled Somerville to secure a thirty-year lease on 33 Woodstock Road, thus providing additional accommodation in the group of three Woodstock Road houses which became known as 'East Houses'. In a lightning transformation, staircases were torn down to make way for corridors between the three houses; a passage was cut through a top floor room to provide an exit down an external emergency staircase, three new windows were put in, electric light was installed, and the whole building was redecorated in time for occupation by students on 10 October. On 28 October the Council passed a resolution of gratitude to the ASM for the endowment fund and jubilee gift 'without which College would have been unable to purchase leases and properties when they came into the market.'

The jubilee itself was celebrated in great style. At a dinner in hall (Plate 35) on 25 May 1929 current members of the college celebrated the recent election of Eleanor Rathbone to parliament and the appointment of Miss Pope as the university's first woman Reader, and were entertained by Miss Margaret Roberts and Miss Emily Kemp to accounts of student life in Somerville's earliest days. On the last Friday of Trinity Term the JCR was taken *en masse* to the New Theatre to see Henry Lytton as the Lord Chancellor and Bertha Lewis as the Queen of the Fairies in the D'Oyly Carte production of *Iolanthe*. The domestic staff were dispatched in a charabanc to the seaside. That summer's gaudy was attended by a record number of old members. The AGM of the Association of Senior Members on 6 July was held in the Oxford Playhouse, and in the evening 500 old Somervillians, representing every generation since 1879, attended a dinner in college at which speeches were given by Professor Gilbert Murray, the Vice-Chancellor (Dr Pember of All Souls), Miss Maude Thompson (one of Somerville's first students), Eleanor Rathbone, and Dame Emily Penrose. In the course of the evening the Principal announced the election of four honorary fellows (the college's first, apart from Dame Emily herself): Miss Bruce, Miss Kirkaldy, Miss Rathbone, and one non-Somervillian, the medieval historian Kate Norgate.[35] Sunday morning devotions reflected Somerville's diverse religious tradition:

---

[35] Miss Norgate (1853–1935), friend and disciple of J. R. Green, and author of *England Under the Angevin Kings* etc., was one of the last of the old 'pre-academic' generation of historians. Her election (on the proposal of Maude Clarke) to an honorary fellowship of Somerville is thought to have been the only official recognition she ever received.

1. John Percival

2. Mary Ward

3. Thomas Hill Green

4. Charlotte Green

5. The Ladies' College, Somerville Hall, Oxford

6. Miss Shaw Lefevre and students, 1885

7. Miss Maitland and students, 1890

8. Woodstock Road frontage, 1910

9. The Gatehouse (1891) shortly before its demolition in 1932

10. The pre-1933 approach to House

11. The new Woodstock Road frontage, October 1933

12. West Dining Room, *c*.1906

13. Hall JCR, *c*.1906

(14–15) *Demeter*
14. The original 1904 production

15. The 1954 revival

16. Commemoration Dance, 22 June 1914

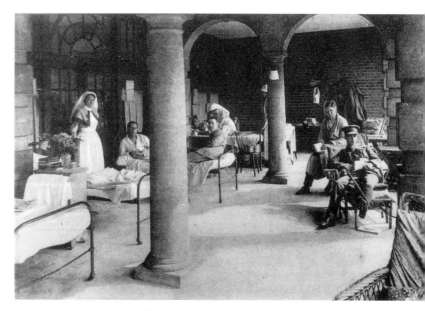

17. Somerville Section 3rd Southern General Hospital

19. Somerville graduates returning to College after the first Degree Ceremony

(18–19) Degrees for women, 14 October 1920
18. Miss Penrose with Professor Gilbert Murray

20. Visit of Queen Mary, 1921

21. Visit of Queen Elizabeth II, 1968

22. Miss Penrose and the JCR Committee, 1923–4

23. The Jiu-Jitsu Club with their coach (and Miss Lorimer), 1924

24. Dorothy L. Sayers in rehearsal for
Pied Pipings, June 1915

25. Winifred Holtby and Barbara Bell
in *The Professor's Love Story*, 1919

26. Barbara Ward (Lady Jackson) and
Jean Taylor (Lady Medawar) in
Arlequin poli par l'amour, May 1933

27. Joyce Sugg as the Slave in
The Frogs, 1946

28. Work in the library, 1932

29. An undergraduate tea party, 1944

30. An early hockey match

31. The tennis four, 1944

32. The Somerville Eight, 1925, with their Coach, Mr Best

33. The Somerville Eight, 1981

34. Margery Fry, 1929

35. Jubilee dinner in Hall, 1929

36. Miss Darbishire and the SCR in 1932

37. The SCR in 1934 as depicted by the Junior Fellow, Isobel Henderson

38. The college kitchen, 1944

39. Firefighting: the trailer pump outside Maitland

40. The Chapel

41. Hoeing for Victory
on the chapel lawn

42. The Tutorial

43. The Lecture

(44–45) Tutors and pupils
44. May McKisack and Indira Gandhi

45. Dorothy Hodgkin and Margaret Thatcher

46. Dame Janet Vaughan and Mrs Pandit, October 1964

47. The opening of the Wolfson Building, November 1967

48. Daphne Park presiding at dinner in Hall, 1981

49. Somerville's first Proctor, March 1990

50. Somervillians Say No, February 1992

51. Somerville's last all-women Governing Body, June 1993

early communion celebrations were held both at St Mary's and in Mansfield College chapel, and at the main noon-day service in the University Church the sermon was preached by the Principal of Mansfield, Dr Selbie. The weekend culminated in a garden party on Sunday afternoon, attended by some 900 Old Somervillians and their guests. Among these, and making what was to prove her last appearance in college, was Charlotte Green, widow of one of Somerville's founders, great-aunt of a future Principal, and herself for forty-five years a member—and for eighteen years vice-president—of the college Council. In the course of the jubilee festivities the Principal's cat Grizzle escaped from her temporary incarceration in Radcliffe House and—with unerring feline instinct for an ailurophobe—sought out Dame Emily.[36]

Margery Fry was herself out of sympathy with many aspects of Oxford, which in a moment of particular irritation she described to her mother as 'full of mediocrities entrenched in privilege.'[37] The only head of house with whom she felt politically much in common was Lindsay of Balliol (though she conceded that this was the best possible company).[38] Apart from LMH's Lynda Grier, 'a person one could be real friends with', she did not warm to her colleagues in the other women's colleges, one of whom, she told her mother after an initial meeting, 'looks very Daisy-Chainish'.[39] She found Oxford politicking tiresome and self-indulgent, writing at the time of the Limitation controversy: 'I believe really people can't get on here without a row now and then to enliven things, and circulars and meetings and canvassings and votings are meat and drink to them. I *hate* these things.'[40] And she was unimpressed by university ceremonial. After officiating on one occasion as dean of degrees for Somerville she described the proceedings as 'a nasty cold-blooded little ceremony', adding that she couldn't quite bring herself 'to address the commonplace Mr Pember as Weekeekankaylahrayee as the really knowing do.'[41] Above all, she was disenchanted by the university's treatment of her brother Roger, whose candidature in 1927 for the Slade Professorship of Fine Art was successfully opposed 'on a frivolous pretext'[42] by people who objected to the irregularity of his private life.

[36] SMF, 26 May 1929 (Fry MSS).   [37] SMF, 9 Nov. 1927 (Fry MSS).
[38] SMF, 30 Jan. 1927 (Fry MSS).   [39] SMF, 25 Jan. 1927 (Fry MSS).
[40] SMF, 20 Feb. 1927 (Fry MSS).
[41] SMF, 26 Jan. 1929 (Fry MSS). Degree candidates are presented to the Vice-Chancellor in a Latin formula beginning '*Insignissime Vice-Cancellarie* . . .'
[42] *DNB* article by Kenneth Clark.

In the event, Margery Fry remained in Oxford for less than five years. The death of her mother in the spring of 1930 freed her sister Agnes from the cares of long years of nursing, and made possible the extended travel which they had long hoped to undertake together. In her letter of resignation Miss Fry apologized for putting the Council to the trouble of so speedy a change of headship: 'It was, I think, understood by them when they did me the honour of electing me that it was unlikely that I should hold the office for any very long period.'[43] Whatever the feelings of the 'outside' members of Council, those of the fellows were conveyed in a special resolution recording 'their deep sense of personal loss on the resignation of Miss Fry from the Principalship and their appreciation of the great service she has rendered to the College as a whole and to the members of the College individually.'[44] The undergraduate body was shattered by the news. 'We feel there won't be anyone like the Fry' wrote Elisabeth Murray to her family: 'She is so fine and so live and vigorous and keen on everything. And we always feel she is on our side where work is concerned—laughing with us at the Tutors' reports and telling us not to be badgered into doing too much work.'[45] The imprint of her vivid personality was indeed stamped on the college, to which she remained devoted, for many years after her departure.

The election of her successor was speedy and uncontentious. A special meeting of Council on 11 November 1930 had only one nomination before it: Helen Darbishire. Two other names—including that of Dame Bertha Phillpotts[46]—had been mooted, but neither found a proposer. Miss Darbishire, proposed by Miss Pope and seconded by Miss Escreet, was unanimously elected and welcomed immediately by the Council. She was granted partial leave of absence for Hilary Term to enable her, before taking up office, to complete a piece of work which required her presence in London. Miss Young was appointed tutor in English language and literature for the remaining four years of her current appointment—an arrangement which was to be cut short by her marriage the following year to Hugh Macdonald.

One of Margery Fry's last acts as Principal was to secure the appointment as assistant tutor in ancient history of a young graduate from

---

[43] SMF to E. Craig, 20 Aug. 1930.   [44] Minutes of Council, 9 Oct. 1930.

[45] KMEM, 12 Oct. 1930 (Murray MSS).

[46] Bertha Phillpotts had resigned as Mistress of Girton in 1925 and was now a Research Fellow and Director of Scandinavian Studies. It was thought that the recent death of her father made it possible that she might be prepared to stand. Minutes of Council, 11 Nov. 1930.

the Oxford Home Students, Miss Isobel Munro. Undecided whether to accept the appointment, and reluctant to tie herself down to the routine of tutorial work, Miss Munro consulted her friend and mentor, Gilbert Murray. She was advised, on balance, to accept. Somerville, he assured her, 'is more fun than a man's college because it is new and growing and in fact "not a tram but a bus" '.[47]

[47] Gilbert Murray to Isobel Munro,. 20 Dec. 1930 (Bodleian MSS Gilbert Murray 144: Letters to Isobel Henderson).

9

Controversy and Consolidation under Helen Darbishire, 1931–1939

THE task of guiding the college through the economic crises of the 1930s, the anxious period leading up to the Second World War, and finally the war itself, now fell to the least worldly of all its Principals, Helen Darbishire, English tutor at Somerville since 1908 and an authority on the works of Milton and Wordsworth. The daughter of an Oxford doctor, and educated at the High School, Miss Darbishire at the age of 50 had spent only four years of her life outside Oxford, three as a lecturer at the Royal Holloway College and one in America as visiting professor at Wellesley.

Her election provoked an unedifying correspondence in the pages of *Time and Tide*—a journal owned and edited by Lady Rhondda, and with a wide Somervillian readership. The 29 November issue contained a letter signed 'Somervillian' lamenting Miss Darbishire's appointment as a return to 'the purely academic precedents of the past' and rebuking the college Council for failing to retain the services of Miss Fry, whose 'contact with wider problems gave her a new understanding of the opportunities awaiting graduates of the college, and the difficulties of youth at its most sensitive and troublesome period':

> There was never a time when Oxford needed more the influence of a woman principal with a wide knowledge of the competitive world of conflicting interests outside its sheltering walls. The divorce between university life and the world outside is wide enough already. Any attempt to render it wider is a tragedy.[1]

These sentiments were supported the following week by 'Another Somervillian', and deplored by a third, Miss M. G. Lloyd Thomas, now a lecturer in English at Girton, who suggested that the original writer would have done better to address her remarks to the college Council than to write under a *nom de guerre* to a public journal.

---

[1] *Time and Tide*, 29 Nov. 1930.

'Whilst Somerville has undoubtedly been on one occasion at least unhappy in its choice of entrance candidates', she concluded, 'it continues to be enviably fortunate in its elections to the Principalship of the College.'[2] Her intervention prompted another anonymous Somervillian, 'Educator', to weigh in the following week to denounce Miss Lloyd Thomas's 'rigid and superior tone', express gratitude to Girton 'for having removed such a menace to modern life from the walls of Somerville', and profess pity for Cambridge 'that such a would-be Mussolini has succeeded in penetrating into Girton College.'[3] The correspondence closed with a letter from two recent Somerville graduates 'J.W. and V.A.D.'[4] protesting at the use of the word 'tragedy' to describe Miss Darbishire's election, and one signed 'Not a Somervillian' which questioned whether Miss Fry herself would welcome such testimonials as those forthcoming from her supporters:

If the Women's Colleges still consider themselves to be, primarily, places of learning, would it not appear normal that their Principals should be scholars?

If an *agent de liaison* is required for the benefit of those who combine with a temperament suited to the 'rough and tumble professions' a desire for a preliminary shove, would not the appointment of a special officer, not the Principal, meet the case?

In other words, do not both writers seem to confuse the functions of a College with those of a first-class agency?[5]

Joan Browne, then an undergraduate, said that her contemporaries regarded the publicly expressed hostility to Miss Darbishire as in bad taste. 'We came to regard her with a slightly superior affection' she recalls—adding that undergraduates 'did not always appreciate her slightly cryptic comments.'[6] Writing home at the time, Elisabeth Murray described the *Time and Tide* letter as 'disgusting': 'Although it is in a way what one feels it is certainly not what one would have publicly said.'[7] It was, she said, the general opinion in college that the Council had been rather unenterprising in its choice, but that perhaps it was nice to have someone who would carry on on the same lines:

[2] *Time and Tide*, 6 Dec. 1930.   [3] *Time and Tide*, 13 Dec. 1930.
[4] ? Janet Watson and Vera Agnes Douglas (later Mrs Lucas).
[5] *Time and Tide*, 13 Dec. 1930.   [6] Recollections of Joan Browne (1930).
[7] KMEM, 29 Nov. 1930 (Murray MSS).

As a matter of fact the Darb is very little known as she lives out of College and really very rarely appears—hardly ever to Hall and at most not more than once a week to lunch, though she always turns up at College prayers. She is bosum [*sic*] pals with the Dean and one rather feels the Dean is the stronger partner . . . Also she is a slave driver and won't have the Fry's sane attitude to work.[8]

Later generations of undergraduates came to appreciate the humanity and wisdom behind the cryptic comments: Nina Bawden is not the only Somervillian whose affection for the college is 'centred almost entirely on the small, warm, dignified person of Helen Darbishire.'[9] The somewhat withdrawn, almost mystical, manner which they characterized as 'communing with the soul of Wordsworth' masked a shrewd head for business and much sound common sense. But any attempt by the new Principal to tighten up discipline after the somewhat lax sway of her predecessor could hardly fail to arouse resentment.

The college administration felt the full force of the new spirit. 'Suddenly every petty detail of office work was supervised and checked,' recalled Hilda Bryant, whose predecessor as Principal's Secretary had found it impossible to adapt to 'such a drastic change in personality as that presented by Miss Fry and Miss Darbishire.'[10] Under the new regime, 'one almost always knew exactly where [the Principal] was at any given moment.':

In one term she gave her lectures . . . In another term she gave a class to English students on Milton . . . Most of her day was spent in the 'Milton Room' at Radcliffe House; except on meeting days in term I never saw her after 11 a.m. until she came over for dinner. Every evening except I think Saturday we had two undergraduates at High Table, getting through the whole College in a year.

Miss Darbishire herself liked to tell how, when an item of college business required urgent attention, the college messenger would seek her out in her accustomed seat in the Bodleian and produce the necessary documents for her signature.[11]

Against the backcloth of this unchanging routine, in the course of the 1930s both the appearance of the college and the composition of

[8] KMEM, 15 Nov. 1930, ibid.
[9] N. Bawden, *In My Own Time: Almost an Autobiography* (London, 1994), 74.
[10] Recollections of Hilda Bryant.
[11] M. Lascelles, *A Memoir* (privately printed, 1989), 57.

its teaching staff underwent a major transformation. The early years of Miss Darbishire's principalship were dominated by building works. In the long vacation of 1932 a sanatorium was built on ground between the back of the Penrose building and Bedford House lecture room—just in time to accommodate the many victims of the following winter's flu epidemic. Council's decision to employ Morley Horder as architect for this project was taken strictly on the understanding that it 'did not put the College under any obligation to employ him permanently as a College architect.'[12] But when, three months later, the advisability of rebuilding Somerville's Woodstock Road frontage (Plate 8) came under consideration—building costs being at that time low, and the existing buildings in constant need of repair—it was agreed to ask him to prepare sketch plans and submit estimates for two sides of a quadrangle.[13] A special meeting in July to consider the plans was interrupted by the arrival of a telegram from Horder: 'What about guarantee supervision fees £750, not paid if £14,000 exceeded.' It was decided to proceed, provided that the total cost could be kept below £20,000.[14] The undertaking was to be financed by means of a £12,000 loan from Christ Church, which offered a more favourable rate of interest than the bank.

The recently refurbished East Houses soon stood in isolation, as the buildings around them—the Cottages, the Gatehouse, and the Waggon and Horses—were demolished to make way for the new quadrangle. The following term, some of the students thus made homeless were accommodated, together with the Librarian, in a house in Norham Road called 'St Charles', which was leased from LMH. The previous occupants had been Jesuits, who had left behind them in the dining-room some welcome vermouth and a rather distressing picture of Jephte's rash vow. The house had one bathroom—with, says Joan Browne, the slowest waterflow on record—to serve twelve students, and rats ('or large and active mice and other moving creatures') behind the fireplaces. When the time came for them to leave, the Somerville refugees solemnly cursed St Charles with bell, book, and candle.[15]

College followed with avid interest the progress of the new East quadrangle. The side facing the road was built in stone, the side facing the main door of the college in brick; the ceremony of topping the

---

[12] Minutes of Council, 1 Mar. 1932. [13] Minutes of Council, 7 June 1932.
[14] Minutes of Council, 20 July 1932. [15] Recollections of Joan Browne.

roof was performed by Miss Darbishire on 3 December, in the presence of representatives of the builders, the SCR, the JCR, and the domestic staff. In 1933 the building was completed by the erection of the Woodstock Road frontage (Plate 11) and the Council Room, up a flight of stairs over the traffic entrance, built with the help of an anonymous gift of £1,000 from an old student.[16] The new quadrangle provided accommodation for thirty undergraduates, two sets of fellows' rooms, and a treasurer's office. The entrance from the Woodstock Road was through an archway with porter's lodges on either side—the waiting-room on the south side rapidly becoming known, on account of its divided door, as the horse-box. The arms and motto of the college were carved by Mr E. Ware on the façade facing Woodstock Road; those of Bishop Percival, Miss Shaw Lefevre, and Miss Darbishire inside the quadrangle. The old plane tree was retained in one corner, a gesture to college piety.

'Our new building is internally everything that we could wish,' reported the Oxford Correspondent, going on to enthuse about 'the interesting, convenient, varied and beautiful rooms, decorated in schemes of green or blue or yellow, . . . the cleverly devised cupboards and book shelves, and the luxurious washing and bathing arrangements.' The first occupants of the new rooms, in Trinity Term 1933, were the returning exiles from St Charles House, 'the historically remarkable pair who had sojourned in LMH', and the freshers from the crumbled rooms of East Houses and the Waggon and Horses. In the chaos which still prevailed on the building-site outside their windows, the hero of the hour was the college porter, Payne, 'whose only habitation was a small wooden hut precariously perched in the midst of ruins from which he would emerge, ever punctual, cheerful and unmoved, to attend to his evening duties at the Gate in the hoarding.'[17] A clock, the gift of Eleanor Rathbone, was set up over the entrance to the Council Room, whose elegant furnishings were completed by the purchase of three handsome china vases from Professor Sayce's collection and two black Wedgwood vases. On a cold evening in December 1933 a dinner was given in the hall for the workmen, with their wives, of the builders (Messrs Hutchins) and the other contracting firms who had worked on the building. It was officially opened the following June by the college's Visitor, the Chancellor of the University, Lord Halifax—one of the first public engagements of

---

[16] Minutes of Council, 31 Jan. 1933.   [17] Oxford Letter 1932/3.

his term of office; and at Encaenia Somervillians had the satisfaction of hearing their new quadrangle praised in the Creweian Oration: *Collegio Somervilliano frons nova, docti opus artificis, est praefixa, varii generis aedificiis additamentum nobile.* ('For Somerville College a new front [quadrangle] the work of a skilful architect, has been erected, a notable addition to buildings of varying style'.) Soon afterwards Dorothy L. Sayers was to describe it for a wider public in the opening paragraph of *Gaudy Night*.

Undergraduates who had observed the 'courteous gallantry' with which Mr Horder conducted himself in his frequent conversations with Miss Darbishire hoped for a romance, but came to realize that he was 'probably ingratiating himself in case of delays or other problems.'[18] That there were indeed problems is clear from the wording of the vote of condolence proposed by Miss Darbishire at Council on the architect's death in 1944: 'Many of us remember stormy Committees and incidents with Mr Morley Horder. But if you choose an architect of genius you must expect storms.'[19]

It would be unjust, however, to attribute these simply to an artistic temperament. Horder's work on the Woodstock Road quadrangle was complicated throughout by the reverberations of a much more controversial enterprise on which the college was simultaneously engaged.

In Trinity Term 1932 a then anonymous old Somervillian—subsequently identified as Emily Georgiana Kemp—signified to the Council her wish to present to the college 'a beautiful, simple, and significant house for the purpose of meditation, prayer, and other spiritual exercises.'[20] In deference to Somerville's non-denominational tradition, she proposed that the building, which she hoped might be known as 'Christ House', should be dedicated rather than consecrated. Council, taking the view 'that a building for religious purposes would have real value in the life of the College', but balking at the title of Christ House, authorized the Principal to negotiate further with the donor. In the course of these negotiations Miss Kemp reluctantly abandoned her preferred name, but insisted on her own choice of architect. Morley Horder was summoned to a special meeting of Council on 23 June and asked if he could incorporate in his plans for the Woodstock Road quadrangle a chapel to the design of Mr Courtenay Theobald. Somewhat surprisingly, he agreed.

[18] Recollections of Joan Browne.   [19] Minutes of Council, 31 Oct. 1944.
[20] Minutes of Council, 7 June 1932.

Throughout the summer, negotiations continued between the Principal, the donor, and the two architects. The idea of the Woodstock Road site for the chapel was abandoned in July, and a series of alternatives proposed. Communications between the four parties were less than perfect: while Council considered one site, Miss Kemp instructed Mr Theobald to prepare plans for another. The question of both site and plans was referred to the Structural Committee, with instructions to consult Mr Horder.

By Michaelmas Term rumours in college were rife. At the meeting of Council on 25 October the chairman of the ASM read out a letter from fifty-five former students protesting against the building of a chapel. It was agreed that they should be sent a placatory letter asserting Council's right to take a decision and its determination to preserve the non-sectarian character of college prayers and services. The Principal was, however, authorized to consult the opinion of the scholars and the JCR committee; and as a result of this consultation it was decided that a College Meeting Extraordinary should be held, to obtain a full census of opinion. On 9 November Miss Darbishire gave the JCR as much information about the proposed chapel as she was able at that point to disclose; two statements were then read out, one accepting and one rejecting the offer, and those present were invited to sign statements for or against the chapel, and (in the event of its being accepted) for or against the site currently proposed at the eastern end of the fellows' garden. In consequence of the meeting, three petitions from the JCR were submitted to the Council: one, with thirty signatures, supporting the idea of a chapel; one, with fifty-eight signatures, objecting to it; and one, with ninety-six signatures, objecting to the proposed site.[21]

A letter was drafted to Miss Kemp, assuring her that 'some members of the Council admired some features of the plans', but requesting further consultations between Mr Theobald and Mr Horder 'or another consultant architect of established reputation.' She replied by suggesting three possible architects, including Mr Theobald's father-in-law, Maxwell Ayrton. Council selected one of the others, Walter Tapper, while referring the question of the future lay-out of the Little Clarendon Street site as a whole to Mr Horder. Meanwhile, letters of protest were received from a former member of Council, Mrs Fisher, a current member, Mr Gillett, and from an intending benefactor

---

[21] Log Book, MT 1931; Minutes of Council, 11 Nov. 1932.

who had decided against a bequest on the grounds that the proposed chapel 'committed the College to the Christian idea.'[22] During the Christmas vacation there was a meeting of the ASM which Miss Darbishire reported as 'lively'.

The whole chapel episode was, indeed, an important test of Somerville's new constitutional arrangements. At the AGM of the Association of Senior Members on 3 June 1933 a motion was brought forward regretting the way in which the Council had accepted the offer of the chapel without reference to the old students. The contention of the proposer and seconder of the motion, Matilda Snow and Eva Dessin, was that the Council was becoming tyrannical in the exercise of its functions, and that its action in this instance amounted to a breach of faith. Opposing speakers took the line that the Council was not only legally but actually the only body competent to judge what was best for the college, and that to have submitted its decision to the ASM beforehand would have been to surrender authority and shirk responsibility. In a crucial speech, Miss Pope reminded the meeting of the change which had come about in the relation in which members stood to the university, which had necessitated the sacrifice of democratic principle by the concentration of executive powers in the hands of a comparatively small Council; such a step once taken—and taken because everyone concerned, including the ASM, believed it to be for the good of Somerville—could not be retraced. When the question was put to the vote, eight members supported and forty-three opposed the resolution, those members of the ASM who were also members of Council abstaining. Proceedings ended with a vote of confidence in the Council which was carried with acclamation, but which none the less fell short of the vote of thanks which the college Treasurer, Miss Beauchamp, had hoped for.[23]

The Council at this point had still not decided where the chapel should be built. Between January and June 1933 four possible sites were considered, one of them involving the purchase from University College of a 7 ft. strip of land on the far side of Somerville's southern boundary wall. Miss Kemp wished for a stone building; the Council's preference was for brick faced with stone. On 6 June revised plans for a stone building within the existing college grounds were presented to Council by Mr Theobald and approved; in October, at the donor's request, the estimate of the builders Wooldridge and Simpson was accepted.

---

[22] Minutes of Council, 22 Nov. 1932.   [23] Minutes of ASM Committee, 3 Apr. 1933.

As work progressed through 1933/4, attention was focused on the chapel's internal arrangements. Asked by the Council to have special stalls made for members of the college staff, Miss Kemp replied that she regretted that she could not agree to a request which 'would be contrary to the spirit of this House of Prayer where all worshippers are on a level and where the simple, informal daily prayers which have been carried on for the first 55 years will be continued with ever-deepening significance.'[24] She herself was beginning to get anxious about the expense of the undertaking; so when problems over the acoustic arose in the long vacation of 1934 Miss Darbishire offered on the college's behalf to pay £100 towards the cost of the work. In October Miss Kemp announced her intention of providing the chapel with an organ, and of enlisting the help of Dr Albert Schweitzer in selecting a suitable instrument; the following February the offer was withdrawn, and Council informed that, though Dr Schweitzer had been most kind and generous, circumstances had unfortunately arisen which made it impossible for her to avail herself of his offer.[25]

There remained a final hurdle to be surmounted: a request by Miss Kemp that she should be entrusted with the arrangements for a simple ceremony one Sunday in term when the chapel would be thrown open to the university. Clearly alarmed, the Council hastily devised its own arrangements for a ceremony of dedication on the Thursday immediately before Hilary Term, and then resolved unanimously that it could not accede to the donor's request, on the grounds that the college must itself be responsible for all services conducted in the chapel in its name, and that a date in January had already been fixed for a ceremony to which the chancellor, vice-chancellor, and proctors would be invited.[26] In the event the ceremony was postponed until 16 February, by which time both Miss Darbishire and the Vice-Principal, Maude Clarke, were absent on sick-leave. It was agreed that a second postponement was out of the question, and that 'in the unavoidable absence of the Principal and Vice-Principal, the dedication would be undertaken by the senior fellow who was both able and willing to do it.' Thus it was that Miss Farnell added to her long list of college offices that of Dedicator of the College Chapel.[27]

With evident relief, on 5 March 1935 Council instructed the Prin-

---

[24] Minutes of Council, 18 July 1934.   [25] Minutes of Council, 5 Feb. 1935.
[26] Minutes of Council, 30 Oct. 1934.   [27] Minutes of Council, 5 Feb. 1935.

cipal to convey to the donor its 'final thanks for the gift of a chapel.'
It was agreed with her that the chapel should be used for daily morning prayers and for Sunday evening prayers which would be conducted as far as possible on the same lines as those formerly held in
the hall; that the Principal should be responsible for the conduct of
the services; that the non-sectarian character of the worship traditional in the college should be maintained; and that, in accordance
with the college charter, attendance at services should always be
entirely voluntary. Miss Darbishire subsequently adopted the practice
of giving an address after the evening service on the first Sunday
of each term; these occasions—in the course of one of which the
Principal, famously, spoke of the sacrifice made by a brilliant young
mathematician of her acquaintance who gave up academic life in
order to become a stockbroker, the better to support his widowed
mother—were attended by quite a number of undergraduates who
did not attend the service itself. Jean Wilks remembers them as 'quiet,
scholarly oases in a fairly hectic life—a pause for reflection on ultimate values, without any syllabus or prescribed learning.'

In the months following the completion of the chapel its surroundings were improved by the construction of an approach from the fellows' garden, by the demolition of the four houses known as East
Court (not to be confused with the East Houses), and by the planting
in front of Maitland at right angles to the chapel of a new rose-bed
with 100 varieties of roses. In 1936–7 an organ, designed by Harrison
& Harrison of Durham with advice from Mr Sidney Watson, and
acquired with the help of a loan of £2,000 from Miss Darbishire, was
installed in the gallery; a carved organ case, designed by Mr Theobald,
was paid for in part by donations from the college's five surviving
original students: Margaret Roberts, Kate Downing, Maude Thompson, Frances Conway Cobbe, and Violet Wild.

The last building project to be carried out before the war—the
reconstruction of the asymmetrical archway connecting Maitland
and House—removed a long-standing college eyesore. The work,
which entailed the construction of a new staircase up to the dining
hall, the extension of the pantry, and the modification of a number of
offices and rooms, was carried out by Hutchins the builders to the
plans of Morley Horder (who on one occasion insisted on attending a
meeting of Finance Committee in order to complain of his treatment
by the college and suggest that his services should be dispensed

with).[28] The bay window from the bursar's office was transferred to the western side of the new archway, and the coat of arms of Miss Maitland, painted in heraldic colours, was carved in stone on the east side. On the inside, the new staircase was illuminated by a striking light-fitting specially designed by the architect to symbolize the college motto. It was the first recorded use for this purpose of the new plastic material called *Novellen*.

The transformation of the college's appearance in these years was mirrored by major changes in the composition of the SCR (see Plate 36). Arriving from Girton in January 1932 to take up the post of principal's secretary, Hilda Bryant witnessed the last days of the *ancien régime*:

> The two 'elder statesmen' were Miss Pope and Miss Lorimer, whose very contrasted characters seemed to fit even their physical appearance—Miss Pope always mild, rather self-effacing except when directly asked her opinion, Miss Lorimer often irritable, quick to sarcasm and contemptuous of anyone who fell below her standards. They were, I think, devoted friends, linked by the fact that scholarship was more important to them than anything else.[29]

Miss Pope, the unmistakable model for Miss Lydgate in *Gaudy Night*, would, she said, 'have been kind to a burglar though not a murderer.'[30] The 'really important people in the SCR' at this date, according to Hilda Bryant, were Maude Clarke and Lucy Sutherland, with Enid Starkie a 'runner-up'. People were wary of Vera Farnell, who was suspected of repeating everything to Miss Darbishire—to the extent that 'this avenue of approach was sometimes used deliberately.' Some—including, according to Miss Bryant, the Principal—were actually frightened of the Treasurer, Miss Beauchamp.[31] Over all of them, and over the wider college community, the Bursar, 'Trix' Stonedale, maintained a 'sardonic but benevolent watch'; when she saw a young tutor wilting, recalled one of them, 'she would take her for a drive

---

[28] Minutes of Council, 14 May 1935.   [29] Recollections of Hilda Bryant.

[30] The resemblance to Miss Lydgate comes across even more strongly in the Report of Council which recorded Miss Pope's death in 1956: 'A burning desire to redress wrongs struggled in her for supremacy with an unquenchable belief in the native disinterestedness and goodwill of everyone. . . . She was incapable of believing that there existed idle or unsatisfactory pupils, but only unhappy or unfortunate ones.'

[31] Agneta Beauchamp succeeded Helene Reynard as Treasurer and Secretary of the College in 1925, after distinguished war service in Salonika, for which she was awarded the OBE in 1919, and was twice mentioned in despatches from the Commander-in-Chief.

on Sunday, and buy her an ice-cream. It was not the ice-cream that mattered.'[32]

The early 1930s saw some important new recruits to the college's teaching strength. With the appointment of Mary Lascelles to succeed Charlotte Young in 1931 the continued distinction of Somerville's English school was assured. The recommendation of Education Committee, when Miss Napier left to get married in 1932, that her successor as Librarian should be 'a scholar of some standing who could combine Librarianship with some tutorial work', provided an opportunity to recall Evangeline Evans from Wycombe Abbey School to take up permanently the post which she had held for two terms during Miss Napier's absence on leave the previous year. In 1933 the Council took a step without precedent in an Oxford women's college, when it elected to a fellowship a tutor who was engaged to be married. Isobel Munro was married to Charles Henderson at the end of Trinity Term; she was, tragically, to return from her honeymoon a widow.

In 1933 a committee was convened to consider again the question of college teaching in the natural sciences. The recommendation, that 'in making a permanent appointment . . . the question of research should be taken into account, and an appointment made of someone who is already distinguished in research or shews likelihood of becoming so,' was made with a particular person in mind. A temporary lecturer in zoology was appointed, and, with an eye to the future, a research fellowship for two years was offered to Miss Dorothy Crowfoot, a recent Somerville chemistry graduate currently working in Cambridge with J. D. Bernal. Dorothy Crowfoot spent the first year of her fellowship in Cambridge, and was then invited to return to Somerville as tutor in natural science. Reluctant—as Isobel Munro had been a few years earlier—to commit herself to the tutorial round, she consulted Bernal, and was advised by him to accept, on the grounds that 'it is far too good to refuse, times are difficult, full-time academic jobs are scarce.'[33] In 1936 she was elected to an official fellowship, and in 1937 she married Thomas Hodgkin, to whom she had been introduced by his cousin, Margery Fry. Dorothy Hodgkin's contribution to science was to bring her in 1964 the Nobel Prize for Chemistry and in 1965 the Order of Merit (the first woman since Florence Nightingale to be so honoured); in Somerville's domestic

[32] Lascelles, *A Memoir*, 50.

[33] D. Hodgkin, 'Crystallography and Chemistry in the First Hundred Years of Somerville College' (Bryce Lecture, 1979).

annals she was to make her mark as the first serving fellow of the college to have a baby.

In 1934 Mildred Pope left Somerville to take up the Chair of Romance Philology at Manchester University. Dorothy L. Sayers, invited to propose the toast to the University at that summer's gaudy, paid eloquent tribute to her former tutor:

> We in this college are this term bidding farewell to a woman who, to all who knew her, has always seemed to typify some of the noblest things for which this university stands: the integrity of judgment that gain cannot corrupt, the humility in the face of facts that self-esteem cannot blind, the generosity of a great mind that is eager to give praise to others, the singleness of purpose that pursues knowledge as some men pursue glory and that will not be contented with the second-hand or the second-best.

It was in the preparation for this speech that the idea of *Gaudy Night* took definite shape in the author's mind.[34]

Miss Pope's successor—her former pupil, Enid Starkie—had been attached to Somerville since 1928 as the Sarah Smithson lecturer in French. In view of this existing connection, she was now dispensed from the probationary period which was customary for new fellows, and also allowed to live out of college, on the understanding that she would be expected to dine in on average three nights a week.[35] 'All the fellows of Somerville live in college' she wrote (inaccurately) in 1940 to a friend, Alyse Gregory,

> but I made it clear that I could not do that and so as a great concession I am allowed to live out. They put my desire for living alone down to the fact of my being a wild Irishwoman and to the fact that I was a student in Paris. I lose financially by the arrangement but I could not bear to live in a community again and I hate a lot of people around me; I particularly hate a lot of women around me. I never really feel at home with my colleagues.[36]

She was to continue to maintain that she was a misfit in Oxford until her death there in 1970. Recording an—at times—stormy relationship with Somerville, her biographer concluded that 'no other women's college would have produced or tolerated or held Enid Starkie.'[37]

---

[34] B. Reynolds, *Dorothy L. Sayers: Her Life and Soul* (London, 1993), 252.
[35] Minutes of Council, 8 May 1934.
[36] Letter from ES to Alyse Gregory, 6 Oct. 1940, quoted in J. Richardson, *Enid Starkie* (London, 1973), 126–7.   [37] Richardson, *Enid Starkie*, 241.

In 1933 a sub-committee to consider the college's provision for teaching in *literae humaniores* recommended the appointment of a tutor in philosophy as soon as a suitably qualified person became available; and the income of the Constance Ann Lee Fund, traditionally used to provide grants for tutors on sabbatical leave, was set aside for this purpose.[38] The following year, Dorothea Sharp's tenure of the Lady Carlisle fellowship came to an end and, after consultation with Gilbert Murray, it was agreed to offer the fellowship to Miss Lorimer 'in consideration of her distinguished services to the College over a period of nearly forty years and of the contribution she has already made to learning during that time.' Miss Mildred Hartley—a Girtonian lecturer at Liverpool University—was appointed tutor in classics, and Miss Lorimer, by special dispensation of the Council, was elected to a tutorship in classical archaeology and an official fellowship until her retirement in 1939. War and illness delayed until 1951 the publication of her great work *Homer and the Monuments*; in 1948, fifty-five years after entering Girton as a student, she was to be one of the first women candidates to present themselves for a Cambridge degree.

In 1933 the illness of Maude Clarke prompted the Council to make provision for sick leave for the Principal and fellows. At the beginning of Michaelmas Term 1935 Miss Clarke submitted her resignation on the grounds of prolonged ill-health. She was persuaded to accept instead two terms of sabbatical leave and to retain the office of Vice-Principal; Miss Stonedale was appointed acting Vice-Principal, Miss Sutherland took on the office of tutor to the history undergraduates, and Miss Clarke's former pupil May McKisack travelled down from Liverpool to do her medieval teaching. Maude Clarke died on 17 November 1935: a great historian and a great tutor, on whose wisdom and judgement and taste Somerville had come to depend in all sorts of ways. Fifty years later, those who knew her spoke still of her loss as irreparable.[39] The following May, Miss McKisack was unanimously elected as her successor. At the meeting of Council of 27 October 1936, Mildred Hartley, Dorothy Crowfoot, and May McKisack were admitted as fellows in the order of their appointment as college tutors. On the domestic front, Mrs Adams, the College Cook, retired in 1934 after 25 years of service.

The 1930s were in many respects a time of expansion and hope for

[38] Minutes of Council, 28 Feb. 1933.
[39] For the impression which she made upon a junior colleague, see Lascelles, *A Memoir*, 47–8.

Somerville. 1933 saw the formation of the Somerville–Girton alliance, cemented with a dinner in either college and a mutual exchange of gifts; the inaugural dinner in Girton was held in the new dining-room panelled in memory of Dame Bertha Phillpotts, their former Mistress, and Somerville's first Lady Carlisle research fellow.[40] In June 1934 Lady Poulton celebrated the 50th anniversary of her election to the Somerville Council. A bouquet of fifty flowers was presented to her, and she gave the college a mazer bowl, in commemoration of the half-century during which she had attended 313 out of a total of 373 Council meetings. She was to continue to serve for a further five years. In 1936, on the proposal of the Director of Education for Oxfordshire, Somerville 'adopted' Bicester County School, a connection which was to be maintained for some forty years, with Somerville nominating a succession of its fellows as governors.[41] That summer, the Principals of the women's colleges were invited for the first time to take part in the procession at Encaenia, and Somerville decided to hold an annual gaudy instead of one every two years, to enable a third of the members of the ASM to be invited each time. (The original spelling of 'gaudy', abandoned in 1911 in favour of 'gaude', was reinstated in 1934.)[42] In 1939, at what was to prove the last gaudy for some years, the principal announced that Enid Starkie had become the modern languages faculty's first D.Litt.—an event marked by Beatrice, the Somerville cook, with a special ice-pudding inscribed 'E.S.D.Litt.'[43]

In the course of the decade the college received a number of valuable endowments, including a gift of £3,000 from Lord Buckmaster to establish a post-graduate scholarship in memory of his daughter Margaret Dighton Pollock, and a bequest of £2,000 from Mrs Margaret Irene Seymour to endow a scholarship for proficiency in music, painting, sculpture, maths, classics, or natural science. On the death in 1932 of Lady Bousfield, the college received under the will of her husband (the Clothworkers' Representative on the college Council from 1900 until his death in 1910) a valuable collection of books and pictures, a sum for building purposes, and £1,000 for the establishment of a scholarship tenable by former pupils of the Girls' Public Day School Trust (of which he had been chairman).[44] In 1936 a bequest of some

---

[40] An LMH–Newnham alliance was formed in the same year.
[41] Minutes of Council, 26 May 1936.   [42] Minutes of Council, 5 June 1934.
[43] Richardson, *Enid Starkie*, 122.
[44] An earlier instalment of books and pictures had been received on Sir William's death in 1910.

£10,000 from Mrs E. M. Holme, a former headmistress of Dewsbury Grammar School who had nominated Somerville as her residual legatee, enabled the college to pay off its outstanding debt to Christ Church. The same year brought bequests commemorating the college's first two Principals: from Miss Emily Shaw Lefevre the silver tea-set which had been presented to her sister on retirement, and from the anthropologist Mrs Katherine Routledge a sum of £500 to commission a posthumous portrait of Miss Maitland.

When Winifred Holtby died in 1935, at the age of 37, she bequeathed to the college the proceeds of her unpublished manuscripts; should this sum exceed £3,000 a scholarship was to be endowed in memory of her friend Dorothy McCalman for the benefit of students who, like Dorothy, had previously earned their living for at least three years. The manuscripts in question were found to consist of a number of short stories, published in 1937 as *Pavements at Anderby*, and a large novel. *South Riding*, published in February 1936, went through eight impressions before the year was out, and has been selling ever since. In 1937 it was awarded the James Tait Black Prize for the best English novel of the year; it has since been filmed, televised, and translated into most European languages, with titles whose English equivalents range from 'Red Sarah' to 'Take It and Pay for It'. Within four years of Winifred Holtby's death Somerville had received some £7,000 for the Dorothy McCalman scholarship.[45] The fund supported a succession of mature students until 1961 when, changes in government funding having rendered such provision redundant, the terms of the trust were altered to enable the partial support of two tutorial fellowships: the Dorothy McCalman fellowship in politics and the Winifred Holtby fellowship in modern history.

Conferences continued to provide a useful additional source of income. The American summer schools organized jointly by the women's colleges were particularly profitable: Somerville's share of the proceeds of the 1932 summer school was over £600, in addition to the £573.16.11d. received by the Bursar for use of college rooms.[46] When an appeal was made to the colleges in 1932 for the new Bodleian Library extension, the Council agreed that Somerville 'would be glad to contribute as generously as its means allow,' and committed itself to twenty annual instalments of £50.[47] The following year the Society

---

[45] The first recipient of the McCalman award—Mary Dimishky—was nominated by Winifred Holtby's mother.   [46] Minutes of Council, 25 Oct. 1932.

[47] Minutes of Council, 7 June 1932.

of Home Students addressed a memorandum to Hebdomadal Council on the inadequacy of the grant allocated to it by the University; the Women Students' Property Committee (which administered the property held in common by the women's societies) responded with the suggestion that the residential women's colleges might feel able to forgo part of their government grant in favour of the Home Students. The Somerville Council agreed that, though this was out of the question for the current quinquennium, it would consider supporting the Home Students in an application for a government grant thereafter. In communicating this decision to the WSPC it added, somewhat priggishly, that

> the attention of the Society of Oxford Home Students should be drawn to the fact that the residential colleges have reluctantly raised their fees in order to put their finances on a sound basis and consider that the basis of the composition fee, in conjunction with the establishment of a bursary fund for poor students, is the only efficient method of dealing with the problem of providing adequate tutorial stipends.[48]

Despite domestic preoccupations, international developments were never far from mind in these years. The plight of Jewish scholars in Germany in the 1930s was followed with deep concern in Oxford, and in October 1933 Professor Brierly—a member of the Somerville Council—chaired an important public meeting at Rhodes House to consider projects for their relief. Miss Darbishire was one of those most active in schemes to provide practical assistance, and on her proposal Somerville agreed to offer temporary appointments to two eminent women scholars who had been dismissed from their posts: Fraulein Noether of Göttingen University, and Frau Doktor Margarete Bieber, formerly Professor of Classical Archaeology at the University of Giessen.[49] Fraulein Noether in the event found a permanent lecturing post at Bryn Mawr—thereby depriving Somerville of association with one of the outstanding creative mathematicians of the time—but in 1934 Dr Bieber was elected to an honorary research fellowship, provided with accommodation by Miss Bruce, and engaged to give a course of lectures to be financed jointly by the women's colleges. Her book on the development of Greek dress *Entwicklungsgeschichte der Griechischen Tracht*, published in Berlin in 1934 with the help of

[48] Minutes of Council, 24 Oct. 1933.   [49] Minutes of Council, 24 Oct. 1933.

funds collected by Miss Darbishire, was dedicated in gratitude to the Principal and Fellows of Somerville College.

In January 1939 a special meeting of Council was called to consider whether the college could provide more substantial assistance for refugee academic women. It was agreed to allocate £150 from the research reserve fund, and to provide board and—if possible in term-time—residence, to one or two women scholars, 'choosing specially those to whom study in Oxford would be most valuable, and whose future, through this opportunity, is likely to be improved and secured.'[50] Research grants and hospitality were offered to the Egyptologist Dr K. Bosse and the classical scholar Dr Herzog Hauser; the foundations of a much longer connection were laid with the offer of a term's meals to Dr Lotte Labowsky, already in Oxford working with Dr Raymond Klibansky.

As the decade wore on, the chances of Somerville enjoying peaceful use of its new buildings must have seemed increasingly remote. In December 1935 a letter from the Town Clerk requested permission to inspect the college premises with a view to their use as a first-aid centre in the event of air-raids. The Bedford House school-room was subsequently designated for use as a decontamination centre, Council agreeing in May 1936 that it should be put at the disposal of the City authorities if and when necessary. The following year, the college fire-precautions were revised in consultation with the City Engineer. A meeting of domestic bursars, summoned to discuss air-raid precautions, was told that the City was prepared to issue gas-masks, but not to contribute to any expenditure by colleges.[51] In Michaelmas Term 1938 the Principal told Council that in her opinion 'it would be advisable to ascertain, if possible, whether in the event of an international emergency, university education would continue, and, if so, on what basis.' While Miss Jebb and Mr Jacks took up this matter with the Board of Education, two of the college servants were sent to join the Clarendon Press fire brigade, and—perhaps most significant of all—the Senior Common Room purchased a wireless set.[52] In February 1939 the vice-chancellor summoned a meeting of heads of house to discuss the functions of the university in a national emergency. It was agreed that the university should act as a clearing-house; all questions, whether from the government or the colleges, would be referred

---

[50] Minutes of Council, 24 Jan. 1939. [51] Minutes of Council, 23 Nov. 1937.
[52] Minutes of SCR, MT 1938.

to the vice-chancellor; and all negotiations, including the use of college buildings, would be conducted by a committee of Hebdomadal Council.[53] The meeting of the Somerville Council to which these arrangements were reported also received a request from Miss Lascelles (who was famously accident-prone) for sabbatical leave in Michaelmas Term 1939, with a view to travelling on the continent. College legend has it that one fellow passed to another a note which read 'Now war is certain.'

[53] Minutes of Council, 14 Feb. 1939.

10

'A Wider World':
College Life Between the Wars

'Before the War they passionately had College Meetings about everything. Now, they won't be bothered. Half the old institutions, like the College debates and the Third Year Play, are dead or moribund. They don't want responsibility.'

'They're all taken up with their young men' said Miss Burrows.

Gaudy Night (1935)

IN *Gaudy Night* Dorothy L. Sayers, herself a student at Somerville from 1912 to 1915, portrays an Oxford women's college of the mid-1930s through the eyes of a heroine who had been there in the early 1920s. Harriet Vane at one point attempts to explain to a group of current Shrewsbury undergraduates the perplexity of the pre-war generation at their 'sad lack of enthusiasm':

'In their day,' said Harriet, 'I think people had a passion for meetings and organisation.'

'There are plenty of inter-collegiate meetings,' said Miss Layton. 'We discuss things a great deal, and are indignant about the Proctorial Rules for Mixed Parties. But our enthusiasm for internal affairs is more restrained.'[1]

The 1920s saw a steady erosion of the old social self-sufficiency of the women's colleges. Somerville, which in the war had experienced a more complete break than any of the others with its own past, was perhaps the readiest of them for change. Four years at Oriel had engendered a powerful *esprit de corps*, but had also detached the college from its roots. Somerville students, returning in 1919 to buildings which only one of them—Vera Brittain—had known before the war, had no collective memory of ordinary peace-time collegiate life. The old, passionate division between Hall and West, which had provided the basis of so many past arrangements, was incomprehensible to the

---

[1] D. L. Sayers, *Gaudy Night* (London, 1935), 137.

post-war generation. The rationale for many traditional practices—and sometimes the practices themselves—had been lost to memory. In a general review of constitutional procedures, a students' committee was instituted (Plate 22), with elected representatives from each year; the title of President of the JCR was substituted for that of Senior Student; and a secret ballot was instituted for the election of college officers. Poring over old minute-books of College Meetings in an attempt to clarify their own constitutional position, the JCR were at times obliged to resort to the longer memory of the dons. At a meeting in June 1922 the Senior Student explained that

> in 1909 the JCR had empowered the SCR to supervise the final election of the President and Secretary, but since then people had forgotten the actual position and there was a general feeling that the part played by both the SCR and JCR should be clearly defined.[2]

Miss Darbishire, attending on behalf of the SCR, assured the meeting that it was for the JCR alone to elect. Earlier in the term she and Miss Pope had been called upon to explain the original aims of Amalgamation, and the principles on which it had been run, to a meeting desirous of combining the JCR funds with the funds of the games clubs.

Janet Vaughan, who as Principal twenty-five years later was to install hens in the garden of Radcliffe House, made an early impression on College Meeting with a proposal that Somerville should revert to the ancient tradition of keeping pigs.[3] The suggestion was presumably facetious, and certainly unsuccessful. The following year, noting that attendance at daily morning prayers had dropped to four or five at most, the JCR President urged students 'to make a real effort to uphold a tradition which is as old as the College itself.'[4] As time went on, the JCR became increasingly less amenable to appeals to past tradition. 'The very close personal relations of the earlier years when the College was much smaller and outside the University were over,' commented Lucy Sutherland of her undergraduate years, 1925–7—adding that she and her contemporaries thought this an excellent thing: 'We considered the reminiscences of our predecessors sentimental and mawkish and prided ourselves on the wider world in which we lived.'[5]

[2] College Meeting, 21 June 1922.   [3] College Meeting, 9 Mar. 1920.
[4] College Meeting, 18 Oct. 1921.
[5] Paper on 'Women at Oxford' given at seminar, 1973. She said she had no doubt that later generations in their turn felt the same about them.

In a letter home in 1929, Elisabeth Murray described a heated discussion at College Meeting over the fate of two pictures given by Ruskin in 1884 (see Plate 13):

> These always used to be in the JCR but were taken down when it was redecorated in grey, pink, blue and gold according to Roger Fry's design, and only brought back for the Jubilee. They don't suit the JCR a bit . . . so someone moved a motion that they be removed. (The Fry had said the final decision would rest with the SCR but that we might express our opinion.) Miss Darbishire then rose up and said that as Ruskin had given them etc we should respect the gift. Then other members of the SCR rose up in arms and said the JCR had no right to remove the pictures at all—that the JCR belonged to the College and not to us, that at any rate one year couldn't legislate in a thing like that for ever and ever etc., etc. It was all most heated and amusing.[6]

The gulf between senior and junior common rooms, which Vera Brittain identified as one of the distinguishing features of Miss Penrose's principalship,[7] was by now thoroughly established. To Alix Kilroy, who as an undergraduate in 1922 prided herself on spending as little time in Somerville as possible, Miss Bruce, Miss Darbishire, and Miss Pope were 'just white-haired elderly ladies of no personal interest to me.'[8]

Such detachment would have been inconceivable to earlier generations. But relaxation of tension after the war, the new status of women as members of the university, and the greater social freedoms of the post-war era now combined to create an environment in which the university, rather than the college, gradually became the chief focus of undergraduate life. A crucial shift in emphasis occurred at about the turn of the decade. An undergraduate who was up between 1929 and 1933 writes of her impression that she hit the very end of a period when undergraduate life was largely centred in college: 'Before I came down it was much more outward looking. At first JCR meetings were very well-attended and lively. This was quite different at the end.'[9]

---

[6] KMEM, 20 Oct. 1929.

[7] V. Brittain, *Testament of Youth: An Autobiographical Study of the Years 1900–1925* (London, 1978), 508.

[8] A. Meynell, *Public Servant, Private Woman: An Autobiography* (London, 1988), 68–9. Miss Darbishire was 41 at the time.

[9] Unattributed Recollections in the College Archives.

As membership of the university opened up to women students a whole range of new social and intellectual opportunities, the old college-based clubs and societies lost much of their charm. The college institutions which survived into the 1930s were, by and large, those which provided a springboard for activity on a wider university stage, or which—like the sports clubs—were sustained by inter-collegiate rivalry. Those which owed their existence to the pre-war necessity of members of the college spending most of their leisure time in each other's company inexorably declined. The days of the large captive college audience had passed. The most popular form of college entertainment in the 1920s was the Saturday evening dance.

A dance marked Somerville's return to its own buildings in Michaelmas Term 1919, a hundred couples dancing till midnight to the 'inspiriting' music of a professional jazz band. Informal dances, with piano accompaniment and an earlier deadline, were held three evenings a term—even in January 1921 when the college was in quarantine for mumps.[10] (The informality of these occasions was relative: students were expected to introduce their partners to the Principal on arrival, and Edith Standen referred to her partner, even in her diary, as 'Mr——'.) Dancing formed part of the programme for the annual Christmas party for the college scouts, and for the party given by science undergraduates in 1923 for their professors, lecturers, and demonstrators. Heated College Meetings debated the desirability of engaging the services of a dancing mistress and of a professional accompanist. In 1923 a college jazz band—consisting initially, rather improbably, of fifteen drummers, a banjo, a violin, and a 'cello—made its first appearance at an impromptu fancy-dress dance, and thereafter played regularly on Saturday evenings.[11] When an Academic Dance Club for men and women members of the university was set up, with the proctors' blessing, in 1927, the Oxford Correspondent reported that it 'in no way detracted from the enjoyment of our usual college dances.'

The Somerville Parliament was an early casualty of the new enthusiasms. Already reduced by 1919 to one meeting a term, the House

---

[10] College Meeting, 18 Jan. 1921: 'The SS announced that as we were in quarantine for mumps the dance could not be held on Feb 5th. It would however be perfectly safe to hold it the week before the risk of infection became serious. She asked for a show of hands in favour of holding it on the coming Saturday Jan 22nd. There were 45 in favour . . . and this was considered a sufficient number to make the dance possible.'

[11] Log Book, HT 1923.

resolved itself in March 1920 into a committee to discuss the report of the Royal Commission on Academic Fatigue. The report itself was detailed and entertaining, but the debate disappointing. In May the first-year students expressed willingness to hold a Parliament should the rest of college wish them to do so; a long discussion as to how the final-year students could signify their wishes in a strictly constitutional way was resolved by a proposal by Winifred Holtby 'that the second, third, and fourth years would be very glad if the first year held their Parliament'.[12] The institution struggled on for another term. The Coalition Party was dissolved; a proposal that Parliament should represent college opinion rather than the parties at Westminster was defeated; and it was decided to hold one more Parliament in Hilary Term in order to give the new first year an opportunity to decide whether they wanted to keep it on. Evidently they didn't. By the following year Parliament had disappeared.

College spirit sustained other traditional institutions for a little longer. The old pattern of entertainment—second-year play in Michaelmas Terms, first-year play in Hilary, and going-down play in Trinity—was resumed after the war. Occasional entertainments were put on by members of the SCR. At a 'delightfully arranged Hallowe'en Party' in 1922 final-year students were required to identify a series of Victorian tableaux in which members of the SCR appeared as figures in famous pictures; Miss Penrose, it was said, 'gave an extraordinarily real impersonation of the famous Huxley portrait.'[13]

The first play to be performed back on home territory in Michaelmas Term 1919 was the second-year production of Barrie's *The Professor's Love Story* (Plate 25). This was parodied in Trinity Term by the going-down students in *The Sleeping Beauty; or The Provost's Partiality; or The Curse of Croxford*, a work whose plot brought together many topical themes:

Princess Charmian, cursed by the malignant power of Oxonia Borealis, the Northern Blight and the Spirit of Chap[erone] Rules, falls into a sleep from which she is forced to wake up in Winterchill College, Croxford, where she will be imprisoned as a student until she is kissed by a prince in the shape of an undergraduate. She is however aided by the Spirit of Degrees for Women, who becomes a don at Winterchill in order to help her. The rest of the play dealt with

---

[12] College Meeting, May 1920.   [13] Log Book, MT 1922.

the progress of the romance of Charmian and Merton New, the undergraduate, affording opportunities for showing College life, and with the love of the Provost of Boreal for Miss B. A. Degrees, which he himself does not suspect. Finally, in spite of the strenuous efforts of Oxonia Borealis to hinder both romances, the Provost and B. A. Degrees and Merton and Charmian are united, while Oxonia is banished from Croxford for ever. The play ended with the conferring of degrees by the Provost as Vice-Chancellor upon undergraduates and women students hand in hand.[14]

The part of Merton New was played by Winifred Holtby; and most of the costumes were made, in the course of a visit to Oxford, by her elder sister Grace. Because of her year's absence on war service in France this was not in fact Winifred Holtby's final year, and she was to figure still more prominently in the 1921 play, of which she and Vera Brittain were co-authors. *Bolshevism in Baghdad: A Psycho-analytic Experiment*, took the form of a psycho-analysed dream in which the Caliph of Baghdad (played by Winifred Holtby in 'most heavenly orange trousers') sends to Oxford for four women dons to found a college in which his wives (who have become converted to Bolshevism) will be restored to order. 'It isn't very funny' wrote Winifred Holtby to her friend Jean McWilliam, 'but has infinite possibilities of caricature and topical allusion, which are the main thing.'[15] The cast included Janet Vaughan as the Minister of Finance, and Vera Brittain as 'the most charming of all the dons', Miss Cleopatra O'Nesbitt—a romantic combination of Maude Clarke and the popular actress, Cathleen Nesbitt.[16] (The following year Helen Waddell prevailed upon Miss Nesbitt to come to Somerville with C. B. Ramage and a company of friends to give a performance of Massinger's *The Great Duke of Florence* and the balcony scene from *Romeo and Juliet* in aid of the Endowment Fund.) The quest for endowment was itself the theme of the 1922 going-down play, *Donec Rursus Impleat Orbem*—a production memorable for Mary Redman's impersonation of Payne the college porter, and the partnership of Elspeth Dundas and Dominica Legge as the Archaeologist and his Dun-legged Ass.

The going-down plays had a further ten years of life, generally, as Vera Farnell said, 'hitting off very happily the events of the year'; in her joint capacity as Librarian and Dean she tended to suffer the worst

---

[14] Log Book, 1920.   [15] W. Holtby, *Letters to a Friend* (London, 1937), 41.
[16] Log Book, 1921. See also Brittain, *Testament of Youth*, 513.

hits, 'but often inspired the best songs.'[17] The 1923 play—a parody of a *Cinderella* pantomime, in which a Somerville student was enticed away from her godmother's choice, Prince B. A., by the Temptations of College: hockey, tennis, dancing, and the river—made much comic play with an article on Somerville which had recently appeared in *The Sphere*, and included a series of tableaux in which an archaeologist sought to prove from relics (i.e. lacrosse sticks, red hockey skirts, etc.) found on the site of Somerville, that the college was a cannibal island. In 1929 'Miss Fry's Young Ladies' presented a revue entitled *Oxford in Aspic*; the 1930 going-down play, *The Red's Progress; or, Seraphina through the Spheres*, was pronounced 'as lively as ever'. But despite these successes, the tradition was nearing the end of its life. Writing of the 1931 production, *The Crown Jewels*, the Oxford Correspondent concluded that it was 'lamentably uninteresting and ill-produced, and made one hope that this worn-out tradition will not survive another year.' In the event, it staggered on for two more years. In 1933 *A Day in the Life of the Mind* 'fell rather flat, whether through exhaustion on the part of the authors and performers, or because of a miserably small audience, we do not know.' The 1934 Oxford Letter recorded simply that 'The Going Down Play has died a natural death.'

It was survived for a short time by the first-year play. This, too, tended towards parochial comment on college life—though with occasional forays into melodrama, such as the 'lurid and realistic' performance of *Bluebeard* given by the 1924 freshers. The 1925 first year, having presented a revue, *The Freshers Explain Themselves*—in which they portrayed what they considered to be the outstanding features of each school: the clever Classics, aesthetic English, frivolous French, hard-worked Historians, methodical Mathematicians, puzzled PPEs, and solitary Scientists—as part of a triple bill in Hilary Term, stepped into the breach in Trinity Term (when as a consequence of the General Strike all examinations were postponed for a week, and the going-down play was cancelled) with a skit in which they imitated the third year at College Meeting, Sunday music, and other college functions.

The standard of acting and production on these occasions was generally high, and the original compositions were often ingenious. The 1931 offering, *The Sneezer of Somerville*, in which the same plot was given after the manner of Edgar Wallace, Greek tragedy, Shakespeare, and Gilbert and Sullivan, was praised in the *College Report* as 'extremely

---

[17] V. Farnell, *A Somervillian Looks Back* (Oxford, 1948), 48.

clever and amusing'. In Hilary Term 1932 the freshers gave a 'more than usually promising' performance of Tennyson's *The Princess*: Anne Scott-James in the title role, 'grand, epic, homicidal, six feet high', was reported by a contemporary to have been superb 'especially in the cold and ferocious bits'; while Mary Fisher, clad in a flowing grey chiton and sandals, with a silver fillet round her hair and a marble pillar to lean on, 'looked the very spirit of classicism, and sounded it too, when she began to declaim blank verse in clear, modulated Oxford tones.'[18] In Hilary Term 1935 the freshers returned to more traditional lines with a revue entitled—in rather worn reference to a favourite theme of Miss Darbishire's—*The Life of the Mind*. But what had started life as a spontaneous entertainment was by now coming to be regarded as an imposition on actors and audience alike. 'It ought to be great fun—at least that's the idea of it,' reported Audrey Brodhurst to her parents in 1932: 'As it is, it is just hateful to everyone.' The end came when in 1937 Joy Dickinson was informed that one of her duties as Senior Scholar was to organize the first-year play, and she simply refused.[19]

With the disappearance of Parliament and the decline of the traditional 'year' theatricals, debating and acting ceased to be activities in which everyone, regardless of talent or inclination, was expected to participate. The succession of debating and dramatic societies which took their place were the province of the enthusiastic few.

One reason for the demise of Parliament was that it did not provide the right kind of practice for the inter-collegiate debates which were now increasingly in vogue. To this end a new Debating Society was established in 1919, one of whose first engagements was a joint debate with the Sutton Society of Brasenose, held in Somerville on Hallowe'en, on the motion 'That this House views with apprehension the use of the strike as a political weapon'. A Brasenose account of the event speaks of the cordiality of their reception, the beauties of the place, and the severity of the treatment meted out to the Brasenose proposer of the motion by his Somerville opponent Miss [Janet] Vaughan.[20] Shortly afterwards the Somerville Debating Society paid a nostalgic return to Oriel to debate with the Arnold Society the motion 'That this House regrets the obsolescence of parental control'. Joint meetings were subsequently held with Ruskin, St John's, the XX Club of

[18] Brodhurst, HT 1932.   [19] Recollections of Christina Roaf (Drake, 1937).
[20] Log Book, MT 1919.

New College, and the Diagnostic Club of Wadham, and with the Spanish and French Clubs—the latter taking place, in French, in the Somerville JCR.

The Debating Society survived, on and off, throughout the 1920s and 1930s. In 1928 its president, Nancy Samuel, was selected to represent the Oxford women's colleges, together with representatives from Cambridge and London, on a debating tour of America organized by the National Union of Students. As Principal, Miss Fry attempted to improve standards by giving instruction classes in public speaking, and instituting a competition in which undergraduates spoke for three minutes each and were placed for matter, style, and delivery.[21] Joint debates were held with a number of the men's colleges—a Somerville undergraduate complained that the men always suggested frivolous subjects, such as 'That love is a waste of time'—and in 1933 a mock trial was held in conjunction with Oriel. The society reconstituted itself in 1938 and 'in company with societies from other colleges, gallantly undertook discussion of subjects which would have daunted dialecticians.'[22] But it is clear that those who remembered the great days of Parliament had a low opinion of modern debating skills.

College drama likewise flourished intermittently, sustained by the prolonged refusal of OUDS to admit women to full membership and from a proctorial regulation which prohibited inter-collegiate drama as infringing the OUDS charter. The gift in 1924 of a real stage by a current undergraduate, Lady Iris Capell, signalled Somerville's growing professionalism, and enabled the college Dramatic Society to undertake more ambitious productions. A play was attempted most years: in 1928 Pirandello's *Cosi e se vi pare*; in 1930 a production, notable for its stage effects, of Dryden's *Siege of Granada*. Though unable (or, as the Oxford Correspondent suggested, unwilling) to attempt a play in 1931, the Dramatic Society revived the following year to organize fortnightly drama readings and a spirited production of *Arden of Feversham*, and at the scouts' party in Michaelmas Term 1932 provided as entertainment a charade illustrating the word PENROSE—a performance which, though agreed to be well acted, was generally thought to be too esoteric for the occasion. A double bill in Trinity Term 1934 provided a contrast between John Ingelind's sixteenth-century interlude *The Disobedient Child*, and John Underhill's translation of *The Cradle Song* by Martinez Sierra—the latter chosen largely because

---

[21] *Fritillary*, 1 Dec. 1928, 24.   [22] Oxford Letter, 1937–8.

of the almost complete absence of male parts. After a year in which the Dramatic Society's only production was a thriller for the scouts' party, it returned in 1936 to a Spanish theme with Alejandro Casona's *The Devil Again*, in a translation by two Somerville undergraduates, Inez Pearn and Marghanita Laski. This unusual play, whose unorthodoxy, according to the ASM Oxford Letter, 'tested the intelligence of the audience somewhat severely' was performed not in college but in the new hall of the Taylorian Institution. The society's last two pre-war productions were more conventional: Congreve's *The Way of the World* in 1937, and a 'very spirited' performance of Dekker's *Shoemaker's Holiday* in March 1938.

The transformation in 1921 of the Somerville Glee Club into the Music Club, and in 1927 of the Music Club into the Musical Society, is an indication of a growing ambition which carried Somerville's musicians far beyond their traditional brief of providing simple entertainment for the rest of college on Saturday evenings. It may well have been the only college society which actually increased in vigour between the wars. The 1920 Oxford Letter recorded, as a 'somewhat novel departure' a number of concerts held in college, and also a series of Sunday evening musical gatherings organized by Miss Bruce. In the course of the next twenty years, the musical life of the college was to benefit enormously from the presence as students of some outstanding musicians, and by their contacts with a larger musical world. In 1924 a song recital was given by Mrs John Seeds; in 1927/8 a concert was given by Harriet Cohen (whose sister Myra Verney was currently reading English at Somerville) and the New Philharmonic String Quartet; and Jean Hamilton returned to Somerville to give a rehearsal of the programme for her forthcoming London piano recital. Under the presidency of Margaret Paterson, the Somerville Musical Society in the early 1930s organized an ambitious series of Sunday evening concerts which attracted large audiences from outside college. Among the professional musicians who gave their services free of charge were Vera Moore, Joan Elwes, Rachel Monkhouse, Gladys Noon, Dorothea Fraser, and John Engleheart. The tradition survived Miss Paterson's departure for the Royal College of Music in 1933, and the following year saw performances by Margaret Deneke and Gabriel Joachim, Sylvia Spencer, and Franz Usborne, as well as a purely Somervillian concert given by the Madrigal Society at which Barbara Ward sang and Eve Kisch, Gladys Low, and Margery Turner played flute and piano solos and duets. In 1935 the Musical Society inaugurated the

tradition of holding a carol service, to which old Somervillians resident in Oxford were invited; the installation of the chapel organ in 1937
gave added dignity to this occasion, replacing the piano and string
accompaniment by which Somerville singing had long been supported. A song recital given by the Musical Society that November
included a composition by Somerville's first organ scholar, Barbara
Bryer. In March 1938 a number of distinguished Old Somervillian
musicians returned to the college to join in a concert given by past
and present members of the Musical Society.

A multiplicity of other societies and clubs made a more or less brief
appearance in college to cater for the interests of the day. One hardy
survivor from the 1890s, the Archaeological Society, was still going
strong in 1928, when Elisabeth Murray described a typically idiosyncratic Sunday outing:

> We assembled in the drive at 10 and were given a set of solutions
> sealed to be opened when lost—each opening to deduct 10 minutes.
> Then we were given the first solution and told to cycle in any direc-
> tion for 5 minutes till out of sight of everyone else. We [Elisabeth
> Murray and Helen Tansley] cycled slowly up the Banbury Road. The
> first clue said 'The Western Stable whence the steed in 3 weeks time
> away with us will speed'. So we were in completely the wrong direc-
> tion and had to fly off to the station. Here Norah Joy handed us
> the second clue: 'A small replica of a big capital.' ... We scoured
> our maps and after about 4 minutes found Little London beyond
> Kennington.[23]

But even ARK was now nearing the end of its long life. The Society
for the Suppression of Printed Matter, founded in 1928, had a predictably short one.[24] The 1920s saw the formation and decline of at least
two scientific societies: the X Club, and the more dashingly-named
'Hotch-Potch of Philosophers', which in 1928 organized a tour of the
Observatory and a series of papers on scientific subjects. A Literary
Society survived from 1921 to 1925 on the strength of a series of popular open lectures. One of the first guest speakers, Alfred Noyes,
appeared, thinly disguised as 'Noyes-Vachelli, the Court Poet', in the
1921 going-down play, reading his own poetry to the assembled court
of Baghdad; his successors included Hugh Walpole, John Masefield,
and Roger Fry, who gave a 'very stimulating and delightful' lecture on

[23] KMEM, 24 Nov. 1928.   [24] *Fritillary*, 1 Dec. 1928.

modern French art, with lantern illustrations, in aid of the Appeal Fund. But despite an ambitious programme for 1924–5 which included G. K. Chesterton on 'The unhistorical novel' and John Buchan on 'The old and the new in literature', attendance failed to match the distinction of the speakers; and at the last College Meeting of the Trinity Term the Society's president, Miss Farnell, announced its decease.

In the course of the 1920s the open lecture came largely to replace old-style society meetings. In 1924 Professor Garstang gave a lantern lecture on 'Birds and their Songs' in which he 'charmed a large audience by his wonderful imitation of their notes, which rivalled the songs which were reproduced on a gramophone'; and the Somervillian anthropologist Mrs Aitken (Barbara Freire-Marreco) a course of six lectures (also with lantern slides) on the Tewa tribe in Arizona, 'enriched by many stories of her personal experiences among the natives.'[25] In 1925/6 Somervillians were able to hear Mr Salter speak on 'Inns of Oxford, 1600–1800', Mr Weaver on 'Cities and churches of Northern Spain', the Warden of New College on 'Coal and railway problems', and Miss Porter, the Lady Carlisle Research Fellow, on 'Growing crystals'; they could also attend classes in speech-training and a recital of verse by Miss Irene Sadler, and a talk (with demonstrations) on Jiu-Jitsu by Mr Pagose. The following year Sir Charles Oman discoursed on cataclysmic history, and Margaret Morris gave a lecture demonstration on methods of movement, assisted by some of her pupils and by enthusiastic first-year students who had been practising her dancing exercises throughout the summer.

But by the late 1920s most college-based societies had fallen victim to the superior attraction of university clubs and societies, where men and women undergraduates were at last able to meet on an equal footing as members, and where speakers of international reputation might be heard. Somerville's French Club was dissolved in 1923, on the amalgamation of the OU Women's French Club with the OU French Club, it being felt that as the latter held meetings every week it would be 'almost impossible to get a good attendance at private meetings.'[26] One of the University French Club's attractions was that—unlike OUDS—it was allowed to have undergraduate actresses take part in its theatrical productions. But there were chinks even in the OUDS armour—one of them recorded by Jean Hamilton:

[25] Oxford Letter, 1924.   [26] Log Book, TT 1923.

[In 1925] I was playing with the orchestra accompanying *Peer Gynt*, conducted by the New College organist, Dr. William Harris. Permission for my taking part was asked of the Proctors. The answer was that I could play as long as I stayed the audience side of the footlights! Fortunately it became necessary for me to accompany the well-known Solveig's Song on a dulcitone, which meant that I had to be close beside her in the wings. Having got across the footlights I became part of the OUDS, and was invited to their club in George Street.[27]

Soon afterwards women undergraduates were allowed to take guest roles in OUDS productions, and in 1927 two Somervillians, Molly Blissett and Dulcie Martin, were selected to take, in turns, the part of Miranda in *The Tempest*.

Proctorial regulations on mixed societies—which required that if meetings were held in a men's college, it must be in a public room, with the written permission of the dean of the college concerned, and in the presence of a member of staff of one of the women's colleges—did nothing to ease the assimilation of women into the social life of Oxford. But neither did the prejudice of male undergraduates. In 1923 opponents of a (successful) motion to admit women to membership of the OU Archaeological Society contended that: '1) Women don't have a "soul" sufficient to appreciate antiquities in anything but a frivolous manner. 2) Amongst ladies, members might find some difficulty in recounting the various improper stories that animate their visions of mediaeval life.'[28] The assertion of one member that 'ladies would spoil the Society's Annual Dinner' was to be replicated in many other university institutions, at both junior and senior level, for years to come.

Joint ventures by the women's colleges provided a half-way house between the purely college societies of the past and the fully mixed university societies which were still, in some cases, a thing of the future. A Central Committee of Oxford Women Students was formed in 1921 to represent the public opinion of the women's colleges; it joined the NUS the following year, but found difficulty in raising the £5 subscription.[29] An Inter-Collegiate Women's Dramatic Society was

[27] Recollections of Jean Redcliffe-Maud (Hamilton, 1924).
[28] Letter from 'A Clerk of Oxenford', *Isis*, 11 June 1924.
[29] College Meeting, 7 Nov. 1922.

founded in 1920 in the unrealized hope that its members would be permitted to accept an invitation to act in OUDS. In Trinity Term 1923 a new Women's Inter-Collegiate Debating Society arose from the ashes of the Oxford Students' Debating Society, which had been declared defunct in 1920. A Somervillian, Grace Kuai, in Michaelmas Term 1924 opposed the motion 'That the academic woman is a mistake'; Lady Rhondda— whose own Somerville career had lasted only two terms—came down from London to speak fourth. *Fritillary*, the magazine of the women's colleges, was reconstituted in 1923 in the hope of becoming 'more of a review and less of a news sheet';[30] the first issue contained an article by Rose Macaulay and a review by Dilys Powell of Vera Brittain's jaundiced novel of Somerville life, *The Dark Tide*. A women's Inter-Collegiate Music Society was founded in 1925, with Jean Hamilton as its first president. In 1923 Amy Dale was elected first president of a society for women Greats students, 'The Megalomaniacs'. Many of these enterprises were short-lived. When the women's colleges combined to form a play-reading society in 1927 they appealed in the pages of *Fritillary* for help in finding a name for it: 'It is open to any suggestions, but quite decided that it must not be called anything "Inter-Collegiate", as such societies seem always to be doomed.'[31] The most ambitious joint venture of the 1930s, the establishment of the Pentagon Club, with rooms in the High Street, to provide for women some kind of social equivalent to the Union, failed after six years for lack of funds.

Despite the enthusiasm of individual Somervillians for such enterprises, Somerville as a whole had a reputation for holding aloof from joint activities with the other women's colleges. A story serialized in *Fritillary* in 1926 mocked, but also exemplified, what was widely perceived as the 'Somerville style':

A dangerous spirit [was abroad] of inter-collegiate fraternisation, a slackening of enthusiasm for those healthy athletic rivalries which have made us Oxford women what we are. Even Somerville was infected, and some of the more sensible of us, believing in the good old collegiate exclusiveness that is the backbone of Somerville Style, had made up our minds that this must stop. We had drafted a resolution . . . which College Meeting would discuss this very evening. It ran: 'That no member of the JCR shall be permitted to join

---

[30] Editorial, Dec. 1923.
[31] Letter from Audrey Falk (St Hilda's) *Fritillary*, 12 Feb. 1927.

any intercollegiate organisation whatever unless she has satisfied the JCR Committee that she is an active and regular member of at least six clubs or societies of good standing belonging exclusively to Somerville, of which said clubs or societies not less than three shall be athletic.'[32]

The concluding words date this passage very precisely to the 1920s, a decade when—thanks largely to the presence in college of a succession of athletic sisters, Angela, Ethel, and Amy Bull[33]—Somerville's sporting reputation was at its uncharacteristic height. In 1921 cricket was put on the same footing as hockey and lacrosse with regard to Amalgamation. A swimming club was formed, and the following year the inter-collegiate swimming cup joined the two hockey cups on Somerville high table. Rowing, hitherto forbidden to women students (largely for fear that it might impair their reproductive faculties), gained grudging acceptance by the authorities, and was taken up enthusiastically by the women themselves. A college rowing club was formed in December 1921, acquiring a togger eight from New College two years later; in 1926 a Somervillian, Enid Jeeves, became the first secretary of the OU Women's Rowing Club. But women's rowing remained hedged round with many restrictions. Council's refusal in 1922 to allow the Somerville Rowing Club to take part in bumping races provided a highlight of the going-down play that summer.

ON REFUSAL OF PERMISSION FOR BUMPING RACE
WITH THE REASONS THEREOF
(Tune: 'O Foolish Fay', *Iolanthe*)

> Your strange request
> We must refuse
> When you suggest
> With rival crews
> Here to contest
> Your strength of thews.
> To show your face
> In feats of skill
> In public place

---

[32] '*Nunc Integritate Stat*: The Story of the Inner Life of a Great College', *Fritillary*, 13 Feb. 1926, 6.

[33] In 1959 the Herbert Bull and Ethel Mary Bull Fund was established in memory of their parents under the will of Ella Angela Bull, for scholarships or exhibitions in classics or English.

Most surely will
Bring dire disgrace
On Somerville.
O Somerville!
This of all sights the oddest
When clad in shorts
In river sports
You prove yourselves immodest.

We can't allow
That you like men
Should make a row
Crying 'Give her ten!'
Or 'One on Bow!'
—Don't ask again.
No girlish charm
Is their's who train;
The brawny arm
Is merely plain;
And with alarm
We view the strain.
'Gainst horrid strain
Must we make then oration
And beg that you
Will keep in view
The future generation.

When in March 1927 the Principal reported that a Somerville student would be rowing in an eight, with students from St Hilda's and the Society of Home Students, in a contest in style and speed against a Cambridge eight, she assured Council that it was not considered a race as the boats were not starting at the same time: the $\frac{3}{4}$ mile course would be arranged on the lower river in the afternoon, and the river would be cleared of other boats. After much deliberation the Council agreed that Miss Gibbs should be allowed to take part in the contest, provided 'that it be not regarded as a precedent, that there be only one boat on the river at once, that the course be not more than $\frac{1}{2}$ mile, and that the test be not rowed on the river in the afternoon.'[34]

---

[34] Minutes of Council, 8 Mar. 1927.

'I'm afraid we can't stop it' reported Margery Fry to her mother, 'but we've made it as harmless as we can.'[35]

Such controversial enterprises coexisted alongside more traditional river pursuits. In 1925 the *Urmila* was finally scrapped, after over thirty years in service, and replaced by *Thyi*. In the same year the Boat Club acquired a new canoe, *Mollusc*, and a new punt, *Mightier than the Sword* (an oblique tribute to Miss Penrose, 'The Pen'), to replace *Farthest from the Pole* which had been in use for over sixteen years. In the course of 1924 the college boat-house—which tended to suffer badly from floods—was thoroughly overhauled and repainted, and the hockey field was re-drained and levelled. The writer of the Log Book expressed the hope 'that it will now rival the excellence of the LMH field, which has long been the envy of the Somerville Hockey Club.' Thanks perhaps in part to these improved facilities, Somerville won the first and second eleven hockey cups that year as well as the first eleven cricket cup and the second six tennis cup. The College Letter for 1926/7 reported that 'the athletic students see to it that there are always plenty of silver cups on the High Table'; 1927/8 was 'a year of triumph for Somerville', in which the first eleven won every hockey match of the season, and Somerville held the inter-collegiate cups for hockey, lacrosse, and tennis.

Throughout the decade, serious sport was interspersed with a series of fashionable crazes. In 1921 and 1922 early-morning 'rag regattas' were held on the Cherwell in Trinity Term, with swimming and diving competitions, and racing in crafts of various kinds; a small entrance fee was charged, and the proceeds handed over to the Endowment Fund. A sufficient number of competitors and spectators fell into the river to make the regattas a great success, but hopes that they would become an annual event remained unfulfilled. In 1924 jiu-jitsu was all the rage (see Plate 23); a class (including Miss Lorimer and the Treasurer's assistant, Miss Wingfield) gave a display of the art to an appreciative audience in Hilary Term, and was featured in the going-down play that summer. 1926 saw the formation of a Ping Pong Club, one of whose attractions was the opportunity it offered to play 'endless matches (always on Sundays) against the men's colleges.'[36] In 1928 Somerville was possessed by a passion for tenna-quoits, the Oxford Correspondent reporting that 'the yew hedge [in the Shaw Lefevre Garden] . . . is not yet either thick or high enough to preclude from

[35] SMF, 11 Mar. 1927 (Fry MSS).　　[36] College Letter, 1927/8.

those interested in sport the vision of members of the SCR engaged in Tenna-quoits—the more professional players equipped with Lenglen shades and sports socks.'

1929 was a year of losses and gains on the sporting front. Miss Bruce—for over forty years, first as a player and then as a spectator, one of Somerville's keenest sports enthusiasts—retired; and the college finally acquired some playing-fields of its own at Cutteslowe.

> There is a hockey ground, a lacrosse ground, and 5 hard tennis courts, with plenty of room left for grass courts if needed later on. A pavilion has been erected. . . . Amalgamation contributed £100 to the cost of the building, the main burden of which was borne by the College. It has been arranged for a private 'bus to take the teams to and from the field, which is on the Banbury Road about two and a half miles from College.

reported the Oxford Correspondent in triumph. But, with Parkinsonian inevitability, the acquisition of these longed-for facilities was marked by a rapid decline in Somerville's sporting reputation. 'All games challenge cups lost—save one half of the swimming cup', she reported of the 1930/1 season, noting, in compensation, that the college had gained twelve first classes that year, ten in final schools, and two in classical honour mods.

Throughout the 1930s the word most frequently used to describe Somerville's sporting record was 'undistinguished',[37] the Oxford Correspondent for 1931/2 reporting that, despite the increasingly good condition of the field and hard courts on the Cutteslowe Ground, 'a larger and larger proportion of Somervillians play no games at all, or are content with Tenniquoits when they can get it.' The popularity of swimming revived in the hot summer of 1933, though women who wished to bathe after 9 a.m. were obliged to retreat high enough up the river to escape the watchful eyes of the Curators of the Parks— a grievance which was removed by the opening in 1934 of the new women's swimming pool in Mesopotamia—known officially as 'The Ladies' Roller Bathing Place', and unofficially as 'Dames' Delight' or 'Spinsters' Splash'. But on the river, as elsewhere, standards were in decline. The Oxford Correspondent for 1933/4 lamented that 'The river, in the Summer Term at any rate, whether for sculling, punting,

---

[37] College Letter, 1931/2, 1932/3, 1933/4, 1934/5, 1935/6.

canoeing, idle or peaceful meditation, is not what it was.' The following year she had worse to report: 'Old members of the Boat Club will be shocked to hear that Punting and Canoeing tests have been abolished, and that members of the College are now at liberty to disgrace themselves, and us, in College boats on the river!'

In a decade when Somerville frequently had difficulty in raising a team in sports like lacrosse and hockey, it nevertheless produced a number of fine individual sportswomen to play for the university—among them a future honorary fellow of the college, Kathleen Timpson (Dame Kathleen Ollerenshaw), who captained the Oxford United Hockey Team in 1933. In 1937/8—a year in which the best that could be reported of the sports clubs was that 'in hockey Somerville first drew with St Hugh's and then were defeated by only 3–2 in the replay'—Somerville provided the captain and two other members of the university lacrosse team, four of the crew of the women's eight, which suffered no defeat, and six members of the women's cricket team, which won the cup presented by the Vice-Principal. The following season, four Somervillians won their blues in lacrosse, two in hockey, and three in cricket, and three rowed in the women's eight. In the last summer term of the peace Somerville could once more boast a tennis six of its own.

In all their activities, from the athletic to the academic, women students throughout this period were subject to elaborate codes of conduct which were largely designed to propitiate conservative male opinion in the university. During the war, Miss Penrose had steadily resisted pressure to modify the chaperone rules, on the grounds that 'the probable extension of the degree to women in the near future made any revolutionary movement at the present very imprudent.'[38] The women who in 1920 were admitted to membership of the university remained subject to restrictions which even before the war had been widely regarded as anachronistic. To older students, like Vera Brittain, who had interrupted or postponed their studies in order to undertake war service, they were intolerably irksome. In 1974 Hilda Whitaker recalled the circumstances in which in 1920 her Somerville contemporaries were permitted to entertain ex-servicemen friends:

In West there was a dreadful cell with hardly any furniture, located on a kind of mezzanine on the main staircase, and looking out on to a high wall with Walton Street beyond. Here two or more girls might

[38] Log Book, TT 1918.

arrange a teaparty for two or more men. This is hard to believe, but I think I have not exaggerated.[39]

She also recalled being summoned to appear before the Vice-Principal, Miss Bruce: 'Gazing at me over her spectacles, she said very gently, "Miss Street, I have been told that last Sunday you were seen in a canoe with an undergraduate. I hope you can tell me this is untrue?"' With admission to membership of the university the conduct, and the dress, of women students now came for the first time under the scrutiny of the proctors:

> Women undergraduates are to wear their gowns going to and coming from the theatre but they are not to wear them if they sit in the gallery. They are allowed to sit only in reserved seats on Saturday nights. The proctors also requested women undergraduates not to ride on the back of motor bicycles in academic dress or to walk arm-in-arm with their male friends in the streets.[40]

A petition to the Principals and proctors resulted in some slight modifications to the rules relating to attendance at the theatre and 'mixed' expeditions on bicycles or in motor cars. But the rules issued in 1921 reaffirmed the prohibition on women undergraduates entering a man's rooms or attending mixed parties in cafés without leave from the Principal and the company of an approved chaperone, deprecated any conversation with men undergraduates before and after lectures, and permitted attendance at cricket matches and boat races only on conditions sanctioned by the Principal.[41] Further restrictions were subsequently imposed, as new hazards—such as leaving Oxford by train without permission, and walking on the towing path on week days—presented themselves to the mind of the authorities.

Undergraduates—both male and female—chafed under the perpetuation of such outdated rules, denounced in *Isis* in 1924 as 'a disgrace to Oxford'.[42] In Trinity Term 1922 the President of the JCR reported to College Meeting the fate of a petition to the five women Principals organized by the Central Committee of Women Students:

> The Principals had consulted with the old Proctors and . . . the old Proctors had consulted with the new Proctors, and . . . the outcome

---

[39] Reminiscences of Hilda Whittaker (Street, 1918).
[40] The first proctorial rules, reported to College Meeting, 16 June 1920.
[41] College Meeting, 27 Apr. 1921: see Appendix.
[42] 'Discipline in the women's colleges', *Isis*, 4 June 1924.

of these consultations was that they agreed that they must go very slowly; but, while refusing to grant leave for river or theatre parties etc, they ceded the clause relating to mixed parties for golf.[43]

Chaperonage was finally abolished in 1925 and, following the practice of the men's colleges, Somerville appointed a Dean to take charge of college discipline. The office was held for the next 22 years by Vera Farnell, in a spirit which may be deduced from the advice she passed on in 1947 to her successor: 'Encourage undergraduates to talk to you about rules and restrictions, giving them, if possible, the impression that the rules are based on reason and are to be taken seriously.'[44] Coming back to Somerville as Principal in 1927, Margery Fry found it 'a relief to feel I needn't look the other way when I meet [students] walkin' out with their young men in the streets.'[45] But tête-à-tête visits to men's rooms were still discouraged, until 1935 by a 'two women' rule, and thereafter by proctorial prohibition of women visiting men's colleges after evening hall.

Anne Scott-James found Oxford social regulations 'idiotic and annoying'; they did not, however, prevent her from receiving three proposals of marriage before she decided to leave at the end of her second year.[46] How seriously the rules should be taken as an indication of actual undergraduate behaviour is open to question; they may well provide a safer guide to what did happen, than to what did not. Taken for lunch in an Oxfordshire pub shortly before her death in 1993, Kathleen Taylor (Byass, 1917) confessed to her host that the last time she had been there had been in 1920, with a male undergraduate, on the back of a motor-bike.[47] The reminiscences of Somervillians of the period convey little sense of a community starved of male company. College and university rules supplied a useful grievance, and rarely appear to have inhibited enjoyment of life. It is clear, indeed, from the frequency with which being chased by the Bulldogs (members of the university police force) and climbing in to college feature in the recollections of the inter-war generation, that they often constituted a positive enhancement.

---

[43] College Meeting, 4 May 1922.   [44] Farnell, Notes for Successor as Dean.
[45] SMF, 25 Jan. 1927 (Fry MSS).
[46] She took a first in mods. in 1933, but a term's philosophy convinced her that she was not cut out for Greats, and she left at the end of Trinity Term 'in a storm of college and parental protest.': A. Scott-James, *Sketches from a Life* (London, 1993), 33 ff.
[47] Funeral address in Elsfield Church, May 1993.

The admission of women to membership of the university certainly removed a powerful guarantee of their good conduct. The letters home of Edith Standen in the mid-1920s bear witness to a frivolity which would have been unthinkable even to her recent predecessors. 'I must tell you of a heavenly rag we have just had', she wrote in February 1924:

> There is a feud, of course, between the men and women of the 'varsity; I mean, we meet them, as individuals, in a most friendly fashion at dances and so on, but as groups we are opposed. It's all quite harmless and above board, there is no bad blood about it as there is at Cambridge. Well, this was the scheme. About twelve of us sat in the back row of chairs at a lecture and prayed for men to sit in front of us. One seat unfortunately was filled by a girl from another college and two were left vacant, but we got eight. Then when the lecturer was well under weigh and pens and pencils were scratching busily we got to work. All had come armed with large safety pins and we twisted and pinned their gowns to the chairs of the unfortunate men with absolute impunity. A commoner's gown has long streamers behind which makes it specially vulnerable. Then, when the lecture was over, we got up quietly and walked away—but those men didn't.[48]

Elated by the success of this venture, Miss Standen and her friends planned another, more ambitious, one: to decorate with placards bearing the names of the most admired men in Oxford—the captain of the rugger team, the president of the boat club, the secretary of the Union, the editor of *Isis*, etc.—the statues of the Roman emperors surrounding the Sheldonian Theatre. 'All up at 6,' records her diary for 14 February, 'for the Imperial Idols rag which was successful.'

In the intervening week she had perpetrated another 'rag' within college, inventing an alarming story of a male intruder in her room; her graphic account of the incident took in not only her fellow-students but also Maude Clarke, who dispatched her back to bed with milk and a hot water bottle, and was extremely angry when the truth subsequently came out.[49] Miss Clarke was not opposed to practical jokes in principle. Shortly after coming to Somerville as history tutor she had, indeed, conspired with some of her old friends at LMH in an

---

[48] Edith Standen to 'Happy', 8 Feb. 1924.
[49] Diary of Edith Standen, 12 and 14 Feb. 1924.

elaborate hoax designed 'to throw Somerville into a turmoil'.[50] But remembrance of this episode did not save Miss Standen, who was summoned to see Miss Penrose and rusticated for three weeks; in 1988, after an illustrious career at the Metropolitan Museum, New York, as one of the world's leading experts on French tapestries, she was elected by Somerville to an honorary fellowship.

Another delinquent undergraduate who subsequently became an honorary fellow was Dilys Powell, rusticated for two terms in 1924 for climbing into college after a clandestine meeting with a Christ Church undergraduate, Humfry Payne—conduct which, she was told by Miss Penrose, had 'dragged the name of Somerville in the dust.' (She subsequently married Payne, a future Director of the British School at Athens, and some years later, at an official dinner at which Miss Penrose was a guest, had the satisfaction of hearing her husband greet her former Principal with the words 'I think we've met before?')[51] While rusticated, Dilys Powell continued to write a column, 'What every woman thinks', for *The Isis*, and in June 1924 collaborated with the President of the Union (and future Lord Chancellor) Gerald Gardiner and a Wadham undergraduate, Arthur Tandy, in an article attacking the system of discipline in the women's colleges. A hoax pamphlet purporting to tell *The Truth about Somerville*—'What about "Push" and "Side" in Somerville? What about the "Gossip Club"? What about the Wine Parties of the Somerville Senior Common Room?'—was hastily suppressed by the proctors.[52] Gardiner was rusticated; in a letter to Miss Penrose he apologized for 'anything which might reasonably be construed as a serious attack on the behaviour of the women students or their authorities (other, of course, than an attack on their regulations, as to which I still feel strongly).'[53] Tandy was gated for the rest of the term. Miss Powell, already in exile in London, was beyond the proctors' reach.

Audrey Brodhurst, outraged a few years later by a controversial

---

[50] A piece of LMH statuary which everyone wanted to get rid of was crated up and delivered to Somerville in the wake of a cable message—'Promised statue just dispatched'—from America, and followed by a letter announcing the imminent arrival at Somerville of the donor, 'Homer P. Rigg'. Account by Christine Anson, in papers collected by Anne de Villiers (Somerville Archives).

[51] Evelyn Irons, 'Somerville, 1918–1921', *ASM Report*, 1993, 65.

[52] A copy of the 'Pink Pamphlet' was deposited in the College Archives in 1978 by Dominica Legge. She could throw no light on the Gossip Club or the SCR Wine Parties, but identified 'Push' as a 'clique of noisy bounders led by the unspeakable Vera Brittain.'

[53] Gardiner to EP, 11 June 1924 (Discipline file).

proctorial ruling (subsequently withdrawn) which prohibited any criticism of the Officers' Training Corps in a forthcoming university debate, deplored the 'heavy pall of the Proctors' limitless discretionary powers'. 'It will be our duty' she wrote to her parents '—I should rather call it our pious aspiration—to try to sweep away, eventually, the whole vicious system.' She derived some consolation from the support of Miss Darbishire, who was 'very much against the Proctors over the free speech fuss.'[54] Somervillian encounters with the proctors were generally, however, of a more trivial nature. Elisabeth Murray describes walking through town on the eve of the general election in May 1929, when many of the men's colleges were holding bump suppers—a combination of events which gave rise to much drunken disorder in the streets:

> Having wriggled between two converging lines of drunkards I went up the Corn which was full of them and had just ridded myself of a couple near the Super who had followed me shouting 'Well of Loneliness banned, disgustin' detiles' in a would-be newspaper boy style—when round the edge of the Ashmolean well out of harm's way I ran into the Proctors just in time to see Margaret Whitley the senior student doing her bow having been run in for not wearing her gown (which she had with her). Several other Somerville people were progged for not having gowns on . . . Instead of doing some good by coping with the youths the Proctors occupied themselves by telling harmless females to put their gowns on.[55]

'I suppose' she concluded contemptuously 'they were afraid to tackle the men and thought they had better look as if they were doing something.'

Under Margery Fry, college discipline was considerably relaxed. The requirement for undergraduates who wished to be out after dinner to sign a book before 6.30 p.m., with details of where they were going, was abolished, and they were simply asked to initial a list at the lodge as they went out. It was made easier for students in their third and fourth years to get occasional permission to stay away overnight. When Miss Fry met on Oxford station two Somerville undergraduates who were off to London without permission (not having realized, indeed, that it was necessary) she 'kindly pointed out to us our sins of omission, but at the same time conveyed the impression that she

[54] Brodhurst, n.d.   [55] KMEM, 2 June 1929.

thoroughly approved the object of the expedition'—to see the exhibition of French art at Burlington House.[56]

There were, however, some matters on which not even she was prepared to take a relaxed view. After hall in January 1930, reported Elisabeth Murray,

> Miss Fry had a very solemn meeting of all the College—anyone who couldn't be there had to write and tell her—about the *library* and the slackness about putting down books taken out in the register etc. I am very glad she has taken steps as it really was desperate getting hold of books as people wouldn't sign for them. She said that at the end of last term things were so bad she had authorised the Librarian to have a raid on all rooms. She read us out the black list—headed by someone who was found to have no less than 54 library books in her room . . . and someone else with 25! She did not say who had what books— but read out a separate list of names of those having more than 5 books and these people were asked to stay behind.[57]

The instincts of a former librarian clearly died hard. Obliged in 1928 to send a student down, for unspecified offences, Miss Fry confessed that she had been afraid it would 'complicate relations with the rest, but happily they all took it very sensibly—including the sinner.'[58]

If discipline was tightened up in Miss Darbishire's day, it was not always rigorously enforced. In *Gaudy Night* Harriet Vane itemizes to the delinquent Miss Cattermole the catalogue of offences which a woman undergraduate of the 1930s could perpetrate in the course of a single evening out:

> 'You've attended a meeting in a man's rooms after Hall without leave, and you oughtn't to have got leave, because you gate-crashed the meeting. . . . You were out after nine, without putting your initials in the book. That would cost you two bob. You came back to College after 11.15 without extra late leave—which would be five shillings. You returned, in fact, after midnight, which would be ten shillings, even if you had had leave. You climbed the wall, for which you ought to be gated; and, finally, you came in blotto, for which you ought to be sent down.'[59]

But *Gaudy Night* bears witness also to the capacity of senior members to turn a blind eye to infringements of the rules. This capacity was not

---

[56] Recollections of Marjorie Jenkins.   [57] KMEM, 18 June 1930.
[58] SMF, 5 Mar. 1928 (Fry MSS).   [59] Sayers, *Gaudy Night*, 165.

confined to fiction: when Miss Darbishire caught another budding Somervillian novelist, Nina Mabey, climbing over the college wall at night she simply told her to go and have a hot bath and not get a chill.[60] Jenifer Wayne recalls a case in the late 1930s, when a Somervillian reported by a landlady for spending the night in her boyfriend's lodgings was reprieved by Miss Darbishire on the grounds that she was 'too valuable a member of the College, and too admirable a person, to be so penalized when others had slipped through the net.'[61]

Not all offenders, however, got off so lightly. In 1937 a Somerville undergraduate was sent down for having spent the night with her boy-friend—a decision of Council from which the junior fellow, Dorothy Crowfoot, recorded her dissent.[62] The JCR's indignation was exacerbated by the fact that the young man in question was merely rusticated by his college for a term. In the course of the ensuing furore, Joy Dickinson, fresh from her northern grammar school, was accosted on her first evening in college by a second-year student demanding to know if she believed in free love.[63] An attempt to organize a petition from other Somervillians prepared to admit to equal guilt foundered on the understandable reluctance of many of the potential signatories to commit their names to paper.[64] Miss Darbishire, herself unhappy about Council's decision, explained to the JCR that if Somerville, already regarded in some quarters as a dangerously radical place, were seen to be taking a lenient line in such a matter, it would risk losing the support of parents and schools. The agitation gradually subsided, but the double standards by which men and women undergraduates were treated in such cases remained a source of bitter resentment into the 1960s.

For all the petty discipline, life at college was decidedly freer for most undergraduates than life at home. And poverty was on the whole a more effective constraint on social life than were the proctors' regulations. In 1930 college fees for tuition, board, and lodging

---

[60] N. Bawden, *In My Own Time: Almost an Autobiography* (London, 1994), 73–4.

[61] J. Wayne, *The Purple Dress: Growing Up in the Thirties* (London, 1979), 62.

[62] Minutes of Council, 26 Oct. 1937; Henderson file. Two years previously, Miss Crowfoot had not only threatened to resign her tutorship if a Somervillian involved in a similar, but less publicized, episode were sent down, but persuaded the first-year senior scholar, Barbara Chapman, to lay her scholarship on the line also; the girl in question was eventually rusticated for a term: BDC, 'Recollections of Dorothy Hodgkin' (*ASM Report*, 1995). [63] Recollections of Christina Roaf.

[64] Conversation with the 'class of 1936' at the 1994 Gaudy.

were £150 a year. Undergraduates on state scholarships had an additional £10 a term to cover all other expenses: travel to and from home, the JCR subscription (25/-), books, clothes, laundry, entertainment, subscriptions to university societies. Audrey Brodhurst found that there was nothing left over for vacations: 'I lived at home, travelled by bicycle, and depended on my parents for holidays, food, lodging and clothes.'[65] Many of those receiving allowances from their families were no better off. But if few undergraduates could afford to live luxuriously they could, according to their tastes, enjoy at little cost the many resources which Oxford had to offer:

> I punted and canoed, rubbed brasses in New College Chapel, walked in Dr Jack's garden at Headington, was moved by the eloquence of Dr Selbie's sermons in Mansfield College, took tea with Miss Beauchamp in her cottage at Marston, and with Mrs T. H. Green, the wife of the philosopher, who was a trustee of the fund which provided travelling grants. . . . With my compatriots I sang a funeral dirge in a play by a Welshman at the old Playhouse opposite College.

recalled Marjorie Jenkins. The opening in 1923 of the Oxford Playhouse in the 'Red Barn' immediately opposite Somerville's front gate had added immensely to the college's social amenities. By the suburban standards of the women's colleges, Somerville was in any case by far the most central—a decided advantage at a time when women undergraduates were required to be back in college by 11 p.m. Somervillians were much more likely than students from the other colleges to be able to attend a meeting, or see a play, through to the end. With balcony seats at 1/10d, theatre-going was within the reach of most of them. Nora Joy, on an allowance of £10 a term, went to the New Theatre most weeks: 'We ordered a packed meal from college and set off with our cap and gown, supper and (if pushed for time) our work, and hired a camp stool and settled down till the doors opened.' On the other hand, they rarely ate out. Marjorie Jenkins could not recall ever having a meal in a restaurant, except when relatives came to visit: 'It never occurred to me or to my friends to do so.' Her clothes were home-made; and, like many of her contemporaries, she saved money by sending her laundry home, by post, for her mother to wash and iron.[66]

---

[65] Note on finances by Audrey Brodhurst (1931).

[66] cf. Elisabeth Murray: 'I sent home some blouses for the wash on Friday. I have 3 more so you needn't rush to get them done.' (KMEM, 21 Oct. 1928).

The financial crisis of 1931, when all awards were examined, and some local authority grants were converted into loans, compounded existing difficulties. Successive Principals did what they could—often by stealth—to alleviate hardship and propitiate the Treasurer. In her introductory address to freshers, Miss Darbishire would make the point that Somerville students ranged in wealth from the rich to the very poor, with most at the poor end, and that at some stage some of them would find themselves in financial difficulty; in this event they were to go to her or the Dean, who would always be ready to lend them half a crown (pronounced 'haf a crown'). Jean Wilks, who tells this story, herself experienced Miss Farnell's help when a delay in receiving her scholarship money from her old school left her temporarily unable to pay her college fees. A few years previously, Joan Browne had received similar assistance from Miss Fry.[67]

But poverty was not a problem for all. Edith Standen's diary for 19 October 1923 reads: 'Out shopping all afternoon, spent pounds at William Bakers, sent the bills to mother.' One of her contemporaries, Nina Maclean, actually owned a car.[68] And another, Rachel Footman, who, though extremely impoverished—after her father's death in her first term she had less than 10/- a week to live on—had wealthy friends with grand cars, was taken to the Aldershot Tattoo in a chauffeur-driven Daimler, and to lunch at the Lygon Arms in Broadway in a Chrysler. In 1930 the money to build the new Reading Room was donated by one of the college's going-down students.

According to their means, Somervillians were active and generous in supporting good causes. At Cicely Williams's suggestion, the practice of taking a Sunday collection, begun in the war, was continued afterwards, the proceeds being donated to the New Hospital for Women. In Trinity Term 1920 the JCR, having rejected a suggestion by Vera Brittain that they should forgo having a college photograph taken and send the money to the Starving Europe Fund, agreed instead to donate to the Fund the money which would normally be spent on an accompanist for the term's dances.[69] In 1922 they raised £120 for the Russian Famine Fund, to support a kitchen in Saratov. Like generations of Somervillians before them, they gave both money and time to the work of the Women's University Settlement in Southwark, and they funded a bursary for a student at the Working Women's

[67] Recollections of Joan Browne (1930).
[68] Recollections of Rachel Varcoe (Footman, 1923).
[69] College Meeting, 29 Apr. 1920.

College. Nearer to home, they contributed to the support of the Mary Somerville research fellowship and to the College Endowment Fund.

They often displayed considerable ingenuity in devising ways of raising money. The tradition of carol-singers touring the college early on the last Friday of Michaelmas Term to raise money for the WUS Christmas party operated partly on the Danegeld principle; in 1922 the inhabitants of Maitland combined to pay 6d. a head to be left undisturbed.[70] Their enterprise was sometimes less altruistically motivated: two undergraduates who were arrested by a policeman in 1931 for riding bicycles without lights set up in college as 'washers and ironers, hairdressers, puncture-menders etc.' to raise money in anticipation of an expected fine.[71] And the entrepreneurial group who in February 1925 invested £2.10/- in the purchase of twenty camp stools, which they then hired out at 3d. a session to people in the Gilbert and Sullivan queue at the New Theatre, were inspired purely by the profit-motive: after a week of mixed fortunes, the venture was just beginning to show an upturn when it was put an end to by the Dean.[72]

In January 1920 College Meeting approved a proposal by Cicely Williams—then in her final year—that first-year students might celebrate leap-year by asking their seniors to take them in to dinner for the rest of the term.[73] It was agreed to limit to 29 February itself her further suggestion that the first year should have the right of 'propping' their seniors. Deference to seniority and the use of surnames were both by now on the verge of a marked decline. The diaries of Edith Standen (1923–6) record a transitional phase, her contemporaries, after a brief initial period of formality, being variously referred to by first names, surnames, or nicknames. A characteristic entry, for 21 May 1924, reads 'With Legge, Hellhound, Gwen and Rob to take our punt from Tims on the Cher.' In the course of May 1924 Dominica Legge appears first as 'Legge', then as 'Dominica', and finally as 'Domin'; Katherine Garvin and Muriel Wiggin remained 'Garvin' and 'Wiggin' to the end. Mary Trevelyan ('Poesje' in the letters of another contemporary, Margaret Mann) appears on 17 October 1923 as 'Miss Trevelyan' and on 2 November as 'Trevelyan'; on 22 January 1924 'Trevelyan' is crossed out and 'Mary' substituted. For Marjorie Jenkins, who came up in 1927, first names were the norm; in other undergraduate circles (including, to judge from *Gaudy Night*, those observed by

---

[70] Log Book, MT 1922.   [71] Brodhurst, MT 1931.
[72] Edith Standen's Diary, 16–24 Feb. 1925.   [73] College Meeting, 26 Jan. 1920.

Dorothy L. Sayers) surnames continued to be used throughout the 1930s. Dons addressed their pupils formally as 'Miss——'—a custom which some undergraduates by the end of the period considered 'quaint', but which Iris Murdoch for one much appreciated: 'I remember my joy when I came up, having been called "Iris" at school, when they said "Miss Murdoch." I was delighted to be called "Miss Murdoch"!'[74] In Marjorie Jenkins's day this formality was maintained throughout a student's undergraduate career; in the late 1930s tutors tended to switch to first names in the third year, an indication of the imminence of finals which often caused 'alarm rather than gratification' in their pupils.[75] By the time that Joyce Sugg came up in 1944, most tutors resorted to first names after a term or so. This arrangement was, of course, unilateral. Amongst themselves, undergraduates most commonly referred to senior members by their surname or a nickname derived from it, preceded by the definite article: 'The Pen', 'The Lorry', 'The Pope', 'The Stone'. Whether it was more correct to refer to Miss Lascelles as 'The Lass' or 'The Lasc' was a matter for some academic debate.

Such familiarity was nurtured by constant daily contact. Most tutors lived in college, and like their pupils, they took most of their meals in hall. Convention required that undergraduates should occasionally join senior members at high table for breakfast. ('Good college women go up about once a week', says an undergraduate in Christine Longford's novel *Making Conversation*, explaining that the main advantage from the student's point of view is that on 'the High' they are supplied with two forks to eat their kippers with, and might even get real butter.)[76] When in 1919 the JCR sought the abolition of this practice, they were told that Miss Penrose—unlike most of the dons—enjoyed the students' company.[77] Convention also determined where people sat in hall at dinner, first-year students occupying the two long tables nearest the serving hatches, second-years the middle ones, and final-year students the tables at the window end.[78] A special table was reserved for those who needed to leave early, its occupants being expected to bow to the Principal on their way out—a convention which survived until the late 1960s. Before dinner, undergraduates assembled in the JCR before proceeding to hall arm in arm with a partner. In sporadic attempts at fraternization they issued

---

[74] E. Whitley, *The Graduates* (London, 1986), 65.   [75] Wayne, *The Purple Dress*, 64.
[76] C. Longford, *Making Conversation* (London, 1931), 183.
[77] JCR Committee, 9 Nov. 1919.   [78] Wayne, *The Purple Dress*, 45.

invitations to members of the SCR; and occasionally—alarmingly—
they themselves were summoned, by note, to dine at high table.
Kathleen Byass, who before coming to Somerville in 1917 had never
set foot outside her native Yorkshire, found herself placed at dinner
on her first evening next to Miss Penrose. 'And what are your feelings,
Miss Byass' enquired the Principal suddenly, in the middle of a conversation on her other side, 'on the Turks' reported treatment of Santa
Sophia?'[79] Miss Penrose's reputation for terrifying small-talk had preceded her from Holloway;[80] in the 1920s she told her secretary that a
good way of drawing out shy undergraduates was to ask them which
end of the bath they sat.[81] Miss Fry, though a more relaxed conversa-
tionalist than her predecessor, could be disconcerting in her own way,
particularly to students whose homes did not run to drawing-rooms,
let alone gold-painted fireplaces. Miss Darbishire specialized in prolongued silences which drove many undergraduates to nervous and
desperate gibbering. One of Joyce Sugg's friends 'swore that she
often told Miss Darbishire involved and pointless lies, affirming, for
instance, [on returning from vacation] that her home town had just
had a heavy fall of snow, though it had had no such thing, when Miss
Darbishire enquired, after a long pause, what sort of weather she had
been having.' But invitations to dine at high table were always issued
'so implacably far in advance' that, short of being laid low with flu,
or whipped into the Radcliffe for an emergency operation, it would,
said Jenifer Wayne, have been 'more than one's gown was worth to
refuse.'[82]

Except on high days and holidays—to celebrate Miss Penrose's DCL
or George V's Silver Jubilee—when cider was provided for the whole
college, the staple drink for undergraduates was water; at high table
there was a modest round of wine on nights when there were special
guests. In the 1930s Dorothy L. Sayers, 'monolithic in black velvet . . .
pillar-like and sleeveless', was one of the more frequent visitors
(doubtless in search of local colour for *Gaudy Night*); occasional male
guests were subjected to the eager scrutiny of the undergraduates
below, on the look-out for 'any signs of embarrassment on the part
of the sole male in that female assembly.'[83] On the evenings of cup
suppers the victorious teams, clad in red flared skirts, white blouses

[79] Recollections of Kathleen Taylor (Byass, 1917).
[80] C. Bingham, *The History of Royal Holloway College 1886–1986* (London, 1987), 93–4.
[81] Recollections of Hester Thomas (née Johnson), Principal's Secretary 1922–3.
[82] Wayne, *The Purple Dress*, 46.   [83] Ibid. 46.

and black stockings, were led into hall each on the arm of a don, and the Bursar provided wine for a loving cup. Elisabeth Murray described one such occasion in 1929:

> At the end of the meal Miss Fry and the [lacrosse] captain stand up and Miss F. offers one of the silver cups containing some drink to the captain. They stand facing each other, Miss F. with the cup and the captain with both hands up. The captain passes the cup on to the next person and Miss F. stands behind her with her hands raised and so on in turn round the table. . . . Meanwhile College claps. At the end Miss F. rises and makes a speech. . . . She says she hopes the college was not going to be divided into those who played games and those who made speeches and so she had written out a speech for each of the lacrosse team to make. Papers were handed round—then they rose up and each had to say one word off their paper one after another as fast as they could go six times round. It was a sort of rhyme about lacrosse but we couldn't quite follow it. Then the captain . . . made a speech and the Dons went out. The team then chair the Captain round the Hall.[84]

In her first letter home from Somerville in 1928 Elisabeth Murray had reported that 'they don't dress much here apparently. . . . I wore the Liberty and black coat and felt quite right.'[85] The convention of changing for dinner was one of the respects in which Miss Darbishire attempted to reverse the decline in standards which had set in under Miss Fry. In a letter home, Audrey Brodhurst summarized an early speech by 'the Darb' on the subject of formal dress in hall:

> *Old* tradition, therefore *good* tradition. (Some Fourth Years will remember this *good old tradition*.) Pity to let G. O. T. die. This is the best modern Hall in Oxford. Maids wait on us in a seemly fashion. Therefore we should dress in a seemly fashion. No compulsion, OF COURSE, but still 'We hope College *will* cooperate etc . . .'

The speech, she said, provoked groans and grumbles of disgust in all quarters; protests were planned and petitions signed—'though of course they'd only have the effect of jerking the Darb into even longer flights of eloquence on the subject of G. O. T.s and may cause her to revive other fossilized O. T.s to support this one.' In a subsequent letter she reported that 'all College except a meagre half-dozen or so' was protesting about dressing for dinner. A Sunday evening meeting to

---

[84] KMEM, 2 Mar. 1929.   [85] KMEM, 12 Oct. 1928.

discuss the matter 'came to precisely nil, because whereas she looks on Hall as a sacred ritual or traditional banquet, we regard it as a meal, just like any other meal.' A counter-suggestion by the undergraduates, that 'for the honour of the College' they should wear gowns at dinner instead of changing, was rejected by the SCR. The rule that undergraduates should change for dinner was reasserted, though never strictly enforced; a few lingering protesters stationed themselves at the table nearest to high table clad in backless evening dress.

In March 1920 the Senior Student was instructed by College Meeting to suggest 'unofficially and tactfully' to the Bursar the provision of less rabbit and stronger tea at meals; the following year the JCR Committee undertook to pass on such written suggestions on the subject of food as they deemed to be sensible. The traditional cuisine of the Oxbridge women's colleges, immortalized in Virginia Woolf's *A Room of One's Own*,[86] provided an irresisible target for successive going-down plays.

BURSAR'S SONG
(1933)

I produce from my larder (and what could be harder?)
   New dishes in endless variety.
It provides an incentive to genuine inventive,
   I claim it without impropriety.
If at breakfast there's fish and you don't like the dish
   And in fact you refuse to partake of it,
Next day I may choose to produce it in stews,
   Or rissoles or Scotch eggs I may make of it.
I never despair tho' you turn from jugged hare;
   It can soon undergo metamorphosis,
It's not recognised when it's subtly disguised,
   And as curry with rice quite amorphous is.
If you sneer at rice kernels they change their externals;
   As soup they're an absolute winner:
If it comes to the worst they may well be dispersed,
   As savory scallops at dinner.
But why should I do all these wonders for you,
   When you show the most shocking ingratitude.
I've tried and I've tried but you're not satisfied,
   I can't sympathise with your attitude.

[86] V. Woolf, *A Room of One's Own* (London, 1929), 26 ff.

You disdain kedgeree, you want cake for your tea,
   You want grapefruit for breakfast each morning.
Caviare for your hall, but it won't do at all,
   For the whole kitchen staff would give warning.
I don't like to boast but there's plenty of toast
   And it's only your greed that reduces it.
In my College the food is remarkably good,
   And 'tis envy alone that traduces it.

But Jenifer Wayne, in the late 1930s, found college food 'generally good, fresh and plentiful',[87] and Somerville undergraduates—unlike their male contemporaries—knew that, whether good or bad, the same food was shared by senior and junior members alike. They supplemented the college diet with lavish teas in their own rooms, and hastened to accept any invitation out. At an undergraduate tea-party in her first term Audrey Brodhurst was offered 'toast, doughnuts, chocolate roll, spotted bread and honey'; four years later, during finals, she was given a free pass to the New College 'schools teas' organised by Mrs Fisher (the mother of her contemporary Mary Fisher), and noted with approval that the food was all from the Co-op.[88] Undergraduates were expected to invite their tutor to tea once a term; the standard fare on these occasions was Fuller's walnut cake.

Smoking, reluctantly tolerated in Somerville before the war, was now taken for granted. Cigarettes were on sale in the college shop, together with other necessities of life such as chocolate and soap powder. 'I smoked too too expertly, didn't choke once' boasted Elisabeth Murray, who on arrival at Somerville in 1928 was shown round college and offered a cigarette by an old schoolfriend, Naomi Hurnard.[89] At a tea-party in her first term Audrey Brodhurst reported that 'a considerable amount of smoking was done.' But Jenifer Wayne, a few years later, thought that most of her contemporaries smoked very little; she herself was presented by her grandfather at the beginning of each term with 100 Cyprus cigarettes, and found that they lasted her easily for the whole term, including offers to friends.[90] The SCR, freed from the obligation to set a good example, abandoned the self-denying ordinance of pre-war days, acquired a number of silver cigarette boxes, and instituted a rota of fellows with responsibility for keeping them

[87] Wayne, *The Purple Dress*, 44.   [88] Letters of Audrey Brodhurst.
[89] KMEM, 12 Oct. 1928.   [90] Wayne, *The Purple Dress*, 59–60.

topped up.[91] In a 1934 cartoon by Isobel Henderson of the members of the SCR, Lucy Sutherland is depicted offering a cigarette to Maude Clarke (Plate 37).

In 1921 Miss Penrose took the step—unprecedented, she said, in her twenty-eight years as the head of a college—of summoning a whole year and rebuking it for idleness.[92] Her reminder of the family sacrifices or public funds to which many of the students owed the opportunity to study at Oxford was a familiar one: it had been used frequently during the war, and would be used again in 1926, when those who 'felt an impulse to enlist' at the time of the General Strike were urged to consider the viewpoint of their parents and others who had sent them to Oxford.[93] Women undergraduates, labouring under the obligation to prove themselves worthy of their membership of the university, were expected to work hard. 'The Tutors say that [the students] don't work enough' reported Miss Fry to her mother, shortly after taking over as Principal—'and *I* rather doubt—under my breath—whether they don't work too much.'[94] Audrey Brodhurst's timetable for her second term suggests that they were indeed hard-pressed:

> I shall have 12 lectures and 3 tutorials per week—rather too many, I think. On Tuesday . . . I start off 'at nine very prompt' with the Lorry on Tacitus, here in Somerville. She lets us go at 9.55. At 10 we have to be at Balliol for Virgil. At 11 we trot round the corner to Trinity for Horace, and then at 12 I have to race back to Somerville to be slaughtered by the Lorry over Greek prose.

Classics may, of course, have been a special case; Miss Lorimer's fierceness as a tutor was as legendary as her geniality as a lecturer. ('I think', she once began a lecture on Homeric armour, 'we had just reached the point where the midriff was set up like a fence about the beating heart.')[95] Audrey Brodhurst later described a chance encounter of five first-year Somervillian classicists in Penrose JCR: 'I am glad to hear that *their* proses are always bad too, and that they make unclassical and barbaric, unscholarly and uncivilized mistakes. . . . We all had a good old grumble together and felt for a short moment very much the fellowship that a small and persecuted sect must feel.'[96]

[91] SCR minute books. [92] EP: Talk to first-year undergraduates, 13 June 1921.
[93] EP: Talks to undergraduates, 1926. [94] SMF, 6 Mar. 1927 (Fry MSS).
[95] Brodhurst, HT 1932.
[96] Two of this particular sect were to get firsts in mods., and two of the others—Mary Fisher and Audrey Brodhurst herself—firsts in Greats.

A different insight into Miss Lorimer's teaching method is provided by Mary Lascelles, to whom—a young tutor desirous of keeping up her Greek—she proposed that they should read Theocritus together: 'We would sit over our (not very easy) text, and, in one of the many pauses, she would exclaim: "Ah, I see that your attention is caught by that rare Doric form"—and I would answer: "Miss Lorimer, I'm still looking for the verb." '[97]

Elisabeth Murray, who read history, reported on her second day at Somerville that she was enjoying everything very much 'except the work which turns me simply green with horror.'[98] The university lectures, of which she attended seven a week, were to prove disappointing:

> They really are awful, no new ideas, simply our set books put in words of one syllable as if we were feeble-minded. All the lectures are designed for the men and last two terms as the men do the exam in two terms. They are therefore very detailed and we shall only do about a quarter of them.[99]

This was work for pass mods., which most Somervillians cleared off after one term, before moving on to what their tutors considered to be 'real work'. Joan Browne, summoned back from Manchester in the Christmas vacation (at the cost of 17/-) for a viva at which the examiner's most serious question was 'Do you usually spell the Canon of Canon Law with two N's?', received the commiserations of Miss Fry for this 'waste of time and money'. Work for Schools was to prove more satisfying, but while Joan Browne appreciated the 'genuine scholarship and breadth of vision' to which her tutors (especially Maude Clarke) introduced her, she regretted that Somervillians did not have the stimulus of more outside tuition, and that their research ambitions were not more fostered. One of the attractions of PPE was precisely that of being sent for tutorials in other colleges, Somerville being unable to provide tuition across the whole range of subjects.

Nora Joy (Mrs Macleod), who settled for pass finals having—as she said—scraped though maths mods, had a more relaxed time, taking economics with Lucy Sutherland (who was evidently less demanding than with her own pupils, among whom she had the reputation of a slave-driver) and French with Enid Starkie: 'I remember going for

---

[97] M. Lascelles, *A Memoir* (privately printed, 1989), 49.   [98] KMEM, 14 Oct. 1928.
[99] KMEM, 21 Oct. 1928.

tutorials in Miss Starkie's rooms somewhere at the other end of St Giles and she would brew up something (? tea) in her samovar.' Some years later Nina Mabey, having read out a 'long, pompous essay on Baudelaire' was asked by Enid Starkie 'Nina, tell me. Do you know anything *at all* about sex?'[100] Her view that Miss Starkie was 'less tolerant than Miss Darbishire' may not have been shared by Jenifer Wayne, who, having turned up at a tutorial with the Nonesuch rather than Saintsbury's Oxford edition of Milton, was summoned to see the Principal and asked if she considered 'that a student who has not troubled to use the standard edition of Milton is worthy of a scholarship at this college?'[101]

Anxieties about work, and about the prospect of finding employment on leaving Oxford, were for many a major preoccupation. 'We did not worry about the state of the world or take up the cause of the afflicted and the oppressed in distant lands', recalled Marjorie Jenkins, an undergraduate from 1927 to 1931. Like many undergraduates who came from a depressed area at a time of high unemployment, she felt that she and her family had problems enough of their own to contend with. In some other cases, family problems were more closely linked to public affairs. 'Sir H. Samuel came the other day' reported Margery Fry to her mother in February 1927, 'and after we had finished about his daughter [Nancy], was quite interesting and forthcoming on Palestine—I didn't ask him to hold forth on the Liberal Party or the Coal Strike!'[102] The presence in college from 1929 to 1932 of Ramsay MacDonald's daughter, Sheila, gave even to the politically most disengaged a vicarious sense of participation in the affairs of the nation; she herself was too busy electioneering to join her contemporaries in West JCR to listen to the results of the 1931 general election on Kathleen Timpson's portable radio.[103]

Joan Browne's experience was probably typical of the moderately political undergraduate of her time:

The great events of Oxford political history in the thirties, I followed from the side lines. I heard the 'King and Country' debate, but could

---

[100] A. Thwaite (ed.), *My Oxford* (London, 1977), 157. In Nina Bawden's later account of this incident in *In My Own Time* (1994), 68, Enid Starkie addresses her as 'Miss Mabey'.

[101] Wayne, *The Purple Dress*, 63.

[102] SMF, 20 Feb. 1927 (Fry MSS). Sir Herbert Samuel (created Viscount Samuel, 1937) was High Commissioner for Palestine 1920–5, and Chairman in 1925–6 of the Royal Commission to examine the problems of the coal industry; early in 1927 he was appointed Chairman of the Liberal Party. His daughter Nancy read PPE at Somerville 1925–8.

[103] Brodhurst, MT 1931.

not, of course, take part.[104] I saw the attack on the Cutteslow wall on a film which broke down in the middle.[105] I contributed my mite to the unemployed as they marched through Oxford. I was at the Oxford Majlis great meeting to receive Gandhi.

A member of the OU Liberal Club, the greatest political event of her undergraduate years was hearing Lloyd George speak at the Union.

Audrey Brodhurst, an active member of the Labour Club and of the Anti-war Committee, witnessed—sometimes dangerously closely—the fascist rallies and counter-rallies of the early 1930s. In Michaelmas Term 1933 she secured the use of Bedford House as a workshop for the construction of banners for a big Armistice Day anti-War demonstration at which Oliver Franks was to be the main speaker; the banners mysteriously disappeared only hours before the start of the rally, and new ones had to be hastily constructed with the help of a Ruskin student who was a professional sign-writer. Though the culprits were never discovered, Audrey Brodhust darkly suspected them to be fellow-Somervillians.[106] Once again, she took comfort from the sympathy of Miss Darbishire.

Like other left-wing undergraduates, she noted with approbation the display of Socialist League pamphlets in Isobel Henderson's rooms at tutorials, and the frequent visits of their hero, A. L. Rowse, who had been a great friend of Isobel's husband. When Franco came to power Mrs Henderson, a passionate Hispanophile, vowed never to set foot in Spain again until he had fallen. Jenifer Wayne—though once invited to tea by a young man who donned a black shirt for the occasion and spoke, to her mystification, of his ambition to have a sabre-scar on his cheek—said that it would have been unthinkable in her day to be pro-Franco.[107] In 1936 Inez Pearn married the poet Stephen Spender within three weeks of their meeting at an assembly in Oxford for Spanish Aid, and almost immediately before his departure for the front.[108]

---

[104] In a celebrated debate in the Union in February 1933 the motion 'That this House will in no circumstances fight for its King and its Country' was carried by 175 votes to 153.

[105] This 7-ft. high wall, erected in 1934 by the Urban Housing Company to separate its new private housing estate from the adjacent council estate (and obliging the inhabitants of the latter to take a 1 mile detour to reach the nearby Banbury Road) became a notorious symbol of English class division. A well-publicized attempt by activists to demolish the wall in May 1934 was thwarted by the police. After a long legal battle the Council had it taken down in 1959.   [106] Letters in Somerville Archives.

[107] Wayne, *The Purple Dress*, 58–9.

[108] The marriage broke up in 1939 and she subsequently married the poet and sociologist Charles Madge.

Audrey Beecham spent the long vacation of 1936 actually fighting on the Republican side in Barcelona, dressing in men's clothes for the occasion; it was only when her Catalan fellow-freedom-fighters mocked her for using a hairnet after she had just washed her hair that she realized how effective had been her disguise.[109]

Iris Murdoch, who came up in 1938, described to an interviewer fifty years later an undergraduate social life overcast by wars and rumours of wars:

> A lot of it was connected with meetings, gatherings, demonstrations —not just left-wing politics, but all sorts of other high-minded groups one belonged to, peace groups and so on. And then just a lot of fun and dancing. There was plenty of perfectly ordinary frivolity. Many undergraduates weren't thinking about politics at all, they were just happy creatures enjoying the *dolce vita* and the Commem. Balls and so forth. Of course, we were so high-minded that we didn't go—we thought it a terrible waste of money to spend £5 on a ticket for a dance! I rather wish we had been a bit more frivolous, but we were immensely idealistic and we thought all this money could be spent on better causes.[110]

Throughout these years each of the five women's societies continued to develop a distinctive style of its own. Writing in *Time and Tide* in July 1929, Winifred Holtby quoted the proverb current in her undergraduate days: 'LMH for Young Ladies, St Hilda's for Games, St Hugh's for Religion and Somerville for Brains'—or, in the version favoured by some of the other colleges, 'Somerville for Freaks':

> But however you take it, Somerville has actually stood for intellectual independence, innovation and the eccentricity that so often accompanies these qualities. . . . The Somerville Freaks have their tradition, and an unkind critic might say that they have little else. 'The ugliest buildings of any Oxford College'—well, well. Ugliness may sometimes be an asset. No student is tempted to remain isolated in idle dreams of beauty in one of the Maitland bedrooms, or looking across to the St Giles entrance. LMH young ladies may stroll down to their lovely curve of the River, and St Hugh's sun themselves on their paved and flowery terrace; but Somervillians jump on their bicycles and whirl off to the Bodleian or Magdalen Bridge, when desirous of

---

[109] Notes by BDC.   [110] E. Whitley, *The Graduates* (London, 1986), 65.

contemplating beauty. So perhaps they keep in closer touch with the university itself than do the students of other colleges.[111]

Though the St Giles entrance was to be transformed in the course of the next few years by Morley Horder, Somervillians showed no greater disposition to stay at home to enjoy the improved view. As the women's colleges emerged between the wars from the enforced self-absorption of earlier years, they rather congratulated themselves on having emerged the furthest.

APPENDIX:

General rules governing the conduct
of women undergraduates (Trinity Term 1921)

1. A woman undergraduate may not enter a man's rooms either in College or in lodgings without obtaining leave from her Principal, and must have a chaperone approved by her.
2. It is understood that conversation between men and women undergraduates before and after lectures is not encouraged.
3. Students must obtain leave from their Principal before accepting invitations for the evening or for picnic or boating parties, or, as a rule for lunch parties.[112]
4. They may not go out after dinner without permission; they must always be back by 11 o'clock, and must report their return. They are not allowed to go out alone in the evening except by special permission.
5. They may not reside in Oxford during vacation without permission.
6. Two or more students may invite their men friends to tea in public rooms or in the grounds of the Society to which they belong after obtaining permission from the Principal. A student may receive her brother in her own room, but not other men friends.
7. Women undergraduates may go to matinees or afternoon performances with their men friends if leave is obtained from their Principal, and if there are two ladies in the party.
8. Mixed parties may not be held in cafes and restaurants without a chaperone approved by the Principal.

---

[111] 'The Somerville Tradition', by GREC: *Time and Tide*, 5 July 1929.
[112] The rule about lunch parties was not enforced in Somerville.

9. Women undergraduates may go to dances in private houses at the discretion of the Principal and subject to the 11 o'clock rule.

10. *Joint Societies.*

    a. Joint Societies must be approved by the Principals.

    b. Women students may join mixed societies provided that a member of the staff of one of the women's colleges is present at the meetings if held in Men's Colleges or in a public room.

    c. Such meetings may be held in public rooms in Men's Colleges, provided written permission has been obtained from the Dean of the College.

    d. Such meetings may not be held in men's rooms either in or out of College.

    e. Leave to be renewed annually for the meetings of each Joint Society.

11. *Games, etc.*

    a. Women students are allowed to play Golf on the North Oxford Links.

    b. They are not allowed to play mixed hockey.

    c. They may only be present at football or cricket matches or boat races under conditions approved by their Principals.

    d. A woman undergraduate may not go for walks, bicycle or motor rides alone with a man undergraduate other than her brother. Permission for mixed parties may be given at the discretion of the Principal.

    e. A woman undergraduate may boat with her brother but not with any other men friends.

Part III

1939 – 1993

II

Somerville and the 'Isle of Man', 1939–1945

ON the outbreak of war in 1939 there were fears that the college buildings might once again be requisitioned as an annexe to the Radcliffe
Infirmary. This time, the Holywell building of New College was proposed as Somerville's alternative home, and the Principal and Bursar
spent the early days of September planning a move unwelcome to
all parties concerned.[1] In the event, thanks largely to the diplomacy
of Miss Stonedale, only West was taken over. The building was used
chiefly to accommodate nurses from the Radcliffe Infirmary, apart
from four ground-floor rooms which were isolated in order to house
the clinical section of the medical school. It was the Regius Professor
of Medicine, Sir Farquhar Buzzard, who coined the name by which
this area became universally known—even in the college accounts—
the 'Isle of Man'.

Pressure on accommodation was eased by the withdrawal on the
outbreak of war of six students and six prospective freshers. College
rooms were rearranged to house as many as possible of the remainder,
and LMH once again came to Somerville's aid by providing accommodation for Miss Lascelles and thirty students.[2] College opened
in Michaelmas Term 1940 with full numbers, and maintained these
throughout the war. As in the Great War, the government's general
advice to women was to stay the course, and, though a number did
withdraw in order to take up war work, their places were quickly
filled, and the waiting-list remained as long as ever.

For the first year of the war the daily life of the college was relatively little affected. The writer of the 1940/1 Oxford Letter opined that

---

[1] According to Vera Farnell, the Matron at the Radcliffe was as concerned at the
prospect of a 'mixed party' of nurses and medical students sharing Somerville between
them as the Somerville authorities were at the prospect of their undergraduates living in
close proximity to New College men: V. Farnell, *A Somervillian Looks Back* (Oxford, 1948),
73.

[2] This number was reduced to eighteen the following year, when Miss Lascelles
returned to Somerville and twelve students were housed in nearby lodgings.

'if an intelligent Old Somervillian were to wake up after a three-years' sleep, in the College precincts, it might take her several minutes to deduce the fact of a European war.' Apart from the universal blackout,

> an abrupt interest in vegetables along the south side of the garden quad; a large bath, font, or Mercury in front of the Chapel; the Library loggia bricked up, and brick accretions about the doors of Penrose and Maitland—these are the only obvious signs, unless you catch sight of a nurse's uniform whisking through West.

But thereafter the signs rapidly increased. During the long vacation of 1940 steps were taken to provide an adequate air-raid shelter for each of the college buildings, the accommodation previously provided by the Clarendon Press having been judged unsuitable. An emergency meeting of Council was held in the long vacation of 1941 to consider the proposals of the city's new Chief Officer to link college fire precautions with the main city scheme; Somerville's arrangements were entrusted to a committee consisting of the Principal, Dean, Treasurer, and Bursar, two of whom were to be available at any given time, and any one of whom might, in an emergency, have to act at her discretion. A second water tank was installed in the East quadrangle, and expenditure of up to £1,000 on fire-fighting equipment was authorized. In Michaelmas Term the Vice-Chancellor chaired a meeting at which it was agreed that Somerville should co-operate for fire-fighting purposes with the Radcliffe Infirmary (which was designated an action station) and the University Press. 'The study of college geography is becoming an exact science' notes the Log Book for 1942/3, while the Oxford Correspondent reported that 'A smart trailer pump is now housed in its own shed, and may been seen most afternoons chugging up and down the path, while fire-parties play a powerful hose on chance passers. Trial runs for members of the staff take place in the privacy of the early morning.'

On 9 September 1940 Somerville suffered its first casualty through enemy action when Jean Darling (1924), a London air-raid warden, was killed in a shelter in Chelsea. When candidates for the degree ceremony that October presented themselves in uniform, it was noted that Somerville was the only college in which all three services were represented.[3] 'If anyone doubts the practical value of University

---

[3] Letter from the ASM Chairman (Miss Pope), *ASM Report* 1939/40.

training in war-time,' commented the Oxford Correspondent for 1940/1, 'Somerville graduates are there to prove it in all the Services, most of the Ministries, and many odder jobs.' Among the latter she instanced those Somervillians who 'are said to make excellent Fifth Form masters in famous boys' schools.' Others were more directly involved in the war effort. One old Somervillian, Mrs Wilberforce (Ogilvie-Forbes, 1922), a captain in the Air Transport Auxiliary, visited college in February 1942 with a view to recruiting students for work flying aeroplanes from factories to UK aerodromes. Another, Kathleen Kenyon, now a Red Cross divisional commandant, came in May to discuss with the Bursar their training in first-aid, home nursing, and child welfare.[4] Among the many Somervillians in Whitehall were two fellows of the college. In May 1940 Miss Evans was recruited as temporary principal and senior assistant in the Industrial Supplies department of the Board of Trade. She was joined the following year by Miss Sutherland, and shortly afterwards by the Principal's Secretary, Miss Simpson. In return, Somerville regained one of its recent history graduates, aircraftswoman Betty Jackson, from the WAAFS as temporary tutor in PPE.

When Miss Lorimer's tenure of the Lady Carlisle research fellowship came to an end in 1939, Somerville elected in her place Dr Dorothy Wrinch—a familiar figure in Oxford, where she had taught mathematics for the women's colleges for most of the inter-war period. Dr Wrinch, the proponent of a controversial theory on protein structure which was to bring her into conflict with Linus Pauling, currently held a lecturership in chemistry at Johns Hopkins University, and it was agreed that she should remain there for the first year of her fellowship. Her return to England was subsequently twice postponed in view of the national importance of the research on which she was engaged; in October 1941 she married Professor Otto Glaser, and resigned her fellowship without ever having taken up residence in college.[5] Council agreed not to advertise the Carlisle fellowship for the duration of the war, but to hold it open in case 'any persons of distinction and standing'—preferably a scientist or mathematician—should present themselves.[6] The Mary Somerville research fellowship

---

[4] PF, 13 May 1942.

[5] For an account of Dorothy Wrinch's career, See P. G. Abir-Am, 'Synergy or Clash: Disciplinary and Marital Strategies in the Career of Mathematical Biologist Dorothy Wrinch', in P. G. Abir-Am and D. Outram (eds.), *Uneasy Careers and Intimate Lives*, 252 ff.

[6] Minutes of Council, 28 Oct. 1941

was similarly put on ice when Winifred Hackett's tenure came to an end in 1940.

The college had been looking to Dr Wrinch's arrival as a partial solution to an urgent problem: to provide teaching for the growing numbers of women who were coming to Oxford to read mathematics. With maths tutors—prime targets for secondment to war service—in increasingly short supply, Miss Busbridge of St Hugh's, who exercised tutorial control of the mathematicians from all five women's colleges, could no longer cope unaided with the numbers involved. After consultation with the other colleges, which agreed to share between them the costs of superannuation, a temporary lecturership at Somerville was advertised, and in 1942 Miss Kathleen Sarginson was appointed to work under Miss Busbridge's direction for the duration of the emergency.

As in the Great War, undergraduates were now pressed into various forms of war work, the JCRs of the five women's societies deciding that each member should give a minimum of six hours a week to National Service. Some worked alongside senior members at the Principal of St Annes' fuse-testing factory at Hartland House.[7] Many qualified as air-raid wardens. Nina Mabey, whose allotted task was 'entertaining American soldiers', served as a waitress at the Red Cross club in Beaumont Street, while noting that some of her contemporaries appeared to interpret their duties more boldly: 'It was clear that one undergraduate, who changed from her drab working clothes into butterfly garments made from home-dyed cheese cloth when she left college at six every evening, was not just setting forth to cut sandwiches.'[8] Christina Drake, as general organizer of wartime activities in Somerville, found that the job for which it was most difficult to raise volunteers was helping Mrs Lobel to dig up the University Parks and plant potatoes. The knitting parties organized by Miss Darbishire in her college room after supper on Sundays were less exacting: 'We were all expected to knit squares out of odd scraps of wool and these were then made up into brightly coloured blankets and dispatched to countries considered to be in need: Norway, Finland, Greece. As each blanket was sent off the country fell to the enemy.'[9] Miss Farnell attended these occasions, but as Miss Darbishire did not consider her to be capable of knitting, she was assigned the task of reading aloud—

[7] See R. F. Butler, *A History of Saint Anne's Society*, ii. *(1921–1946)* (Oxford, 1957), 78–9.

[8] N. Bawden, *In My Own Time: Almost an Autobiography* (London, 1994), 71.

[9] Recollections of Christina Roaf (Drake 1937).

mostly Henry James—to the assembled company. The Principal herself—in every other respect a model of probity—was suspected of cheating, by buying new wool instead of reusing old scraps.

Somerville also adopted an elementary school evacuated to the parish of St Barnabas from Bow, undergraduates teaching the boys country dancing and Scottish reels, and producing plays for them to act in. As producer, Christina Drake found it simplest to borrow costumes and scenery, and spend the £2 allocated for this purpose by the JCR on currant buns with which she could bribe the actors to attend rehearsals. In Trinity Term 1940 the boys acted the Bottom scene from *A Midsummer's Night's Dream* on the lawn outside Penrose, for an audience of wounded soldiers collected by Miss Beauchamp from the Radcliffe Infirmary. In return for such entertainment, the masters and boys helped transform the chapel lawn into a vegetable plot (Plate 41). The undergraduates' own theatrical ventures were severely curtailed by wartime, though play-readings—particularly those done in conjunction with men's colleges—were popular. The 1941 freshers gave a performance of *Twelfth Night*; and in 1943 permission was given for a production of *Much Ado About Nothing* 'without the elaboration of a special set.'[10]

There were, however, other outlets for their talents in this regard. In Hilary Term 1943 a number of undergraduates volunteered to take part in a mock blitz organized by the City Council to test Oxford's preparedness for an emergency; Miss Darbishire was subsequently congratulated by the Town Clerk on the histrionic ability of one Somervillian 'whose realistic impersonation of a hysterical foreigner deprived of house and sense and all coherent speech had shown up some weak spots in the city organisation.'[11] The undergraduate in question was later identified as a modern linguist in her final year, Daphne Park. Towards the end of the war several members of the SCR and JCR responded to an appeal to women students by the Army Malaria Research Unit for guinea-pigs in the testing of a new drug. The volunteers were assured that 'experience with the drug to be used indicates that poisonous effects following administration are very rare', and that 'it is not considered that the drug will interfere with study'; in the event, according to the Log Book, they suffered little inconvenience beyond a tendency to turn yellow.[12]

---

[10] PF, 14 Oct. 1942.   [11] Farnell, *A Somervillian Looks Back*, 74–5.
[12] Log Book, 1943–4.

Vacations were taken up with harvesting, work in canteens and munitions factories, and various other forms of national and domestic service. Some undergraduates remained in Oxford during the vacations as full-time fire-watchers. Nina Mabey recalled an 'eerily unpleasant week' on duty in the University Museum, sleeping on a camp-bed between a mummy in a glass case and a stuffed alligator, and a more agreeable time playing planchette on the roof of the Bodleian Library.[13] In the summer of 1942 the Ministry of Labour, concerned at the exceptional shortage of labour in the Oxford area, appealed for students to undertake clerical work in connection with the issue of new unemployment cards. College did what it could to protect its students' interests, stipulating that those who worked for the Post Office at Christmas should not be allowed to undertake night work, and setting a maximum of six weeks for those working in factories during the long vacation.[14]

In Michaelmas Term 1941 Miss Darbishire instituted a termly lecture on some subject connected with reconstruction after the war. From time to time she addressed the undergraduates on the importance of making regular contributions to the national savings certificates, and in June 1940 she joined with the other women principals in appealing in the press for a fund to provide a Red Cross ambulance for the Lord Mayor's Fund. Between November 1939 and June 1943 the Somerville group of the National War Savings Scheme, consisting largely of the domestic staff, collected £1,600. 'Wings for Victory Week' in 1943 raised £251.3s.0d.—enough to provide five parachutes (£175), two dinghies for four-engined bombers (£60), two dinghies for fighters (£16), and one pair of chemically heated socks (3/-).[15]

No gaudies were held during the war, and college entertainment was cut to a minimum. A shortage of maids meant that members of the SCR were reduced to washing up their own coffee cups after lunch, engaging in endless—and sometimes acrimonious—debate over the form the rota should take.[16] One of the few social events which did survive was the Principal's Sunday afternoon tea-party for first-year undergraduates, to supply which Miss Farnell and Miss Bryant used to join the long queue outside Oliver & Gurden's factory on Saturday mornings for the one unrationed cake allowed to each customer.[17]

[13] Bawden, *In My Own Time*, 73.   [14] PF, 5 Nov. 1941 and 20 May 1942.
[15] ASM Meeting, 12 June 1943.   [16] SCR Minutes, MT 1944, HT 1945.
[17] Recollections of Hilda Bryant.

But wartime conditions also generated a social life of their own. Hospitality at high table was offered to a number of Somervillian civil servants whose departments had been evacuated to Oxford from Whitehall after the London blitzes of 1940, while the weekend visits of Lucy Sutherland and Anne Evans brought the welcome spice of metropolitan gossip. Somerville was also able to enjoy the company, though it lamented the plight, of a remarkable group of refugee scholars from Germany: the Egyptologists Miss Bosse (later Mrs Griffiths) and Mrs Baumgartel (whose monograph on the dating of the prehistoric civilizations of Egypt was the first publication undertaken by the Griffiths Institute, and whose daughter read PPE at Somerville 1940–1943); the Hittite scholar Miss Leonie Zuntz, who had obtained work as a reader at the University Press; and Miss Lotte Labowsky, who was asked to take charge of the college library during Miss Evans's absence in Whitehall.

The conversion of sports fields into allotments, the time-consuming obligations of war-work, and a university ban on matches held more than 50 miles away from Oxford combined to relegate sport to a low position on the undergraduate agenda. The musical life of the city, on the other hand, positively thrived. The Oxford Letter for 1940/1 reported that the College Musical Society had filled the hall on all its occasions, 'although it has had to compete with a great multiplication of concerts in Oxford since the war drove London life into the provinces.' In Hilary Term Terence White played a medley on the college organ, and Eve Kisch—now a professional flautist—returned to Somerville with the pianist Dorothy Moggridge and the 'cellist Sela Trau for a concert of music by Bach, Beethoven, Schubert, and Lennox Berkeley. 'The Somerville Bechstein plays Bach as though butter was melting in its mouth' commented the Oxford Correspondent of a concert given that summer by James Ching. 1943 saw the formation of a partnership with the Exeter College Musical Society, the first fruits of which were a concert given in Exeter by the Menges Quartet, and a piano recital by Denis Matthews in Somerville. During the war years the Somerville choir also extended its range beyond the routine provision of music for chapel services and occasional concerts in college. Under the enterprising leadership of Anne Reynell it gave two performances of Debussy's *La Demoiselle Elue* with the London Symphony Orchestra in the Sheldonian in March 1944, and the following May took the part of semi-chorus in Holst's *Hymn to Jesus* sung by the Bach Choir. On 20 May some of its members joined in the performance of madrigals and motets in the Sheldonian to celebrate the creation of a Music Faculty.

In 1940 the college received a bequest of £500 from Lady Bryce in memory of her husband, a friend of many of the Somerville founders, and a life-long supporter of women's education. The money was used to endow an annual lecture, at which the college played host to large audiences from both within and outside the university. The first Bryce lecture was given in June 1942 by the American Ambassador, Mr John Winant, on the subject 'Inherited qualities of the British and American peoples'. Mr Winant—who arrived at the Walton Street gate of Somerville while the reception party awaited him in the Woodstock Road—returned his 15 guinea fee to the college to be used for the benefit of the undergraduates. When, soon afterwards, General Sikorsky came to Somerville to visit a group of Polish students attending a British Council conference, the *Oxford Mail* photographer was heard to remark that it would save trouble to keep a picture of the front quad and just paste in the celebrities as they came.[18] Old Somervillian visitors of the period included Eleanor Rathbone, who spoke to the undergraduates about Miss Maitland at the 1943 commemoration service, and Dr Rose Graham, Mrs H. A. L. Fisher, Miss A. F. Davies, and Margery Fry, who dined in hall in October 1944 to celebrate the 50th anniversary of their admission to Somerville as students—an occasion marked by gifts from Dr Graham and Mrs Fisher of a chased silver bowl and a silver sugar bowl.

Conference trade in wartime being minimal, the college buildings were used in vacation to provide free hospitality for civil defence workers, to accommodate relatives visiting military hospitals in Oxford, and to provide a refuge for present and former students whose homes were in dangerous areas. In the long vacation of 1940 Somerville was host successively to Southover Manor Girls' School and to forty boys and staff from the Caldecott Community. With the introduction of 'shortened courses' in 1942 a voluntary vacation term was organized for a month in the summer for the benefit of first-year undergraduates who would be affected by the new regulations on conscription.

Despite the many calls on their time and the inroads made on their sleep by air-raid warnings and fire-drills, undergraduates managed to maintain a remarkable academic record. The Schools results in 1941

---

[18] Oxford Letter, 1941–2.

among men doing shortened courses were described by the retiring vice-chancellor as 'a retort in the grand manner, avenging centuries of rebuke';[19] Somerville in this year got eight firsts, including four out of four in English. In 1942 the Oxford Correspondent reported with pride the achievement of Mrs John Austin (Jean Coutts), scholar of the college, who

> was married in March 1941, . . . wounded in a blitz in April, took a First in Greats in June, and had a daughter in February 1942. This daughter is being kept under our eye. The Tutor in Literae Humaniores looks forward to having a pupil with pre-natal experience of the examination.[20]

The presence of married and, indeed, pregnant undergraduates was one of the many wartime phenomena to which the college was learning to adjust. Requests to continue in residence after marriage were regarded with a new sympathy, particularly in cases when a fiancé was likely to be ordered to the front at short notice; in June 1943 the Principal and fellows were given authority to deal with such cases without reference to the Council.

The National Service Act of 1942 exempted women tutors, many of whom were air-raid wardens, and brought the call-up age for women forward to 20. This meant that all undergraduates who entered college above the age of 17 and who were not intending to take up teaching or special scientific work (including medicine) were obliged to take a two-year shortened honours course. In the Oxford Letter that year, Isobel Henderson lamented the academic effects of the new arrangements:

> Somerville begins the fourth year of the war without a broken window or an empty room, but its intellectual life is no longer intact. Women undergraduates will now be guillotined—academically speaking—at the age of $20\frac{1}{2}$. . . . Exemption was . . . promised for unusual ability, but in this category the Ministry of Labour has not yet found the woman of whom it dreamed. We sent it a short list of undergraduates whom we thought intelligent, judging by a First in Mods or some other of our rough local criteria; but it turned them

[19] Vice-Chancellor's Oration, 8 Oct. 1941.
[20] Oxford Letter, 1941/2. Mrs Austin subsequently became fellow and tutor in Philosophy at St Hilda's. Though this daughter did not come to Somerville, a younger sister—Lucia Mary Coutts Austin (b. 1951)—did, in 1968.

all down. Some clearer document of genius is required: perhaps a horoscope.[21]

She conceded that the new regulations came as something of a relief to many undergraduates who, like their predecessors twenty-five years earlier, felt uneasy at enjoying the privileges of university life in time of war, but went on to express her own anxiety for the future:

> Shortened courses can turn out more BAs for less money; parents and the State may get to like the taste of dehydrated learning. Does a third year make much difference to efficiency in most bureaucratic or commercial jobs? Does not a modern State need a million good second-rate graduates rather than a thousand scholars? It is not so easy to remember that when academic scholarship declines general education cannot keep its level, or to believe how quickly a technical tradition can be lost, in scholarship as well as in industry or art.

The college did its best to minimize the evils of the shortened courses, organizing vacation terms for those affected and making grants for special courses available to students still in their first year. To safeguard the three-year courses, Somerville admitted each year a proportion of students below the usual admission age of 18. Some candidates too old to qualify even for the two-year course were enabled to beat the deadline by coming into residence a term early. Looking back on this period, Vera Farnell recalled the 'sense of rush and confusion' created in college by the extreme youth of some of the undergraduates, combined with the fact that some were working to a two-year and others to a three-year syllabus.[22] As Principal's Secretary, Hilda Bryant reckoned that she worked almost as much for the Ministry of Labour as for the college, as 'week by week fresh sets of complicated forms poured in, all to be filled in in triplicate.' She strongly suspected that most of the completed forms were never even looked at.

It was with a mixture of academic relief and administrative consternation that the college learned in July 1944 of a new regulation allowing those undergraduates who were to have completed their two-year course in 1945 the option of staying for a third year. In Michaelmas Term Council appealed to the university to introduce legislation to raise the statutory number of undergraduates from 150 to 160, and in

---

[21] Oxford Letter, 1941/2. In 1942/3 only two exemptions were granted.
[22] Farnell, *A Somervillian Looks Back*, 74.

an anguished letter to the Registrar put the case for the admission of a further twenty students *extra numerum*:

We had expected 75 of these [2-year course] undergraduates to go down in 1945, leaving an equivalent number of vacancies. Now, since almost without exception they are taking up the option of a third year, we shall have only 15 or 16 vacancies to offer in 1945 instead of the normal 50. . . . We expect about 380 candidates in 1945.[23]

Both applications were successful. The Bursar's task after the war was clearly not going to be easy.

Exigencies of wartime forced on the college a number of changes, some of which were to prove permanent. In Trinity Term 1942 representatives of the Oxford and Cambridge women's colleges and of the Head Mistresses' Association met to discuss the scholarship and entrance examination, and recommended unanimously the holding of a simultaneous examination in March of each year.[24] In 1943 the college by-law which required a minimum of four tutors to be in residence was suspended to enable Miss Hartley to spend a period of leave in government service, and the JCR constitution was modified to take account of the new conditions of shortened courses. The need to make major decisions quickly, at a time when pressure of other commitments made it extremely difficult for 'outside' members of Council to attend meetings, thrust the burden of responsibility increasingly upon the small resident body of the Principal and fellows. An emergency sub-committee had been set up in 1939; at a special meeting in Trinity Term 1940 its powers were vested for the coming long vacation in 'the Principal together with such Fellows as are resident or available.'[25] Throughout the war the Principal and fellows met most weeks during term, matters of special importance being reserved for discussion on Saturday evenings or Sunday mornings when Miss Sutherland and Miss Evans could be present. The meetings were informal, and had no statutory or executive powers, and—initially—no minutes; but it was through them that lasting habits of self-government were forged.

Relations with the university were also permanently affected by the

[23] Minutes of Council, 31 Oct. 1944.
[24] Minutes of Council, 26 May, 16 June 1942. In the event, St Anne's—whose syllabus was very different from that of the other colleges—withdrew from later negotiations to arrive at a common syllabus and a joint examination: PE, 17 Nov. 1942.
[25] Special Meeting of Council, 11 June 1940.

war. When in 1942 the Estates Bursars Committee drew up a scheme for the reduction or rebate of war damage contributions on college buildings, it did not occur to it to inform—let alone include—the five women's societies. The latter, after consultation with the University Registrar, agreed to press for representation on the committee. The bursars, disconcerted by a proposal which was incompatible—they said—with their practice of meeting over dinner, came up with a counter-proposal: after meetings of the standing committee the chairman might routinely go through the business with a representative of the women's colleges—provided the women contributed to the cost of circulating the papers. The secretary of the committee was subsequently authorized 'to pass on to the women's colleges at his discretion and in any manner he might find convenient, such items of bursarial business as he might think desirable', on the understanding that this decision might be revoked without any suggestion of bad faith should it prove to be unworkable. There was clearly some way to go before the women's colleges achieved their aim of constitutional representation; but they had at least put down a marker.[26]

In 1943 Miss Beauchamp retired after eighteen years as Treasurer and Secretary of the college. She herself argued energetically for a permanent appointment to be made at once; but Council took the view that, with so many potential candidates locked up in war work, this was undesirable, and Miss Stonedale was asked to step from the Bursar's shoes to the Treasurer's for the duration of the war. There was a general post among the college administration, Miss Stott replacing Miss Stonedale as Bursar, and Miss Bryant returning from the Red Cross to her old post of Principal's Secretary, to enable Miss Gillies to take over as her assistant.

In the same year, Miss Darbishire asked the Council to consider the question of her retirement 'in view of the general national situation and the pressure of her literary work' and the desirability of her successor coming into office before the problems of the post-war period became matters of immediate moment.[27] At the request of the fellows she agreed to stay until the end of July 1945, but expressed her willingness to go sooner if it would be in the college's interests for her to do so. The meeting of Council summoned in June 1944 to set in motion the search for a new Principal was chiefly preoccupied with

---

[26] Minutes of Council, 27 Oct. 1942; 16 Feb. and 1 June 1943.
[27] Minutes of Council, 23 Nov. 1943.

the question of whether the ASM should be represented on the selection committee; it was eventually agreed by a narrow margin that membership should be restricted to the vice-chairman (A. D. Lindsay) and the fellows.[28] A letter from Lady Margaret Hall inviting suggestions of suitable candidates for its forthcoming principalian election was answered non-commitally.[29] According to Hilda Bryant, the atmosphere in college for the ensuing months approximated very closely to that depicted in C. P. Snow's *The Masters*. The fellows, equally divided between two outstanding candidates (and all protesting that they would be happy to serve under either), were eventually rescued from deadlock by Lucy Sutherland's offer to withdraw from the contest.[30] Her offer was accepted with gratitude and relief, and on 6 February 1945 Dr Janet Vaughan, medical officer in charge of the North-West London blood supply depot for the Medical Research Council, was unanimously elected Principal as from the beginning of August.

[28] Minutes of Council, 3 June 1944.   [29] PF, 7 Nov. 1944.
[30] Correspondence between Lucy Sutherland and A. D. Lindsay, Dec. 1944–Jan. 1945 (Lucy Sutherland MSS, Bodleian Library).

12

Post-War Reconstruction: The Principalship of Janet Vaughan, 1945–1967

JANET Vaughan was the first scientist, and the first married woman, to be Principal of Somerville.[1] Once told by a headmistress that she was too stupid to be worth educating, she took a first in natural sciences (physiology) at Somerville in 1921 and went on to become a leading haematologist. During the war she ran West London's blood transfusion service from its headquarters in Slough, and in 1945 she was one of the first scientists to go into Belsen, an experience which no doubt put the problems of Somerville into a certain perspective. She was to remain a practising scientist throughout her time as Principal, publishing forty-eight scientific papers in twenty-two years; a college play one Christmas portrayed her constantly crossing and recrossing the stage in cap and gown muttering 'Just off to the lab; just off to the lab.' Like Margery Fry, whom she much admired, she found considerable difficulty in adjusting to Oxford, and Somerville, ways. On her arrival in college she was, as she says in her reminiscences, 'aghast' to find that the Principal had no telephone, and that the college telephone was switched off at 5 p.m. When she protested, she was told 'We do not telephone, we write notes'.[2] After one of her early parties in Radcliffe House, which had gone on, characteristically, until 2 a.m., her secretary said 'I think I should tell you Principal that Oxford dinner parties end at 10 p.m.'

Having overcome her initial doubts about Oxford, Janet Vaughan stayed for twenty-two years, continuing throughout to pursue her own scientific work, and serving on numerous committees within and outside the university. She sat on the Royal Commission for Equal Pay, became a trustee of the Nuffield Foundation, chaired the Regional Hospital Board, and got the first new hospital after the war

---

[1] She had married David Gourlay, co-founder of the Wayfarers Travel Agency, in 1930.

[2] JV, 'Jogging Along'. The question of the college telephone service was raised at the first Meeting of Principal and Fellows of the new regime (11 Oct. 1945).

to be built at Swindon. Within the university, she fought for the right of foreign students to bring their wives and families to Oxford with them, campaigned for the provision of psychiatric care for students, and was responsible for planning the first college accommodation for graduates in Oxford. Her medical contacts enabled Somerville to be in at the outset of initiatives to establish a Student Health Service, as one of the three participating colleges in a pilot scheme undertaken in 1946 by the Director of the Institute of Social Medicine, Professor Ryle, and subsequently extended to the whole university. In 1955 she represented Oxford as the only woman delegate—and, apart from the representative from Outer Mongolia, the only scientist—at the bi-centenary celebrations of the University of Moscow. In 1957 she was made a Dame of the British Empire; on her retirement in 1967 Oxford conferred on her the degree of Doctor of Civil Law.

In retirement in North Oxford she continued her scientific work. Her major book *The Physiology of Bone* was published in 1969 and went through three editions. She became a Fellow of the Royal Society in 1979, and was awarded the Osler Medal for outstanding services to medicine in 1981. She continued to be active in the Labour Party until, prompted in part by affection for Shirley Williams, she joined the Social Democrats. When asked in a radio interview how she had managed to fit so many activities into her life, she replied 'I never played bridge.'

For the undergraduates up in 1945 she could not have presented a more startling contrast to her predecessor. 'She was tall' recalled Joyce Sugg, 'with large features, black hair knotted in her neck. She often wore black or figured dark material which floated or billowed about her in a rather splendid manner. Her evening dresses did not look at all like cosy dressing gowns'—a reference to the celebrated 'plum coloured comfortable woollen garment' in which Helen Darbishire had been accustomed for years past to appear at dinner. The austere formality of Miss Darbishire's college room, with its large flat desk, uncomfortable chairs, and almost complete lack of decoration, was transformed into an elegant sitting-room, with large arm-chairs and sofa, antique furniture, and family portraits. Among the venerable college possessions consigned to storage was the blue and gold credenza presented in 1921 by Lady Mabel and Lady Jane Lindsay, to which the new Principal took an instant and violent dislike; it was removed, according to Hilda Bryant, 'in the nick of time at the end of the first long vacation, to avoid an explosion.'

As Principal's Secretary, Miss Bryant found that the leisurely tempo of morning routine was a thing of the past:

> By 8.30 or even earlier she had opened her post (insisting on her own pigeon-hole instead of everything coming to her secretary) and by 9 a.m. had dealt with the day's routine. Gone also was the system by which undergraduates had to make appointments to see her through me—they were given 'carte blanche' to call on her at all times, both in college and in Radcliffe House. Tea had to be provided at any hour between 10.30 a.m. and 5.30 p.m. A direct-line telephone was installed, sherry and glasses stored in the cupboard in the bureau. Radcliffe House also changed, with children in the house and hens at the bottom of the garden.[3]

To the college at large Janet Vaughan brought an energy and optimism and persistence which were of crucial importance in surmounting the difficulties and uncertainties which lay ahead.

Somerville had emerged from the war with greatly increased undergraduate numbers, a reduced teaching strength, run-down buildings and precarious finances. It was only gradually that it, and the rest of Oxford, was able to return to anything approaching normality. In the long vacation of 1945 the baffle walls in front of the library and Maitland loggias and the front door of Penrose had been taken down, the mosquito-infested water-tank in front of Maitland was demolished, and preparations were made to restore the vegetable garden to lawn. Black-out curtains were converted into commoners' gowns. But the West buildings—with the exception of the 'Isle of Man' and eight rooms on the ground floor—were not finally derequisitioned until January 1946, and undergraduates coming up in Michaelmas Term 1945 found themselves accommodated in rooms hastily converted from singles to doubles, with three students housed in the West JCR.

Undergraduate numbers throughout the university were hugely inflated by students resuming courses which they had broken off in order to do their national service, and by those whose entrance scholarships, won during the past four years, had been held over till the end of the war. In recognition of these exceptional circumstances, the university allowed the women's colleges to increase their statutory number of undergraduates, Somerville's quota being increased by ten to 160. By 1945/6, the total number of members of the college

---

[3] Recollections of Hilda Bryant.

(including those reading for research degrees or the diploma in education) was 236. 'The whole university is having the same experience' reported the Oxford Correspondent:

> Queues form before 9 o'clock at the doors of all the libraries; by 9.05 every seat is taken. The shortage of books in nearly every subject is serious, booksellers' supplies of new copies of reprints of standard works are cleared in half a day and no library can replace its worn-out books; the editions of newly-published academic books are very small.

In Michaelmas Term the Council explored the possibility of renting and equipping an emergency canteen to cater for the many students who could not be accommodated in hall and were finding it difficult to obtain adequate meals elsewhere.[4] The problem of accommodation was so acute the following year that the University Registrar canvassed the idea of providing colleges with Nissen huts—an offer which Somerville declined, believing shared rooms to be a lesser evil.[5] Conditions were exacerbated by the weather—by a cold spell in January 1946 in which the ancient central heating system in West collapsed and the electrical wiring was suddenly found to be defective and dangerous, and by the cold, wet summer (in which, claimed the *ASM Report*, only the newly sown college lawn flourished) and terrible winter which followed. 'Life is not easy for the undergraduate in these days' reported the Oxford Correspondent in 1947, 'with shortage of fuel, shortage of food and shortage of books. Hilary Term was suggestive of medieval conditions when in the half-darkened streets people stumbled over frozen snow to seek in lectures some compensation for their lack of books and in lecture-rooms a modicum of warmth.'

During the worst of the weather undergraduates were supplied by college with mid-morning Namco to warm them up.[6] Senior members were sustained by food parcels sent by the American Oxonians, the butter being kept for SCR tea, and the other contents of the parcels distributed among the fellows by lot.[7] A plea for gifts of books for the library and plants for the garden met with a generous response from old Somervillians. Mrs Erskine Muir presented lilies for the old water-tank in the East quadrangle; Mrs Hicks and Mrs Snow gave

---

[4] Minutes of Council, 27 Nov. 1945 and 19 Feb. 1946.   [5] PF, 17 June 1946.

[6] National Milk Cocoa features largely in Girtonian recollections of this period: see 'Surviving Girton on NAMCO', *Girton College Newsletter*, 1993, 9–10.

[7] SCR Minutes, MT 1947.

some rock plants, the Principal a rose-bed. Old members contributed to the establishment of a lily-of-the-valley bed in the fellows' garden. The bursars did what they could to improve the appearance of the college. The new installations necessitated by the collapse of the heating system in West enabled the college to obtain permits to re-decorate one of its buildings, if only on austerity lines; elsewhere Miss Garstang and Miss Gillies and the college men 'managed a little dis-tempering and cheerful painting and an almost incredible amount of carpet cleaning.'[8]

The resumed rhythms of everyday academic life were interspersed with celebrations and feasts. Somerville joined enthusiastically in the 'liveliness and gaiety' of two great ceremonial Convocations and the first peace-time Encaenia, and celebrated privately the return of the politics tutor Mary Macdonald from a long vacation in America as Mrs Malcolm Proudfoot, bearing welcome supplies of rich Ameri-can wedding cake.[9] In June 1948 Enid Starkie was invested with the cross of *Chevalier de la Légion d'honneur* by the French Ambassador at the opening garden party of the new Maison Française.[10] The college gaudy was reinstated that summer, though invitations to the garden party had to be restricted to Oxford residents and those attending the dinner, new regulations from the Ministry of Food forbidding a meal being provided for over a hundred people, however simple the fare. In 1950, at the request of the university, Somerville hosted a dance in honour of Princess Margaret, to which selected members of all the women's societies and their partners were invited. In 1953 the JCR hired a television for the day to watch the Coronation, and the new college flag was flown for the first time to mark Miss Tyler's marriage to John Armstrong of Hertford. 1954 saw the revival of two venerable pre-war occasions—Open Night (with coffee and biscuits) for old Somervillians living in Oxford, and the SCR party (with sherry and cigarettes) for current graduate students.

In June 1946 the views of colleges were sought on a proposed increase in undergraduate numbers consequent upon the Barlow Report on Scientific Manpower.[11] Somerville declared itself prepared to contemplate an expansion from 160 to 180 or 200, exclusive of advanced students, provided that admission standards could be main-tained and that capital was made available for adequate teaching

[8] Oxford Letter, 1945–6.   [9] Ibid.
[10] In June 1958 she was promoted to the rank of *Officier*.
[11] *Report on Scientific Manpower*, May 1946 (Cmd. 6824).

and accommodation. Expansion beyond this point was, in the Council's view, both undesirable on educational grounds and impracticable without building on a scale impossible on the existing site.[12]

In the matter of undergraduate numbers, the women's colleges faced a harsh dilemma. Despite the many problems caused by the inflated numbers of the immediate post-war period, heavy dependence on fee income made the prospect of a sharp decline when the concessionary period drew to an end a matter of deep concern. In presenting the college accounts for 1946–7 the Treasurer noted that the satisfactory margin of income over expenditure was less than the anticipated fall in revenue should numbers be reduced to the statutory maximum of 160.[13] A joint letter to the vice-chancellor from the five women principals requested a change in the statutes to enable a gradual rise in numbers in the women's societies to 180 (with a possible extension to 200 in the more distant future), pointing out that raising the quota would for some time to come mean not an increase in numbers but a check on their decrease. The letter was favourably received, and in 1948 Hebdomadal Council agreed to propose an increase of twenty for each college. Rumours that strong opposition might be expected aroused fears of a repetition of the events of 1927, and ensured a full house for the debate; Janet Vaughan reported seeing several members of Congregation being wheeled into the Sheldonian in invalid chairs. The case for an increase was defended—'in spite of his well-known conservatism'[14]—by the President of St John's, A. L. Poole (a former member of the Somerville Council), the Warden of New College, A. H. Smith (a current member of the Council), and the old Somervillian Principal of St Hilda's, Miss Mann; the opposition was led by the President of Corpus (Sir Richard Livingstone) and the Principal of St Edmund Hall (A. B. Emden). The result—228 votes for the increase and 11 against—was a triumph beyond all expectations for the women's colleges. 'If the "woman question" is not yet dead in Oxford it may be presumed moribund' reported the Oxford Correspondent, noting with satisfaction that the majority had included representatives of every college and faculty in the university, and adding as 'an appropriate comment on this notable debate' the fact that the last Sunday of Trinity Term had seen a number of academic women—including Dr Vaughan, Miss Lorimer, and four

---

[12] Special Meeting of Council, 17 June 1946.   [13] Minutes of Council, 11 Nov. 1947.
[14] JV, 'Jogging Along'.

members of the Somerville SCR—dining on high table at Magdalen as the guests of the President and fellows.[15] When, some years later, Janet Vaughan herself moved a further statute giving another small increase in the permitted numbers of women, she spoke to an empty house, and there was no debate. In 1956 the Warden of Wadham was unopposed when he proposed the abolition of the fixed quota.

Increased undergraduate numbers necessitated a larger staff. As the teaching and administrative arrangements into which Somerville had entered for the duration of the war came to an end, there was a welcome infusion of new blood into the SCR. The Mary Somerville and Lady Carlisle fellowships, unfilled since 1940, were promptly advertised, and in 1946 Elizabeth Anscombe and Lotte Labowsky became the first post-war holders. Miss Stonedale agreed to stay on as Treasurer for a further year; but Miss Stott, having reached retirement age, declined reappointment as Bursar, and was replaced by the Treasurer's assistant, Miss Garstang. Miss Sutherland, released in Trinity Term 1945 by the Board of Trade, had instantly been snapped up by Lady Margaret Hall as Principal; her wartime replacement, Miss Jackson, left to take up a post at Durham. Somerville entered the long vacation of 1945 with tutorial vacancies in PPE and history and the possibility of one in maths, and with the prospect of having to find successors in the near future for Mrs Turville-Petre and Miss Farnell in English and French. At a meeting of the Principal and fellows called in May 1945 to discuss a successor to Miss Sutherland as PPE tutor, Dorothy Hodgkin drew attention to the serious shortage of science teachers, and Enid Starkie pressed the claims of Romance philology.[16]

In the event, one of the wartime appointees—Kathleen Sarginson—stayed on, taking over tutorial control of Somerville mathematicians from Miss Busbridge in 1946, and in 1947 becoming Somerville's first fellow and tutor in mathematics. An internal solution was also found for the treasurership, which was offered to Anne Evans, on her release from Whitehall, in exchange for the library.[17] In making new academic appointments, there were many competing claims on very limited resources. Enid Starkie's elevation to a university readership in 1946, the year before Vera Farnell's retirement, gave special urgency to the question of modern languages (Somerville's largest school), and

---

[15] Oxford Letter, 1947–8. [16] PF, 15 May 1945.

[17] In 1948—at Miss Evans's request—the college secretariat was reorganized so as to enable the Principal's secretary to take over the Treasurer's erstwhile function as Secretary to the college (PF, 16 Nov. 1948).

led to the immediate appointment of Miss Elizabeth Tyler as tutor in French. Meanwhile, at a time when the college was not in a position to make many permanent appointments, it succeeded in attaching to itself as lecturers or research fellows or assistant tutors a number of promising young scholars who in succeeding years were to form the core of its teaching strength: Olive Davison (later Mrs Sayce) in German, Philippa Foot in philosophy, Ursula Brown (later Mrs Dronke) in English, Margaret Hall in economics. One appointment which was intended as permanent lasted for only a few months, the economist Helen Makower resigning within the year to take up a post at the London School of Economics. Her departure coincided with that of Mary Proudfoot, to join her husband in America. In 1947 tutorial control of the PPE school was taken over by Mrs Hall, Mrs Foot being appointed lecturer in philosophy and Miss Lucy Brown—a graduate of Girton—assistant tutor in history and politics. When in 1949 it was decided to make all inter-collegiate lecturers a charge on the Common University Fund, Somerville—with five eligible fellows— was one of the colleges which stood to benefit most.[18]

In a college whose statutes until 1993 required its Principal and fellows to resign on marriage (albeit in fair expectation of re-election) the influx of so many young married women marked a significant break with tradition. In 1938 Dorothy Hodgkin had made college history as the first serving fellow to have a baby (and the first in the university to seek maternity leave). In 1944, faced with the prospect of two more Somerville infants—another Hodgkin and a Turville-Petre—Council agreed that all members of the tutorial and administrative staff should be expected to take paid leave for at least one month before, and two months after, the birth of a child. With Janet Vaughan—a mother of two—now chairing college meetings it was difficult to maintain traditional doubts about the compatibility of family and college responsibilities. By the early 1960s over half the fellows were married, several of them with young children—Elizabeth Anscombe holding the record, with seven. ('I shall be having a baby on Monday', she is reputed to have informed a pupil on one occasion, 'You had better come for your tutorial on Tuesday.') Somerville presented to the post-war world numerous role-models for young women who aspired to combine academic and domestic life; but the traditional model of the college as a residential community of scholars was inevitably weakened.

[18] J. P. D. Dunbabin, 'Finance since 1914', in *HUO* viii, 652–3.

In the course of the 1950s, however, the resident community had a number of important reinforcements. Jean Banister, who had been appointed Somerville's first lecturer in physiology in 1949, was elected to a fellowship in 1951. In 1952 Somerville appointed as fellow and tutor in modern history the editor of the recently published *Political Correspondence of Mr Gladstone and Lord Granville*, Agatha Ramm. When, three years later, May McKisack left to take up a chair at Westfield College, she was succeeded by her former pupil Barbara Harvey. These all lived in college; Anne Cobbe, who in 1955 succeeded Kathleen Sarginson as fellow and tutor in mathematics, obtained permission to live out.

The resignation of Anne Evans on her marriage in 1951 to Sir Nicolas de Villiers prompted another review of the treasurer's office. Once again, it was decided to appoint an academic: the new Treasurer, Rosemary Syfret, an expert on Sidney and Milton, was a welcome asset to Somerville's large English school—so much so that in 1957 she resigned the treasurership in order to teach full-time. The post was now taken up, again part-time, by Mary Proudfoot, who, recently widowed, returned to Somerville as lecturer in politics. In 1961 the college at last recognized that the office was too heavy to be held in conjunction with an academic post, and entrusted it to Jane Hands, whose rapid rise through the administrative hierarchy began in 1954 with her appointment as Assistant Bursar.

In financial matters the college long remained dependent on the advice and expertise of the 'outside' members of Council; and it was fortunate in having among these one of Oxford's most distinguished financial administrators, Sir William Goodenough. The Finance (Universities & Colleges (Trusts)) Act of 1943 had empowered colleges to make a scheme for property held on trust to be administered as a single fund. On the advice of Sir Frank Newson-Smith (adviser to the University Chest and the Radcliffe Infirmary as well as to several other colleges), Somerville realized a number of its investments, established a sinking fund, and sought specialist advice on the wisdom of investing in land.[19] In Hilary Term 1947, after making enquiries about the policy of other Oxbridge colleges, the Council approved an investment scheme proposed by Newson-Smith and Goodenough. Recognizing that a widening of investments was likely to necessitate the establishment of machinery to guide a part-time unprofessional

---

[19] Minutes of Council, 16 Feb. 1943.

Treasurer and to safeguard the interests of the college, Council agreed to strengthen the Finance Committee with a view to its exercising active and constant control over future investment policy. In Hilary Term 1948, the scheme having been approved by the King in Council, Sir William Goodenough, Mr Robert Hall, and Mr Charles Bosanquet were co-opted on to Finance Committee to advise college on the use to be made of its new powers of investment.

Somerville needed all the financial expertise it could muster to weather the economic uncertainties of the late 1940s. Introducing a proposal to raise fees in June 1948, the Treasurer pointed out that if the college had so far avoided financial crisis it was only because of the temporary increase in undergraduate numbers and the restraints upon expenditure imposed by shortages and rationing. The post-war cost of living was conservatively estimated at 60 per cent above the pre-war level. The college's estimated income for 1949–50 (by which time undergraduate numbers would have stabilized at about 180) was c. £42,000, an increase of 50 per cent over the 1938–9 figure; estimates of expenditure showed an increase of 5 per cent over the 1946–7 level and of 61 per cent over the pre-war level. What was particularly disquieting was the extent to which rising expenditure was concentrated upon the household, maintenance, and general establishment items: the combined cost of stipends, scholarships, and library, which before the war represented 56 per cent of the year's expenditure, accounted for only 29 per cent of the 1949–50 estimates. The situation, concluded Miss Evans, in words which ring down the years, 'calls for ingenuity and discrimination in allocation of existing resources, for enterprise in attracting benefactions which will relieve the pressure on general revenue (e.g. by the endowment of fellowships), and possibly for a renewed application for a UGC grant in some shape or form.'[20]

With little endowment to fall back on, and anxious to remain roughly in step with each other, the women's colleges had no choice but to increase their fees. A rise of 25 per cent—from £150 to £187.10.0d.—in 1946 brought Somerville to the same level as St Hugh's and St Hilda's, and slightly below that of LMH. In the summer of 1948 a further increase to £255 p.a. was agreed, to take effect from Michaelmas Term 1949. Alarmed at the proposed increase, the JCR requested a meeting with the Treasurer and asked to see the college

---

[20] Minutes of Council, 1 June 1948.

accounts; they were told that these were too complicated for under-graduates to understand.[21] The sum set aside for bursaries, however, was doubled from £75 to £150, and the maximum award in any one case raised from £20 to £50. In presenting the accounts for 1948/9 Miss Evans drew attention to the capital depreciation resulting from the sharp decline in the value of gilt-edged investments, and reported that the college's financial advisers were unable with any certainty to predict future trends. The receipt in February 1952 of an anonymous gift of £1,000 'to meet any deficit on the annual expenditure of the College, either in the current year or in 1952/3' could not have been more welcome.

Ironically, while Somerville was struggling in general to make ends meet, it was encountering considerable difficulty in making use of some of its more restricted trust funds. Candidates for the richly endowed travelling scholarship in Mediterranean archaeology established in 1945 by bequest of Lady Woolley (Katharine Menke, 1910) were so few that in March 1948 Sir Leonard Woolley was approached—unsuccessfully—about the possibility of opening it to women candidates from other universities, or even to men.[22] The scholarship was subsequently converted into a travelling fellowship, and attracted a succession of distinguished holders, including, from 1954 to 1956, Somerville's future Principal, Barbara Craig.

By means of regular fee increases and careful investment Somerville steadily improved its financial position. A decision to put one-third of the college's investments in property (the remainder being divided equally between gilt-edged securities and equities), resulted in the acquisition in 1950 of 35 Regent Street, Swindon and 87 High Street, Winchester. In November 1954, on the advice of Mr Russell, it was agreed to reduce gilt-edged securities to 25 per cent and change the balance to equities. Finance Committee was to keep the investment situation under constant review; and the Principal, Lady Hall, and the Treasurer, together with any other member of Finance Committee available, were empowered to take action in vacations, should necessity arise. In 1956 there was a further switch from gilt-edged to equities. The college's financial position steadily improved, despite the general trade recession.[23]

A first call on the college's resources was to maintain its teaching

[21] Recollections of Barbara Harvey.   [22] PF, 8 Mar. 1948.
[23] Minutes of Council, 3 Dec. 1958.

strength. In 1952 a fellowship endowment fund was established with a donation from the Cadbury Trust and the promise of annual donations and a future capital sum from Mr R. D. Richardson.[24] Later that year Philippa Foot was elected the first holder of the Alice Cobb research fellowship in philosophy, established by gift of Miss C. V. Chapman in fulfilment of the wishes of her sister, Mrs Cobb. A bequest received from Mrs John Spedan Lewis in memory of her elder son, who had died in childhood, was used to endow the tutorial fellowship in English held by Mary Lascelles. In an unsuccessful appeal by the women's colleges to the Ford Foundation for fellowship endowment in 1955, Somerville put history and economics as its top priorities.

In December 1952 colleges were invited to comment on a proposed university application to the University Grants Committee. The five women principals wrote a joint letter to the vice-chancellor setting out the special financial circumstances of their colleges:

> By the most careful budgeting and frugal living the Women's Colleges have succeeded in paying their way out of a combination of undergraduates' fees and the profits of letting to vacation conferences. They have met the great increase of costs since the war by increase of fees and conference charges, by redoubled economy and by a good deal of concealed delay in repairs and replacements.[25]

The overriding need, they said, was for capital. At a subsequent meeting, the vice-chancellor undertook to prepare a paper on the subject , it being agreed that the question needed to be considered on a national basis and as a matter of university policy. In 1956 the women's colleges decided to launch a joint public appeal for general endowment, undergraduate and graduate accommodation, and the endowment of fellowships and graduate awards. Somerville's target of £460,000, regarded by the other women's colleges as too high, was vigorously defended by Janet Vaughan on the grounds that the college had yet to acquire the land necessary for future building.[26]

In the event this appeal was overtaken by the university's own major appeal for the restoration of Oxford's ancient buildings. Colleges were asked to co-operate by circularizing old members with a covering letter stating their own needs under the terms of the

---

[24] Minutes of Council, 19 Feb. 1952.   [25] Minutes of Informal Council, 2 Dec. 1952.
[26] Minutes of Council, 13 Nov. 1957.

university Appeal; in the case of the women's colleges these particular needs, of course, were negligible. The idea was briefly entertained of combining the women's appeal with one planned for the new men's college, St Catherine's, or in collaboration with Girton and Newnham. But in June 1958 a *Times* leader on the needs of the women's colleges fell on deaf ears; the President of the Federation of British Industries, Sir Hugh Beaver, gave it as his view that it was not a cause in which industry was at present interested.[27]

It was now becoming clear, however, that in future money was more likely to be available from the university for loans to the women's colleges. An increase in the UGC block grant to the University in 1959 resulted in an annual grant of £100 to all college libraries, and a 25 per cent increase in the university's contribution to the colleges for services rendered. The following year the UGC grant was used to raise all CUF salaries by £150. In 1961, as a means of relieving the women's colleges of some of their financial commitments, the UGC offered a contribution towards the stipends of the women principals; the offer was accepted gratefully but with hurt pride, Somerville's letter of thanks expressing 'regret . . . that the women's colleges had been singled out as a separate group in the University.'[28] (St Hilda's was the only college whose pride was sufficiently hurt for them to consider refusing the offer.)[29] In the event a similar offer was made to four poor men's colleges.

When the Colleges Contributions Scheme was set up in 1960 with the object of building up the endowment capital of the poorer colleges by means of a levy on the richer ones, Somerville noted that it was unlikely to have to pay any contribution for the foreseeable future. It was, indeed, to benefit considerably from the scheme, and from the generosity of other colleges, in the coming years. Especially welcome was a gift of £10,000 from Nuffield College in 1964 for general educational purposes; the Warden of Nuffield expressed pleasure at Somerville's decision to use this gift to contribute towards a tutorial fellowship in economics (to be named the Nuffield fellow), but hoped that the college would not feel bound to do so for ever 'as we want your Governing Body to be quite free to use the income in the way they think most beneficial to your College, and not to feel too obliged to the source.'[30] Jesus College soon afterwards followed suit,

---

[27] Minutes of Council, 3 Dec. 1958. [28] Minutes of Council, 15 Feb. 1961.

[29] Minutes of Council, 14 June 1961. [30] Minutes of Council, 11 Mar. 1964.

with a gift of £1,000 to each of the women's colleges to augment their endowments. When a rating revaluation that year resulted in men's colleges receiving substantial repayments from the City while the women's colleges remained in deficit, the Estates Bursars Committee recommended that the repayments to the men's colleges be paid into a pool from which the deficits of the women's colleges should be met.[31]

The University's policy of restricting the number of women in Oxford had resulted in an enforced selectivity which maintained academic standards at a very high level. Somerville's reputation as the blue-stocking college flourished in these years. In 1950 Margaret Hubbard, a Dorothy McCalman scholar with a first degree from the University of Adelaide, was awarded the Hertford Scholarship, never before won by a woman, following this within two years by a Craven Scholarship, and the Ireland Scholarship, the most distinguished classical award open to members of the University. In 1954 the Gibbs Scholarship in Chemistry was awarded for the first time to a woman, Marjorie Aitken, and the Gladstone Memorial Prize was won by Edna Diamond, who read part of her essay at Encaenia. In 1958—a year in which Sally Hinchliff was awarded the Thomas Whitcombe Green Scholarship and Stephanie Pickard the First Craven Scholarship— eleven Somerville undergraduates were placed in the first class in the final honour Schools.

The discontinuance in 1952 of the practice of publishing women's examination results separately from those of the men was one small indication of the gradual absorption of the women's colleges into the mainstream of university life. Another came the following year with the merging of the Women's and the Men's Appointments Committees.[32] A major advance was made in 1960 when the Estates Bursars Committee at last overcame their problems about dining arrangements and admitted the treasurers of the women's colleges to membership. Women dons even began to impinge on university politics. In 1956 Elizabeth Anscombe mounted a lonely protest in Congregation against the granting of an honorary degree to President Truman, the man responsible for the bombing of Hiroshima and Nagasaki;[33] in

[31] Ibid.
[32] When the OUAC was set up in 1936 a successful campaign had been launched to oppose women being included in its brief.
[33] G. E. M. Anscombe, *Mr Truman's Degree* (privately printed [1956]). Her only supporters in Congregation were Philippa and Michael Foot and Margaret Hubbard.

1961 Enid Starkie—unsupported, to her chagrin, by any current fellow of Somerville—made her first unsuccessful bid for the Professorship of Poetry.[34]

The increasing prominence of women in the university was matched by an increasing self-reliance at home. In Hilary Term 1950 the Somerville Council, on the motion of its vice-chairman, Lord Lindsay of Birker, resolved to seek authority to amend the statutes so as to vest the government of the college in the hands of the Principal and fellows. There were consultations with those who had served on the Council in the past, and with the ASM; and Janet Vaughan was dispatched to pay a personal call on Miss Pope, who said that the proposed changes had long seemed to her inevitable. For seventy years the 'outside' members of Council, with their wide range of expertise and influence, had played a crucial role in moulding the character of Somerville as an institution. But, despite natural feelings of regret at the passing of the old order, it was now generally agreed that the time had come for the college to remodel its constitution on the pattern of the older academic societies within the university. For a transitional period no new elections to Council were made, existing members consenting to serve until the revised statutes came into force. Special provision was made for Professor Gilbert Murray, the last surviving life-member, who retained his seat under the new constitution as a welcome and honoured Councillor, and who continued to chair the Library Committee until his death, in 1957, at the age of 91. The last step towards self-government was made in 1961 when Dr Russell resigned from the Finance Committee, saying that he felt college should now dispense with its outside member, the internal members being fully competent. The continuance of Dr Russell's long connection with Somerville, begun in 1943 with his nomination as the University Representative on the Council, was happily secured by his marriage in 1956 to the college's Librarian, Norma Hodgson (Lewis, 1921).[35]

In revising the college statutes one of the Council's chief concerns was to safeguard the interests of old members of the college, and in particular to offer some compensation for the loss of ASM representation on Council. LMH provided the model for a scheme proposed by

---

[34] J. Richardson, *Enid Starkie* (London, 1973), 222 ff.
[35] After Dr Russell's death in 1972 she married, as his second wife, Sir Weldon Dalrymple Champneys, Bt. (d. 1980).

Anne Evans, whereby each year two distinguished old members were elected for a three-year term as 'Guests of High Table', with an entitlement to a week's free hospitality a year in college. A dinner was given annually in their honour, preceded or followed by a party to which undergraduate scholars and exhibitioners were invited. The first four guests to be elected—Mrs Spedan Lewis, Miss E. M. Merrifield, Mrs Michael Roberts (Janet Adam Smith), and Miss Jean Fisher—established a pattern of Somervillian achievement in business, education, literature, and law which later generations were to maintain and elaborate. Among their successors were several who were subsequently to be still more closely attached to the college as honorary fellows: Cicely Williams, Nancy Fisher (later Mrs Trenaman), (Dame) Kathleen Kenyon, Muriel St Clare Byrne, Eirene Lloyd Jones (Baroness White), Dilys Powell, Hazel Stuart (Lady Fox), Shirley Williams, (Dame) Anne Mueller, Emma Kirkby. For forty years the Guests of High Table provided the college with a regular stream of visitors from the wider world, and undergraduates with an opportunity to meet some distinguished predecessors. But by the 1980s, though the range of potential Guests was far from exhausted, gathering them together for a celebratory dinner was beginning to prove difficult. After one such occasion which, in the event, only one of the six current Guests was able to attend, Governing Body agreed to try a new format whereby they would be invited instead to join in the regular college occasions—such as Michaelmas Dinner—of their term of office. It was, however, increasingly apparent that the fixed rhythms of university life were rarely compatible with the busy schedules of women of the world; in 1991 Governing Body concluded that other ways should be sought of drawing old members into the life of the college, and the institution of Guests of High Table was regretfully abolished.

Somerville's charter and statutes were revised again in 1959, when the five women's societies were at last admitted as full colleges of the university. This new status, established by a statute passed by Congregation on 20 October, opened up the office of vice-chancellor to women; that of proctor was still, however, considered an unsuitable occupation for a woman. It was not until 1977—by which time the majority of men's colleges had opened their fellowship to women—that this last bastion fell; meanwhile, the university sought to safeguard the interests of the women's colleges by instituting the office of Representative of the Women's Colleges, an *ex officio* and voting member of the Hebdomadal Council and of all university committees on which the proctors served. The first Somerville fellow to be elected to this office was Jean Banister in 1962/3. By the time that Barbara Harvey was elected in 1967 the title had changed to 'Assessor', and its scope had been widened to include representatives of the new graduate colleges. Miriam Griffin, elected in Hilary Term 1977 to serve for the proctorial year 1978/9, was the last assessor to serve under the old dispensation. Thereafter, all colleges took turns to elect proctors and assessor, and Somerville, now at the foot of the list, had to wait until 1990 for its first proctor.

These constitutional developments were common to all the women's colleges. But each of these retained a strong individual ethos, and Somerville's was very much determined by the personality of its Principal. She herself felt frequently under censure, not least from the spirit of her formidable great-aunt, Charlotte Green, portraits of whom gazed down—disapprovingly, as she believed—from various vantage points on the college walls.[36] Though in 1945 the fellows had deliberately chosen a scientist as Principal, they appeared at times distrustful of a scientist's capacity to conduct ordinary college business. With a mixture of irritation and amusement Dame Janet recalled in her memoirs how, whenever a paper was needed for Governing Body, the Vice-Principal was instructed to help her in its composition.

Scientist heads of house were a rarity in Oxford at this period—at one stage Janet Vaughan was the only one—and her mere presence did much to raise Somerville's scientific profile. The prospect of having Dorothy Hodgkin as a colleague had doubtless been one of the factors which attracted Janet Vaughan back to Somerville in the first place; the college now shared in the excitement of discoveries about the structure of insulin which were to lead in 1964 to her gaining the Nobel Prize for Chemistry and in 1965 to the Order of Merit. In 1955 Dorothy Hodgkin exchanged a tutorial for a professorial fellowship on her appointment as University Reader in X-Ray Crystallography. The election to a professorial fellowship in 1952 of the Margaret Ogilvie's Reader in Ophthalmology, Dr Antoinette Pirie, completed a distinguished scientific triumvirate whose shared social concern did much to confirm Somerville's reputation for political radicalism.

Within the college Janet Vaughan worked hard to redress the ingrained imbalance, at both junior and senior level, between the

---

[36] JV, 'Jogging Along'

sciences and the arts. The appointment of Jean Banister as tutor in physiology was an important sign of the college's tutorial commitment to the sciences. The offer of dining rights was used as a means of bringing into college a number of women scientists who lacked any other form of college attachment. Distinguished visiting scientists whom the university had asked the Principal to entertain on its behalf were brought in to dinner at high table. Somerville became known as a college where the sciences were cherished. Giving evidence to the Franks Commission in 1964, Janet Vaughan reported with satisfaction that—counter to the general trend in the university—the number of candidates applying to read physics at Somerville was on the increase. 'It is an exciting world, is it not, Physics?' she replied to Sir Lindor Brown's question why this should be.[37] In the past, the college had rarely admitted more than two physicists a year; in 1965 there were seven. Somerville's first lecturer in physics, Rosemary Coldwell-Horsfall, was appointed in 1957; two years later she went to America, and was succeeded by Frank Neville Robinson of Wadham College, the first male member of Somerville SCR. A further attempt to build up the science fellowship was foiled in 1962 when, after only three years in post, the chemist Marjorie Harding (Aitken, 1953) followed her husband to Edinburgh.

But Janet Vaughan's interests were not narrowly confined to the sciences. If medicine was in her genes, so was literature: John Addington Symonds was her grandfather, Virginia Woolf her cousin. When her husband was out of Oxford, she often called upon Joyce Cary to help host formal dinner parties in Radcliffe House: 'I could never read his novels', she confessed, 'but his talk and his friendship are one of the best memories of Oxford days.'[38] It gave her immense pleasure to know that Wittgenstein was a frequent visitor to tea in the senior common room, the guest of Elizabeth Anscombe. She valued excellence of any kind, and delighted in the company of writers, scholars, politicians, and public figures of all kinds and any nationality. A steady stream of distinguished visitors experienced the haphazard hospitality of Radcliffe House, rubbing shoulders with an equally steady stream of undergraduates in search of the Principal's somewhat bracing sympathy.

Some of these visitors came as guests of the college to deliver the Bryce Lecture: Norman Baynes to speak on 'The Hellenistic civilization and East Rome', R. W. Chapman on 'Lexicography', Sir Leonard

---

[37] Evidence to Franks Commission, 19 Nov. 1964.   [38] JV, 'Jogging Along'

Woolley on 'Middle East archaeology', Mary Cartwright on 'The mathematical mind'. In 1947 the most remarkable lecture of all happened almost by accident. The intended speaker that year, the French politician Edouard Herriot, was obliged by pressure of political events to cancel his visit at short notice. As it chanced, Enid Starkie was currently in correspondence with André Gide about the possibility of his delivering a lecture in Oxford at some future date; moving quickly, she persuaded him to deliver the Bryce Lecture on 5 June, and persuaded the university to confer on him an honorary degree later that week. The hastily thought-out scheme almost foundered when Gide showed his intended lecture to Roger Martin du Gard, and was told that it was 'médiocre et insuffisant'; his attempt to withdraw was parried by a long telegram from Enid telling him that everything was ready and the official speeches written. In the event, the lecture, entitled 'Lendemains de guerre', was delivered to a packed hall, with the Reading Room and the staircase and the quadrangle outside crowded with people hoping to catch a glimpse of the great man. He was accommodated overnight in Radcliffe House, and won the heart of Janet Vaughan's maid by carrying down his own breakfast tray.[39]

Another distinguishing feature of Janet Vaughan's principalship was the growth of the Middle Common Room as a force in the college. The number of graduate students coming to Somerville, many of them from abroad, rose steadily through the 1950s and 1960s. 'We like graduates' Dr Vaughan told the Franks Commissioners in 1964, in response to a question as to whether Somerville had any conscious policy about the proportion of graduate to undergraduate students in the college: 'We have always liked them. We find them interesting people. We think them very important. The women are usually going back to big jobs in their own country. We have never made any effort to limit them as long as their academic credentials have been satisfactory.'[40] The Principal, an unregenerate élitist, welcomed the presence of this diverse body of what she (with some justification) saw as future leaders in distant lands. But the warmth of her own hospitality could not disguise the inadequacy of college provision for its graduate students. In the early 1950s a room on the ground floor of the East building was made over to them as a common room, but as it contained nothing but chairs it was rapidly abandoned. The first attempt to pro-

---

[39] J. Richardson, *Enid Starkie* (London, 1973), 170 ff.
[40] Evidence given to the Franks Commission, 19 Nov. 1964.

vide the graduates with any kind of social organization came from one of their own number, Hannah Stanton, who read theology at Somerville as a mature student from 1954 to 1956, and subsequently became a household name when she was imprisoned and deported from South Africa after the Sharpeville shootings of March 1960.[41] A visit by Janet Vaughan to a sick graduate student from Nepal brought home to her the inadequacy of the lodgings in which many students were obliged to live; and the provision of decent accommodation for graduates was thereafter placed high on the college's list of priorities. The Margery Fry and Elizabeth Nuffield House was the first house for graduates to be planned—if not quite the first to come into use—in Oxford.[42] Fourteen nations were represented among the original twenty-four occupants who in 1965 drafted the first MCR constitution.

One of Janet Vaughan's most firmly held beliefs was that any institution should always have plans for future development sufficiently worked out to enable it to move instantly if funds suddenly became available: 'Always have your plans on the drawing board. . . . Someone may ring up any moment and offer you money to put them into practice.'[43] It was a principle which was triumphantly justified on more than one occasion during her time at Somerville.

In May 1947, in anticipation of grants being made available from the UGC, the University Registrar asked colleges to supply estimates of building and maintenance work over the next five years. At the head of Somerville's list of priorities was the provision of at least seven additional undergraduate rooms; library extension was to have precedence over any building project not designed to increase undergraduate accommodation. The Principal, determined that Somerville should be able to stake a claim to a UGC grant when opportunity arose, called a meeting to consider possible building sites and architects. In consequence, informal approaches were made to Balliol about the possibility of acquiring the Radcliffe House site and adjacent Balliol properties, and to University College about the corner site from 24 Little Clarendon Street to Bedford House. Several architects were interviewed, and in March 1948 Mr Geddes Hyslop was asked to

---

[41] Notes on overseas students by Janet Vaughan.
[42] The Balliol/St Anne's building in Holywell opened shortly before the Somerville building.
[43] Interview with Polly Toynbee in L. Caldecott (ed.), *Women of our Century* (London, 1984), 124.

submit detailed plans for a new residential block on the north side of the gravel quad, linking Hostel and House, and rough plans for a library extension and a staff hall. In Michaelmas Term the Licensing Committee of Council and Colleges gave provisional approval for the residential extension, stipulating that work should not begin until 1950.

The new building, financed with the help of a loan from the university and the proceeds of the sale of the college sports ground at Cutteslowe, provided eight undergraduate rooms, some of them furnished with gifts in kind from donors to the Building and Furniture Fund. In 1952, emboldened by an unexpected bequest of £7,000 from a former student, Mary Cassels Ross, 'to be used for the benefit of the library', and by the promise of a loan of £5,000 from the university, the Council appealed to old members for contributions towards the building of a westward extension to the library which would provide additional accommodation for undergraduates as well as stack-room for books. It was late in 1956 before the building was completed; in the meantime one of college's small properties ('Pooh Corner') in Walton Street next to Bedford House was taken over to provide accommodation for four undergraduates.

While the college scrimped and saved to finance these new buildings, it was committed to heavy expenditure in maintaining its existing premises. In 1952–3 extensive repairs had to be carried out to the stonework of House. Growth of student numbers necessitated a major reorganization of the kitchen quarters and domestic staff hall, and the replacement of much out-of-date equipment. The new kitchens, financed by a grant from the UGC, came into use in October 1959. In recording its gratitude to the UGC, the Council expressed its delight at being able at last to offer meals in Hall to all its graduate students.[44]

With the removal in 1956 of university restrictions on undergraduate numbers, the women's societies were free, in principle, to determine their own size. In practice, although the fixed quota had been perceived as an indignity, Somerville had little desire to expand beyond it: in welcoming its abolition in 1956, the Council agreed that there should be no change in the policy of admitting a maximum of 200 undergraduates. The rapid expansion of the women's colleges in the years ahead was not of their own seeking, but a somewhat apprehensive response to governmental pressure to increase the number of

---

[44] Council Report for 1959.

women at Oxford. In Somerville the mid-1960s saw a spate of building activity, the Graduate House and Vaughan and Wolfson buildings transforming in the space of four years the appearance of the college, which had not changed much for the previous thirty.

A still more drastic change, however, had first to be averted. Among the many road plans proposed in the course of the 1950s to alleviate Oxford's notorious traffic problems, one of those most seriously considered involved the widening of Little Clarendon Street to carry the flow of north-bound traffic, and the construction of roundabouts at the junctions with Walton Street and St Giles. The implications for Somerville, and for its own building plans, were alarming. At the Public Inquiry held in February 1956, the college was ably represented by its young law lecturer, Hazel Fox (whose husband, Michael, performed a similar function for Magdalen); in response to her questioning the Principal made the memorable assertion that even in existing traffic conditions it often took her as long as five minutes to get her car out of the college traffic entrance on to the Woodstock Road. (No one in Somerville had ever seen Janet Vaughan—an impatient driver—wait much longer than five seconds.) More powerful interests than Somerville were also opposed to the plan which, after a further alarm in 1960, was eventually dropped; in 1968, after considering a variety of alternative routes, the City opted instead for a scheme of traffic management and restricted parking.

Meanwhile, Somerville steadily pursued its own development plans. In 1957 the opportunity at last arose of purchasing Radcliffe House and, with it, the houses at 15–17 Woodstock Road. In 1958, with the threat to Little Clarendon Street in abeyance, the college announced its intention to go ahead with a development on its southern boundary. At Dorothy Hodgkin's suggestion, Philip Dowson of Ove Arup & Partners was approached as a possible architect, and commissioned to draw up plans for a graduate house to accommodate twenty-four students, and an undergraduate block with accommodation for forty-eight students and two tutors; the two buildings were to be linked with each other and with the existing college grounds by gardens and courtyards. In September 1959 an appeal was launched for the graduate house, the cost of which was estimated at £80,000 out of a total for the whole development of £200,000. Though old Somervillians, as always, contributed generously to the appeal, by the summer of 1961 the college was still far short of its target, and Governing Body decided that building should not proceed until a further £20,000 had been raised. Janet Vaughan moved swiftly into action with an approach to Lord Nuffield, and by the end of the vacation was able triumphantly to report a gift of £45,000 from the Nuffield Foundation in memory of his wife, a generous supporter of women's education. The building had already been earmarked as a memorial to Margery Fry, who died in 1958; it was now agreed that Elizabeth Nuffield's name should be associated with hers, and a circular plaque, where neither name would have precedence, was commissioned for the entrance.

Building work on the graduate house and arcade of shops in Little Clarendon Street began early in 1962. It was decided to lay the foundations of the undergraduate block at the same time, although the building itself could not be proceeded with until a further capital sum of around £131,000 had been collected. At this point the UGC, which had recently made substantial grants to St Hugh's and LMH, indicated that it might be prepared to consider applications from St Hilda's and Somerville, which still had large numbers of undergraduates accommodated in lodgings. In a curious accession of high-mindedness, Governing Body resolved that, pressing as was the need for further accommodation, 'it would be inappropriate at this time to ask for further aid for the women's colleges, in view of the help they had recently received, and in view of the needs of other poor men's colleges.'[45] It was, however, noted that, if another undergraduate block was built, it might be possible to ask the UGC to furnish it.

The recommendations of the Robbins Committee for university expansion, published at this time and accepted in principle by the university and the college, led to a rapid change of policy. In an attempt to meet the recommendation for increased numbers of undergraduates, Philip Dowson was instructed to modify plans for the new building so as to accommodate sixty undergraduates instead of the forty-eight originally intended, and to keep costs down to the UGC specification of £1,000 per study bedroom. Somerville's readiness, should funds prove forthcoming, to proceed immediately with a building programme which would enable it to increase its total numbers to 230, stood it in good stead with the UGC. A grant was quickly obtained, and work on the undergraduate block was well in hand when on 15 October 1964 the Margery Fry and Elizabeth Nuffield House was opened by the President of the United Nations, Mrs Pandit

---

[45] Minutes of Council, 14 Mar. 1962.

(Plate 46), in the presence of the Chancellor and Lady Dorothy Macmillan. The East quadrangle had recently been renamed in memory of Helen Darbishire, who died in 1961; there was no question but that the new undergraduate building should be 'Vaughan'.

Other Principals might have rested on their laurels. At the beginning of the 1964 long vacation Janet Vaughan summoned a special meeting of Governing Body to consider future building plans in the light of an offer of £100,000 just received from the Wolfson Foundation for a hall of residence. Philip Dowson was again the college's choice of architect, and produced plans for a striking building along the Walton Street wall, joining West and Penrose, and incorporating a lecture theatre to replace Bedford House.

The Vaughan building was completed in the spring of 1966, and undergraduates out in lodgings were able to move into it at the beginning of Trinity Term. The rooms, reported the JCR President in that year's Newsletter 'are light, comfortable, and gaily coloured, and if, even now, not all undergraduates have a room in College, this is because admissions have been increased since more places for women are needed at Oxford.' As always, the acquisition of a new building was a signal for changes in the use of some of the old ones. The sanatorium at the back of Penrose was converted into three flats for research fellows, and a new sick-bay, more centrally placed, and therefore easier to look after, was constructed out of three rooms in Darbishire.

The Wolfson building was opened on 21 November 1967, the first major event of Barbara Craig's principalship (Plate 47). In October she had taken over from Dame Janet Vaughan a college of 270 undergraduates and nearly 100 graduates. Somerville had doubled its size in ten years.

13

Barbara Craig and the Beginning of the Co-residence Debate, 1967–1980

A SOMERVILLE classicist, with wartime experience as Assistant to the Professor of Greek at Aberdeen University and Principal in the Ministries of Home Security and Production, Barbara Craig had spent most of the past twenty years abroad, assisting her husband James in his work for the British Council in Brazil, Iraq, Spain, and Pakistan. He was now to prove equally devoted as a principalian consort. During their time in Baghdad Mrs Craig had been able to pursue her own archaeological interests in the relations between Greece and the Orient, work for which Somerville elected her to the Woolley fellowship in 1954. She brought to the post of Principal a wide knowledge of the world and its young people, a reputation for hard work and endurance in adverse conditions, exacting standards of scholarship, and sympathy for most manifestations of human frailty except the inability to spell. A welcoming article in *Oxford* noted the 'enigmatic fire in her eye', speculating on whether it should be attributed to 'single-minded purpose' or to 'strong emotion sternly controlled.'[1] It was probably more often attributable to suppressed laughter than Somerville realized at the time.

Barbara Craig succeeded to the principalship on the crest of a wave. All five Oxford women's colleges at this date had Somervillian heads, with Lucy Sutherland at LMH, Kathleen Kenyon at St Hugh's, Mary Bennett at St Hilda's, and Nancy Trenaman at St Anne's. An ambitious building programme had just been completed. Undergraduate numbers were steadily increasing, graduate numbers rapidly so. The college's teaching strength was being consolidated and extended. Its position at, or near, the head of the Norrington Table was established. In the summer of 1967 thirteen Somerville undergraduates—including six out of the nine candidates taking PPE—were placed in the first class in Schools. The following year Somerville achieved overall the

---

[1] *Oxford*, 21/2 (May 1967), 13 ff.

highest percentage of firsts of any college in the university: two in classical honour mods., and seventeen in the final honour Schools. It was at about this time that a number of the men's colleges began to think about the advantages of opening their doors to women.

The first serious discussion of 'co-residence', by New College in 1964, had been cautiously welcomed by the Somerville Governing Body. The much more widespread movement of the early 1970s caused inevitable anxiety in the women's colleges, which feared, with some justification, that many of their best candidates would be creamed off by competing mixed colleges. Somerville, while rejoicing that its own graduates were leading the way into the former male bastions—in 1973 Carol Clark was appointed French tutor at Balliol, and became the first woman fellow of a former men's college—saw its own academic prestige begin to decline. Women undergraduates were enthusiastic for change: a JCR survey in 1969 indicated that 90 per cent of Somervillians favoured all or some of the Oxford colleges going mixed, and that a majority of them wished Somerville to admit men. The Governing Body—more evenly divided in its views—decided to wait and see what happened.

As colleges throughout the university began to consider whether to go mixed, an alternative possibility—of entering into some sort of alliance with an existing college of the opposite sex—occurred to several of them. In November 1969 tentative negotiations between Somerville and its nearest neighbour, St John's, were abandoned when it became known that St John's was itself considering admitting women.[2] A college working-party set up in 1971 to explore the possibility of Somerville admitting men concluded that there would be no advantage in doing so at present, but suggested that—if a suitable partner could be found—an alliance with one of the men's colleges might still be worth pursuing. Discreet enquiries established that Corpus Christi College might perhaps be interested in an association of some kind, and during the long vacation the Principal was authorized by an informal meeting of fellows to proceed further, without committing Somerville in any way. In Michaelmas Term a joint committee was set up to explore the proposal in greater detail; the JCR presidents of both colleges were consulted and expressed enthusiasm for the possibility of an interchange of lunching and dining rights. In Hilary Term 1972 a joint statement announcing the

---

[2] GB, 12 Nov. 1969.

establishment of a Somerville–Corpus Alliance was approved for circulation, and it was agreed to review arrangements at the end of the next academic year, when the alliance might take 'a more defined and positive shape'.[3] As a first step, Somerville fellows examining in the Schools that summer were offered lunching rights at Corpus.

The alliance bore its first institutional fruit in the appointment of Dr Valentine Cunningham to a lecturership in English at Somerville in conjunction with his tutorial fellowship at Corpus; in 1974 Jennifer Loach was appointed to a similar post in modern history, with the fellowship attached to Somerville. Reciprocal lunching and dining arrangements were negotiated, and the possibility of some limited exchange of library facilities explored. The possibility of offering mixed accommodation in Somerville's graduate house was raised, 'rather to face it than seriously to pursue it', there being general agreement that a building in which there was joint accommodation from the start would be more satisfactory. Reviewing the alliance at the end of the year, Governing Body concluded that it had been 'both useful and agreeable', and agreed to suggest deferring a further review until Hilary Term 1977, when Council was to initiate a general review of arrangements for the admission of women to the mixed colleges.[4]

It was understood from the outset that the alliance should preclude neither college from going mixed if it wished to do so. In 1974 an informal meeting of Somerville fellows to consider the possibility of the college opening its fellowships to men concluded that there should be no move for the time being, but that the question should be re-opened in a year's time. The Sex Discrimination Act, due to come into force on 29 December 1975, threatened new—but, as yet, uncertain—complications. Three letters sent by the college to government departments asking for clarification of the position having met with only formal acknowledgements, it was agreed on 26 November to seek legal advice. The gist of this was that, while colleges whose statutes were protected by the Universities of Oxford and Cambridge Act 1923 could continue to restrict their fellowships to members of one sex, the university itself—a co-employer in the case of most academic appointments—could claim no such protection.[5] Somerville, about to advertise for a successor to Mary Proudfoot as fellow and tutor in politics, adopted the lawyers' suggestion that no mention of gender should be made in the advertisement itself, leaving it to the

---

[3] GB, 22 Apr. 1972.   [4] GB, 30 May 1973.   [5] GB, 21 Jan. 1976.

further particulars to make clear that the college statutes precluded anyone but a woman being appointed.

The position university-wide was by now extremely complicated. In 1974 Brasenose, Jesus, Wadham, Hertford, and St Catherine's became the first colleges to admit women undergraduates. In Trinity Term 1976 the 'St Hilda's Report' on co-residence cast doubt on the desirability for the time being of more men's colleges opening their doors to women; a counter-report commissioned by the Oxford University Students' Union, which advocated the most rapid transfer possible to a mixed society, was enthusiastically endorsed by the Somerville JCR. In Michaelmas term the Conference of Colleges reported that

> Three men's colleges intended to admit women at all levels as soon as possible, five were likely to admit women at all levels within a few years, three may wish to open fellowships to women, two planned no change, two expressed no view, and three had not replied; one women's college was likely to admit men at all levels, one may wish to open fellowships to men, one planned no change at present, and two expressed no view.[6]

The following term Somerville voted to remain single-sex at all levels, and to seek advice on the legal implications of its decision. Corpus had meanwhile decided to admit women undergraduates from 1979; asked if it wished to be released from its obligations to Somerville, it gallantly protested continuing devotion. In the event, the two existing joint appointments were soon afterwards unscrambled, and the alliance came to a natural end.

In the university at large there was majority support for a policy of gradual, phased transition from 1979. The Committee on Co-residence reported in Trinity Term 1977, recommending that until 1983, when all restraints would be removed, colleges should enter into a voluntary scheme for the orderly increase in the number of mixed colleges, and urging the need to take special measures to protect the interests of the women's colleges.[7] By Michaelmas Term all the men's colleges except Christ Church, Oriel, and Merton had signalled their intention eventually to admit women, and—in a fateful development—two of them had declared their intention of ignoring any majority decision in favour of gradualism.[8] Solidarity thus breached,

[6] GB, 24 Nov. 1976.   [7] GB, 25 May 1977.   [8] GB, 15 June and 9 Nov. 1977.

any attempt at an orderly progression was abandoned, as the men's colleges rushed pell-mell to open their doors to women. Congregation declined to intervene to stop the rush. The consequences for the women's colleges were—predictably—catastrophic.

They themselves opted for a variety of solutions. St Hilda's, like Somerville, determined to remain single-sex for the time being. Lady Margaret Hall and St Anne's decided to go mixed at all levels, though delaying the admission of male undergraduates for a year or two while they built up a substantially mixed fellowship.[9] St Hugh's chose to open its fellowship to men in 1977 while maintaining a single-sex undergraduate and graduate entry. All plummeted from near the top to near the bottom of the Norrington Table. It was clear that—whether mixed, single-sex, or hybrid—they were in for a difficult time.

Co-residence, though a constant preoccupation, was far from the only issue confronting the university and colleges at this period. Oxford did not escape the waves of violent student unrest which in the late 1960s and early 1970s threatened academic institutions throughout Europe and North America. Like other universities, it was increasingly vulnerable to intervention from central government, to the see-saw of academic expansion and contraction engendered by a fluctuating government policy which made forward planning virtually impossible, and to the problems of making financial ends meet at a time of economic crisis. To these widely felt difficulties Somerville added some of its own: the consequences of over-rapid expansion in the 1960s, and the realization, reinforced by a series of costly repair bills, that the mid-1960s had not been the best of times for putting up new buildings.

The Governing Body, which was responsible for steering Somerville through these shoals, was itself in process of rapid change. The retirement of Mildred Hartley two years after her marriage in 1963 to William Taylor, the death in 1967 of Isobel Henderson, and the departure in 1969 of Somerville's two philosophers—Philippa Foot to America and Elizabeth Anscombe to a chair in Cambridge—effected a complete transformation in the school of *literae humaniores*, and deprived the college prematurely of four senior fellows. The retirement in the mid-1970s of Margaret Hall and Mary Proudfoot had similar—though not in this case unforeseen—consequences for PPE.

---

[9] St Anne's opened its fellowship to men in 1976 and its entrance examination two years later. LMH admitted its first male fellows in its centenary year, 1979.

In the course of the decade Somerville suffered two more cruel losses. The sudden death at Christmas 1971 of Anne Cobbe, fellow and tutor in maths since 1955, robbed the college at a crucial moment of one of its wisest counsellors. A protracted illness prepared the college for the death in 1978 of Rosemary Woolf. During her sixteen years as English tutor at Somerville her writings on medieval literature and drama had won her an international reputation; in college she was renowned for her encyclopaedic knowledge of modern detective fiction. Many solemn tributes followed her death; the lines composed by her junior colleague, Katherine Duncan-Jones, in happier times perhaps provide a better clue to her college *persona*:

> Should anyone ask what duty or task
> Miss Woolf's sabbatical chore is,
> She spends her days reading Mystery Plays
> And her nights reading mystery stories.

A sudden influx of young tutors filled the new posts created to cater for expanding student numbers and the vacancies left by retirement, resignation, and death. In the late 1960s the size of the Governing Body increased, and its average age dropped, dramatically. Though the new appointees came preponderantly from within Oxford—many of them, indeed, from Somerville itself[10]—the college was now beginning to recruit more widely. Miriam Griffin, who succeeded Isobel Henderson in 1967, was Somerville's first American fellow. In the years which followed the Governing Body was to become increasingly cosmopolitan, with Julie Jack, Nancy Waugh, and (briefly) Jenny Harrison from the United States, Anna Morpurgo Davies from Italy, Anne de Moor from Belgium, Karin Erdmann and Almut Suerbaum from Germany, Aviva Tolkovsky from Israel, and Niamh Hardiman and Gráinne de Búrca from the Republic of Ireland.

The new generation of fellows injected into the college a broader range of experience and a new set of expectations. Many of them had family commitments; in 1974, with a bumper crop of SCR babies in prospect, Somerville became one of the first Oxford colleges to establish a crèche. But even the unattached tended increasingly to live out

[10] Lesley Brown (Wallace, 1963), fellow and tutor in philosophy 1970; Jane Bridge (1963) fellow and tutor in mathematics 1971; Margaret Adams (1958) fellow and tutor in inorganic chemistry 1972; Judith Heyer (Cripps, 1956) fellow and tutor in economics 1975; Frances Stewart (Kaldor, 1958) additional fellow 1975; Marian Dawkins (Stamp, 1963), fellow and tutor in biology 1980.

of college. In 1979 the by-law which required fellows to be resident in Oxford was altered to the effect that they must be able to reach college from home within half an hour. To fill the gap at the common table left by the exodus of the young and unmarried, a new core of regular week-day diners emerged from among those whose partners worked and lived at a distance and appeared in Oxford only at weekends. As fellows became increasingly protective of their private lives, the difficulty of finding volunteers to undertake the office of dean, with its liability to be called on in an emergency at any hour of day or night, was compounded. The burden of pastoral care fell increasingly on the Bursar, who was resident in college, and on the Principal, whose knowledge of students' problems was equalled only by her discretion in dealing with them.

Fellows with experience of other organizations were also more apt to question traditional Oxonian ways of proceeding. In her evidence to the Franks Commission in 1964, Janet Vaughan had made a plea for greater secretarial resources to be made available to relieve the 'paper drudgery' which was the lot of most college tutors: 'I think this is one of the faults of the academic world. We do not adapt ourselves readily to using modern devices.'[11] Now, in a gesture towards relieving the growing administrative burden which fell upon fellows, in Hilary Term 1968 Somerville acquired its first dictating machine together with two tapes—one for the use of those who wished to practise, and the other for those (viz. Miss Banister) already expert in the new technology. In 1978, after an animated Governing Body meeting (for there was no fellow who did not have strong views on the subject), a Xerox machine was installed in the fellows' secretary's office. In her retirement speech to the SCR in 1993 Barbara Harvey attributed to this period the college's decisive transition from a predominantly oral to a predominantly written culture.

Perhaps the most significant feature of the new fellowship appointments of these years was the number of them which went to scientists. Janet Vaughan's principalship had established Somerville's scientific reputation; to provide the necessary tutorial underpinning to sustain this was a major preoccupation of her successors. The first Governing Body meeting of the new regime agreed to use a farewell gift of £1,000 from Dame Janet to help endow an additional fellowship in science. A donation from Dorothy Hodgkin enabled the

---

[11] Evidence to Franks Commission, 19 Nov. 1964.

college to proceed to an immediate appointment, and in Hilary Term 1968 Louise Johnson, a departmental demonstrator in molecular biophysics, was elected as Somerville's first Janet Vaughan lecturer. Five years later, on her appointment as a university lecturer, the college elected her to an additional fellowship.

In Trinity Term 1969 the new Long-Term Planning Committee was asked to consider the question of fellowships in the sciences, bearing in mind not only the importance of appointees having continuing research interests, but also the desirability of their being able to secure outside support and funding. These deliberations were given added urgency when Eva Richards announced her wish to reduce substantially her teaching hours in chemistry on her husband's election in 1970 to the wardenship of Merton. The college advertised for a tutor in chemistry, was unable to decide between two of the candidates, and proceeded to appoint them both: Josephine Peach was elected fellow and tutor in organic chemistry from October 1970, and Margaret Adams—who was committed for the next two years to a research project in the USA—was offered a tutorship in inorganic chemistry from October 1972. The future of Somerville's chemistry school was assured, albeit at considerable financial cost. Part of this was met by a series of gifts from the EPA Cephalosphorin Fund; in acknowledging the third of these in 1977, the college announced that Margaret Adams would be the first holder of the newly established Dorothy Hodgkin/E. P. Abraham tutorial fellowship. In 1971 association with a university lecturership in human experimental psychology, for which a woman was the successful candidate, paved the way for the expansion of Somerville's combined school of psychology, philosophy, and physiology (PPP); Nancy Waugh, an expert on memory loss, joined the fellowship from America in June 1972. The prospect of a permanent solution to the problem of physics teaching came in 1974 when, after a series of temporary appointments of lecturers, and a protracted saga involving the possible return to Oxford from California of the Janet Watson visiting fellow, Nina Byers, the college eventually secured a promise of a CUF lecturership. In October 1975 Carole Jordan—later to become the first woman President of the Royal Astronomical Society—was elected Somerville's first tutorial fellow in physics. When in Hilary Term 1976 the Governing Body took stock of its own composition, it noted that since 1951 the number of fellows had risen even faster than had the number of undergraduates, and that the current proportion of science to arts fellows roughly paralleled the ratio among undergraduates.[12] Three years later a gift from the Mary Snow Charitable Trust for the endowment of a fellowship in the biological sciences enabled the college to set about filling the teaching gap left by the resignation of Wilma Crowther, a fellow of LMH and lecturer in zoology at Somerville since 1959. Despite some misgivings at the long-term implications of making a third permanent appointment in the sciences without the security of a university association, Governing Body decided to proceed to an election, and gained Marian Dawkins as its first tutorial fellow in the biological sciences.

In the arts subjects, the main area of growth at this period was in law. Somerville's small law school, looked after initially by a succession of temporary part-time lecturers, had for some years been organized—to its great advantage—by the law tutors at Lincoln. This happy arrangement began to break down after the departure of Mr Simpson for a chair at the University of Kent at Canterbury, and in Michaelmas Term 1974 Somerville set about considering alternative arrangements. Without a CUF lecturership there was no hope of creating a permanent tutorial fellowship; but, at this juncture, the college had the great good fortune to secure the services of Hazel Fox, who—as Hazel Stuart—had taught for Somerville in the 1950s at the beginning of a distinguished legal career. Her return in January 1977 as a college lecturer and additional fellow breathed new life into Somerville's law school. The number of undergraduates admitted to read law was increased, and—with the unscrambling by St Anne's in 1977 of the co-operative arrangements for the Geldart Law Library— a college law library was established. By the time that Lady Fox returned to London, to take up the directorship of the British Institute for International and Comparative Law, Somerville had secured its long-desired CUF lecturership and Anne de Moor was established as the college's first tutorial fellow in jurisprudence.

The five women's colleges had been exempted, together with Hertford and St Catherine's, from a request by the vice-chancellor in November 1966 for an overall standstill on undergraduate numbers. Somerville, which had grown rapidly in the previous decade, had no wish to expand further. Governing Body agreed in Michaelmas Term 1967 that the estimated figure for the following year—270—was the maximum desirable, and proposed as alternatives to the further expansion of the existing women's colleges the establishment of a

---

[12] GB, 10 Mar. 1976.

new mixed foundation at Oxford or the expansion of some of the smaller universities.[13] On learning that the college was likely to come under pressure to increase its numbers to 300 it determined to put up as much resistance as possible, and, if obliged to expand, to aim to settle for a few more candidates in those schools it was most eager to strengthen: the biological sciences and psychology. By 1969 undergraduate numbers had crept up to 280, and by 1970 to 300. Governing Body repeatedly asserted its concern that any further increase would cause serious pressure on college accommodation and facilities, noting in 1970 that the number of women undergraduates in Oxford as a whole was already greater than the figure of 1,500 recommended by the University's Size and Shape Committee as the minimum aim for 1977. In Michaelmas Term 1971, with a sense that things were getting out of hand, it accepted a recommendation of Education Committee that the college should aim at gradually reducing its total numbers.

But financial pressures were now irresistibly working in the opposite direction. The university, which in 1971 asked colleges not to go beyond their forecasted numbers, was by 1973 urging them not to fall short. Somerville's decision to reduce its intake was rapidly reversed. Noting in November 1975 that Somerville had the lowest fee income of all the women's colleges but the highest spending on the education, research, and internal accounts, Governing Body agreed that undergraduate numbers for 1976 might be increased to a maximum of 320.[14] In 1980 it admitted the financial necessity of maintaining numbers at as high a level as possible.

These decisions were taken against a background of declining applications. In 1970 changes in the Cambridge admissions procedure meant that women candidates no longer had the option of taking the entrance examinations for both universities. The Governing Body, convinced that the importance of retaining the existing joint examining arrangements with the men's colleges in Oxford far outweighed the maintenance of the Oxford–Cambridge option for women candidates, declared itself unwilling to accept as binding in discussions with Cambridge a majority view of the Oxford women's colleges.[15] As more and more colleges in Oxford and Cambridge opened their doors to women, the number of applications to the women's colleges began to fall dramatically. Accustomed for most of their history to having far more applicants than places, they found themselves in the novel

---

[13] GB, 25 Oct. 1967 and 19 June 1968.   [14] GB, 12 Nov. 1975.
[15] GB, 18 Feb. 1970.

position of having to work hard to attract candidates. Tutors went out to visit schools, and parties of sixth-formers were invited to visit college. Weekend and evening conferences for schoolteachers were organized. Contacts with schools were fostered by the institution of 'schoolmistress studentships' for teachers seconded to Oxford for a term to pursue some form of study or research. Undergraduates, particularly keen to support any project which might increase the number of applicants from state schools, were themselves responsible for a number of initiatives. In Trinity Term 1974 the JCRs of all the women's colleges except LMH co-operated in organizing an open day attended by 120 sixth-formers from some sixty schools; similar occasions were subsequently organized by individual colleges. The number of applicants increased with the opening to women in 1976 of the system of 'conditional offers', by which the offer of an undergraduate place was made conditional upon the attainment of specified A-level grades. But this also increased substantially the burden of administration, traditionally shouldered in Somerville by the Principal and her secretary. In 1979 the office of Tutor for Admissions was instituted, with Miss Dunbar as its first holder.

Initially, the Tutor for Admissions was responsible for graduate as well as undergraduate admissions. In 1969, at a time of rapid expansion, Governing Body had agreed that 120 graduate students was the maximum that the college could comfortably provide for (though Barbara Craig, who had a softness for the MCR, confessed that she was sometimes bad at counting when a particularly interesting candidate applied).[16] Over the next few years sharp increases in graduate fees, and growing uncertainty as to their financial support, effected a steady reduction in the number of applications throughout the university. The position was especially serious in the case of overseas students, who traditionally made up a high proportion of the graduate body. University figures published in Michaelmas Term 1980 showed that applications for undergraduate courses had dropped by 5 per cent (more in the arts than in the sciences), and graduate applications by 8 per cent, the decline being greater for women than for men.[17] The sight, earlier that year, of Barbara Craig walking at the front of a protest demonstration through the streets of Oxford had brought home to many Somervillians the gravity of the situation. The following spring her successor took part, together with the heads of Queen's,

---

[16] 'Reflections in Retirement', *ASM Report*, 1980.   [17] GB, 26 Nov. 1980.

Balliol, and Wolfson, in a delegation to the Secretary of State for Education, to voice the university's concern at government policy in this regard.

In college, an important bridge between the graduate body and the SCR was provided by the junior research fellows—a lively, diverse, and expanding body in these years. Lack of endowment for research was one of the respects in which the women's colleges most keenly felt their poverty. Somerville, justifiably proud of the college loyalty which had sustained the Mary Somerville fellowship—however pre-cariously—for so long, was eager to extend its range of support to young scholars. To this end, the Mary Ewart Fund, previously used for scholarships, was redeployed after 1961 to finance a second junior research fellowship. In 1964 Somerville gained its first association with the University-administered Joanna Randall-MacIver junior research fellowship, tenure of which circulated among the women's colleges, bringing them a welcome succession of art historians, musicologists, and students of literature. When in 1969 Rhodes visiting fellowships were opened to women, the Rhodes Trustees facilitated the election of married women by providing Somerville with a house outside col-lege where they might be accommodated with their families. In the college's centenary year Claudine Dauphin was elected to the Lady Carlisle fellowship, which had been in abeyance for some years in order to build up capital; and the Ernest Cook Trust funded a junior research fellowship in environmental studies, to which Trudy Watt was appointed. In 1980 the one-off allocation to Somerville of the Gordon Milburn junior research fellowship (to promote the theolo-gical or philosophical study of mysticism and religious experience) enabled the college to enjoy the presence in the SCR of Janet Martin, and to learn to appreciate the paintings of her artist fiancé, Oliver Soskice. The possession of a Soskice still-life is a distinguishing charac-teristic of Somerville fellows of a certain generation.

Although over the years a number of scientists were elected to the Mary Somerville and Mary Ewart fellowships, the disproportion between arts and science applicants was a cause for concern. It was not merely a reflection of the general bias of women towards the arts, but an indication of the inappropriateness for many experimental sci-entists of the traditional terms of research fellowships of this kind. The desirability had long been felt of establishing some form of col-lege association better geared to the needs of young scientists whose primary attachment was to their laboratory and whose research was funded by outside bodies. In 1978 a small beginning was made with the use of a bequest from Dame Catherine Fulford to establish a non-stipendiary post-doctoral research fellowship in the sciences. A Somervillian chemist, Elizabeth Austin, was the first of a series of Fulford fellows whose presence in the SCR helped bring home to their colleagues in the arts the vast range of research being undertaken in the university's science departments.

Barbara Craig's principalship spanned two periods of student unrest. In the event, the troubles which rocked European and North American universities in 1968 impinged relatively lightly on Oxford. The local discontent had three main strands: the demand for student representation on the decision-making bodies of the colleges and university, dislike of the system of proctorial discipline, and the desire to establish a central Union which would provide a non-collegiate focus for student organization. The university responded by referring all three matters to a Committee on Relations with Junior Members, set up in Trinity Term 1968 under the chairmanship of Herbert Hart. One of the members of the committee was Barbara Harvey, Somerville's nominee as university assessor that year.

The Hart Committee met and took evidence against a background of increasing unrest, culminating on Whit Monday in an occupation of the Clarendon Building. College deans were summoned to a meeting with the proctors to discuss the desirability of increasing student involvement in college and university policies. The Somerville Governing Body responded by inviting the JCR officials and any other junior members who were interested to attend a special meeting in Wolfson Hall on the last Sunday of Trinity Term. Discussion focused on the desirability of the JCR seeing the College estimates, so that its financial position could be made clear to them; the appeal procedure incorporated in the Dean's Regulations; and the possibility of fuller participation by junior members in the business of House Committee.[18] As a result of the meeting it was agreed to set up a Joint Exploratory Committee, where senior and junior members could meet regularly to discuss matters of mutual concern.

During the long vacation which followed the university and colleges prepared for the worst. It was agreed that in the event of a sit-in at Somerville the police should be sent for only if there was serious damage to persons or property and, if possible, only after an *ad hoc*

---

[18] Report by Miss Cobbe, GB, 16 Oct. 1968.

meeting of such fellows as were available. The principals and deans of the five women's colleges met to consider how to deal with any disruption of catering arrangements; their proposal that, in the event of a sit-in affecting dining-hall arrangements at any of the women's colleges, the others would help by offering to feed some of the undergraduates affected, was accepted by Governing Body with the proviso that the JCR should be consulted first. At the first, apprehensive, Governing Body meeting of Michaelmas Term the fellows agreed that 'a great effort must be made to meet undergraduate requests promptly, when these were reasonable', and that when their requests were not practicable, on financial or other grounds, the JCR officers should be promptly informed of their rejection. Those fellows who had been elected to serve on the newly formed Joint Exploratory Committee were enjoined 'to proceed with reasonable caution, and to be careful to make no specific commitments.'[19]

The new academic year opened tensely. In November the proctors issued a warning to all junior members that any further attempt to disrupt the conduct of university business by unruly behaviour would be treated as a serious offence. But in Somerville life was already beginning to return to normal. The issues raised at the second meeting of the Joint Exploratory Committee—described by those who attended it as 'lively'—were, first, the possibility of a college ball; secondly, proposals for a JCR bar; thirdly, changes in the college prospectus; and, fourthly, the desire for an exposition by the Treasurer of how undergraduate fees were used.[20] In the event, Somerville's main disciplinary action in this year of student unrest proved to be the gating for two weeks in January of an undergraduate brought back to college at 1.30 a.m. by a police inspector and a constable for climbing scaffolding in Beaumont Street and singing hymns.[21]

The Hart Committee reported in May 1969. It came down in support of revision of the disciplinary statute and of the establishment of a Students' Union; in the matter of student participation in the business of the university it favoured the establishment of joint consultative committees rather than student representation on decision-making bodies. Its recommendations were generally accepted, and consultative committees duly sprang up at every level of college and university life. They were time-consuming and expensive to service,

---

[19] GB, 16 Oct. 1968.   [20] GB, 4 Dec. 1968.
[21] GB, 24 Jan. 1968; and Dean's file.

and they—predictably— failed to satisfy the more radical students; but they bought a brief spell of peace and they fixed the pattern of university business for years to come.

In the spirit of Hart, the Somerville Governing Body set about reviewing its committee system with a view to securing greater undergraduate involvement. Junior members had long been represented on the Library Committee. In 1969 provision was made for limited JCR representation on Finance Committee, and also on the newly established Long-Term Planning Committee. A recommendation of the Joint Exploratory Committee that two undergraduates should attend Governing Body meetings whenever JCR business was discussed (but leave before any decision was taken) was accepted in 1971. But the following year—when the question of representation of junior members on college governing bodies was under consideration by the Conference of Colleges—a JCR proposal that three undergraduates should attend Governing Body as non-voting delegates was rejected. Governing Body's counter-proposal—that the standing of the Joint Exploratory Committee should be raised so as to make it a real forum for discussion of substantive business—was unacceptable to the JCR, which responded that, in these circumstances, it no longer wished for representation on that body.[22] The Committee was thus in abeyance during the next period of student unrest, to be revived at the JCR's request in Michaelmas Term 1975.

Somerville was more directly drawn in to the student troubles of 1973/4, which in Oxford focused on demands for a Central Students' Union—a building worthy of the social and political aspirations of the newly established, but meagrely housed, students' union. The cry 'What do we want?—CSU. When do we want it?—NOW' rang through the streets and quadrangles of Oxford, doing little to endear the student population to townspeople already beginning to feel the rumbles of recession. From their vantage-point in Little Clarendon Street Somervillians were well-placed to observe some of the more exciting demonstrations; rumour had it that the college chapel was a designated storage depot for a planned occupation of the new University Offices in Wellington Square. While the troubles lasted, feelings ran high in college as elsewhere; it was not a happy time. Somerville undergraduates were active in the campaign, and two of them were among the eighteen junior members rusticated by the university disciplinary court for their part in the occupation in February of the Indian Institute. No one envied the Dean her job.

[22] GB, 15 Nov. and 6 Dec. 1972.

The angry confrontations of the early 1970s were succeeded in an astonishingly short time by a period of almost preternatural calm. There was one obvious economic reason for this: the overriding pre-occupation of most undergraduates in the second half of the decade was to secure a job when they went down. What Somerville owes to the long hours spent by Barbara Craig simply listening to the anxieties and aspirations of the young it will probably never know. Whatever the explanation, within a year of two of its members being rusticated the JCR was fielding a team to compete—unsuccessfully—against Trinity College Cambridge on television in 'University Challenge'.

Communication with undergraduates at this period was beset with difficulties. In Michaelmas Term 1972, in pursuit of greater egalitarianism, the office of JCR President was abolished; the system which briefly replaced it—a division of functions among the members of the JCR executive, each of whom held office for half a term—was cumbersome and confusing, and a nightmare for anyone who had to have dealings with them. Undergraduate hostility to any manifestation of 'élitism' affected many aspects of college life. The 1970 Michaelmas Dinner was organized with a view to overriding the traditional distinction between high and low table, with junior members seated on the dais with the Principal, and other senior members dispersed through the body of the hall—a practice which was maintained for nearly twenty years. The following term, the undergraduate members of the Joint Exploratory Committee called (in vain) for the abolition of high table at lunch. In Michaelmas Term 1972 it took up the cause of equal pay for women, with particular reference to the wages paid to college scouts. When the JEC was revived in 1976 undergraduates insisted that members of the domestic staff should be entitled to attend; their willingness to do so proved, however, to be beyond JCR control. Distinction between award-holders and commoners in the matter of vacation residence charges—the former were charged for services, but not for their room—was a recurring bone of contention; it was finally abolished, at the JCR's reiterated request, in 1980, whereupon disapprobation was focused on the remaining convention that award-holders should have priority in the allocation of college rooms. In 1983 an undergraduate refused to accept an exhibition on the grounds that she opposed élitism.[23]

Provision for undergraduate representation on Finance Committee had been made in 1969 in the hope that undergraduates 'would feel

---

[23] GB, 16 Feb. 1983.

that their representatives were in the confidence of the college, and so that there should be some undergraduates, at least, who have some understanding of the financial problems of the college.'[24] An attempt in Trinity Term 1971 to explain to a wider undergraduate audience the need to impose higher maintenance fees fell on unresponsive ears: the Principal reported that those attending the special meeting called for this purpose (mainly from among the first years) 'had not shown themselves ready to accept any of the arguments put to them.' A subsequent meeting, at which the Treasurer and Lady Hall addressed 'a packed and reasonable' audience on the college's financial position, proved more satisfactory. A letter was sent to all current and prospective undergraduates and also to the Local Education Authorities to explain that Somerville could no longer hold itself bound to maintain fees at a fixed level for three-year periods. In 1973 Governing Body informed the Committee of Estates Bursars that 'the only condition on which College could accept a continuing restraint in fee increases would be a substantial increase in income from endowment (i.e. capital which would bring in an annual income of *c*.£10,000)', adding that, even with such subvention, it might not be possible to keep pace with inflation.[25]

The fee increases which now became an annual feature of college life hit undergraduates hard. Governing Body was sympathetic to their plight, but, in the face of the college's own financial difficulties, helpless to do much more than protest in the appropriate quarters. A letter from the Principal, expressing concern at the academic implications of the reduction in students' living standards and their increasing inability to afford to buy books, received a sympathetic reply from the local MP, Evan Luard, and an unhelpful one from the Department of Education and Science.[26] In 1976 Governing Body acceded to a request by the JCR that undergraduates should be allowed to live in college while in gainful employment in Oxford during vacations, while deploring the hard fact that such employment should be necessary.

The college itself was endlessly preoccupied with small economies. Working parties to consider possible savings were convened in 1971 and 1974, and made a number of practical suggestions to reduce expenditure on such items as college entertaining and telephone charges. But a mounting deficit pointed to the necessity of more

[24] GB, 19 Feb. 1969.   [25] GB, 28 Nov. 1973.   [26] GB, 28 Apr. 1976.

stringent measures. A special meeting of Governing Body, convened during the Easter vacation of 1975, agreed a package of measures to help meet the estimated deficit for 1975–6, and to maintain thereafter a change of direction in financial policy. The recently agreed limitation on undergraduate numbers was to be relaxed to admit up to ten extra in the coming October; also to be relaxed was the college's long-maintained rule that undergraduates in their first year should not be allowed to live out. Nancy Waugh was asked to convene a working-party to consider whether teaching resources were being used to best advantage; domestic and administrative expenditure was to be rigorously reviewed.[27]

In response to the recommendations of these various review bodies, many small luxuries of college life, hitherto taken for granted, were reduced or abolished. Heating was turned down, or even off. Meals became simpler, and college hospitality was curtailed. As one of a series of experiments with weekend meals, which were particularly costly in staffing, hot soup and sandwiches were made available on Saturday and Sunday evenings to those who had signed and paid for them by Saturday lunch-time. The SCR dining-room was closed at weekends after Saturday breakfast. During the periods in vacation when the college was officially closed no domestic service or meals were available. In a subsequent round of economies, the annual dinner for Guests of High Table was shifted from a Saturday to a (less expensive) Friday evening.

But clearly economies, by themselves, were not enough; increased endowment was essential for the college's financial survival. This became the main plank of the Centenary Appeal, launched in 1975 with the services of a professional fundraiser. Old Somervillians responded generously, particularly in support of teaching and the college library, which was enabled to establish a fund for the purchase of science books to balance the generous provision for the humanities made in 1963 under the will of Dr Rose Graham. It was agreed that funds not earmarked by their donors for some specific object should be used to endow an existing tutorial fellowship; modern history was chosen as the first school to benefit, and Jennifer Loach was designated the first Centenary Fellow.

It was an encouraging start, but many other posts remained under-endowed, and tutorial costs were rising at a rate even higher than that

[27] Special Meeting of GB, 26 Apr. 1975.

of inflation in general. Women dons had, traditionally, been paid less (and had fewer benefits in kind) than their colleagues in richer men's colleges. With the rise of co-residence, a practice which had long been seen as undesirable was no longer a sustainable option. In 1969 the Treasurer had urged the desirability of Somerville making an effort to bring its tutorial and administrative stipend scales more nearly into line with those prevailing in the men's (and therefore potentially mixed) colleges.[28] In 1973, with the advertisement of a university lecturership in chemistry which would be associated with Wadham regardless of the sex of the appointee, Governing Body took note of 'the new situation created by the competition of the mixed colleges electing men or women to their fellowships.'[29] For better or for worse, in future the women's colleges would have to pay the going rate.

Somerville's ability to support research was also now coming under threat. In 1977 the committee which administered the Mary Somerville research fellowship was forced reluctantly to the conclusion that, in view of the rate of inflation and the increase in university fees for graduates, no election should be made for 1978–81. The fellowship's precarious finances were rescued in 1981 by a handsome bequest from one of its former holders, May McKisack; but the future of the college's other research fellowships remained insecure. It was agreed that, for the time being, unallocated gifts and bequests should be added to the Research Reserve Fund, and that the funding of research fellowships should be given high priority in any future appeal.

In these unsettled years, colleges encountered considerable difficulty in matching their building programmes to the housing requirements of their undergraduates. The completion of Somerville's major residential development in the late 1960s was succeeded almost immediately by a fashion—attributed by some to the intolerable level of noise in Vaughan building, but probably owing more to a general reaction against all forms of institutionalism—for living out of college. When in Trinity Term 1971 the college surveyor made suggestions for replanning the back of West, concern was expressed that the scheme might give the college more residential accommodation than it could actually use.[30] Two years later, with plans for library extension under way, the Long-Term Planning Committee identified future building priorities: sound-proof rooms for music and language practice, a crèche, and a buttery or coffee bar for the JCR. Plans for

[28] GB, 12 Nov. 1969.   [29] GB, 28 Nov. 1973.   [30] GB, 26 May 1971.

additional undergraduate or graduate accommodation were to be dropped for the time being. Galloping inflation was soon, in any case, to put them out of the question.

But the same economic pressures which rendered new building projects impracticable increased their desirability. The rising cost of living and heavy pressure on accommodation in central Oxford soon made college rooms seem much more attractive. In Trinity Term 1974 the JCR expressed concern at the difficulty of finding accommodation out of college and reported indignantly that in the coming academic year thirty-six second-years would be obliged to live out. A similar protest was voiced at the Joint Exploratory Committee two years later, in response to the news that college was proposing to increase its undergraduate intake. As the decade progressed and the college, reluctantly, increased undergraduate numbers in a desperate attempt to make financial ends meet, these difficulties were compounded. Contemplating the exceptionally high intake proposed for 1977, Governing Body accepted the need to acquire additional lodgings close to college. But accommodation could no longer be planned simply with undergraduates in mind. In its centenary year Somerville acknowledged the need 'to use the college site to bring in additional income as well as to provide additional accommodation.'[31] Future building projects were to have more than half an eye to the conference trade.

During Barbara Craig's principalship, the outward appearance of the college changed remarkably little. The conversion to library use of the residential accommodation on the ground floor of the Champneys building profoundly affected the internal arrangement of the library, but, apart from the glazing of the central loggia, was virtually undetectable from outside. With the help of grants from the Pilgrim Trust, the Goldsmith's Company, and the Gilchrist Charitable Trust, the original upper library was redecorated, its lighting improved, and its floor carpeted. The new arrangements, which provided at last a self-contained library, brought home the desirability of giving some other name than 'Library' to the residential part of the adjacent 1956 building, and in 1977 it was agreed that this should be 'Holtby' in commemoration of the posthumous bounty of one of Somerville's most distinguished alumnae. In 1978 the library itself achieved a brief flash of international publicity when the Ivy Gurney

---

[31] GB, 20 June 1979.

Fund for the purchase of modern French literature, established by Miss Margery Abrahams in memory of a college friend who for many years had organized the Oxford French Circulating Library Club, was entered by its founder for the Whitbread Award for the Promotion of Franco–British Cooperation, and was commended jointly with Raleigh Bicycles. (The prize went to Concorde.) A luncheon in Paris to celebrate the commendation was attended on behalf of the college by Miss Gurney's niece, Mrs Wainwright, and her husband.

The main outward changes of these years were not to the college buildings, but to its gardens. A violent storm in the new year of 1976 robbed Somerville of one of its most notable landmarks—the stately cedar, older than Walton House itself, which stood at the entrance to the main garden quadrangle. (Distressed observers of the fallen giant consoled themselves with the reflection that, had the cedar fallen in a different direction it would have taken a large part of the Hall with it.) The following year Dutch elm disease struck the garden, and one affected tree was felled in an attempt to protect the others. The ensuing replanting included three trees presented by the JCR to mark the college centenary. In May 1976 Mr Harold Macmillan, in his capacity as the college's Visitor, inaugurated the centenary celebrations by planting a replacement cedar at a somewhat greater distance than its predecessor from the hall.

The centenary year, with its round of celebrations, provided a temporary respite from austerity. The gaudy weekend in July, attended by old Somervillians and their families in huge numbers, was a triumph for the bursar, Denise O'Donnell, and her staff. It was also a security nightmare—for the old Somervillians included the new Conservative Prime Minister, Margaret Thatcher (Plate 45). Preaching the following day at the centenary service in the University Church, her old political opponent Baroness White voiced the college's pride in the achievement of one whose politics many of its members deplored: 'It could have happened to a member of another college, but I fear that most Somervillians feel that it was right that it should be one of us.'

Reflection on the achievements of Somerville's first century, and the massive odds against which many of them had been accomplished, was the best possible antidote to despondency about the future. If there were hard decisions and lean times ahead there were harder and leaner ones behind. In this spirit, the fellows in 1978 set about the process of finding a new principal to succeed Barbara Craig in 1980. Leafing through *Who's Who* in hope of inspiration, their attention was drawn to the entry for an old Somervillian diplomat recently back from service in Ulan Bator.[32] 'Hobbies—' they read: 'Good talk and difficult places.' Confident of qualifying at least on the latter count, they approached Daphne Park.

---

[32] They had no idea of the nature of her work until a programme on BBC Panorama in November 1993 revealed that she was a senior officer in MI6 .

14

'Difficult Places': The Principalship of Daphne Park, 1980–1989

How Daphne Park rated Somerville beside her previous postings—Moscow in 1954, Leopoldville in 1959, Lusaka in 1964, Hanoi in 1969, Ulan Bator in 1972—she was too diplomatic to say. Her presence ensured that life in college in the 1980s, however difficult, would not be dull.

She was a high-profile Principal: a member of the British Library Board, chairman of the Legal Aid Advisory Committee, Governor of the BBC. Within the University she served as a pro-vice-chancellor. She travelled energetically in the cause of the college Appeal, making frequent visits to the USA, the Gulf States, and the Far East. A popular figure in America, she was invited in 1987 to give the Commencement Address at Chatham College, Pittsburgh, and the Norman Angell Lecture at Ball University, Indiana; the following year, in the intervals of a whistle-stop tour of Somervillians in New York, Chicago, and San Antonio and meetings with the presidents of a number of American women's colleges, she was guest speaker at an Oxford and Cambridge dinner in New York and was the subject of a dashing profile in the *New Yorker*.[1] An incurable optimist, she ensured that, in one of its darkest decades, Somerville never lost confidence and hope.

The 1980s were difficult times for higher education in general. A women's college faced these difficulties with even less control than a mixed institution had over its own future. Alternating governmental injunctions to expand and to contract, the withholding and occasional sudden release of funds, increasing bureaucratic interference in every aspect of academic and domestic life, combined to create an atmosphere of uncertainty, of which the Long-Term Planning Committee was an early, and symbolic, casualty: it was suspended in

---

[1] *New Yorker*, 30 Jan. 1989.

1983 when it became clear that planning for more than a year or so ahead was a virtual impossibility.

The need for retrenchment led the university to freeze established posts as they became vacant, and to shift teaching costs, wherever possible, on to colleges. In the case of CUF appointments a waiting-period—normally of two years—was instituted, during which time colleges were obliged either to appoint a temporary lecturer or to bear the entire cost of a 'titular' CUF replacement. This placed a heavy financial burden on colleges, but at least reserved for them the initiative in determining their course of action. The retirement of a fellow who held a university lecturership, on the other hand, might well signal a permanent, or protracted, diminution of the college's teaching strength. Under these various pressures, Somerville's recently expanded fellowship began inexorably to contract.

In the Christmas vacation of 1979 a special meeting of Governing Body, called to consider a paper from the General Board on retrenchment in university expenditure, had reluctantly agreed to support the proposal for a waiting period for CUF lecturerships. It was a matter of particular concern for Somerville, whose two senior fellows were approaching retirement. The following term Governing Body discussed what arrangements should be made for the teaching of modern languages and history on the departure in 1981 of Elizabeth Armstrong and Agatha Ramm. In the case of history, which had two other fellows to bear the intervening burden, it was agreed to make a temporary appointment for two years, pending the release of a replacement CUF lecturership. Modern languages, Somerville's largest school, and a peculiarly complicated one to organize, presented greater difficulties. Until the retirement of Christina Roaf in 1979 it, too, had been a three-fellow school; her successor as university lecturer in Italian was a man, who, being ineligible for a fellowship at Somerville, was assigned to the recently mixed Lady Margaret Hall. A two-year interlude before the appointment of Mrs Armstrong's successor would now cast the whole burden of administering Somerville's modern languages school on its one remaining fellow, Olive Sayce. Governing Body agreed that, if the college's plea for an immediate replacement CUF was unsuccessful, it would bear the cost of proceeding at once to a substantive appointment. In the event, the university programme of retrenchment was deferred for a year and, having secured a replacement CUF in French for 1981, and being assured of obtaining one in history for 1983, the college agreed to advance by a year the election of a tutor in history. Adrianne Tooke thus joined the Governing Body in Michaelmas Term 1981 as fellow and tutor in French, and Joanna Innes a year later as fellow and tutor in modern history.

The college could more easily plan for the retirement of its fellows than for other personal or professional eventualities. The marriage and departure to America of Jane Bridge in 1978 ushered in an unsettled period for the mathematics school, which was only resolved in 1984 with the election of Karin Erdmann. Politics was without a fellow from 1984 to 1986 between the resignation of April Carter and the election of Niamh Hardiman. Julie Jack's early retirement in 1988 involved the college in a long interregnum before the reinstatement in 1994 of her CUF lecturership in philosophy. In 1990, in response to the university's need to cut posts in the faculty of *literae humaniores*, Miriam Griffin's CUF lecturership in ancient history was reallocated to Somerville and Trinity jointly. When Olive Sayce retired that year uncertainty about her replacement meant that the modern languages school was again, briefly, faced with the prospect of being left with only one fellow. The one tutorial gain of these years was in law, where, after a series of unsuccessful attempts to secure an appointment in association with some other college,[2] Somerville was eventually assigned a second CUF lecturership, to which Gráinne de Búrca was elected in 1989.

In the case of CUF lecturerships, where the college was the primary employer, it could at least count on eventually securing a woman appointee. With university lecturerships there was no such security. Jean Banister's retirement in 1984 after 35 years as tutor in physiology, threw into question the whole future of Somerville's flourishing physiological sciences school. The college made bid after bid for association with any university post which might provide the necessary teaching; time after time the association went to some other college, or the appointment went to a man. Somerville was fortunate in its interim arrangements—securing the services as director of studies of Dr John Walker, recently retired from Worcester College—but a heavy burden of moral tutoring, and responsibility for co-ordinating tutorial arrangements in this complicated school, fell on the other science tutors. It was not until October 1987, with the appointment of Dr

---

[2] The 'joint/joint' appointment, in which two colleges combined to seek association with a university post, became an increasingly common feature of these years.

Aviva Tolkovsky to a university lecturership in neurosciences, that Somerville regained a tutorial fellow in physiology.

The problem of how to maintain the tutorial strength—particularly in the experimental sciences—of the remaining single-sex colleges was one of which the General Board was well aware, and to which it proposed a series of more-or-less unsatisfactory solutions.[3] Association with one of the 'new blood' posts released in 1982/3 offered a faint ray of hope. But, as with other appointments in which the university was the primary employer, it was necessary to secure a back-up mixed college to which a male appointee might be assigned. When considering the further particulars of one such post with which Somerville was associated in 1983 Governing Body noted that 'the differences between the stipend and benefits received by fellows of Somerville and those received by fellows of other colleges would be very obvious to female candidates for university lecturerships, who would be sent particulars by two colleges.'[4] Evidence was accumulating that assignment to a single-sex college was open to interpretation as a form of discriminating against a successful woman candidate.

The main growth areas in the university—engineering and information technology—were ones for which Somerville had no existing tutorial provision. In 1984, for the first time, Somerville included in its prospectus a director of studies in engineering—Dr T. V. Jones of St Anne's—and agreed to aim at taking two undergraduates a year in the subject. The support of engineering became one of the main objects of the new college appeal. In 1985 GEC offered to fund a research fellowship, to be associated with a college research fellowship or—in the case of a man being appointed—a research lecturership. The latter proved to be the case, and in October 1985 Kevin Warwick joined the SCR as Somerville's first research lecturer in engineering. In the same year Somerville was successful in a bid to be associated, jointly with Pembroke College, as the junior partner in a new blood post in information technology, which brought with it three additional undergraduate places to each college; Carroll Morgan was duly elected a fellow of Pembroke and appointed to a lecturership at Somerville. Negotiations with IBM had meanwhile secured for the college a two-year secondment in arts-related computing, to be held in conjunction with a visiting fellowship. In the course of her secondment Kit Cowlishaw not only played an active part in the life of the college but,

---

[3] GB, 19 June 1985.   [4] GB, 27 Apr. 1983.

through her institution of a course on 'Computing for the Terrified', made a lasting impact on that of the university. At the end of her term of office, a similar arrangement with ICL secured the services of Sarah Pettitt and the equipping of a fine new computer room for the use of undergraduates.

The presence of so many new lecturers and research fellows made for a lively Senior Common Room. A succession of Polish visiting scholars to whom the college gave hospitality—as part of a wider Oxford scheme—from 1982 onwards, provided a further welcome diversification. Their visits were generally brief, and in the depths of the vacation; but some established more lasting links, and their presence served as a salutary reminder that Somerville's problems were as nothing compared with those faced by some academic institutions elsewhere.

To those on the spot, the problems were none the less pressing. The contraction of the Governing Body did not simply mean a reduction in the college's teaching strength; it placed an almost intolerable administrative burden on the remaining body of fellows. Liability for service on the college's many committees came round with increasing regularity. Filling the major, time-consuming, college offices—Vice-Principal, Dean, Senior Tutor, Tutor for Admissions, Secretary of Governing Body—became increasingly difficult. Minor offices were held in multiples of two or three. The convention that new fellows should be eased gently into their responsibilities—being spared, for the first year of their appointment, from serving on college committees, or being burdened by college office or excessive teaching demands—was gradually abandoned.

A similar process was at work among the college's graduate body, which was hard hit by swingeing increases in graduate and overseas students' fees. The MCR was not merely contracting in size; its members were increasingly enrolled for one-year courses. This meant a lack in social continuity from one year to another, a diminishing pool of people available to take on the responsibilities of office, and a reduced subscription income with which to finance common room activities. The early 1980s saw a number of initiatives to halt the decline. A tutor for graduates was appointed; and the college began to offer graduate scholarships. The establishment in 1985 by Dr Jenny Teichmann,[5] in memory of her mother and aunts, of the Levick Sisters' Research Fund

---

[5] Mary Somerville Research Fellow 1957–60.

for Philosophy and Philology, enabled Somerville to attract a succession of young graduate students in these fields. The Janet Watson Fund provided top-up funding for American, and the Indira Gandhi Fund (established in 1985 to foster the college's connections with India) for Indian graduates. In the late 1980s the college's participation in the Soros scheme brought to the MCR an impressive series of visiting graduate students from Eastern Europe. Concern throughout the university at the facilities available to graduate students led to a review of their needs, the first fruit of which in Somerville was the installation in 1986 of a computer for their use. Christine Franzen, moving from MCR to SCR on her election in 1985 to the Mary Somerville research fellowship, provided an invaluable link between the two. At her suggestion a number of initiatives were taken to draw members of the MCR more closely into the social life of the college, the most lasting of these being the establishment of termly MCR/SCR symposia at which representatives from each common room give a brief account of their current field of research. But despite all these initiatives, by the end of the decade Somerville had the smallest graduate body of any college in the university.

Undergraduate numbers remained large, but they were drawn from a diminishing pool of applicants. The advantages of an all-women's college, however obvious to those who had actually experienced them, were proving difficult to convey to the current generation of school-leavers. Those who had been educated in all-girls' schools were generally, by the age of eighteen, eager for change; most of those who had hitherto experienced nothing but mixed education found the prospect of a women's college strange, if not actually abhorrent. During the annual entrance exercise in December the mixed colleges, themselves under pressure to admit more women, were increasingly reluctant to pass on promising candidates. Some of those whom they did pass on told the tutors interviewing them at Somerville that they would rather not come to Oxford at all than come to a women's college.

Efforts at recruitment were energetically supported by the JCR, which was particularly anxious to attract more candidates from state schools. But in attracting candidates, Somerville laboured under a further handicap—that of poverty. Between 1979 and 1986 student grants fell in value by 20 per cent. At a time when vacation jobs were hard to get, and when undergraduates living out of college had to pay rents well above the national average, many of them were coming under severe financial pressure. This was exacerbated by the abolition in 1986 of the Housing Benefit Scheme, and by the increasing failure of parents—often under financial pressure themselves—to meet their grant obligations. Substantial student bank overdrafts became common form. Book-buying, on the level taken for granted by previous generations, became a rarity. The popular colleges to apply to were the rich ones, which had the means—from guaranteed accommodation to the offer of bursaries and book grants—to soften the prevailing hardship.

By the beginning of the 1980s it was clear that all but the richest educational establishments were destined for the foreseeable future to be in a state of constant appeal for funds. Over the next decade most colleges attempted to introduce their old members to the notion— taken for granted in the United States—of regular giving by alumnae to supplement appeals to industry and large foundations. Somerville appointed a part-time Appeal Secretary in Michaelmas Term 1981, and launched the new Appeal late the following year. Old Somervillians, who had only recently contributed to the College's Centenary Appeal, responded with a predictable mixture of enthusiasm, resignation, and outrage to this new call on their generosity. While the Principal set off to canvass support in America and the Middle East, an energetic committee under the chairmanship first of Dame Gillian Brown, and then of Lady Bingham, identified potential benefactors in this country, and organized fund-raising events. In an effort reminiscent of the 1920s, college gaudies were enlivened by raffles, tombolas, and sales of books, pictures, and antiques. (A collection of watercolour landscapes by Miss Penrose which Nesta Clutterbuck donated to a picture sale in 1991 may indeed have included some of those sold in 1922 in aid of an earlier Appeal.) A series of Literary Luncheons celebrated the work of a distinguished line of Somervillian novelists, from Dorothy L. Sayers to Michèle Roberts. Emma Kirkby gave a concert in the Sheldonian Theatre. Current undergraduates joined old members in a sponsored walk round Blenheim Park, and donated the proceeds of the 1988 Ball (one of the few in living memory to make a profit) to the Appeal for books for the Library. Regional groups of Old Somervillians organized talks and cheese-and-wine parties, and sold each other home-made jam and chutney. In a particularly imaginative venture, the London Group set up the 'Mary Somerville Art Fair', with the dual aim of helping the college appeal and promoting the work of young artists.

The forging of links with industry was one of the main features of

Daphne Park's principalship. She urged the college to take advantage of the opportunities for contacts opened up in 1984 by Women's Year in Science and Engineering, and in March 1987 she was guest speaker at a dinner given in London by the Engineering Employers Federation. She invited captains of industry to dine in college, and instituted an Open Evening for Industry to which representatives from high technology industries were invited to meet second-year undergraduates who were considering their future employment prospects. This event, which became a regular feature of Somerville's calendar, had some unexpected spin-offs in addition to the hoped-for industrial sponsorships—not least an offer of euphonium lessons from a visiting industrialist who discovered in one of his undergraduate hostesses a shared passion for brass bands.

In the course of the decade large sums were raised, in addition to several substantial bequests. But Somerville's needs constantly outstripped the generosity of its benefactors. In 1985 the Ernest Cook Trust gave £200,000 to endow a junior research fellowship in environmental studies; rising inflation meant that by 1989 the fund was already insufficient to enable the immediate appointment of a successor to the fellowship's second holder, Dawn Bazely, and it was agreed that it should in future be offered for three years in six. Older-established trust funds were similarly affected. It became standard practice to allow a fallow period between appointments to the Mary Ewart research fellowship, to enable capital to accumulate. By 1992 it was clear that, even with fallow periods, the Lady Carlisle Fund could no longer support a senior research fellowship, and its funds were merged with those of the Constance Ann Lee Fund to provide periods of study leave for existing tutorial fellows.

The Treasurer's Report in Michaelmas Term 1987 made worrying reading.[6] The age composition of the fellowship, combined with the fact that college was having to bear the full cost of three tutorial appointments in the sciences, meant that Somerville's expenditure on teaching fellows per undergraduate was substantially above the Oxford college average. The uncertainties engendered by the system of conditional offers, which prevented first-year numbers from being finalized until a month or so before the beginning of the academic year, meant that the college too often found itself in Michaelmas Term with unoccupied rooms on its hands. The college's financial

---

[6] GB, 11 Nov. 1987.

difficulties were compounded by the sharp decline in the number of graduates, an increasing drop-out rate among undergraduates, and a dwindling conference income. To embark on an ambitious building plan at such a time was clearly a risk; but Finance Committee concluded that it held out the best hope for the future.

The importance of conferences in helping to balance the college's books had been a fact of life for at least half a century; in the 1980s they were to become crucial to its financial survival. The practice of closing the college down for a three-week period in the long vacation, with all employees taking their holiday simultaneously, was abandoned in 1980, in order to maximize conference occupancy. The following year Governing Body accepted a recommendation of Finance Committee that undergraduates should be actively discouraged from staying up during vacations except for academic purposes. In 1982, acknowledging that some SCR sacrifices to Mammon were also necessary, it agreed to the use by conferences of the Vaughan Senior Common Room and the surrender to conference organizers of up to six cherished places in the SCR car park.

Throughout the university, colleges upgraded their rooms with a view to conference occupancy, and planned new buildings less with the needs of undergraduates in mind than those of vacation visitors: Somerville began to instal shaver points in its rooms long before admitting male undergraduates. In 1983 the acquisition of the freehold of 19–21 Woodstock Road enabled the college to contemplate a major new development southwards from St Aloysius church. The refusal of the City Planning Committee to give permission for the demolition of the existing shop frontage at 11–21 Woodstock Road added considerably to the architects' problems, and reduced the number of rooms which could be built (and therefore the amount of income which could be generated). In the event, the constraints of a difficult site proved a spur to architectural ingenuity, and the resulting building—strikingly different in its eastern and western aspects—contrived to please both the conservationists and the innovators. Designed not simply to provide undergraduate accommodation, but also to attract the top end of the profitable conference trade, the Dorothy Hodgkin Quadrangle, begun in 1988, symbolically had at its heart a lavishly equipped conference centre named for the Prime Minister.

But, coinciding as it did with the need to undertake major repair works on the Margery Fry and Vaughan buildings, it was a heavy drain on the college's resources. The enterprise—a monument to the vision and energy of Daphne Park—would have been impossible without the emergence of Mr (later, Sir) Geoffrey Leigh as a major friend and benefactor, and the support of many admirers of the Prime Minister, both at home and overseas, who financed the conference centre named in her honour. One of these, Dr Damon Wells, compounded his generosity by funding the construction in Darbishire of a much-needed set of archives rooms.

In February 1983 Mrs Thatcher lunched informally with the SCR, before proceeding to the New Council Room to unveil a portrait bust presented to the college by the sculptor Oscar Nemon. An orderly group of sub-fusc-clad Somervillians protested inside the college grounds against the government's educational policy; a larger and rowdier group of demonstrators massed in the Woodstock Road to voice more general grievances. Individual Somervillians will have their own views about Margaret Thatcher as a politician; and many communicated them, in forceful terms, on this occasion. The college as an institution is greatly in her debt. She has been a generous supporter of the Appeal—hosting a reception in 10 Downing Street; speaking, together with Shirley Williams and Eirene White, at a fundraising dinner in Goldsmiths' Hall; and agreeing, at the urgent wish of a group of the college's friends in America, to lend her name to the 'American Margaret Thatcher Appeal' which contributed a large sum towards the cost of the Woodstock Road development. In 1986 she was to give important moral support to Somerville's battle to maintain its single-sex status.

In May 1985 Harold Macmillan, now Lord Stockton, attending a dinner in college in celebration of his ninetieth birthday, gave a remarkable demonstration of continuing political quick-wittedness. 'Now when was it' he enquired of the deputation of senior fellows who greeted him on arrival 'that you changed the college statutes?' It was explained to him that Somerville was still a single-sex institution. Shortly afterwards, in an after-dinner speech which brought the packed hall to its feet in a standing ovation, he congratulated the college on its wise refusal to swim with the tide.

The wisdom of remaining a women-only college was a subject on which the fellows by now had very mixed feelings. By Michaelmas Term 1980 Oriel was the only remaining all-men's college. In what was possibly a last bid to stave off the inevitable, tentative overtures were made to Somerville about the possibility of some form of association.

Four Somerville fellows met informally with four Oriel fellows and concluded that there was no future in the proposal.[7] In 1984 Oriel admitted its first women, and Somerville reopened the question of admitting men. When it came to the vote, there was a majority in favour of change which fell just short of the two-thirds which the college statutes required.[8] It was agreed to reconsider the matter in two years' time.

As 1986 approached, tension in college mounted. During the Christmas vacation papers were invited from the JCR and the MCR, and the current junior research fellows were canvassed for their views. Representatives of all three bodies attended the last Governing Body meeting before the vote was due to be taken, and voiced solid support for Somerville remaining single-sex. Of the 274 votes cast in a JCR poll, 226 were against the admission of men and 34 in favour; 14 declared no preference. 90 per cent of the MCR was opposed to change. For the next three weeks the college's junior members lost no opportunity to press home their arguments. On Wednesday 12 February fellows walked to the crucial meeting through two silent lines of sub-fusc-clad students. Inside the New Council Room they rehearsed again the familiar arguments. The proposal was put that the charter and statutes of the college be amended to permit the election of men as fellows and the admission of men as undergraduate and graduate students. It was—to the general astonishment—overwhelmingly defeated.[9]

Among the fellows who voted on this occasion to maintain the status quo there were several whose instinct was for change, but who thought it right, particularly in view of the strength of undergraduate feeling, to allow the college one last opportunity to make a success of remaining single-sex. In North America there was some evidence that women's colleges, after a period in the doldrums, were entering into a phase of renewed popularity; there were hopes that Somerville, having sat out the hard times, might now be poised to benefit from a similar shift in public opinion. The size of the majority was seen as giving a positive mandate—lacking after the 1984 vote—for Somerville as a single-sex institution. It invested the college, and the college Appeal, with a new lease of life and brought it a new burst of publicity. An undergraduate, Sophie Mills, appeared on Channel Four TV to put to

[7] GB, 26 Nov. 1980, 11 Mar. and 17 June 1981.   [8] GB, 7 Mar. 1984.
[9] GB, 12 Feb. 1986.

the viewing public the case for retaining an all-women's college; the Principal was interviewed on the *Today* programme, and the college featured in a programme on *Women's Hour*. A Special report on Somerville appeared in *The Times*.[10] In the summer of 1986 the Principal visited the United States, meeting enthusiastic groups of Somerville alumnae in Washington, Chicago, Pittsburgh, and New York. The college prospectus was thoroughly revised to stress the advantages of an all-women's college. A schools liaison officer was appointed from among the fellows to work closely with the JCR in putting the message across to schoolgirls, by means of visits to schools and open days for sixth-formers in Oxford. As part of this programme, the JCR received professional help and funding to make a video about life in Somerville for circulation to schools.

But within months of the college's decision to remain single-sex its ability to do so came under threat from an unexpected direction. The European Commission, reviewing the operation in the United Kingdom of the 1975 Sex Discrimination Act, was putting pressure on the government to remove remaining anomalies: these included the protection afforded to single-sex colleges by section 51 of the Act, which upheld their right under the Oxford and Cambridge Act of 1923 to advertise posts exclusively for one sex. In mid-May the colleges concerned—Somerville and St Hilda's in Oxford, and Newnham and Lucy Cavendish College in Cambridge—learned that the government was minded, in a new Employment Act currently before parliament, to introduce a clause which would effectively remove this protection. Prompt action by the four principals, aided by a sympathetic presence in Downing Street, secured a postponement 'to allow time for consultation with the institutions most closely affected and for further representations to be made to the European Commission'.[11] It transpired that it had not occurred to the Commissioners, one of whose objectives was to improve opportunities for women, that it was women's jobs that the single-sex colleges were seeking to protect. (The last of the single-sex men's colleges, Magdalene at Cambridge, was already in process of changing its statutes.) Statistics were produced to show that the rapid expansion in the number of women admitted to Oxford and Cambridge as undergraduates had not yet been matched by any increase in the number of teaching appointments going to women, and that there was still a marked imbalance between the

---

[10] 29 May 1987.   [11] *Hansard*, 10 June 1986.

numbers of men and women applying for academic posts.[12] Torn between the wish in principle to bring single-sex recruitment to an end, and in practice to instigate some form of positive action in favour of women, the Commission reluctantly conceded that the women's colleges might have a temporary role to play in redressing the employment imbalance. There was a long period of anxiety before the Principal was able to report to Governing Body, in November 1988, that the forthcoming Employment Bill would include provisions to protect, for the time being, the position of single sex colleges. It was emphasized that once a healthier employment balance had been achieved, the government was committed to bringing single-sex recruitment to an end. Somerville had secured, at best, a stay of execution.

---

[12] The Oxford figures for 1984 showed that of the 618 fellows in former men's colleges seventeen were women; of the 81 fellows in the three former women's colleges 28 were men. (Principal's speech to the AGM of the ASM, 5 July 1986). The number of women undergraduates had risen from just over 2,000 in 1970 to 4,630 in 1985.

15

College Life since 1945

AT one of the first college meetings of Janet Vaughan's principalship it was agreed (subject to the Dean's permission in individual cases) to allow beer and cider to be served at parties in the students' common rooms.[1] Twenty-two years later she began her last term as Principal by addressing the undergraduates on the subject of drugs.[2] The retirement in 1967 of Somerville's longest-serving Principal marks a natural watershed in a period of rapidly accelerating social change. Traditional structures of university and college discipline were already by then being called in question; in the years that followed they were to be repeatedly—and sometimes violently—challenged. The publication of the Franks and Hart Reports were to have profound implications for the way the university was organized, and for relations between its senior and junior members. With the reduction in 1970 of the age of majority from 21 to 18, colleges were released from the responsibility of standing *in loco parentis* to most of the student body, and the legal basis of much of the traditional discipline was removed.

Somerville sought advice from Hazel Fox on the implications of this change in the law, and revised its by-laws and regulations accordingly.[3] The Dean, relieved from endless collection of small fines for minor misdemeanours, was enabled to concentrate her energies on more pressing matters, such as the impounding of the python which, in the early 1970s, an undergraduate was discovered to be keeping as a pet in her college room. (The clause in the Dean's regulations which prohibits undergraduates from keeping animals 'of any description' in their rooms dates from this incident.) In 1974 the college instituted a new set of procedures by which serious offences were to be taken before a disciplinary committee of three senior and three junior members. The pastoral remit of tutors was reduced, and though the more approachable of them continued, no doubt, to provide a shoulder for

[1] PF, 26 Oct. 1945.   [2] GB, 8 Mar. 1967.   [3] GB, 11 Mar. 1970.

311

distressed undergraduates to cry on, the formal relationship between tutor and pupil became more purely academic. In the 1980s an advisory panel of senior members, backed up by the university counselling service and a wide range of specialist help-lines, took over many of the responsibilities of the 'moral tutors' to whom, in the past, undergraduates had notionally confided their personal problems.

As colleges concerned themselves less and less with the details of how undergraduates lived their lives, much that had been distinctive about that way of life disappeared. The trend was reinforced by other contemporary developments: by a hostility to élitism which prompted undergraduates to play down their Oxford credentials, and by a pervasive youth culture which gradually blurred the distinctions between town and gown. From the mid-1960s onwards the life-style of undergraduates, their way of dress and mode of speech, approximated increasingly to that of their peer-group in the country at large. Their lives, which had long ceased to be bounded by the college, were becoming focused almost as much on the town—its cinemas, supermarkets, clubs, and pubs—as on the university. The word 'student', once reserved for women to indicate that they were not members of the university, came to be generally adopted by undergraduates of both sexes to stress their solidarity with students elsewhere.

In comparison with the changes which came about in college after 1967, those of the earlier period seem extremely modest. But every small advance was significant at the time. From 1946 onwards, beer and cider were allowed at dinner on Saturday nights. In 1947 somewhat reluctant consent was given for drinks to be provided at the college dance, after a campaign by undergraduate ex-servicewomen who had been appalled the previous year at having to offer their partners fruit cup.[4] Though Council rejected a JCR request to seek proctorial permission for undergraduates to attend the weekly tea-dances at the Carfax Assembly Rooms, it agreed—in conscious departure from the practice of the other women's colleges—that 'in suitable cases' undergraduates might be allowed to attend proctorially approved Eights Week dances, provided that care was taken to be quiet on return.[5]

A protracted—and often comic—campaign was waged by the JCR in the vexed matter of visiting-hours. In 1946 their request to be allowed to entertain men guests in college rooms till 10 p.m. on Saturdays was turned down, as contrary to the known wishes of the

---

[4] PF, 18 Feb. 1947; Recollections of Barbara Harvey.   [5] PF, 29 May 1946, 4 May 1948.

vice-chancellor. It took until 1960 to wring from Governing Body the concession that 'for one experimental term . . . each undergraduate be allowed to give the Lodge the names of three men friends who, on any one Saturday or Sunday, would be admitted to college from 7–10 p.m'.[6] The 1960s saw a steady erosion of remaining restrictions. Visiting hours in lodgings were pushed back, in stages, from 7 p.m. to 11.30 p.m. In Hilary Term 1963 it was conceded that undergraduates who invited male guests to dinner in hall might give them coffee in the Reading Room or House JCR till 8.30 p.m., and that dinner parties in undergraduate rooms on the night of the college dance might continue until 10 p.m. The rule requiring undergraduates to register in advance the name of any male guest who was expected to call between 8.30 and 10 p.m. on Saturday and Sunday evenings was abandoned soon afterwards, perhaps because it was so patently susceptible both to fantasy and to sabotage. In a JCR poll on the subject of visiting hours, 165 members declared themselves in favour of extension, and three against. In Hilary term 1964 it was agreed that guests should be allowed up to 10 p.m. both in term and vacation, though 'for the protection of undergraduates from unwanted visitors all evening visitors must be signed in.'[7]

In the early 1960s, the main thrust of the Dean's annual address to the first-year was to impress upon them the importance of not kissing their boyfriends goodnight in the traffic entrance. It was never quite clear whether her concern was for propriety or for road safety (the latter a serious consideration in the days when Janet Vaughan's erratically driven Mini was apt to erupt at any moment on to the Woodstock Road). A familiar sight outside any of the women's colleges at this period was the cluster of embracing couples as the evening deadline approached, and hordes of young men prepared to sprint back to beat their own college curfew. The case for Somerville employing a night porter was made by the Dean in 1958, after a survey revealed that in the course of Michaelmas Term seventeen undergraduates (of whom seven were deemed to have valid excuses) had come in by the front gate after midnight.[8] Statistics, of course, did not reveal how many bolder spirits had simply climbed over the wall. In 1964, the search for a night porter having proved unsuccessful, Somerville became the first college in Oxford to issue latch-keys to undergraduates who

---

[6] Informal Council, 27 Apr. 1960.   [7] GB, 11 Mar., 24 Apr. 1964.
[8] GB, 3 Dec. 1958.

wished to be out late. Shortly afterwards, college abolished the requirement—which over the years had been the source of much resentment and no little forgery—to sign the roll in hall by 9.30 a.m. each day. It was one of the very few matters, apart from the election of fellows or a change of statute, on which the Governing Body is recorded as having gone to a formal vote.[9] The academic year ended, however, with a stark reminder that Somerville had not entered into a phase of complete *laissez-aller*. An undergraduate was rusticated for being absent one night without leave; and, at the prompting of Enid Starkie, the Governing Body sent a reminder to landladies of their obligation to let the college know at once if one of their lodgers was away overnight.[10] The novels of Margaret Forster and Caroline Seebohm make it clear that the obligation was frequently, in practice, neglected.

The strictness of the college rules in Janet Vaughan's day was mitigated by the humanity of the Principal herself. Obliged in the late 1950s to rusticate an undergraduate who, returning from an unauthorized visit to Cambridge, had been unfortunate enough to hitch a lift from a friend of one of the fellows, she wrote apologetically to the girl's parents to express the hope that they would not be hard on her. At a time when overnight guests in college were forbidden, visiting fiancés were frequently accommodated in Radcliffe House. Their girlfriends were usually instructed to report in time to cook breakfast in the morning, but at least one young man had his Sunday morning sausages cooked for him by Dr Vaughan herself, clad in dressing-gown.[11] Under her successor, undergraduates were issued as a matter of course with a key to college, and gate hours—like cooked breakfasts, watchful landladies, and the rope-ladder stored in West for helping latecomers climb into college—rapidly became a thing of the past. The hour by which visitors were required to leave the college was pushed gradually forward, to the point when it clearly made more sense—and caused less disturbance—to allow them to stay overnight. By the 1980s the main purpose of the Dean's regulations in this regard was to minimize inconvenience to neighbours, to satisfy fire regulations, and to prevent permanent double occupancy of college rooms.

[9] GB, 15 Feb. 1961, 11 Nov. 1964. For grant purposes, undergraduates had to supply evidence of being in residence for at least 42 days a term.   [10] GB, 2 and 16 June 1965.
[11] Recollections of Jennifer Taylor (Everest, 1954) in *Janet Maria Vaughan: A Memorial Tribute*.

The war had accustomed Somerville to having married under-graduates in residence. For some time afterwards the relevant by-law, which stated that only in 'exceptional circumstances' would an undergraduate be permitted to continue her course after marriage, was generously interpreted with respect to ex-servicewomen who could not reasonably be expected to comply with regulations designed for 18-year-olds. But the 1950s saw a return to the old severity, which undergraduates were not alone in finding irksome. In Hilary Term 1960 seven fellows (Mrs Armstrong, Miss Banister, Miss Brown, Miss Cobbe, Mrs Hall, Miss Harvey, and Miss Syfret) petitioned the Governing Body for the by-law to be revised: 'We think that the time is coming when there will be more married undergraduates, both men and women, than in the past. We should therefore like to see the rule about marriage expressed positively rather than negatively.'[12] Their intervention secured the redrafting of the by-law to the effect that 'Undergraduates who wish to continue their course after marriage must, before they marry, obtain the consent of the Governing Body'; and the Principal was instructed, for future guidance, to keep a case-book recording the decisions taken in individual cases.[13] Contrary to undergraduate belief, the college's interest in the matter was chiefly to ensure that the necessary financial support was available to enable the married student to complete her course.

Many years later the writer Victoria Glendinning, one of the Somervillians of this generation who did marry while still an undergraduate, described the episode in a speech at a college gathering. Student marriage was, she said, uncommon in the 1950s, and much disapproved of by the fellows—in particular, she suspected, by her own tutor, Mrs Armstrong; that she was permitted to continue her course after marriage she was inclined to attribute to the advocacy of that great romantic figure, Enid Starkie. Mrs Armstrong, listening to the speech, was seen to shake her head. The truth was exactly the reverse. She had supported her pupil's cause (and her name was among the seven petitioners of 1960); Enid Starkie—always, notwithstanding her Bohemian reputation, a hanging judge in matters of undergraduate discipline—had opposed it. It was a striking illustration of the misconceptions which so often underlie the relationship between tutor and pupil, and a salutary lesson on the dangers of oral history.

[12] Minutes of Council, 17 Feb. 1960.   [13] Informal Council, 9 Mar. 1960.

The new by-laws cannot be said to have prompted an unbridled rush to the altar. Undergraduate marriages continued to be rare—though in the 1950s and 1960s, when it was fashionable to get engaged, a remarkably high proportion of Somervillians married almost immediately after finishing their course.[14] Succeeding generations reflected national trends in marrying later, or not at all. In 1968 Anne Scott-James revisited Somerville, whose rules she had found so oppressive thirty-five years before, to interview undergraduates for an article in the *Sunday Times*. Among the women she talked to, she estimated that two-thirds were sexually experienced; many were in steady sexual relationships; none, she claimed, was looking forward to early marriage or children.[15] The effects of the sexual revolution, already apparent, were to become increasingly marked in the years ahead, with condom machines installed in college cloakrooms, and contraceptive information readily available. Lesbian relationships, generally in the past a matter for concealment, came to be openly cultivated during the 1980s. A generation alerted to the dangers of Aids kept itself informed not only about condoms but also about dental dams.

But contraceptives sometimes failed, and they were sometimes spurned. In the course of the 1980s the college learnt to adapt its rules to accommodate (admittedly infrequent) cases of pregnancy and motherhood—once considered absolute bars to a continued undergraduate career. Undergraduate mothers coped in a variety of ways with the dual claim on their energy and time. Some could count on the support of husbands or boy-friends or parents. Some made use of the college crèche. One finalist refused to attend a whole term's revision classes on the grounds that they would prevent bonding with her new baby, and then confounded her tutors by getting a first. A group of six Somerville undergraduates living in a shared house combined to look after the baby born to one of them in the course of her second year;[16] the baby was made a guest member of the JCR (a privilege shared with the Librarian's cat, Dudley). Somerville gradually became more accustomed to the presence around the place of small children —a development hastened by the increase in the number of mature students who came to college, particularly as graduates, with existing family commitments.

---

[14] See A. Cameron, 'Past Masters', *THES*, 28 Oct. 1994. Date of marriage is not always given in the college Register, but at least one-third of those who came up in October 1959 are recorded as having married by the end of 1963.   [15] *Sunday Times*, 1 Dec. 1968.
[16] 'Six Girls and a Baby', *Today*, 11 Feb. 1991.

One of the most striking—if minor—transformations of the 1960s was in the appearance of the undergraduates themselves. The immediate post-war generation, constrained by rationing, had little opportunity to exercise their fashion sense. They wore 'good suits' or stout tweed skirts and handknitted jumpers by day; changed, if possible, into a silk or woollen dress for dinner;[17] and, if fortunate enough to be invited to a ball, wore their mothers' cast-offs, 'borrowed, and swapped and manœuvred'.[18] The end of clothes-rationing in 1949 was greeted with great rejoicing: 'How glad we were to see so many tired jumpers and slacks give way to the crisp cotton frocks which added a pleasing touch of gaiety to the Somerville garden during the summer months. It was a wonderful summer.'[19] But even in the 1950s women undergraduates did not dress markedly differently from their mothers. Skirts were permanently pleated, and hair was permanently waved. Trousers, regarded in LMH as an indication of membership of the Experimental Theatre Club, or of a late-night essay crisis,[20] were more likely in Somerville to be a political statement. In Caroline Seebohm's novel of late 1950s Somerville life, *The Last Romantics*, the well-born Daphne Fanthorpe signals her conversion to left-wing principles by exchanging the fair isle sweaters, fur coats, and stiletto heels with which she had come up to Oxford for a peajacket, jeans, and boots.[21] The more conventional progression was that described by Averil Cameron, from 'demure suits' to 'bouffant skirts and page-boy hairdos'.[22] But before long, as the fashion-gap between the generations widened, jeans and duffle-coats became the norm, and straight hair began to predominate over the perm. In 1962 black stockings appeared on the first-year photograph for the first time since the 1930s.

Coming to Somerville from North America as a graduate student in October 1959, Ann Hansen felt decidedly overdressed in tweed skirts, cashmere sweaters, and a blazer, and was stared at in the streets when she set out for a punting expedition in 'neatly tailored gray flannel Bermuda shorts and a Norwegian patterned cardigan'; she herself was astounded at the 'general scruffiness' of Oxford students with their

---

[17] Recollections of Joyce Sugg.

[18] Hilary Roe (Vaughan, 1943) in 'Special Report for 1943', *ASM Report*, 1993.

[19] Oxford Letter, 1948/9.

[20] See the chapter by Antonia Fraser (LMH, 1950) in A. Thwaite (ed.), *My Oxford* (London, 1977).   [21] C. Seebohm, *The Last Romantics* (London, 1987), 80.

[22] Cameron, 'Past Masters'.

'skirts above the knees, . . . overly long fishermen's sweaters, and hair hanging like a horse's mane.'[23] The sartorial rot had set in. In the harsh Hilary Term of 1963 Somerville undergraduates were allowed, exceptionally, to wear trousers in hall and at tutorials in college—though not to university lectures. The gradual replacement of stockings and suspenders by tights paved the way—once fabric technology had advanced to the point when tights could be relied on to stay up—for the advent of the mini-skirt. In Trinity Term 1966 Somerville was besieged by reporters and cameramen when a principalian notice warning undergraduates against wearing mini-skirts during Schools was leaked to the press. (In a letter to the women's colleges, the proctors confirmed that 'Extravagantly short skirts are incompatible with the intended sobriety of sub-fusc and we consider that examiners may reasonably take exception to them.') A fellow who asked one of the reporters why there was so much public interest in Somervillian dress was told that it relieved the tension of the seamen's strike.[24]

The boldness of the undergraduate who wore a trouser suit at Isobel Henderson's memorial service in 1967 is still remembered in college.[25] That year the Governing Body supported the JCR in their request to the proctors to be allowed to wear jeans at lectures in the Examination Schools, and, this achieved, went on to press for similar rights for senior members.[26] (For years past, Elizabeth Anscombe had waged a running battle with the Clerk of the Schools, who would not let her past to give her lectures if she was wearing trousers; the proctors eventually hit on the solution of providing her with a changing-room, equipped with a decanter of sherry, where she could keep a skirt for the purpose.)[27] In 1968, in what was to prove the last attempt to legislate for how undergraduates dressed for meals, the Governing Body conceded that trousers might be worn at evening hall 'provided that these were respectable'.[28] How to assess the respectability of subsequent fashions—the flowing robes of the 1970s, the patched and slashed garments of the 1980s, the hotpants, leggings, and 'grunge' of the 1990s—was beyond the fellows' capacity, and they sensibly did not try to do so. Shortly after trousers became an acceptable sub-fusc

---

[23] Recollections of Ann Hansen (1959).   [24] JCR File, May 1966.
[25] Recollections of Barbara Harvey.
[26] GB, 15 Nov. 1967 and 24 Jan. 1968. Permission was given for senior members to wear slacks, trousers, or jeans with cap and gown for attendance on occasions on which the university had jurisdiction over dress, but not on formal or ceremonial occasions.
[27] Recollections of Lesley Brown (daughter-in-law of the proctor concerned).
[28] GB, 1 May 1968.

alternative to skirts a Somervillian candidate presented herself at a degree ceremony in brown cords, and the proctors—less inhibited about pontificating on the subject of female attire—circulated a note that these should be *formal* trousers, 'with a crease'.[29]

The wearing of gowns to tutorials and lectures, once universal among undergraduates, was by now a mark of eccentricity, or else a sign of deference to particularly old-fashioned senior members. But, surprisingly, sub-fusc itself was not seriously challenged during these anti-authoritarian years. A protest demonstration against the university matriculation ceremony in Michaelmas Term 1968 proved to be 'a total fizzle'.[30] When in 1969 the Somerville Joint Exploratory Committee discussed the question of academic dress for examinations junior members expressed no wish for radical change apart from the desire not to have to wear caps.[31] It was, indeed, on the JCR's initiative that in 1977 the traditional first-year photograph was for the first time taken in sub-fusc, on the morning of the matriculation ceremony.

The late 1960s saw a more fundamental break with college tradition when, with the introduction of a system of meal rebates, and the upgrading of pantries to facilitate self-catering, undergraduates ceased to take most of their meals together in hall. Thereafter meal arrangements were constantly tinkered with in efforts, on one hand, to effect economies, and, on the other, to accommodate the changing eating habits of the young. The dressing-bell before dinner was abandoned, and the pigeon-holes outside hall where, in more genteel days, undergraduates had stored their table napkins, were removed. Cooked breakfast was abolished. Responsibility for providing tea was taken over by the JCR. The Sunday evening meal—always the gastronomic low-point of the Somerville week (in contrast to the men's colleges, where it was often the main guest-night)—was abolished after a dismal period of experimentation with soup and toasted sandwiches; Saturday dinner soon went the same way. An early self-service meal replaced formal hall on most weekday evenings, senior members retreating—except on guest nights—to the seclusion of the private

---

[29] Letter from the Senior Proctor (Justin Gosling) to the Dean of Degrees, 9 Mar. 1978: 'I was glad to see that one of your candidates took advantage of the revised rules on sub-fusc at the last degree ceremony. Some surprise has been expressed, however, that anyone should consider that particular design of brown corduroy suitable wear for formal occasions'.   [30] Article by Anne Scott-James in *Sunday Times*, 1 Dec. 1968.
[31] GB, 5 Feb. 1969.

dining-room. Somerville's traditional 'meat and two veg' cuisine was gradually superceded by pasta and curries and other still more exotic dishes (often, confusingly, served with boiled potatoes and cabbage). Vegetarian options were in increasing demand and became decidedly palatable—a far cry from the penitential nut rissoles which, in earlier years, were routinely served up to Roman Catholics on Fridays. Soon after the death of the college chef, Brian Barton, in 1988, Somerville followed the example of a number of other colleges and engaged the services of a firm of contract caterers.

Changes in meal arrangements involved—and to some extent were prompted by—changes in the domestic staff. Until the early 1960s service was provided by a core of resident scouts, who cleaned rooms in the morning, served lunch and tea, and waited, uniformed, at table at dinner. Many of these were long-term employees of the college, and as they came up to retirement they became extremely difficult to replace—particularly in the face of competition from the men's colleges which began at this time to employ women cleaners in the place of male scouts.[32] Somerville began to rely heavily on the services of foreign students who wished to spend a year or two in Oxford to improve their English, and whose style inevitably differed somewhat from that of their predecessors. A succession of glamorous Danes and Germans, installed in the staff quarters in the attics of Maitland and Darbishire, enjoyed a social life of which the undergraduates they were serving were often heartily envious. As cafeteria service replaced formal hall, and undergraduates assumed (in theory) greater responsibility for keeping their rooms tidy, the college looked increasingly to part-time and casual staff, employing local women to clean in the mornings and students from the Oxford Polytechnic to wait at table at the few formal meals which remained.

The fact that, even on formal occasions such as Michaelmas Dinner, the hall was no longer capable of accommodating the whole college was symptomatic of a more general weakening of traditional collegiate life. Daily prayers in the chapel were abandoned in 1969 for lack of a congregation. The Sunday evening chapel service continued, though it was dealt a severe blow when newly mixed men's colleges began to recruit women for their choirs, and Somervillian chapel-goers were lured away by the prospect of a mixed choir and a free Sunday dinner. There was a growing tendency for undergraduates

[32] See K. Thomas, 'College Life, 1945–1970', *HUO* viii, 207.

to go away from Oxford at weekends—a development hastened by the virtual disappearance of Saturday morning tutorials. The shift away from college as the main focus of undergraduate life, initiated between the wars, was now virtually complete. Somerville had become too big, and its buildings too dispersed, for even its resident members to get to know each other easily. Those living outside college might, if they chose, lead a very detached existence indeed. In the early 1970s, with the disappearance of 'recognized college lodgings' and their attendant landladies, undergraduates became responsible for finding their own accommodation—often in rented houses and flats shared with students from other colleges. They ate less frequently in college, and less formally. They had fewer social contacts with graduate students, whose lives were now centred on the Margery Fry House, and with senior members, who were mostly non-resident. Significantly, in the 1970s some tutors began to refer to their college rooms as 'offices'.

Colleges throughout the university were affected by these trends, but from the 1970s onwards their effects were to be particularly marked in the remaining single-sex institutions, whose members were obliged to look beyond their own walls if they wished for mixed company. This was not necessarily seen as a bad thing, though some were nostalgic for what they believed (often erroneously) to have been the old ways. In the 1980s Somerville and St Hilda's undergraduates repeatedly claimed as an advantage the fact that their members were more likely than those from a mixed college to be active in the university at large.

The claim was not new. Winifred Holtby had said something similar (though for different reasons) in 1929. In 1951 the JCR President reported that the fact that college societies were, with some exceptions, on the decline, 'is no cause for anxiety to a JCR that lends its talents to all the undergraduate activities of the university. There is scarcely a club or society in Oxford in which Somerville does not play an active part.'[33] From the 1950s onwards, there are few references in the annual JCR Newsletter to college societies, but many to university societies which had Somervillian presidents, and to the prominence of Somervillians in university journalism, politics, drama, sport, and debate.

The rise and decline of the Malory Society in the late 1950s was symptomatic of the fate of purely college-based societies. A forum for

---

[33] (JCR) Oxford Letter, 1950–1.

the discussion of medieval subjects, the society was founded in 1956 under the joint presidency of Barbara Harvey and Ursula Brown. Its members included historians, English students, and modern linguists from both JCR and MCR. It secured a succession of distinguished speakers—Neville Coghill on Chaucer, Peter Dronke on Dante, Keith Thomas on 'The position of women in the middle ages'—entertaining them after dinner to mulled wine in winter and white bordeaux in summer. But it was unable to sustain the initial impetus for long. Having begun ambitiously by restricting the number of members to fifty, it found itself by 1961—though popular with graduate students and their guests—unable to attract any support from the new first-year. In Trinity Term 1961 Maurice Keen of Balliol addressed the final meeting on the subject of 'Brothers in Arms'. For a college society at this period, the Malory Society had been relatively long-lived; in keeping a minute-book and preserving it for posterity it was unique. A Somerville Philosophical Society survived, on and off, for some ten years in the 1970s and 1980s without leaving any written trace. Only the newly expanded law school, with its range of professional contacts and supporting network of enthusiastic old Somervillian lawyers, was able in later years to sustain anything like a regular programme of meetings. The decline of college societies was doubtless hastened by the rising popularity of the television: the JCR acquired its first set in 1963, largely to satisfy undergraduate demand to watch *That Was the Week That Was*,[34] and never looked back.

Some important university avenues remained closed to women well into the 1960s. An invitation to Ann Chesney to speak in the Eights Week Debate at the Union in 1951 was regarded as a college triumph; but when a new college debating society was founded in 1956, the JCR President reported that 'the majority of the members are over-modest about public speaking, and the few who have a wistful eye on the Union are discouraged by the improbability of female membership in the near future.'[35] In 1958 the news that motions to admit women to membership had once again been defeated, was received in Somerville with 'wry amusement'. Somervillians were still much in demand as guest speakers: in 1961 Frances Kaldor spoke on the necessity for unilateral disarmament, and Lydia Howard, in a debate on the Common Market, was praised for her ability to

---

[34] Oxford Letter, 1963. In 1958 the JCR had rejected suggestions to acquire a television or washing-machine, and decided to purchase a new sewing-machine instead.

[35] Oxford Letter, 1957.

deal with attacks from the floor.[36] When in 1962 women were at last admitted to full membership of the Union, Somerville congratulated itself that such contributions had played an important part in bringing this about. But the goal once achieved, it rapidly became less prized. Later generations of student politicians were less likely to set their sights on the Union than on the OUSU.

It took still longer for women to be admitted to full membership of OUDS, though after the war they were increasingly involved both in helping backstage, and as guest actresses—Shirley Catlin gave a memorable performance as Cordelia in an OUDS production of *King Lear* which toured America in 1950. Though permission was not normally given for undergraduates to take part in more than one major production a year, the Somerville Council in 1948 refused to agree to the adoption by the women's colleges of a fixed rule to this effect, preferring to allow discretion to individual tutors. It did, however, enforce a rule restricting rehearsal time to a fortnight—a considerable disincentive to enterprising actresses and producers.[37] According to Joyce Sugg, 'there was a good deal of half-used or unused dramatic talent in Somerville' at this date. The college Dramatic Society's first major post-war production—the *Frogs* of Aristophanes—was performed in the presence of the translator, Gilbert Murray, dining in hall on his first evening out after a long convalescence. Joyce Sugg (see Plate 27)—who as the comic slave was instructed to be quick in her entrance on the donkey because the girl who played the rear half was subject to fainting fits—recalls that Murray's presence in the audience was very alarming to a cast which (despite Miss Hartley's encouraging presence at the dress rehearsal) was far from word-perfect. A somewhat damning review by Kenneth Tynan in the *Isis* surprised nobody. Among the projects which came to nothing at about this time was one by Christine Brooke-Rose for a slightly risqué play with an all-women cast. In the early 1960s Esther Rantzen was to hit the tabloid press when she fell foul of the Dean by proposing to introduce a naked vestal virgin into a college play: 'Dame Janet did not mind a bit,' she later recalled, 'and the tickets sold out.'[38] The main dramatic event of the intervening years was the sedate revival in 1954—to mark the 50th anniversary of the opening of the library and the 75th anniversary of the foundation of the college itself—of Robert Bridges's

---

[36] Oxford Letter, 1961.   [37] PF, 21 Oct. 1947, 16 Nov. 1948.
[38] 'Somerville Girls', *The Times*, 7 Feb. 1992.

masque *Demeter* (see Plate 15), with a new prologue specially composed for the occasion by the author's daughter Elizabeth Daryush. But by 1963, when a revived college Dramatic Society staged Webster's *The White Devil* in hall, it was considered worthy of note that 'Somerville was the only women's college to attack a production alone, providing all the actresses and administration.'[39] Inter-collegiate drama, banned between the wars, now flourished in Oxford, and purely college productions—like *Comus* in 1972, and *Something out of Nothing* in 1985—were becoming the exception rather than the rule. Even the play put on by the Dramatic Society to mark Somerville's centenary in 1979, Wycherly's *Love in a Wood* (performed in a slight drizzle on the chapel lawn), called upon actors from outside college.[40]

A wry comment on the economics of undergraduate drama is contained in the JCR President's report of the Somerville production in Trinity Term 1977 of Ben Hecht's *The Front Page*: 'This was a great success in Oxford drama terms—it broke even.'[41] The same commercial awareness underlies her account of the newly formed Somerville Make-up Team (SMUT), which, having gained valuable experience by handling such productions as *The Mikado* at the Oxford Playhouse, 'intends to charge suitably exorbitant prices for this expertise next term.' The venture was to prove highly successful, and for many years to come the services of SMUT were called upon for productions throughout the university.

A steady alliance with Worcester gave greater stability to Somerville's musical life. The Worcester and Somerville Musical Society, which replaced Somerville's war-time alliance with Exeter, was launched in Hilary Term 1945 with a concert of local talent. The first of its many guest concerts took place the following term, with an all-Bach programme by the Birmingham School of Music Symphony Orchestra. Subsequent ventures included performances of Purcell's *Dido and Aeneas* in the Holywell Music Rooms in Michaelmas Term 1948, *Venus and Adonis* (with the John Blow Orchestra) in Hilary Term 1952, a cantata by Alan Bush in 1953, Purcell's *Masque from Dioclesian* in Trinity Term 1959, and Benjamin Britten's *St Nicholas* performed in the University Church in 1966. In Trinity Term 1951 the Worcester–Somerville Choir took part in a performance by the Chelsea Opera Group of *Cosi fan Tutte*—an occasion marked by a special buffet

---

[39] Oxford Letter, 1963. [40] JCR Newsletter, 1979.
[41] JCR Newsletter, 1977.

supper served in the college garden. Over the years the Society also sponsored many memorable concerts by professional musicians, most notably a recital by Julian Bream and Peter Pears in 1964, and a concert by the Amici Quartet in Michaelmas Term 1965. In the 1950s it instituted a series of tea meetings and record recitals which achieved considerable popularity at a time when few undergraduates themselves owned gramophones. In 1948 the Worcester–Somerville Choir took responsibility for the annual service of Christmas music held in Somerville chapel—an arrangement which was to continue until 1985, when it was agreed that the service should in alternate years be held in Worcester.

Somerville's musical enterprise was by no means absorbed, however, by the Worcester–Somerville connection. Among the college's own ventures was a concert of Brandenburg Concertos given in 1950/1 by the Boyd Neel Orchestra—the generous, and most imaginative, gift of an old Somervillian, Mrs Spedan Lewis. Individual Somerville musicians continued to be active in the musical life of the university at all levels. The opportunity to hear Emma Kirkby singing with the Schola Cantorum, at the threshold of a distinguished musical career, was a particular pleasure of the late 1960s. She remains a generous friend of the college, of which she became an honorary fellow in 1987, returning in 1980 to give a concert of music by Dowland and his contemporaries in aid of the Isobel Henderson Memorial Fund, in 1983 to sing with the Schola Cantorum in Carissimi's *Jephte* as part of the JCR's 'Women and the Arts' Festival, and in 1986 to give a concert in the Sheldonian Theatre in aid of the college Appeal.

The acquisition by the JCR in 1951 of an upright Bechstein piano for the Council Room to replace the old hired one previously in use marked a distinct improvement in Somerville's musical facilities. But an attempt to improve these further by the provision of a music room in the basement of the new Vaughan building was frustrated by a design fault which relayed every sound to undergraduate rooms several floors away. After some years of intermittent use as a seminar room, it was eventually converted, with the help of a gift from Christina Roaf, into an exhibition room—named after her artist mother, Vera Waddington—for the display of works of art.[42]

Over the years the college had acquired, by gift or bequest, a considerable—and very diverse—collection of pictures. Its only venture

---

[42] In 1992 the lower half of the room was converted into a library stack room.

into the art market came on the initiative of the JCR, which in 1950 decided to establish an art fund to buy pictures for the common rooms in House and West. Powers of selection were delegated to a committee of experts which in the years that followed was to make some extremely shrewd purchases—notably two paintings by John Minton, acquired in 1953. The following year the Art Committee was entrusted, together with the new assistant bursar, Miss Hands, with planning the redecoration of the junior common room, and the Mintons, when not out on loan to exhibitions elsewhere, hung here until it became sadly apparent that valuable objects could no longer be safely left in public rooms. The Art Committee also took advantage of the Arts Council's and the Contemporary Arts Society's hiring systems, to provide three or four new pictures each term for the JCR—an enterprise recorded in Margaret Forster's savage novel of college life, *Dames' Delight*, with its reference to the 'ghastly paintings . . . chosen by a College Art Committee from some godforsaken gallery that loaned them out to needy institutions.'[43] In 1959 the JCR introduced an optional art levy, collected at the same time as amalgamation, which enabled them to acquire in the course of the next few years such works as Cartier's large *Vortex in Grey* and Terry Frost's *Abstract* (loaned to Leicester Art Gallery during the Christmas vacation of 1961/2 for an exhibition of works of art belonging to the JCRs of Oxford colleges), as well as a number of smaller pictures for use in undergraduate rooms. Among the exhibitions which the Committee arranged in Somerville was one of Mexican art, opened in 1964 by the Mexican Ambassador.

The loan in 1962 by an old Somervillian, Mrs Dawkins, of a fine Lurcat tapestry which was hung on the staircase near the hall, helped set the Art Committee to thinking in terms of loans of works of art for the college. It was to achieve some spectacular successes in this line. In 1962 Henry Moore was approached, and agreed to a six months' loan of his bronze *Falling Warrior* for display in the college garden. Emboldened by the success of this venture, the Committee wrote to Barbara Hepworth, who responded gallantly with *Core*. Subsequent loans included *Watcher Five* by Lyn Chadwick, and sculptures by Werthmann, Gerald Gladstone, Oliffe Richmond, and E. R. Nele, providing, as the JCR President wrote in 1965, 'a representative view of the main aspects of modern sculpture.'[44]

[43] M. Forster, *Dames' Delight* (London, 1964), 172.   [44] Oxford Letter, 1965.

In 1964 the Art Committee initiated its most ambitious project: the commissioning of a piece of sculpture to stand between the Graduate House and the new undergraduate building then under construction. Donations were solicited, and an advisory committee—consisting of Henry Moore, John Piper, Philip Dowson and representatives of the JCR—was formed, and charged with the task of selecting a suitable sculpture by a young artist. Hopes that the sculpture would be in place for the official opening of the Vaughan building, however, were not fulfilled, and it was not until 1971, after long negotiations with the Arts Council, that the JCR acquired its sculpture. The chosen work was *Triad*, a three-dimensional Zed of striking size by the young sculptress Wendy Taylor. Unfortunately for the Art Committee's original plan, Miss Taylor was insistent that the Vaughan terrace would be an inappropriate site for the work, and *Triad* was duly installed next to the cherry tree on the chapel lawn. This disappointment worked in the end, however, for good. When the Vaughan terrace did eventually acquire its sculpture, to mark the college's centenary, it was by a rising young Somervillian sculptress, Polly Ionides, who in the mid-1960s, as Polly Richter, had played a leading role on the JCR Art Committee.

Among intermittent attempts to encourage artistic activity among the undergraduates themselves was the establishment in 1970 in the 'Bulge' next to the JCR of a 'Creativity Room' where members of the college could draw, paint, and make things for relaxation. The conversion of the Bulge for this purpose was partly financed by a gift from an old Somervillian, Mrs Morgan of Virginia (Antonia Bell, 1932), whose daughter had spent some time in the Margery Fry House; the JCR President was able to report in 1971 that the room's 'gloriously messy and colourful mixture of powder paints, charcoal and crayons provides not only an inspiration for serious-minded artists, but also ready therapy for anyone in need of it.'[45] Another initiative, associated with the college centenary, was the presence for a year of an Artist-in-Residence. Jennifer Durrant, a young painter of large and vibrant abstracts, exercised her influence chiefly from her studio in Gloucester Green. In 1980, at the invitation of the Art Committee, she returned briefly to Somerville to run a workshop. The institution in 1978 of the new Bachelor of Fine Art degree brought to the college a succession of undergraduate artists who were able to exhibit their

[45] JCR Newsletter, 1971.

work in the Vaughan Exhibition Room, and to reach a wider London audience through the Mary Somerville Art Fair.

One of the more unexpected developments of the period was the re-emergence of Somerville in the 1980s as a sporting college. The immediate post-war period had seen a modest revival in women's sport in Oxford. 'Though fewer undergraduates play games than of old, those who are players play to some purpose', wrote the Oxford Correspondent in 1949, after a season in which Somerville provided the captain and more than half of the united hockey team in a year of victory. In 1951 the JCR went so far as to hire a hockey pitch in the Parks; by 1957 the number of players had become too few to justify the expense. In 1952 the OU Women's Boat Club was forced to close temporarily for lack of funds, it being rumoured that an offer from a sympathetic sailor to contribute regularly from his pay had had to be refused on the grounds that university clubs were not allowed to accept outside support.[46]

In a college where sport was decidedly a minority interest, it was proving increasingly difficult for teams to secure adequate financial support from the JCR, and the establishment by the university in 1960 of the Women's Sports Committee, with a grant of £1,000 to subsidize university games, was warmly welcomed. The sport which attracted most enthusiastic support in Somerville that year, however, was judo. 1961 saw the return of croquet to the Penrose lawn, with the acquisition by the JCR of a second-hand croquet set 'in excellent condition'; and it was reported in 1962 that 'the Chess Club thrives'. Somerville could, in fact, claim one outstanding sportswoman at this period— Sue Dennler, who in 1963 came second in the high jump at the international students' games in Brazil. But, significantly, she was in her day the only member of the OU Women's Athletic Club; in recording her triumph the President of the JCR acknowledged that 'Sport [is] not a fashionable activity for women in Oxford.'[47]

The gift to the JCR in 1960 of a 25-ft. skiff, equipped with oars and a sail, revived enthusiasm for the river. The new boat made its debut on the Cherwell in the summer of 1961, and even appeared briefly at Eights Week, 'to the astonishment and approval of onlookers.'[48] By 1964 a group of Somervillians provided the nucleus of a newly formed Women's Boat Club. Over the next decade rowing gained steadily in popularity, and the college boat club, handicapped by having to use

[46] Oxford Letter, 1952.   [47] Oxford Letter, 1963.
[48] Oxford Letter, 1961.

borrowed boats, determined to acquire one of its own. In 1978 it was able to purchase a lightweight shell from Eton, and won the women's novice section in the Christ Church Regatta. In the College's centenary year, Somerville achieved four bumps in the summer Eights, and held its first bump supper for the whole college in celebration. In 1980 the first eight at last achieved its ambition by coming head of the river in the women's division. Despite the poor state of its equipment, the boat club now had so many members that it was able to put three eights on the river. An article in the 1981 college *Report*, contrasting the poor condition of Somerville's hand-me-down or borrowed boats with the lavish provision made for their women rowers by rich mixed colleges like Jesus, prompted a generous response from an Old Somervillian, Christina Barratt, after whom Somerville's next boat was named in gratitude (and who subsequently bequeathed to the college her fine classical library). The boat club entered a period of mixed fortunes on the river, almost constant debt to the college, and equally constant efforts to raise money by means of discos and cocktail parties.

It was perhaps a sign of the times that the JCR President in 1971 referred in her Newsletter not to sport, but to 'recreational activities': table tennis, bridge, chess, and darts. But the formation in Michaelmas Term 1972 of a Somerville hockey team marked the start of a revival of more traditional games. By the 1980s JCR Newsletters have almost the ring of the 1920s:

> The hockey team is . . . doing well, beating every team in sight, despite the fact that every game is an 'away' game—we have no home pitch. The tennis team was narrowly beaten in the finals of Cuppers, and Somerville now boasts the first women's football team in the University. (1982)

> Our swimming team outclassed the rest of the University to win Swimming Cuppers, while, on land, our hockey team bullied the others into relinquishing the trophy . . . (1983)

> The Somerville Sports team had a more than successful year . . . The Boat Club, despite being plagued with financial crises, managed to win the Oriel Regatta and bumped and bombarded its way through Torpids to get a position which allows Somerville to go Head of the River next year . . . The hockey team successfully defended its reputation as the best in the University by winning the Wadham Tournament for the third time in a row and also added the Cuppers trophy to its collection . . . (1985)

This enthusiasm for sport was partly a matter of fashion. But an important contributory factor was undoubtedly the university movement towards co-education, with the new competitiveness—and new opportunities—which this inspired. The novel prospect of beating a Balliol or Keble team was very attractive to a college which for a century had been restricted to competition with four other colleges. As an all-women's college, Somerville had an obvious advantage in terms of numbers when selecting its sports teams, though its lack of sports facilities appeared the more marked by contrast with the lavish provision of more ancient, and wealthy, foundations. These strands are summed up in the JCR Newsletter for 1986:

> The number of Somerville sportswomen has increased rapidly during the year. The newly-formed netball team already has a regular following of over 20 players, a Somerville table-tennis team has been started up and will be playing in Cuppers, and our already established sports teams have scored their usual successes. The Boat Club was Head of the River in Eights this summer (so what's new?) and our rowers are training hard, determined to be Head of Torpids in Hilary 1987. The famous Somerville Hockey team demolished all opposition once again, retaining the Cuppers trophy and winning the Wadham Tournament for the 4th time in a row, despite the lack of a hockey pitch.

Perhaps inevitably, as Somerville's image became more sporting its reputation for political radicalism declined. Activism has always been a minority interest: 'There *must* have been undergraduates at the time who were devoted to some political party, convinced that their philosophy could do much to put the world to rights after the ravages of the war—but I knew none of them' writes Joyce Sugg of the 1944 generation, describing her own particular group of friends as 'as apolitical as it is possible to be'. Yet her contemporaries included Nina Mabey who, with her friends, marched through Reading during the 1945 election campaign singing 'Vote, vote, vote for Mr Mikardo, chuck old Churchill in the sea', and Margaret Roberts who, disdaining the Labour Club as too fashionable, was beginning to make her mark in the University Conservative Association.[49] Joyce Sugg was probably the most representative figure of the three, and arguably of Somervillians at any date. But the college's reputation was indisputably

---

[49] N. Bawden, *In My Own Time: Almost an Autobiography* (London, 1994), 76–7.

political, and—despite the assurance of the JCR President in 1953 that
activity and interest was 'healthily balanced between all the parties'[50]
—preponderantly left-wing. The impression was reinforced in Janet
Vaughan's time by the known political sympathies of the Principal.
Two future Labour MPs were undergraduates at Somerville in this
period: Shirley Williams (Catlin, 1948) reading PPE, and Shirley Sum-
merskill (1950) reading medicine. The daughters of Hugh Gaitskell
and James Callaghan read PPE a few years later, and were taught politics by a future Conservative City Councillor, Mary Proudfoot.[51]

The SCR, divided in its party allegiance, sought to preserve the
peace by not discussing politics at all; Barbara Harvey recalls the un-
real atmosphere during the Suez crisis, when no one mentioned the
international situation in the common room, or talked of anything
else outside it. The JCR felt no such restraint. A motion of censure
on the government's military intervention in Egypt was passed by an
overwhelming majority at a special JCR meeting, and relayed by telegram to the Prime Minister and Foreign Secretary. Undergraduates
joined in demonstrations, helped organize protest meetings and
petitions, and travelled to London to lobby their MPs. Reporting on
these activities in that year's Oxford Letter, the JCR President felt
bound to add, in fairness, that 'there was a small number of Somervillians who supported the intervention, some of whom were active
in expressing their approval.'[52] Russian intervention in Hungary the
following year, on the other hand, found Somerville united in its
response. An undergraduate, Judith Cripps, was actually caught up
in the uprising, and spent some time in a Hungarian gaol; Janet
Vaughan's words of reassurance to her father—'She'll cope; she's a
Somerville woman'—passed rapidly into college legend. The JCR's
corporate energies were channelled into relief work for refugees, and
especially into support of the Hungarian Student Scholarship Fund;
entrance candidates that year were supplied with needles and wool to
enable them to knit blanket squares for refugees while waiting in the
JCR to be summoned for interview. In the years ahead, many politicians were to be favoured with the views—whether on foreign or
domestic policy—of the Somerville JCR, and many victims of unjust
regimes were to receive their support. The arrest and deportation
from South Africa after Sharpeville of Hannah Stanton, who read

[50] Oxford Newsletter, 1953.   [51] Councillor for Oxford North Ward 1982–6.
[52] Oxford Letter, 1956.

theology at Somerville as a mature student 1954–6,[53] and the arrest and torture in Chile of Sheila Cassidy, who read medicine 1958–63, added a personal dimension to political protest. Over the years the JCR, with the support of the Governing Body, raised funds to enable students from both countries to study at Somerville.

The political concerns of Somerville undergraduates at this time reflected those of students in the country at large. One generation walked to Aldermaston in support of the Campaign for Nuclear Disarmament, another protested outside the American Embassy against the war in Vietnam. In the 1980s they demonstrated against totalitarian regimes in Poland and Chile, and against government cuts at home. They were solidly against apartheid, contributing funds towards the defence in the 1959 treason trials, pressing the college in 1977 for disinvestment in South Africa,[54] and proposing in 1986 that the JCR Bar be renamed the 'Winnie Mandela Room'. (Governing Body, voicing doubts whether this was the most appropriate way of marking Mrs Mandela's fight against injustice, lent its support to an alternative plan—which came to nothing—to associate her name with the JCR Third World Scholarship.)[55]

But, while the JCR's corporate stance remained respectably to the left, activism was once more on the wane. In 1977 the JCR President attributed a lack of enthusiasm for extra-college involvement by the JCR to 'a national trend against participation in political controversy.'[56] It was probably also in part a reaction to Somerville's own recent experience, when during the troubles of 1973/4 the JCR washing-machines had remained unserviced while the Executive applied its energies to the headier cause of student representation. The Left Caucus did its best to maintain Somerville in its traditional allegiance, with a series of open meetings addressed by left-wing and feminist speakers; and in 1988 the JCR banner was taken out of mothballs for a series of demonstrations against proposed anti-homosexual legislation.[57] But, in what one JCR President described as 'the ongoing battle between those who wished to turn the JCR into a consortium

[53] Hannah Stanton gave an account of her experience in *Go Well, Stay Well: South Africa August 1956 to May 1960* (London, 1961).

[54] GB, 16 Feb. and 27 Apr. 1977. Governing Body asserted its obligation to deploy its funds to the college's best advantage, but set up a working party (Dorothy Hodgkin, April Carter, Judith Heyer, and Hazel Fox) to prepare a paper setting out the moral criteria on the basis of which a list might be constructed of companies in which the College would not wish to keep or purchase holdings.   [55] GB, 19 Feb. 1986.

[56] JCR Newsletter, 1977.   [57] JCR Newsletter, 1988.

specializing in the wholesale purchase of domestic appliances and those who wished to keep the Somerville JCR flag flying at the forefront of political, social and cultural activities',[58] the domestic appliance lobby was on the whole in the ascendant.

In this, as in other respects, the 1980s were a time of sharp contrasts. Undergraduates were active as ever in supporting good causes and engaging in good works. In 1979 the JCR set up a Third World Fund to help finance Somervillians working during the vacations on development projects. In 1981 they raised money for cancer research, the NSPCC, Help the Aged, Dr Barnardo's Homes, and Help the Blind. They organized War on Want lunches in aid of famine-stricken regions abroad, and involved themselves in local charities such as the JACARI women's groups in support of battered wives. At the same time, they organized entertainments for themselves on a scale, and at a cost, undreamed of by earlier generations. A Winter Ball held jointly with Mansfield College in 1982—with two heated marquees, multiple covered walkways, revues, cabarets, bands, vodka bar, and supper in hall—bore little resemblance to the sedate college dances of old, and itself seemed sedate in comparison with the (loss-making) 'One World Ball' in the summer of 1991, a double ticket for which cost £115. Such events were, of course, exceptional. The most characteristic forms of in-college entertainment in the 1980s were the Saturday-night disco and the video evening.

The growing prominence of alcohol on most such occasions was a sign of the times. In 1963 the college wine steward, Enid Starkie, had rejected a JCR request for permission to buy spirits as well as wine from the college cellar.[59] In 1969 the installation of a bar in the Reading Room, where sherry might be bought at a shilling a glass, was reported in the popular press as a bold blow for feminism.[60] The range of drinks was gradually extended, but the Reading Room, which had no plumbing, was plainly unsuited to the purpose, and its décor accorded ill with undergraduate tastes of the 1970s. Somerville's buildings provided no scope for a beer-cellar of the kind affected by most men's colleges. In 1981 the JCR itself was refurbished and transformed into a bar; within a short time the annual turnover was sufficient to warrant the employment of a professional barman.

The purpose of the change, according to the JCR President, was to

---

[58] JCR Newsletter, 1985.   [59] JCR File, June 1963.
[60] JCR file, 1969: cuttings from *Daily Mail* and *Daily Express*.

make the JCR 'more of a focus for college life'.[61] In practice it rendered the common room increasingly uncongenial to undergraduates who did not drink or smoke. Heavy drinking among the young—and particularly among young women—was by this date a matter for national concern; and it was a habit which many undergraduates had acquired before coming to Oxford. But there was an equally striking trend in the opposite direction. Earlier generations were often unaccustomed to alcohol; but few of them would have refused on principle a glass of wine at the Michaelmas Dinner. If drinking was now on the increase, so was abstention. At a time when the atmosphere of the JCR was approximating ever more closely to that of a pub, fruit juice was rapidly replacing sherry as the preferred lubricant of social encounters between senior and junior members. A similar contrast was observable in the case of smoking, now also worryingly on the increase among young women. The extent to which this was a generation-linked phenomenon was underlined in Somerville by the contrast between the junior and senior common rooms, the former heavily impregnated with cigarette fumes, the latter—except during Elizabeth Anscombe's occasional visits—virtually a nicotine-free zone.

It was, of course, perfectly possible for an undergraduate to avoid visits to the JCR and still lead a full and active life. Less easily avoided were the weekly essay and the tutorial (see Plate 42). The style of these encounters varied enormously from one tutor, and one period, to another. In the 1950s Enid Starkie's pupils discussed Baudelaire over sherry and Turkish cigarettes; May McKisack's looked on while their tutor unembarrassedly consumed the cup of tea brought in to her mid-morning by a uniformed college maid. From the 1960s onwards there was increasing experimentation with teaching methods: more frequent use of seminars and classes, greater mixing of the sexes, and—with the proliferation of optional subjects—more exchange of pupils between colleges. The shape of the working day changed, with tutorials coming to occupy the afternoon hours once sacred, for senior and junior members alike, to healthy outdoor activity, and being displaced by domestic chores and early hall from the once favoured period between 5 and 7 p.m. A new professionalism began to make itself felt. Tutors were sent off on university courses on how to teach, and came back with their consciousness about body-language and eye-contact raised. Duplicated reading lists, sometimes covering a

---

[61] JCR Newsletter, 1981.

whole term's work, replaced the tentative verbal recommendations which in the past had maintained the fiction that next week's essay title arose spontaneously out of this week's discussion. Undergraduates were often on first-name terms with their tutors; and to those brought up in a more punctilious age they often seemed remarkably casual in their approach to academic engagements. Women dons no longer complained that they were handicapped in their teaching by lack of experience as examiners in the Schools.

But, for all these changes, the basic tutorial format, which brought together for an hour once a week a tutor, one or two undergraduates, and an essay, remained the cornerstone of the college system. It is, as a former tutor has commented, a peculiar form of teaching:

> The tutor is talking, hour after hour, with (not at) a succession of pupils, all supposedly of untold promise, but for the present of very diverse performance. There are no boundaries: any cross-reference may be illuminating: an event, in the history of literature, may call for parallel or comparison in other fields of human experience. And so the only limit is that of time available.[62]

Her conclusion, that the tutor, to outwit a pupil who is fortified with an essay, needs 'the speed and cunning of a hunted animal' may surprise Somervillians who have not been accustomed, in this context, to cast themselves in the role of hunter, or to regard their weekly essay as much of a defence. A system which depends so much for its effectiveness on a meeting of minds can be, where this fails, a misery for both parties concerned. A tutor who inspires one pupil may bore, or mystify, another. In retrospect, it is usually the funny or alarming aspects of particular tutorials which stick most in people's minds. The cumulative effect takes longer to assess. 'She never laid down the law as a teacher, but engaged in a kind of dialogue in which one absorbed information and responded to ideas almost without realising what one was doing' recalled Shirley Williams of Margaret Hall.[63] 'If I am any good as a teacher today' wrote Narayani Menon, eighteen years after reading history under Agatha Ramm and Barbara Harvey, 'it has a lot to do with those tutorials, where we learned that a tutor is expected to make you think, not provide you with final answers.'[64] Of her own tutorials with May McKisack, Barbara Harvey recalled:

---

[62] Lascelles, *A Memoir* (privately printed, 1989), 51.

[63] C. Moir and J. Dawson (eds.), *Competition and Markets: Essays in Honour of Margaret Hall* (London, 1990), p. xii.　　　　[64] 'Special Report for 1964', *ASM Report*, 1985.

We were not put in possession of facts . . . although our worst errors were very briskly corrected. Nor was it the discussion of ideas that was remembered afterwards, but something else. We left these occasions with a clear, strong, often quite chastening sense of the weight of conclusion that the evidence available to us as undergraduates would bear and how far our essays had respected these due limits. The question: 'Did you get that from a reliable source?' was a familiar shot across the bows. For her this meticulous examination of evidence was, I believe, the *raison d'être* of the tutorial, and at the heart of an historical education was a training in the use of evidence. I know that I shall not be alone in feeling a life-time's gratitude for this intellectual experience.[65]

The importance of thinking for oneself was perhaps most austerely inculcated in the school of *literae humaniores*. Mildred Hartley (Mrs Taylor), as Mods tutor, was famous for keeping her pupils away from all secondary literature. Elizabeth Anscombe's pupils might be sent off after their first tutorial, with no reading list and instructions not to write more than half a page, to produce an essay on (as it were) 'Justice'.[66] Exposure, week after week, to the 'scepticism carried to the point of perversity about any reconstruction of ancient history not based on primary sources' which was the hallmark of Isobel Henderson's tutorial method had a profound and lasting effect on generations of Somerville classicists.[67] But it was a student reading English who in the 1950s had an essay returned to her with the comment 'Now tear this up and write what *you* think.'[68]

The impact of such tutors was not simply academic. Contact with Enid Starkie was, for most of her pupils, a life-enhancing experience. Dorothy Hodgkin's pupils, drawn into the life of an exuberant extended family, learned that great science was not incompatible with ordinary human concerns. The elegance and glamour (and, at times, downright frivolity) of Margaret Hall gave added bite to her rigorous analysis of the distributive trades. Isobel Henderson's practice of taking her finalists to the races to mark the end of Greats aroused in them anxieties about dress besides which any worry about the actual examinations paled into insignificance. As hostess at a dinner party in

[65] Address given at the Memorial Service for May McKisack, 3 Oct. 1981.
[66] Cameron, 'Past Masters'.
[67] Obituary by Sally Humphreys (Hinchliff, 1953), in *ASM Report*, 1967.
[68] Ruth Bately in 'Special Report for 1955', *ASM Report*, 1995.

the early 1960s to celebrate the engagement of one of her pupils, she herself appeared memorably clad in 'a long evening dress, fur stole and elbow-length white gloves with diamond bracelets worn over them'.[69] She expected undergraduates to take an interest in current affairs, lamenting, on a visit to America, the narrow-mindedness of pupils who 'take a morbid interest in the Alcamaeonids and none at all in Civil Rights or Vietnam.'[70] The fund established in her memory to buy books for the college library in subjects in which she herself was interested has benefited not only classics and ancient history and archaeology, but also travel, music, art, poetry, the history and litera-ture of Spain. Had the library included sections on horse-racing or cricket, they would most certainly have qualified for a grant. 'One is always wrong', she used to say 'not to like things.'[71] Such transmis-sion of enthusiasm from one generation to another is central to what collegiate life is about, and it helps explain why so many tutor–pupil relationships have developed—often improbably—into friendships for life.

To the undergraduate of the 1990s the constraints which governed the lives of their even quite recent predecessors seem almost unbe-lievably quaint. But their own lives are subject to a combination of pressures which earlier generations were spared: the widespread breakdown in family life which means that undergraduates in in-creasing numbers have no stable home base; the changes in student funding which make a (sometimes very substantial) bank overdraft the norm; the heightened sensitivity to sexual exploitation which has accompanied the achievement of greater sexual freedom; the uncer-tain employment prospects which, in a time of recession, cast anxiety on the preceding years spent at university.

The typical fresher of 1960 arrived in Oxford by train, preceded by a trunk containing her worldly goods. Her 1990s counterpart is de-livered to college by car, family and friends pressed into service as bearers for the array of high-fi equipment, word-processors, cooking utensils, duvets, and pot-plants deemed essential for the conduct of student life. The material expectations of undergraduates have in-creased as dramatically as the rail network has declined. And both their material possessions and they themselves are more at risk. With the college open to all comers, a room left unlocked—even for the time it takes to fetch a kettle from the neighbouring pantry—is only

---

[69] Cameron, 'Past Masters'.   [70] *ASM Report*, 1967.   [71] Ibid.

too liable to be burgled. Young women who spend the vacation trekking in the Himalayas or crossing Australia on a bicycle are now—with some reason—fearful of walking alone in the streets of Oxford at night. Earlier generations of undergraduates, though subject to all manner of restrictions on how and where and with whom they spent their time, would have been as amazed to be issued on arrival at college with a room key as with a rape alarm.

Many of these are matters on which feminism has something to say. But feminism made its appearance relatively late on the Oxford political agenda.[72] Somerville, understandably, was one of the last colleges in the university to institute a Women's Group, or to appoint a JCR Women's Officer. Activism in this respect tended to be spearheaded by women at the former men's colleges who were now discovering as individuals what Somerville had discovered, as an institution, nearly a century before—that Oxford is a place of deeply ingrained, if largely unconscious, male prejudice. By the 1980s a single-sex college, so recently the norm in Oxford, was widely regarded as an anomaly. Somerville's junior members, by tradition not much given to manifestations of community spirit, were in the 1990s to display a quite uncharacteristic *esprit de corps* in rallying to its defence.

[72] See J. Howarth, 'Women', *HUO* viii, 369.

Somerville for Men?

THE election in 1989 of the first non-Somervillian Principal for over eighty years was variously interpreted as a welcome breath of fresh air, or as as an ominous portent of change. Catherine Pestell, a graduate of St Hilda's, bore little resemblance to her predecessor beyond a career in the Foreign Office. Her capacity for springing surprises was rapidly demonstrated, when at the last Governing Body Meeting of Trinity Term 1991, she announced her engagement to be married. It transpired that in the course of the year's meetings of heads of house she had struck up a more than neighbourly acquaintance with the acting Warden of Green College, Dr Trevor Hughes. The announcement provoked a minor constitutional crisis, for the college statutes—never before invoked in this respect—required the Principal to resign her office on marriage. But close study of the small print revealed provisions for re-election; and after a wedding in the college chapel and a fortnight when Somerville was technically without a head, she resumed office in Michaelmas Term as Mrs Hughes. Within a few months it was to fall to her to break a piece of news which many found much less palatable.

The first two years of her principalship had been remarkable ones for Somerville. The Dorothy Hodgkin quadrangle came into use in the course of 1990, and a party to celebrate it, and the associated Margaret Thatcher conference centre, was held in the presence of both honorands on what proved to be one of the few fine days of the following Trinity Term. In the 1990 New Year's honours list Daphne Park was raised to the peerage as Baroness Park of Monmouth. In March that year Joanna Innes took office as senior proctor (Plate 49) and, the last college to benefit from the extension in 1980 of the proctorial cycle, Somerville began to feel the advantages of a system which ensures that every college in turn has a representative at the heart of the university's administration. That spring, the Royal Society announced the election of two women Fellows, both of them—Louise

Johnson and Carole Jordan—fellows of Somerville. Of the three women promoted by the university at this time to *ad hominem* reader-ships, two—Louise Johnson and Barbara Harvey—were from Somer-ville. Louise Johnson's appointment in Trinity Term to the David Phillips Chair in Molecular Biophysics completed a notable hat-trick; the following year Somerville's English tutor, Heather O'Donoghue, was appointed Vigfusson Rausing Reader in Ancient Icelandic Litera-ture and Antiquities, following in the footsteps of her former super-visor, Ursula Dronke. Somerville's delight in these latter achievements was tempered by regret, for both appointments carried with them fellowships at other colleges: Louise Johnson was lost to Corpus, and Heather O'Donoghue to Linacre.

As they joined with the rest of college in celebrating these tri-umphs, the fellows were uneasily conscious of a time-bomb which threatened to shatter the *status quo*. A series of recent legal judgments, in cases affecting institutions outside Oxford, had cast doubt on the safety of existing procedures for associating university lecturer-ships with single-sex colleges. In Trinity Term 1990 Somerville and St Hilda's were invited to send representatives to a committee appointed by the university to look into the matter and take legal advice. The committee took over a year to report, but in the interim the college representatives confirmed that anxiety was focused on the legality of providing a back-up college to which a male appointee might be assigned. A system designed to protect the interests of the women's colleges was perceived as operating against the interests of women candidates, by denying them membership of the (generally, in ma-terial terms, more privileged) mixed colleges to which their male competitors were assigned. As women applicants for university posts began to query these arrangements, the mixed colleges, anxious about their legal position, and eager to recruit more women fellows on their own account, were becoming increasingly reluctant to provide the necessary back-up. Counsel now confirmed that a single-sex college which participated in such an arrangement, though itself protected by the law, might put both the university and the other college concerned at risk. In reaching this conclusion with regard to university lecturerships, counsel went on to raise the possibility—devastating in its implications—that the procedures for CUF appoint-ments in single-sex colleges might also be unsafe.

Governing Body received the committee's report at the beginning of Michaelmas Term 1991. The university, sympathetic to the plight of the women's colleges, scrupulously avoided bringing any pressure to bear on them, and, indeed, suggested various ways in which the legal difficulties might be circumvented. But there was no mistaking the underlying message. Somerville might be able to preserve its single-sex character in the short term if it was prepared to accept a status which would isolate it increasingly from the mainstream of university life. It was a price which very few fellows—even those most committed in principle to the idea of a women's college—thought it right to pay.

The college was given until January 1992 to consider its position. By the time that Governing Body met for this purpose early in November, St Hilda's had already declared its wish to remain single-sex. The Somerville meeting ended with an agreement to explore further the implications of change. This was done at a meeting in December at which, following college practice in questions of major importance, each fellow in turn was invited to speak, and to which, unusually, those fellows who were unable to be present were encouraged to send their views in writing. In a discussion in which almost every conceivable shade of opinion was expressed, the view most commonly voiced was that 'the college had a job to do which had not yet been done, but that circumstances had changed in such a way that it was no longer practical . . . to continue to restrict membership to women.'[1] Fellows also reaffirmed the view—which they had held consistently since discussions on the subject started in the early 1970s—that decisions of principle in relation to senior and junior members should not be separated. They were given the Christmas vacation for further reflection before a vote was taken in January.

Circumstances had determined that so far the main focus of Governing Body's concern had been with appointments at senior level. As the fellows now dispersed to the heaps of examination scripts which awaited them in their rooms, their attention was concentrated on the undergraduate aspects of the problem. The first fortnight of the Christmas vacation in Oxford is given over to interviewing candidates for undergraduate admission the following autumn. In Somerville this had been an increasingly demoralizing experience in recent years. The familiar pattern was now repeated: a declining number of first-choice applicants, the manifest disappointment of many of the candidates sent on for interview at Somerville by the colleges of

[1] GB, 4 Dec. 1991.

their first choice, and the downright refusal of some to consider the possibility of being assigned to a women's college. There were some notable exceptions to the trend—all the successful candidates in English had put Somerville as their first choice—but whereas in the past tutors had been able to take comfort from those candidates who expressed a positive enthusiasm for an all-women's college, this year they were only an added source of unease. So was the sight of the squad of undergraduate helpers, oblivious of the impending thunderbolt, enthusiastically extolling to candidates the merits of the single-sex option. But, overall, the 1991 admissions exercise did nothing to challenge the view that young women, by and large, rightly or wrongly, preferred their colleges mixed. Most fellows emerged from the experience convinced that if Somerville was to be more attractive to women, it must open its doors to men.

There was little doubt, when the college reassembled in the New Year of 1992, that the necessary mandate for change would be secured. On 22 January it was agreed by a large majority to amend the charter to allow the admission of men as junior and senior members, and the statutes to allow the admission of men to the fellowship. The decision set in train a complicated legal process. To take effect, it needed to be ratified by a two-thirds majority at a second meeting of Governing Body, called for 19 February. The change to the charter then required the approval of the Queen in Council; changes to the statutes had to be approved by the university, laid before parliament, and then submitted to the Privy Council. The eligibility of men as fellows would follow automatically on the change of statutes; the timing of undergraduate admissions could be decided, once the charter had been changed, by ordinary Governing Body decision.

The legal threat to the college's existing arrangements made it vital to proceed at fellowship level as quickly as possible. In the course of the past year university lecturerships in biochemistry, engineering, and physics had slipped through Somerville's fingers; the same fate was now feared for a new appointment in plant sciences for which the college was currently bidding. Replacements would soon have to be sought for Nancy Waugh, whose resignation through ill health the previous summer had left Somerville without a fellow in psychology, and for the politics tutor Niamh Hardiman, who had just announced her impending departure for a post in Dublin.

The timing of the admission of men at junior level was more problematic. As fellows considered the options available, it became clear that there was no 'good' time. The sooner the change was made, the harder it would bear on the current generation of undergraduates. To defer the change until after they had left would protract—many thought, intolerably—the college's current difficulties. If Somerville was finding it hard to attract candidates to an all-women's college, it was not likely to enhance its appeal by announcing that it would go mixed in four years' time. Since the transitional period was bound to be painful, there was much to be said for making it brief. There was also a strong argument, if the college was—as it earnestly wished —to continue to promote the interests of women at junior level, for the transition to mixed status being managed by a substantially female Governing Body. After much heart-searching, the fellows eventually came down in favour of proceeding, if no insuperable obstacles presented themselves, to the admission of male junior members at the earliest possible opportunity—in 1992 for 1993.

Having taken its decision, the Governing Body now had to make it public. And here it was faced with a very great difficulty. The reopening of the question in the first place had not been of the college's own seeking. The secrecy with which discussions had been conducted, and the timetable within which they had been compressed, had not been of the college's own choice. The university continued to enjoin the strictest confidentiality with regard to the contents of the report which had sparked off the crisis. In announcing a highly controversial decision, Somerville was debarred from revealing what, for the majority of fellows, had been the clinching argument.

Governing Body had undertaken to convey its decision to Council by Monday 3 February. It clearly could not make a public announcement before this date, and would be unable to maintain confidentiality for long afterwards. A press release was scheduled for Tuesday 4 February. In the preceding week the Principal and fellows set about informing, in confidence, all those who needed to be notified in advance: the Visitor, honorary and emeritus fellows, the Presidents of the ASM and of the Appeal, junior research fellows, the Bursar, the College Secretary. A batch of letters to members of the ASM and Appeal Committees and other interested individuals was timed to arrive by first post on the Tuesday morning. All current members of the college were to be informed, in person or by letter, by the Monday evening.

The most difficult decision was how, and when, to break the news to current junior members. After consultation with the JCR President and the MCR Secretary (deputizing for the President who was away from Oxford at the time), it was agreed that a meeting in hall, to be addressed by the Principal, should be called for the evening of Monday 3 February. But, in the event, the press struck first. In stipulating an embargo on publication until the Tuesday, Governing Body had (naïvely, as Lord Jenkins later said) neglected to take into account the journalists' desire for 'comment'. The reporters moved in on Monday afternoon to prepare their story for the next day. It was a miscalculation which the undergraduates were not likely to forgive, and at 7 p.m. they assembled in large numbers to make their views clear.

The Principal was accompanied to the meeting by the senior fellow, Barbara Harvey. The impression that they were the initiators of change, and not simply spokesmen of Governing Body, was to prove almost ineradicable in the weeks ahead.

Governing Body had not expected the news to be welcome to junior members—hardly any Oxford or Cambridge college had changed, in either direction, without JCR opposition—but it had seriously underestimated both the strength of their feelings, and their sense of betrayal. And it had underestimated still more their capacity to mobilize public opinion. Within hours of the angry confrontation in Hall the college was plastered with red and black notices proclaiming that 'Somervillians say NO!' Within days the notices were sprouting throughout Oxford. Undergraduates were indefatigable in arguing their case within college and in soliciting support for it outside. Reporters and television crews converged on Somerville from Italy, India, Japan. Distinguished old members were canvassed for their views, or proffered them, unsolicited, in the correspondence pages of the press.[2] Letters protesting at the college's decision began to pour in from students' unions, parents, teachers, MPs. The JCR and the women's group of almost every college in Oxford wrote—in terms of greater or less incivility—to express anger and disgust at the proposed change. The Oxford Union voted by 512 votes to 109 to keep men out of Somerville. Fellows of colleges whose rejection in 1979 of a policy of orderly transition lay at the root of many of Somerville's current difficulties upbraided it now for failure to hold the line. Particularly galling were the letters—of which there were many—from old Somervillians who prefaced their rebuke with a sentence to the

---

[2] Shirley Williams, an honorary fellow, wrote to the *Independent* urging the Governing Body to think again.

effect that their own daughters had, unaccountably, been unmoveable in their determination to apply to a mixed college. The correspondence about admitting men soon began to rival the proportions of the 1932 correspondence about building a chapel, and the arguments used were strikingly similar: Somerville had betrayed the spirit of its founders, and its Governing Body had exercised a tyrannical abuse of power. The message was clear: there was overwhelming support for the view that Somerville should remain single-sex for other people, or other people's daughters, to go to.

Though in general the college's old members were not pleased, a number of them now rallied to the Governing Body's defence. Several nonagenarians expressed enthusiasm for the change, and Esther Rantzen in a press interview said she thought it a good thing that men should be given the opportunity to go to Somerville. Daphne Park, whose loyal advocacy of the merits of a single-sex college during her time as Principal had convinced many that this represented her own deepest convictions, now came into the open and revealed—what the fellows had known all along—that her strong personal preference had always been for change. Dame Janet Vaughan said she was only sorry that Somerville had not admitted men years ago. Barbara Craig had made it clear twelve years before that 'if and when the Fellows sense that the best way forward for Somerville would be to admit men, men will certainly be admitted.'[3]

There were two focuses to the protest: the decision itself, and the manner in which it had been made. Many junior members who did not feel strongly about the admission of men, or even favoured it, were outraged at the failure to consult those whom the decision most nearly concerned—a point made forcefully at Governing Body by the President of the MCR, herself a strong advocate of change. The haste and secrecy of Governing Body's present proceedings were contrasted with the period of consultation and debate which had preceded the 1986 vote. Hopes were pinned on the decision being overturned at the meeting on 19 February.

That the fellows had not consulted the college's junior members was undeniable. There was, on the other hand, no argument in favour of an all-women's college with which they were not already thoroughly familiar: they had been hearing (and, indeed, using) them for over twenty years. The desirability of Somerville remaining a

---

[3] BDC, 'Reflections in Retirement', *ASM Report*, 1980.

women's college, and its effectiveness as such in promoting the interests of women, were subjects on which there had always been a wide range of views on the Governing Body; and fellows listened now with varying degrees of sympathy to the case made for maintaining the status quo. But it was at senior level that the arguments in the past had always seemed most persuasive, for it was here that the under-representation of women in the university was most marked; and at this level, they were convinced, the battle had already been lost.

Since the co-residence debate had opened in the early 1970s the Governing Body had been clear that the college should move as a whole, or not at all. The solution adopted for some years by St Hugh's, of maintaining a single-sex undergraduate body while opening the fellowship to men, it had consistently rejected in the belief that it was both condescending to women and constitutionally retrograde. It soon became clear that this was not the view of the current generation of junior members, who—unlike their predecessors in 1986—attached little importance to what happened at senior level; indeed many of them assumed, because of the number of male lecturers around the place, that the Governing Body was mixed already. Their concern was almost exclusively to maintain their own single-sex identity. On this point of principle there was little chance of the two parties reaching understanding, let alone agreement. After four weeks of meetings, memorials, and demonstrations—many of them conducted in a blaze of media publicity—the Governing Body met again on 19 February and ratified its earlier decision (see Plate 50).

At this point, most undergraduate bodies, however disaffected, would have given up the fight. Not so the Somerville JCR, which, in a dramatic development, appealed to the college's Visitor, Lord Jenkins of Hillhead, to intervene in his capacity as internal judge of disputes within the college community. Supported by the financial and legal resources of the National Union of Students, they contended that the Governing Body's decision was in breach of the objects of the college charter, and that its manner of proceeding had constituted both a procedural breach of the charter and a breach of natural justice. On 25 March a preliminary meeting was held with Lord Wilberforce, deputed by the Visitor to hear oral representations from both parties to the dispute. On 11 May, after the submission of written evidence on both sides, Lord Jenkins, assisted by the Hon. Sir Henry Fisher, presided at a hearing in the University Offices. Both parties were represented by counsel, and the hearing was attended by the Principal and five fellows, and by six junior members. The corridor outside was packed with a large number of witnesses on behalf of the latter, ready to enlarge on the written evidence which they had already submitted.

An account of the hearing was given in the Visitor's ruling, released to the Governing Body on 2 June, and published two days later. Lord Jenkins described as 'spirited rather than convincing' the petitioners' contention that the action of the Governing Body was illegal, and that the university and the Privy Council would be acting illegally in pursuing it. He acknowledged the 'dedicated, careful, and even agonized consideration' which the Governing Body had given to the issue, and expressed himself satisfied that it had acted 'responsibly as well as legally' in seeking to add to the charter and amend the statutes of the college. With the manner of the Governing Body's proceedings he was less satisfied. Though conceding the need for confidentiality and the desirability of speed, he questioned the wisdom of trying to take the matter quite so much 'on the run'; and he gave it as his view that the undergraduates did indeed have a moral, if not a legal, right to consultation. In expressing the view that the Governing Body had been 'too unselfish in the weight they gave to shielding the university and the other women's college from any possible embarrassment as opposed to their own need to be able to present the case for change to their undergraduates in as frank, persuasive and timely a way as possible' he was, presumably, wearing his Visitor's rather than his Chancellor's hat. The outcome of his deliberations was to urge the Governing Body to delay the admission of men as junior members for at least a year—preferably two—and to use this time to try to come to a better understanding with the undergraduate body. For their part, he urged the petitioners to desist from further legal action. The purpose of the college, he concluded, was 'to be an educational institution of the highest repute, and not a breeding ground for litigation.'

The Governing Body had signified in advance its readiness to abide by the Visitor's ruling; it now duly rescinded the decision to admit male undergraduates in 1992 for 1993, and agreed to resume discussions with the JCR in an attempt to reach a common position. Some of the undergraduates were still convinced, however, that they had a sound legal case for stopping the proposed changes, and, with the support of the NUS, a group of them sought leave to apply for action in the High Court. Many even of the junior members who were opposed to change regarded this as going too far. As Trinity Term progressed a party opposed to litigation gained increasing support in both JCR and MCR, and on the last day of term a hastily organized petition against continued legal action attracted forty-seven signatures. In the face of this evidence of division within the college, NUS funding was withdrawn. Many of the undergraduates involved in the legal process also withdrew; but some had already departed on vacation and some finalists had gone down for good. When the Principal gave her annual report to the ASM at the gaudy in July the legal position was still unclear. In the event, the junior members did not pursue their application for judicial review; but not all the individuals involved had withdrawn from the suit when the matter went to court on 1 September. The case was dismissed, and costs were awarded to the college.

In the course of the long vacation the changes to the charter were approved by the Queen in Council; the changes to the statutes were still pursuing their more ponderous course from university to parliament to privy council. The legal formalities had not yet been completed when the university lecturership in plant sciences was advertised with Somerville as the associated college; St Hugh's came to the rescue by offering, in the event of a man being appointed, to provide a temporary fellowship until such time as Somerville's statutes were changed. In an equally generous gesture, Lady Margaret Hall, Somerville's back-up college for the recently filled chair of general linguistics, offered—provided his consent could be obtained—to surrender its claim to the new appointee, Professor James Higginbotham, who would not actually be taking up his post until the following year.

In Michaelmas Term the consultative process with junior members about the timing of male undergraduate admissions was resumed. In 7th week there was a 67 per cent turn-out for a JCR referendum in which forty-five undergraduates voted in favour of going mixed in 1993 for 1994, twenty-five for the following year, and 138 for no change in the foreseeable future; there were fifteen abstentions and one spoilt vote. By now the JCR had come to acknowledge that the problem of admissions was a real one, and in Hilary Term support crystallized around a proposal that Somerville should employ a salaried schools liaison officer—on the model of one recently employed by Christ Church to attract candidates from state schools—who would devote herself full-time to the recruitment of women applicants. The experiment, it was argued, should be tried for an agreed period—say three years: if applications improved in consequence, Somerville's problem would be solved; if they did not, the JCR would acknowledge defeat and concede the necessity of admitting men. The Governing Body, conscious of the vigorous efforts at recruitment made after the 1986 vote, remained unpersuaded that the JCR in 1996 would prove more amenable to change than their predecessors in 1993. In March, at the request of the Visitor, a questionnaire was distributed to the 135 undergraduates who were expected still to be in residence in Michaelmas Term 1994, asking whether, in the event of men being admitted in the near future, they would favour 1993 for 1994, or 1994 for 1995. Of the sixty-six replies, forty-three were in favour of the earlier date. In the light of this response, the Visitor indicated that he was not disposed to resist a Governing Body decision. Another vote was taken, and the fellows agreed by an overwhelming majority to invite applications from men in 1993 for admission in 1994. From the beginning of the debate in Michaelmas Term 1991 until now there had never been more than four fellows (out of a total fluctuating between twenty-one and twenty-five) in favour of maintaining the single-sex option; at the final vote there were only two dissenting voices.

When giving evidence to the Franks Commission in 1964, Dame Janet Vaughan had been asked if she thought there were any sex-linked barriers persisting in Oxford; and she had, famously, replied 'I would have said none in Oxford. . . . I would have thought that none existed really, unless people imagine them.'[4] Thirty years later such a view would command little support. In opting to open Somerville to men, the Governing Body was under no illusion that in Oxford at large the battle for equality had been won. Neither the university as a body nor its constituent mixed colleges had much grounds for complacency at the way in which 'co-residence' had been managed during the past twenty years. If the overall number of women undergraduates had risen sharply, the proportion of them who read science subjects had worryingly diminished. In many colleges women junior members were still in a small minority; and in some, rumour had it, they were a harrassed minority. The under-performance of women in Schools—even in subjects such as English and modern languages, where they were traditionally strongest—was giving grave cause for concern.[5] So was their manifest under-representation at senior level— some colleges, nearly twenty years after going mixed, had yet to

[4] Franks Commission evidence, 19 Nov. 1964.
[5] Seminar Paper given by G. McCrum, 26 Nov. 1993.

acquire a woman fellow, and science departments were still, on the whole, overwhelmingly male.

St Hilda's and Somerville had played a crucial role in maintaining a female presence in the university at this period. Between them, they accounted for some 38 per cent of the women appointed to CUF posts in the ten years up to 1992; in 1992 itself they accounted for 20 per cent of the women undergraduates reading mathematics and science. But their effectiveness in these regards was being eroded by legal constraints and by preoccupation with their own institutional problems. Their very immunity from many of the pressures to which women in the university at large were subject tended to cut them off from the important initiatives now coming from the mixed colleges, and from the concerns of such campaigning bodies as the Women Tutors' Group. A large part of the Governing Body's motivation for change was to join the battle on behalf of women where the action was now perceived as being keenest.

Events quickly showed that the Governing Body's fears had been well-founded. In Michaelmas Term 1993 the legal complications which Somerville had been unable to make public were spelled out by the Principal of St Hilda's in an article in the *Oxford Magazine* entitled 'Does Oxford want a women's college?'[6] To satisfy the requirements of the law, university posts associated with St Hilda's were now advertised with the proviso that a woman, if appointed, would be able to choose between a fellowship at St Hilda's and one at the mixed back-up college. A succession of women appointees opting for the latter course had made the point that, in this respect at least, the interests of a women's college might actually be in conflict with the interests of women as individuals. This is not a happy position for an institution dedicated to the promotion of women's interests to find itself in; in practical terms it reduces to less than one in four the chances of securing an appointment in any given instance.

But Somerville's decision had not been prompted by purely negative considerations. In voting for change, the Governing Body had some grounds for believing that it was in fact a good time to do so— that in the university at large the tide, which had for so long been set against the interests of women, was at last on the turn. The vice-chancellor's reference, in his 1992 Oration, to 'the challenge of Somer-

⁶ E. Llewellyn Smith, 'Does Oxford want a Women's College?', *Oxford Magazine*, 97 (1993).

ville' was an indication of the decision's wider implications. It is too soon to say whether the Governing Body's optimism was justified, but the early signs are hopeful. The last university appointment with which Somerville secured association as a single-sex college, and the first with which it was associated after having gone mixed, both went to women scientists: Angela Vincent and Sarah Gurr. In the week that James Logue was elected to a fellowship in philosophy at Somerville, similar appointments at Balliol and Pembroke went to women—in the case of Pembroke to a Somervillian, Martha Klein. In 1992 St John's became the first of the former men's colleges to elect a woman as proctor, for the year 1993/4. The following year Christ Church followed suit and, with a Somervillian, Anita Avramides, representing St Hilda's, for the first time both proctors were women. Inroads were even beginning to be made on the science professoriate, with the election of Susan Iverson to the chair of Psychology, and of Kay Davies—a Somervillian—to the chair of Genetics. Most significantly of all, perhaps, in October 1993 three of the former men's colleges announced the election of women heads of house: Marilyn Butler at Exeter, Jessica Rawson at Merton, and Averil Cameron—a Somervillian—at Keble.

Postscript: The Somerville Tradition

IT is as a college for women that Somerville's character has been decisively formed, its history inextricably bound up with the broader history of women in Oxford. But the fact that it was founded by a splinter group was a portent of things to come: on many subsequent occasions it has adopted a line of its own, and it has tended to count this for virtue. Somerville was the first of the women's societies to see itself as a college rather than merely as a hall of residence. Under Miss Maitland it was the most active in campaigning for the admission of women to degrees, and under Miss Penrose the most insistent that women should seek membership of the university on terms of equality with men. This pioneering energy accounted in part for the sense, which developed very early on, of Somerville being different from the other women's societies—more ambitious, more awkward, decidedly less ladylike. Its students, from an equally early stage, acquired the reputation of being 'difficult'.

The college's distinctiveness has never been simply one of gender. Somerville's non-denominational status distanced it at the outset from a university establishment which remained, for many years after the abolition of religious tests in 1871, overwhelmingly Anglican and clerical. Other distinguishing characteristics were soon developed: a concern for academic excellence, a commitment to science, a reputation for political involvement, an almost Balliolesque tradition of public service at home and abroad. Somerville's strong sense of identity has been fostered and perpetuated by a long line of writers: uniquely among the colleges of Oxford and Cambridge, it has been credited with a 'school of novelists'.

The founders of Somerville were not alone in seeking to promote the higher education of women in Oxford. What distinguished them was their determination to make this education independent of religious affiliation. The principle of non-denominationalism which was Somerville's *raison-d'être* has fashioned—directly or indirectly—much of the College's subsequent development. It enabled Somerville from the start to tap sources of funding and support which were denied to the Anglican foundations: Miss Wordsworth, looking back in 1912 on the early history of LMH, concluded that that Hall's churchmanship 'cost us the favour of many city companies, and deprived us of a good many scholarships, legacies, etc, which we otherwise should have had.'[1] When the Cassel Trustees made a grant to Somerville in the 1920s they first sought an assurance that the college's non-denominational status would be maintained. Over the years some small sacrifices have been made in return: in the 1950s and 1960s the Governing Body carried scrupulousness to the lengths of twice refusing association with a university scholarship restricted to the children of Anglican clergymen.

It was perhaps inevitable that a non-denominational college should acquire the reputation of being 'godless'; and it is a reputation which many Somervillians cherish. But—though a natural home for the agnostic and the freethinker—Somerville has never been an irreligious college. In 1879 proposals for a purely secular constitution were rejected in favour of one which would hold all denominations in equal respect; the college statutes declare it to be a place of 'religion, learning and education'. Prayers were read daily in college from its foundation until the undergraduate congregation dwindled to vanishing point in Hilary Term 1969. Somerville's first President went on to become a bishop; a succession of distinguished Anglican clergy and Nonconformist ministers served on its Council. A survey of the later careers of Oxford women students has shown that those most likely to go on to religious work of some kind were the daughters of Nonconformist ministers—a group which was heavily concentrated in Somerville.[2] The college has fostered a strong missionary tradition; and in Edith Coombs, who gave her life in the Boxer Rising of 1900 while rescuing children from her burning mission school at Tai Yuan Fu, it can, indeed, claim the rare distinction of a martyr. The tally of Somervillian nuns includes the abbess of a Russian Orthodox convent in France, Sonia Hambourg. In 1917 a Somervillian, Constance Coltman (Todd, 1908), was the first woman to be ordained to the Congregationalist ministry. When in 1994 the Church of England admitted women to

[1] E. Wordsworth, *Glimpses of the Past* (London, 1913), 169.
[2] J. Howarth and M. Curthoys, 'The Political Economy of Women's Higher Education in Late Nineteenth and Early Twentieth Century Britain', *Historical Research*, 60 (1987), 208–31, table 3.

the priesthood, Somervillians were, predictably, among the first to present themselves for ordination.[3]

But the college from the start had a special attraction for students from outside the Anglican establishment. At the turn of the century, when Nonconformists were thin on the ground in the university at large, they accounted for roughly one-third of the students at Somerville.[4] Quaker and Unitarian influences on the college were strong from the outset; Jewish influences were later to become so. At the opening of the second phase of the West building in 1894, Lord Herschell praised Somerville's policy of receiving students of all faiths, which, he said, 'gave opportunities to each and all for learning that tolerant sympathy and wide charity which were among the most precious possessions of life'.[5] Emily Kemp's gift to the college in 1932 of a chapel which might be a 'House of Prayer for All Peoples', prompted as it was by long practical familiarity with Buddhism and the other religions of the East,[6] was hardly incompatible with the founders' objectives. But, despite its unconsecrated and ecumenical status, the chapel has always been a focus of controversy in college; to this day, no subject is more calculated to guarantee an uncomfortable Governing Body meeting or to provoke dissension among old members.

If the college has always regarded its students' religious beliefs (or lack of them) as their own affair, it has concerned itself very closely with their academic development. Somerville established a scholarly reputation early on, demanding high standards of its students, assembling a fine library and a formidable teaching staff, encouraging research, and, in the fullness of time, exporting academics in large numbers to universities and colleges throughout the world. A recent historian of women in higher education has described Somerville in the 1880s and 1890s as 'a seminary of Wardens'.[7] It has continued to be a seminary of principals and scholars. In the university at large it soon became known as the bluestocking college. 'What does he read?' was said to be the characteristic Somervillian response to news of a friend's new boyfriend—while at LMH they asked 'Who is his father?', at St Hugh's 'What is his sport?', and at St Hilda's 'Where is he?'[8] The

---

[3] Vera Sinton (1962) was among the first group of women to be ordained in Oxford cathedral, Jane Maycock (1986) in St Paul's, and Elizabeth Pearce (Earl, 1969) in Chester.

[4] College Register.   [5] *Fritillary*, 3, Dec. 1894.

[6] In 1910 she translated *Buddhism as a Religion* from the German.

[7] Carol Dyhouse in conversation with the author, 1994.

[8] D. Balsdon, *Oxford Life* (London, 1957), 192.

policy of Cheltenham Ladies' College when placing its pupils, according to the historian of its sister-foundation, St Hilda's, was to direct the more social of them to LMH and the cleverer ones to Somerville.[9] (A leading old Somervillian headmistress, on the other hand, claims always to have reserved the 'more bolshie' of her pupils for her own old college.) The bluestocking stereotype persisted long after it had ceased to bear much relation to the facts. In the 1980s, when, with the spread of co-education, Somerville was beginning to find difficulty in filling its undergraduate places, it was still plagued by the legend that it was the most difficult Oxford college to get into.

For the greater part of its history, this had indeed been the case. It took the young Janet Vaughan three attempts to get into Somerville in 1919, despite the fact that she was a great-niece of the Vice-President of the college Council, Mrs Green, and god-daughter of a former President, H. A. L. Fisher. Between the wars, when the number of male applicants to Oxford almost exactly equalled the number of places available,[10] Somerville had anything up to eight applicants for every place. A strong meritocratic tradition perhaps helps explain why social divisions have tended to be less marked than at some other colleges.[11] When assembling her first intake of students in 1879 Miss Shaw Lefevre expressed the hope that she would have 'some ladies as well as the professional class.'[12] But even in her day, the socialite who was not academically up to the course was seen by the other students as an object of pity. Frances Sheldon, writing home in 1880, described one girl 'of an entirely different stamp from the rest.':

> She has only been at boarding schools and learned the harp and singing and those things. She has seen a great deal of society . . . been hunting ever so much, played tennis an incredible amount and had a frivolous time generally. . . . Everyone seems to have taken her right in hand to help her get along well. They are continually taking her to their rooms to coach her, and taking pains to escort her everywhere she has to go.[13]

---

[9] M. E. Rayner, *The Centenary History of St Hilda's College, Oxford* (Oxford, 1993), 110.

[10] *HUO* viii, 91.

[11] See Janet Morgan (St Hilda's, 1951–5), quoted in Rayner, *The Centenary History of St Hilda's College*: 'The grammar school girls and the Cheltenham ladies hardly mixed at all socially. There was no hostility, just two quite separate social worlds which very few individuals crossed. I think St Hilda's differed from the other women's colleges in that respect.'

[12] F. M. G. Willson, *A Strong Supporting Cast: The Shaw Lefevres 1879–1936* (London, 1993), 304.   [13] Sheldon, Oct. 1880.

In the event, women at Oxford were to be drawn overwhelmingly from the professional, commercial, and industrial middle classes. There were minor variations between colleges: in its early days Somerville admitted fewer clergy daughters, and more daughters of businessmen than did LMH or St Hugh's.[14] And within the college group there were perceptible differences of wealth, social background, and education. In 1936 Jenifer Wayne noted the arrival at Somerville of a contingent from Downe House, who all got off the same train from Paddington, and 'gave the impression that coming to Oxford was the most natural thing in the world. . . . Oxford was simply a place to be taken in their expensively tweedy stride.'[15] But the boarding-school element has never predominated at Somerville, which had no special relationship of the kind which kept St Hilda's supplied with a steady core of Cheltonians. Jenifer Wayne's own school, Blackheath High School, was rather more representative than Downe House of Somerville's natural constituency. It is from the great London day schools, the foundations of the Girls' Public Day School Trust, and from the (once direct-grant) provincial grammar schools that Somerville has traditionally drawn the bulk of its students; its recruiting efforts in recent years have increasingly been directed to the state sector. A northern element has been strong from the start: if any one school should be singled out for special mention, it is Bradford Girls' Grammar School, which sent its first two students to Somerville in 1880 and has maintained the tradition ever since.

In every generation there have been students sensitive to social distinctions of which others are seemingly oblivious. The culture-shock for the relatively small number of women who came to Somerville from working-class backgrounds was undoubtedly great. Margaret Hill (Haigh, 1937) has described her poignant journeys between two worlds—Somerville and the Lancashire mill-town where she grew up —'when I felt absolutely alone, with no-one to share, or understand, the dichotomy of language and culture that I suffered.'[16] Many students from independent schools, however, were in retrospect to lament their own immaturity, and to express envy of those who had a less sheltered experience of the world. The overwhelming evidence from old members is of life-long friendships formed at college across social and cultural divides. Somervillian snobbery has always tended to be

[14] D. I. Greenstein, 'The Junior Members, 1900–1990: A Profile' in *HUO* viii, 55.
[15] J. Wayne, *The Purple Dress: Growing up in the Thirties* (London, 1979), 38.
[16] M. Hill, 'A Lancashire Childhood', *ASM Report*, 1988.

intellectual rather than social. 'Somerville had the reputation of attracting the most intellectual women . . . while Lady Margaret Hall, like its name, was the most social,' wrote Caroline Seebohm in her novel *The Last Romantics*:

> St Hilda's, St Anne's, and St Hugh's . . . were shrouded in spinster-like anonymity. How we loved to exploit these artificial hierarchies, strutting in our class superiority . . . 'What college', one would be asked. 'Somerville', we would drawl, watching arrogantly for that twitch of suppressed surprise, quickly followed by respectful recognition, that would cross our interlocutor's face.[17]

But even when its academic reputation was at its height, Somerville has been wary of taking examination results as a prime measure of success in life. 'At the moment' said Janet Vaughan to the Franks Commissioners in 1964 'we have a rather high proportion of Firsts and Seconds, which is rather nice for us, but some Third-Class people have been known to do extremely well in the world'—and she instanced the case of her own undergraduate contemporary, Cicely Williams, who launched a distinguished international career as a paediatrician with a third in physiology.[18]

In a university long dominated by the humanities, and where the sciences have too often been regarded as a male preserve, Somerville has taken pride in the fact that it was named after a woman scientist, that it could count a Nobel prizewinner for chemistry among its alumnae-fellows, and that for twenty-two crucial years after the Second World War it had a distinguished scientist as Principal. Both Dorothy Hodgkin and Janet Vaughan were notable in their day for encouraging women to undertake scientific research, and to pursue their scientific work—as they had themselves, and Mary Somerville had before them—in conjunction with family responsibilities. Somerville as an institution has done its utmost to further such efforts.[19] Scientists were prominent among the college's early supporters, their presence (or that of their wives) on the college Council helping to facilitate the acceptance of women students in the science lecture-rooms and laboratories of the university. In 1885 Somerville was the first of the women's halls to appoint a tutor in the sciences. It

[17] C. Seebohm, *The Last Romantics* (London, 1987), 42–3.
[18] Evidence to the Franks Commission, 19 Nov. 1964.
[19] See D. Hodgkin, 'Crystallography and Chemistry in the First Hundred Years of Somerville College'.

later used its research fellowships to support the work of scientists like the physicist Florence Isaac (Somerville Research Fellow 1906–9) and the crystallographer Polly Porter (Lady Carlisle Fellow 1919–29). In recent years the college has funded out of its own limited resources three tutorial fellowships in the sciences; the desire to safeguard its ability to maintain a full range of science teaching played a large part in the decision to open the Governing Body to men.

'Which party?' was Janet Vaughan's immediate response to an undergraduate who sought permission to spend time out of Oxford to help with her mother's election campaign.[20] Although to the Principal's mind the answer in this case was the wrong one, permission was readily given. From the outset, Somerville was the most politically orientated of the women's colleges. Its founders, its first Principals, and many of its early supporters and benefactors were convinced and active Liberals. Though the predominating allegiance has varied over the years, the involvement in politics has persisted. The most popular college society of an unenfranchised generation was—significantly— the Somerville Parliament. The vote once won, Somerville has proved a fertile international breeding-ground of politicians. Five members of the college have gone on to serve as MPs at Westminster, three of them subsequently being created Life Peers.[21] The rise to prime ministerial office of the only Conservative among them may be seen as both the culmination and the contradiction of Somerville's long political tradition.

The tradition has not been confined to British politics. Indira Gandhi (Plate 44) was a student at Somerville from 1937 to 1938, her undergraduate career cut short by homesickness and ill-health; Mrs Radhabai Subbarayan, the first woman member of the Indian Central Legislative Assembly, studied briefly at the college before the Great War. Edith Stuart, the first woman Senatorial candidate in South Africa, and Margaret Ballinger, first National Chairman of the South African Liberal Party, were both Somerville historians. Virginia Tsouderos, whose political career in her native Greece was to include four-and-a-half months' imprisonment in solitary confinement under the Colonels, read PPE from 1942 to 1944, and remained convinced fifty years later that Modern Greats provided the best possible preparation for public life.[22]

---

[20] P. Adams (ed.), *Janet Maria Vaughan 1899–1993: A Memorial Tribute* (Oxford, 1994), 5.

[21] Eirene White, Margaret Thatcher, and Shirley Williams. Somerville's other two Life Peers—Daphne Park and Margaret Jay (Callaghan, 1958)—reached the Lords by other routes.   [22] Conversation in Somerville, MT 1993.

This international perspective, which was by no means the norm in Oxford,[23] characterized Somerville from the start. The college admitted its first North American student in 1880 and its first from India in 1889. Links with both continents have remained strong. The expansion of the Middle Common Room from the 1950s onwards, the opening to women of Rhodes scholarships and visiting fellowships, and the development in the 1980s of the Registered Visiting Students scheme, have maintained the flow of students from overseas, to the college's great enrichment. One of the most potent arguments used in favour of Somerville remaining an all-women college was its ability to attract students from those cultures which insist on the educational segregation of the sexes.

The fund established in 1985 in memory of Indira Gandhi is devoted both to enabling Indian students to study at Somerville, and to enabling Somerville students to visit India. The college's overseas links have always been a two-way affair. Somervillian enthusiasm for travel has produced some notable explorers and anthropologists: Emily Kemp (1881), author of *The Face of Manchuria, Korea and Russian Turkestan* (1911) *Wanderings in Chinese Turkestan* (1912), and *Chinese Mettle*, which in 1921 won for her the medal of the French Geographical Society; Katharine Routledge (Pease, 1891), the only woman on a three-year expedition to Easter Island in 1913–16;[24] Marya Czaplicka (1911), who explored Siberia as Mary Ewart Travelling Scholar in 1914 with two women companions;[25] Beatrice Blackwood (1908), winner in 1943 of the Rivers Memorial Medal of the Royal Anthropological Institute, who, when engaged in fieldwork in North America and Melanesia prided herself on the fact that her tiny stature enabled her to be sent first into caves with small entrances 'to make sure that it would be all right for the men to follow'.[26] A much larger number of Somervillians have made their home abroad, involving themselves as missionaries, teachers, doctors, economists and engineers, in the life of their adopted country. Joan Wicken (1951), who used her tenure of the Alice Horsman travelling fellowship in 1956 to travel round Africa by bus, has spent most of her working life as Personal Assistant to

[23] See *HUO* viii, 97.

[24] Mrs S. Routledge, *The Mystery of Easter Island: The Story of an Expedition* (London, 1919).

[25] M. A. Czaplicka, *My Siberian Year* (London, [1916]). A Fund in her memory was established in 1971 by bequest of her fellow anthropologist Barbara Aitken (née Freire-Marreco, Mary Somerville Research Fellow 1909–13) to assist scientists to attend conferences abroad.

[26] Notes by Janet Vaughan on Somervillians working abroad.

President Nyerere of Tanzania. If Cicely Williams's (1917) unorthodox approach to paediatrics (and to the medical establishment) cost her the recognition in Britain that her work deserved, she was venerated in the developing countries to which she devoted most of her long career, and by her fellow-inmates in the Japanese prison camps where she was confined for much of the Second World War. She spoke little of the latter experience, except to give one piece of advice: 'Remember if you have to be imprisoned get in with a Sikh, he will have a comb in his turban.'[27] This, unfortunately, was not an option for a later Somervillian doctor, Sheila Cassidy (1958), whose imprisonment and torture in Chile in 1975 for treating a wounded left-wing revolutionary did much to bring home to the British public the harsher realities of South American politics, or for Hannah Stanton (1954), who in 1960 shared a cell in Praetoria Central Gaol with the ANC's Helen Joseph and discovered her to be a fellow enthusiast for Jane Austen.[28]

In 1888 the Revd Thomas Lacey sent Gladstone a copy of *Caswell*, an anonymous two-volume novel of religion and seduction in provincial England, with the comment: 'It is not a *pleasant* book, . . . it is an open secret that it was written by one of the ladies of Somerville Hall.'[29] (The authoress was in fact his own sister, Mary Rebecca Lacey, who had entered Somerville as a mature student the previous year.) In the 1920s the popular press identified as the 'Somerville School of Novelists' a group of writers who had been roughly contemporary as students during and just after the Great War: Dorothy L. Sayers, Vera Brittain, Winifred Holtby, Margaret Kennedy, Sylvia Thompson, Doreen Wallace, Hilda Reid. The college's literary tradition stretches back to its first secretary, Mrs Humphry Ward, forward to Iris Murdoch, Christine Brooke-Rose, Maggie Gee, Michèle Roberts. When June Barraclough, at interview for a place to read modern languages, confessed that what she really wanted to do with her life was to write novels, Enid Starkie's immediate rejoinder was 'Well, you've come to the right place.'[30] At the last count over seventy Somervillian novelists and poets were represented in the college library. Many of them have explored in their works the theme of the educated woman; and some, in doing so, have drawn explicitly on their own under-

[27] Vaughan, 'Jogging Along'.
[28] H. Stanton, *Go Well, Stay Well: South Africa August 1956 to May 1960* (London, 1961), 207.
[29] Revd T. A. Lacey to W. E. Gladstone, May 1888 (British Library Add MS 44503, f. 266).
[30] J. Richardson, *Enid Starkie* (London, 1973), 35–6.

graduate recollections. Somerville itself appears thinly disguised as 'Drayton College' in Vera Brittain's *The Dark Tide* (1923) and as 'Springfield' in Christine Longford's *Making Conversation* (1931); undisguised (even to the plumbing in Penrose) in Caroline Seebohm's *The Last Romantics* (1987); most famously, perhaps, as the 'Shrewsbury College' of Dorothy L. Sayers's *Gaudy Night* (1935). The latter work, thought by many at the time to be uncomfortably near the bone, has always provoked mixed reactions in Somerville. Winifred Holtby is cited with greater satisfaction. Somervillians, she wrote, comparing them in 1929 with the students of the other women's colleges,

> are a little more intractable, convivial, apt to scatter their energies over external activities; they are certainly inclined to look more untidy and incongruous, to experiment with clothes and cosmetics; to embrace curious creeds and odd political allegiances, and to make unorthodox but distinguished careers for themselves.[31]

If it is on the record of its former students that a college's reputation largely depends, Somerville's alumnae have served it well. In the early days they both helped dispel the Victorian assumption that a college education would disqualify young women for family life, and demonstrated—despite the limited opportunities available to them—that women, suitably trained, were capable of holding down a career. At a time when there were few professional openings for women outside teaching, and few greater social needs than the provision of decent education for girls, Somerville—like all the women's colleges—produced schoolmistresses in huge numbers. Of the 2,726 students who passed through the college between 1879 and 1950 almost exactly one-third (912) are recorded in the college Register as having spent at least part of their career in teaching of some kind.[32] Outside teaching, the college set an ideal of (often voluntary) public service which was to find its most prominent expression in Margery Fry's work for penal reform, Eleanor Rathbone's for the provision of family allowances, Cornelia Sorabji's for the legal status of women and children in her native India. But it was to lead many less well-known Somervillians into settlement work and medicine, the factory inspectorate and

---

[31] 'The Somerville Tradition' [by GREC], *Time and Tide*, 5 July 1929.

[32] The proportion of Somervillians who went into teaching rose from 37 per cent of those who entered college between 1879 and 1890 to 44 per cent of those who entered between 1900 and 1920, falling back to 22 per cent of the 1930–50 generation.

social work, succeeding generations reinterpreting for their own day the social concerns of their predecessors. Lettice Fisher (Ilbert, 1894) was chairman from 1918 to 1949 of the National Council for the Care of the Unmarried Mother and her Child; the director responsible for introducing the change of name to 'National Council for One-Parent Families'—with the extension of function that this implied—was another Somervillian, Margaret Bramall (Taylor, 1936). The biggest family-planning centre in the world, the Margaret Pyke Trust in Soho Square, was founded by one Somervillian, Lady Medawar (Jean Taylor, 1932), as a memorial to another, Margaret Chubb (1912).

As soon as it became possible to do so, Somervillians began to play a part in local government;[33] in 1920 seven former members of the college were included in the first list of women magistrates.[34] Many such unpaid activities were undertaken in conjunction with daunting domestic responsibilities. Looking back in 1993 over a life in which she had, *inter alia*, raised four children, served for 30 years as a member of the LCC and GLC, and chaired a Government Committee of Enquiry, Peggy Jay (Garnett, 1931) identified as her chief regret the fact that 'all the years of public work and responsibility resulted in no income.'[35] So long as a marriage-bar operated in the professions—in teaching until the Second World War, and in the diplomatic service until the 1960s—few women were able to contemplate the possibility of combining motherhood with a formal career. They were rarely the less busy for that. The Great War opened up unexpected employment opportunities, from pig-keeping to work for the Ministry of Munitions; in 1917 Somerville conducted a survey of the wartime occupations of its old members, which subsequently found a home in the Imperial War Museum as one of the most complete and detailed records of women's work for the period.[36] The momentum was maintained after the war. Among the earliest women entrants to the Administrative Class of the home civil service were two Somerville contemporaries, (Dame) Alix Kilroy and (Baroness) Evelyn Sharp. Three near-contemporaries—Mary Somerville (Mrs Brown), Grace Nisbet (Mrs Wyndham Goldie), and Joanna Gibbon (Mrs Spicer)—

[33] Article by Norah Chesterton (Reid, 1893), *SSA Report*, 1908.

[34] Mrs F. D. Acland (Cropper, 1897), Miss Faithfull, Miss Fry, Mrs C. E. Montague (Scott, 1896), Miss Penrose, Miss Rathbone, and Lady Rhondda. There were in all 169 women magistrates appointed for England, 21 for Wales, and 42 for Scotland.

[35] Year Report for 1931, *ASM Report*, 1993.

[36] *SSA Report*, Nov. 1917. For an analysis of the returns see M. St C. Byrne and C. H. Mansfield, *Somerville College 1879–1921* (Oxford, 1921), 46 ff.

joined the BBC, where they were to exercise a powerful influence over broadcasting policy in the years ahead. Later generations set their sights on politics, the diplomatic service, industry, finance, publishing, accountancy, law. In all these spheres, as in the traditional one of education, Somervillians have made notable—and in some cases, outstanding—contributions. They have also demonstrated that celibacy is no longer the necessary price of a successful career.

The conspicuous achievement of some of the college's alumnae has tended to engender a peculiarly Somervillian form of neurosis: that unless one has raised a family and become a Fellow of the Royal Society by the age of fifty—or, alternatively, been imprisoned by an unjust regime—one has somehow failed to live up to the college's expectations. But the most significant achievements are not necessarily the most conspicuous. Somerville has always prized individuality, and rejoiced in the more idiosyncratic life-choices of its old members. 'I think it is most sensible to do this after academic work' said Janet Vaughan to a former student who confessed apprehensively that she was now working in Oxford market as an apprentice florist.[37] Those Somervillians whom circumstances have obliged to adapt their careers to accommodate the raising of children, the support of partners, the care of the elderly and sick, are bringing a trained intelligence to bear on one of the thorniest social problems of the day: how women can best respond to the competing claims of their personal and professional lives. If the changing of traditional male attitudes is essential to a satisfactory outcome, Somervillians are in a strong position to contribute to the debate. In the 1890s Somerville helped fashion the 'New Woman'; a century later, with this experience behind it, the college has set itself the perhaps greater challenge of educating the 'New Man'.

---

[37] Adams (ed.), *Janet Maria Vaughan*, 24.

Bibliography

SOMERVILLE COLLEGE

MANUSCRIPTS

References not attributed to other sources are to the Somerville College archives. These include, in addition to the college's own administrative records, the following deposits:

Diary of Mary Ward, 1879.
Barnett MSS: Letters home from Charis Barnett, 1912–14.
Brodhurst MSS: Letters home from Audrey Brodhurst, 1931–5.*
Ilbert MSS: Letters home from Lettice Ilbert, 1894–7.
Mann MSS: Papers of Margaret Mann, 1924–8.
Sheldon MSS: Letters home from Frances Sheldon, 1880–3.*
Standen MSS: Diaries of Edith Standen, 1923–6.

*Transcripts

COLLEGE PUBLICATIONS

Somerville College Register, 1938, 1959, and 1971 edns.
Somerville College Report, published annually from 1879.
SSA Report, published annually from 1888 to 1925, and incorporating the 'Oxford Letter'.
ASM Report, published annually from 1926 (since 1950, when responsibility for writing the 'Oxford Letter' was transferred to the President of the JCR, as a Supplement to the *Somerville College Report*).

OTHER MANUSCRIPT SOURCES

BODLEIAN LIBRARY, OXFORD

AEW Papers: MS. Top.Oxon.*c*.817.

MSS Gilbert Murray 144: Letters to Isobel Henderson.
Lucy Sutherland Papers (uncatalogued).

BRITISH LIBRARY
Additional MS. 44503.

HAMPSHIRE RECORD OFFICE
Wickham MSS. 38M49/D19.

INDIA OFFICE LIBRARY, LONDON
Sorabji MSS (MSS.Eur.F.165/1–4).

LADY MARGARET HALL
Council Minute Books.
Wordsworth Papers.

ST ANNE'S COLLEGE
AEW Papers.
Bertha Johnson Papers.

PRIVATE COLLECTIONS
Mrs Annabel Cole: Papers of Margery Fry.
Miss K. M. E. Murray: Letters home, 1928–32.

PRINTED BOOKS

ABIR-AM, P. G., and OUTRAM, D. (eds.), *Uneasy Careers and Intimate Lives* (New Brunswick, NJ, 1987).

ADAMS, P. (ed.), *Janet Maria Vaughan 1899–1993: A Memorial Tribute* (Oxford, 1994).

BAILEY, G. (ed.), *Lady Margaret Hall: A Short History* (London, 1923).

BAILEY, H., *Vera Brittain* (London, 1987).

BAILEY, K. C., *A History of Trinity College Dublin 1892–1945* (Dublin, 1947).

BALSDON, D., *Oxford Life* (London, 1957).

BARDOUX, J., *Memories of Oxford*, trans. W. R. Barker (London, 1899).

BARRETT, G., *Blackfriars Settlement: A Short History 1887–1987* (London, 1985).

BATTISCOMBE, G., *Reluctant Pioneer: A Life of Elizabeth Wordsworth* (London, 1978).

BAWDEN, N., *In My Own Time: Almost an Autobiography* (London, 1994).

BENTLEY, L. (comp.), *Educating Women: A Pictorial History of Bedford College University of London 1849–1985* (Ham, Surrey, 1991).

BINGHAM, C., *The History of Royal Holloway College 1886–1986* (London, 1987).

BOSANQUET, E. S., *Late Harvest: Memories, Letters and Poems* (privately printed, n. d.).

BRADBROOK, M. C., *'That Infidel Place': A Short History of Girton College 1869–1969; with an Essay on the Collegiate University in the Modern World* (London, 1969).

BRITTAIN, V., *The Dark Tide* (London, 1923).

—— *The Women at Oxford: A Fragment of History* (London, 1960).

—— *Testament of Youth: An Autobiographical Study of the Years 1900–1925* (London, 1978).

—— *War Diary 1913–1917: Chronicle of Youth*, ed. A. Bishop and T. Smart (London, 1981).

BURSTYN, J. N., *Victorian Education and the Ideal of Womanhood* (New Brunswick, NJ, 1984).

BUTLER, R., and PRICHARD, M. H., *A History of St Anne's Society, Formerly the Society of Oxford Home Students* (Oxford, 1957).

BYRNE, M. ST C., and MANSFIELD, C. H., *Somerville College 1879–1921* (Oxford, 1921).

CALDECOTT, L. (ed.), *Women of Our Century* (London, 1984).

CARPENTER, H., *OUDS: A Centenary History of the Oxford University Dramatic Society 1885–1985* (Oxford, 1985).

COBBE, F. P., *Life of Frances Power Cobbe as Told by Herself* (London, 1904).

CONWAY, M. D., *Autobiography, Memories and Experiences* (2 vols.; London, 1904).

COURTNEY, J. E., *An Oxford Portrait Gallery* (London, 1931).

CURZON, N., *Principles and Methods of University Reform* (Oxford, 1910).

DALLY, A., *A Doctor's Story* (London, 1990).

DARBISHIRE, H., *Somerville College Chapel Addresses and Other Papers* (Oxford, 1962).

DAVIES, E., *The Higher Education of Women (1866)*, ed. with an introduction by Janet Howarth (London, 1988).

—— *Women in the Universities of England and Scotland* (London, 1896).

DENEKE, H., *Grace Hadow* (London, 1946).

DE VILLIERS, A., FOX, H., and ADAMS, P., *Somerville College Oxford 1879–1979: A Century in Pictures* (Oxford, 1978).

DYHOUSE, C., *Girls Growing Up in Late Victorian and Edwardian England* (London, 1981).

EMERY, J., *Rose Macaulay: A Writer's Life* (London, 1991).

EVANS, G. E., *So Hateth She Derknesse: A Biography of Edith A. Willey 1895–1970* (privately printed, 1971).

FABER, G., *Jowett: A Portrait with Background* (London, 1957).

FAITHFULL, L. M., *In the House of My Pilgrimage* (London, 1924).

FARNELL, L. R., *An Oxonian Looks Back* (London, 1934).

FARNELL, V., *A Somervillian Looks Back* (Oxford, 1948).

FORSTER, M., *Dames' Delight* (London, 1964).

FRANKENBURG, C. U., *Not Old, Madam, Vintage: An Autobiography* (Lavenham, 1975).

GORHAM, D., *The Victorian Girl and the Feminine Ideal* (London, 1982).

GREEN, V., *Love in a Cool Climate: The Letters of Mark Pattison and Meta Bradley 1879-1884* (Oxford, 1985).

GRIFFIN, P. (ed.), *St Hugh's: One Hundred Years of Women's Education in Oxford* (London, 1986).

HARRISON, B. (ed.), *The History of the University of Oxford,* viii. *The Twentieth Century* (Oxford, 1994).

HERBERTSON, B., *The Pfeiffer Bequest and the Education of Women: A Centenary Review* (Cambridge, 1993).

HIBBERT, C. (ed.), *The Encyclopaedia of Oxford* (London, 1988).

HINCHCLIFFE, T., *North Oxford* (London, 1992).

HOLLAND, C. H. (ed.), *Trinity College Dublin and the Idea of a University* (Dublin, 1991).

HOLTBY, W., *Letters to a Friend,* ed. Alice Holtby and Jean McWilliam (London, 1937).

HUWS JONES, E., *Margery Fry: The Essential Amateur* (London, 1966).

—— *Mrs Humphry Ward* (London, 1973).

JOHNSON, R. (ed.), *The Oxford Myth* (London, 1988).

LASCELLES, M., *A Memoir* (privately printed, 1989).

LEONARDI, S. J., *Dangerous by Degrees: Women at Oxford and the Somerville College Novelists* (New Brunswick, NJ, 1989).

LODGE, E. C., *Terms and Vacations,* ed. Janet Spens (London, 1938).

LONGFORD, C., *Making Conversation* (London, 1931).

MABBOTT, J., *Oxford Memories* (Oxford, 1986).

MCCRONE, K. E., *Sport and the Physical Emancipation of English Women 1870-1914* (London, 1988).

MCWILLIAMS-TULLBERG, R., *Women at Cambridge: A Men's University—Though of a Mixed Type* (London, 1975).

MARETT, R. R., *A Jerseyman at Oxford* (London, 1941).

MEYNELL, A., *Public Servant, Private Woman: An Autobiography* (London, 1988).

PFEIFFER, E., *Women and Work: An Essay Treating on the Relation to Health and Physical Development of the Higher Education of Girls, and the Intellectual or More Systematised Effort of Women* (London, 1888).

PHILLIPS, A. (ed.), *A Newnham Anthology* (Cambridge, 1979).

PHILLIPS, C., *Robert Bridges: A Biography* (Oxford, 1992).

PRESTWICH, G., *Essays Descriptive and Biographical; With a Memoir by Her Sister, Louisa E. Milne* (Edinburgh, 1901).

RAYNER, M. E., *The Centenary History of St Hilda's College, Oxford* (Oxford, 1993).

REYNOLDS, B., *Dorothy L. Sayers: Her Life and Soul* (London, 1993).

RHONDDA, VISCOUNTESS, *This Was My World* (London, 1933).

RICHARDSON, J., *Enid Starkie* (London, 1973).

RIDLER, A., *Olive Willis and Downe House: An Adventure in Education* (London, 1967).

ROGERS, A., *Degrees by Degrees: The Story of the Admission of Oxford Women Students to Membership of the University* (London, 1938).

ROWBOTHAM, S., *A New World for Women: Stella Browne, Socialist Feminist* (London, 1977).

SAYERS, D. L., *Gaudy Night* (London, 1935).

SCOTT-JAMES, A., *Sketches From a Life* (London, 1993).

SEEBOHM, C., *The Last Romantics* (London, 1987).

SELBIE, W. B., *The Life of Andrew Martin Fairbairn, D.D., D.Litt., LL.D., F.B.A., etc. First Principal of Mansfield College, Oxford* (London, 1914).

SHAEN, M. J. (ed.), *William Shaen: A Brief Sketch* (London, 1912).

SIDGWICK, E., *Mrs Henry Sidgwick: A Memoir by her Niece* (London, 1938).

SOMERVILLE, M., *Personal Recollections, from Early Life to Old Age, of Mary Somerville. With Selections from her Correspondence. By her Daughter, Martha Somerville* (London, 1873).

SONDHEIMER, J., *Castle Adamant in Hampstead: A History of Westfield College 1882–1982* (London, 1983).

SORABJI, C., *India Calling: The Memories of Cornelia Sorabji* (London, 1934).

STANTON, H., *Go Well, Stay Well: South Africa August 1956 to May 1960* (London, 1961).

STEPHEN, B., *Girton College 1869–1932* (Cambridge, 1933).

STOCKS, M. D., *Eleanor Rathbone: A Biography* (London, 1949).

SWIFT, MRS and MRS T., *Remembrances of Micklem Hall 1887–1933* (Oxford, 1935).

TAYLOR, A. M., *Gilletts: Bankers at Banbury and Oxford* (Oxford, 1964).

TEMPLE, W., *Life of Bishop Percival* (London, 1921).

THWAITE, A. (ed.), *My Oxford* (London, 1977).

TREVELYAN, J. P., *The Life of Mrs Humphry Ward* (London, 1923).

TUKE, M. J., *A History of Bedford College for Women 1849–1937* (London, 1939).

VICINUS, M. (ed.), *Suffer and Be Still: Women in the Victorian Age* (London, 1972).

—— *A Widening Sphere: Changing Roles of Victorian Women* (London, 1977).

—— *Independent Women: Work and Community for Single Women 1850–1920* (London, 1985).

WARD, MRS H., *A Writer's Recollections* (London, 1918).

WAYNE, J., *The Purple Dress: Growing Up in the Thirties* (London, 1979).

WHITLEY, E., *The Graduates* (London, 1986).

Bibliography

WILLSON, F. M. G., *A Strong Supporting Cast: The Shaw Lefevres 1879–1936* (London, 1993).

WINTERBOTTOM, D., *Clifton After Percival: A Public School in the Twentieth Century* (Bristol, 1990).

—— *John Percival the Great Educator* (Bristol, 1993).

WITHERS, A., *Lifespan* (London, 1994).

WORDSWORTH, E., *Glimpses of the Past* (London, 1913).

JOURNALS

Fritillary
Girton College Newsletter
Jackson's Oxford Journal
Journal of the Women's Education Union
Lady's Pictorial
Oriel Record
Oxford Magazine
Oxford University Gazette
Time and Tide
Times Higher Education Supplement

ARTICLES

PUBLISHED

ARNOLD, L. B., 'The Bascom–Goldschmidt–Porter correspondence 1907–1922', *Earth Sciences History* 12/2 (1993).

HOWARTH, J., and CURTHOYS, M., 'The Political Economy of Women's Higher Education in Late Nineteenth and Early Twentieth Century Britain', *Historical Research*, 60 (1987), 208–31.

SUTHERLAND, G., 'The Movement for the Higher Education of Women: Its Social and Intellectual Context in England, c.1840–80', in P. J. Waller (ed.), *Politics and Social Change in Modern Britain: Essays Presented to A. F. Thompson* (Brighton, 1987), 91–116.

UNPUBLISHED

DRAPER, J., 'An Educated Male Elite: Oxford University Undergraduate Behaviour in the Formative Years of the Women's Colleges', B. A. thesis (Oxford, 1994).

HODGKIN, D., 'Crystallography and Chemistry in the First Hundred Years of Somerville College' (Bryce Memorial Lecture, 1979).

PERRONE, F., 'University Teaching as a Profession for Women in Oxford, Cambridge and London, 1870–1930', D.Phil. thesis (Oxford, 1991).

VAUGHAN, J. M., 'Jogging Along' (copy deposited in College Archives).

Index of Persons

Women who appear in the text under both maiden and married name are indexed under the former. Somervillians who appear only under their married name have their maiden name supplied in brackets. Dates refer to year of student entry to Somerville. The references in bold type refer to notes on the illustrations which appear on pp. xi–xv.

378

Piper, John 327
Pirie, Antoinette 268
Poincaré, Jules Henri 112
Pollard, Catherine (1888) 41–2, 108–9
Pollock, Margaret Dighton 190
Poole, Austin Lane 161, 257
Pope, Mildred (1891) **xiv (34)**, 36, 53, 55, 60 n., 68, 76, 79, 91, 94, 101, 103, 113, 122, 123, 129, 134, 140, 153, 155, 161–2, 171, 172, 174, 183, 186, 188, 196, 197, 266
Porter, Mary Winearls 78, 206, 358
Poulton, Edward 39, 114, 128
Poulton, Emily 23, 114, 159, 190
Powell, Dilys (1920) 208, 217, 267
Powell, Eleanor Grace (1884) **xi (6)**, 26, 28, 35, 37, 49, 50, 60 n., 62, 108, 120, 140–1
Prestwich, Grace 14
Procter, Grace (1913) 87
Proudfoot, Mary, *see* Macdonald
Pusey, Edward Bouverie 8
Pyke, Margaret, *see* Chubb

Quiller-Couch, Sir Arthur 153

Ralph, Mary 69
Ramage, Cecil B. 200
Ramm, Agatha 260, 299, 335
Ranking, George 88–9, 99
Rantzen, Esther (1959) 3, 323, 345
Raper, Robert William 118
Rathbone, Eleanor (1893) 3, 58, 60 n., 67, 126, 129, 135, 165, 172, 180, 246, 361, 362 n.
Rathbone, William, MP 23 n.
Rawson, Jessica 351
Redman, Mary (1918) 200
Reid, Constance (1913) 87
Reid, Hilda (1917) 158, 360
Reynard, Elizabeth (1923) **xiii (22)**
Reynard, Helene 155, 158
Reynell, Anne (1941) 245
Rhodes, Doris 155, 170
Rhondda, (Margaret Haigh) Viscountess, *see* Thomas

Rich, Florence (1884) 31, 39–41, 112, 114–15, 117
Richards, Evä 283
Richardson, Revd. R. D. 263
Richmond, Oliffe 326
Richter, Polly (1961) (Mrs Ionides) 327
Riddell, Sir Walter Buchanan 57 n., 165
Roaf, Christina, *see* Drake
Roberts, Janet, *see* Adam Smith
Roberts, John Varley 114
Roberts, Margaret Elizabeth (1879) 172, 185
Roberts, Margaret Hilda (1943) (Baroness Thatcher) **xv (45)**, 3, 74, 296, 307, 330, 358
Roberts, Michèle (1967) 304, 360
Roberts, Sir Owen 22
Robertson, Margaret (1901) 47
Robinson, Frank Neville 269
Rogers, Annie 8–9, 50–2, 58, 60, 82, 134, 164
Rogers, Beatrice (College Cook) 190
Rogers, Harold 170
Rogers, Thorold 8, 38
Rolleston, Grace 14
Romanes, George John 45
Ross, Mary Cassels (1896) 272
Ross (William) David 87
Routledge, Katharine (Pease, 1891) 191, 359
Rowe, Dorothy (1912) **xiv (24)**
Rowse, Alfred Leslie 232
Ruskin, John 9, 26–7, 64, 112, 197
Russell, Alec Smith 57 n., 262, 266
Russell, Bertrand 54
Russell, Norma, *see* Lewis
Ryan, Charles 21
Ryle, John Alfred 253

Sadler, Irene 206
Sadler, Sir Michael 156
Salter, Herbert Edward 206
Samuel, Sir Herbert (Viscount Samuel) 231
Samuel, Nancy (1925) 167, 203, 231

Samuelson, B., MP 23 n.
Sargent, John Singer 160
Sarginson, Kathleen 242, 258, 260
Sassoon, Siegfried 93
Savery, Constance (1917) 92, 98, 118
Sayce, Archibald Henry 180
Sayce, Olive, *see* Davison
Sayers, Dorothy L. (1912) **xiv (24)**, 3, 78, 88, 121, 127, 130, 137, 143, 145, 181, 188, 195, 224, 225, 304, 360, 361
Schweitzer, Albert 184
Scott (Anna) Dorothea (1895) 117
Scott-James, Anne (1931) 202, 215, 316
Scott Stokes, Dorothy (1913) 138
Scroggs, Mr (College Porter) 82
Seebohm, Caroline (1958) 314, 317, 357, 361
Seeds, Mrs John 204
Selbie, William Boothby 173, 221
Seward, Margaret (1881) **xi (6)**, 35, 38, 39, 40, 53, 61 n.
Seymour, Margaret Irene 190
Shaen, William 21
Sharp, Dorothea (1924) 189
Sharp, Evelyn (1922) 362
Sharp, Jane (1880) 43, 117
Shaw Lefevre, Emily 191
Shaw Lefevre, George 21, 23
Shaw Lefevre, Sir John 15
Shaw Lefevre, Madeleine **xi (6)**, **xv (48)**, 15–19, 20–43, 45, 46, 62–3, 66, 69, 74, 83–4, 105, 107, 112, 116, 118, 120, 154, 180, 191, 355
Sheavyn, Phoebe 54, 123
Sheldon, Frances (1880) 34, 105–8, 111, 117, 355
Sidgwick, Arthur 22, 38
Sidgwick, Charlotte 19
Sidgwick, Eleanor 30, 79, 83
Sidgwick, Henry 38
Sidgwick, Rose 66
Sidgwick, William 9, 12
Sikorsky, Wladyslaw 246
Simpson, Alfred William Brian 284

Simpson, Alice Mary 241
Sinton, Vera (1962) 354 n.
Siordet, Vera (1913) 87
Skues, Mary (1884) 28, 107, 112, 120
Smith, Alic Halford 57 n., 257
Smith, Arthur Lionel 57, 136, 145, 157
Smith, Eleanor 9, 14, 62
Snow, Christine Mary, *see* Pilkington
Snow, Matilda (1905) 137, 183
Somerville, Mary 13, 22, 85, 357
Somerville, Mary (1921) (Mrs Brown) 362
Sorabji, Cornelia (1889) **xii (7)**, 3, 34, 85, 107, 110–11, 113–14, 117, 124, 128, 141, 142, 361
Sorabji, Dick 117
Soskice, Oliver 287
Spencer, Sylvia 204
Spender, Stephen 232
Spicer, Eva Dykes (1917) 104
Spicer, Joanna, *see* Gibbon
Stafford, Fiona **xvi (51)**
Stallybrass, William Teulon Swan 164
Standen, Edith Appleton (1923) 198, 216–17, 222, 223
Stanley of Alderley, Henrietta Maria, Lady 25
Stanton, Hannah (1954) 271, 331, 360
Starkie, Enid (1916) **xiv (36, 37)**, **xv (43)**, 92, 170, 186, 188, 190, 230–1, 256, 258, 266, 270, 314, 315, 333, 334, 336, 360
Stevenson, George Hope 115
Stewart, Frances, *see* Kaldor
Stonedale, Beatrice **xiv (36, 37)**, 103, 144, 155, 186, 189, 239, 250, 258
Stott, Laura **xiv (36)**, 250, 258
Street, Hilda (1918) (Mrs Whitaker) 98, 213–14
Stuart, Edith (Pringle, 1903) 358
Stuart, Hazel (1946) (Lady Fox) 267, 273, 284, 311, 332 n.

General Index